A Wilder Shore

A Wilder Shore

The Romantic Odyssey *of*
Fanny *and* Robert Louis Stevenson

CAMILLE PERI

VIKING

VIKING
An imprint of Penguin Random House LLC
penguinrandomhouse.com

Copyright © 2024 by Camille Peri

Penguin Random House supports copyright. Copyright fuels creativity,
encourages diverse voices, promotes free speech, and creates a vibrant culture.
Thank you for buying an authorized edition of this book and for complying with
copyright laws by not reproducing, scanning, or distributing any part of it in any
form without permission. You are supporting writers and allowing Penguin
Random House to continue to publish books for every reader.

Image credits may be found on pages 453–54.

LIBRARY OF CONGRESS CATALOGING-IN-PUBLICATION DATA

Names: Peri, Camille, author.
Title: A wilder shore : the romantic odyssey of Fanny and Robert Louis
Stevenson / Camille Peri.
Description: New York : Viking, 2024. | Includes bibliographical references and index. |
Identifiers: LCCN 2024003460 (print) | LCCN 2024003461 (ebook) |
ISBN 9780670786190 (hardcover) | ISBN 9781101612897 (ebook)
Subjects: LCSH: Stevenson, Robert Louis, 18501894—Friends and associates.
| Stevenson, Fanny Van de Grift, 18401914—Friends and associates. |
Authors' spouses—Great Britain—Biography. | Authors, Scottish—
19th century—Biography.
Classification: LCC PR5495 P47 2024 (print) |
LCC PR5495 (ebook) | DDC 828.809—dc23/eng/20240319
LC record available at https://lccn.loc.gov/2024003460
LC ebook record available at https://lccn.loc.gov/2024003461

Printed in the United States of America
1st Printing

Designed by Nerylsa Dijol

For David, who makes all things possible . . . and sometimes impossible

And for my sons, Nat and Joe, the pulse of my heartbeat

A Wilder Shore

INTRODUCTION

S he was the only woman in the world worth dying for." It was these words, which I came across in a reference to Fanny Van de Grift Stevenson, that first caught my attention. They were written by an admirer, not the man she devoted her life to—her famous husband, Robert Louis Stevenson. But Louis, as he was called, actually did risk his life to get to her, crossing the world when he was in ill health, because he felt he could not live without her. "Honour, anger, valour, fire" were qualities he attributed to Fanny, who sustained him with "a love that life could never tire, evil quench, nor death stir," as he wrote in one poem.

As I delved deeper into their story, I came to realize that, without Fanny, there would be no Robert Louis Stevenson as we know him. He probably would not have written *Treasure Island* or finished *Kidnapped*, and *Dr Jekyll and Mr Hyde* might well have been a different story from the one the world knows today. Without Fanny, Louis probably would not have become one of the most famous and beloved authors in the world.

Theirs was an unlikely Victorian love story: He was a university-educated writer from a prominent family in Scotland; she was a high school graduate from the rustic Midwest. He was ambitious but in frail health and adrift, penning magazine essays that would likely be forgotten. She was forceful and determined—whether she was seeking her fortune in the Nevada silver rush or studying art in Paris. She was ten years his senior and married, with children, when they met. How could a union between them work—or even happen?

It was the fascinating and fruitful partnership between Fanny and Robert Louis Stevenson that compelled me to write this book. When the sickly Scottish writer and the American runaway wife met, improbably, in an art colony in France, both were seeking escape from a bland Victorian bourgeois life. They found it in each other. Their marriage was tumultuous, a ship tossing in a frothing sea. But together they created a beautiful adventure that would not have been possible without the other. *A Wilder Shore* is a portrait of these two extraordinary people and an exploration of the union that stimulated, frustrated, and ultimately sustained them.

Louis was a self-described "chronic sickest," prone to violent, bloody coughing fits that appeared to be caused by tuberculosis. But he had the heart of an adventurer. This book travels the world with him and Fanny as they seek better health for him, a looser lifestyle, and more creative freedom—a journey that included their honeymoon squatting in an abandoned silver mine and ended with them living in Samoa, where they joined the native islanders' fight for independence from imperialist powers. I followed their path—from France and Britain to New York and San Francisco, and ultimately to the Pacific Islands—to bring their story to life.

A Wilder Shore may challenge some readers' expectations of RLS (another nickname), who is often thought of simply as an entertaining author of boys' books and a man who was childish himself. In fact, he heroically overcame incredibly daunting medical challenges to write some of the most towering, indelible prose in Western literature. "He seemed to pick the right word up on the point of his pen, like a man playing spillikens," author G. K. Chesterton wrote. Through it all, with Fanny, Louis retained the imaginative powers of youth that fueled his writing and his life.

Fanny has suffered the unflattering fate of most literary wives, whom critics historically render invisible or pick apart to find evidence of how they helped or hindered their husbands' careers. This leaves them only half formed on the printed page. Depictions of Fanny often vacillate between extremes: She is either a skilled and caring helpmate or, more often, a prickly, selfish drain on her husband. Many previous Stevenson biographies have denigrated her as a "difficult" woman without further exploring her character. No portrayal has captured the complex and dynamic woman she was or the passion, companionship, and creative energy that became the life force of the Stevensons' marriage.

Fanny was integral to RLS's writing process—from handling the practical matters of life (including the formidable logistics of moving around the world to keep him alive) to encouraging him to write fiction and to delve into psychology and politics in his work. But she too had a vivid imagination, which she expressed in her own writing and in the way she lived her life.

Fanny left behind several published nonfiction essays and short stories, along with travel narratives and a novel, *More New Arabian Nights: The Dynamiter*, that she coauthored with Louis. Yet most of her fiction and nonfiction has been dismissed or ignored—even by her own biographers. In part, this began with Louis's literary clique, who branded her primitive—even "savage"—because she was olive skinned and American. A highlight of my research for *A Wilder Shore* was locating pieces of Fanny's work that have received no critical attention. They help reveal some of the themes that absorbed her and shaped her influence on Louis, as well as provide a glimpse of nineteenth-century popular magazine writing—often the most open path to publication for Victorian women. *A Wilder Shore* is the first book about the Stevensons to consider the body of Fanny's work as well as that of her famous husband.

THE STEVENSONS WERE as creative and progressive in their personal life as they were in their writings, and their attempt to build a relatively egalitarian marriage nearly 150 years ago has surprising resonance today. Theirs was an exciting but socially unsettled time, when Victorian norms of gender, social class, race, sexuality, and even marriage were just beginning to erode. Louis admired Fanny for her courage and strong views—qualities then deemed almost exclusively masculine—and she appreciated him for his "feminine" dreaminess and sensitivity. Together they created women characters who broke the rules: a female terrorist, a cross-dressing countess with "manlike ambitions" and a lusty sex drive, a runaway from a religious cult, a dark-skinned British woman impersonating a Cuban slave. Louis wrote of the prejudice against immigrants in the United States, and both wrote of interracial love and marriage. In their South Seas writings, both questioned imperialism and the "scientific" theories about race that were used to justify it. They examined the costs of progress and colonialism on marginalized people and Indigenous cultures.

Achieving parity in marriage was no smooth or easy task. Louis was the peacock in the relationship, the genius and the moneymaker—and, to a great extent, Fanny would see it as her role to keep him alive and writing. There were times when she would feel like a housemaid or nurse; when she had no time even to contemplate who she was; when she resented the expectation that wives should be grateful for money allotted to them as if it were an unearned allowance.

But although Victorian women were considered biologically suited to the "domestic sphere," Louis did not expect his wife to contentedly define her life by homemaking. Despite Fanny's relative lack of education, he depended on her critical insights as much or more than those of his snobby male literary colleagues, much to their annoyance. And he saw to it that she was formally credited as coauthor for a book they wrote together at a time when wives were rarely acknowledged for contributions to their husbands' work. The couple's verbal scuffles were notorious, but they were also part of a lifelong conversation that pushed them to evolve and grow.

There were many times during my research that I longed to step into one of the Stevensons' homes, an experience Fanny's daughter, Isobel Field, likened to "the rising of a curtain in the theatre." Half the time, the couple floated in a somewhat surreal world, on drugs that included laudanum (a tincture of opium) and ergotin (a derivative of the main component of LSD)—remedies that were routinely prescribed for serious illnesses like tuberculosis as well as vague Victorian ailments like "the vapours." Even their dog, Walter, or "Woggs," was sometimes on drugs for his "fits." When Fanny and Louis were well, however, they were lively entertainers, hosting evenings of good food and sparkling conversation. Their eclectic collection of guests ranged from literary luminaries like Henry James to eccentrics like Jane Shelley, who kept the heart of the poet Percy Bysshe Shelley, her dead father-in-law, enshrined in her drawing room.

I'd love to witness Louis as he famously paced the room, brilliantly holding forth in English, French, and Latin, and stopping occasionally to perch on anything but a conventional seat—a dizzying practice that inspired the American historian Henry Adams to liken him to an "insane stork." I might follow my nose to the kitchen to see Fanny, a renowned cook, putting the final touch on dishes from recipes she picked up on her travels, like bouillabaisse or soufflés. In Samoa, where the couple tended to entertain on a grander scale, she might be supervising the roasting of a dozen or more pigs and hundreds of pineapples from their garden.

Fanny once said that Louis "taught me how to live." The Stevensons' unconventional partnership allowed Louis more freedom within the cage of his poor health, and both partners more freedom within Victorian society, than they might otherwise have sought or enjoyed. It drove them to crisscross the globe seeking new and astonishing experiences that neither could have pursued alone. This is an intimate window into how they lived and loved—a story that is at once a travel adventure, a journey into the literary creative process, and, I hope, an inspiration for anyone seeking a freer, more unconventional life.

ONE

It was the beginning of her life or the end. No thinking person would dare consider crossing that bridge—especially in this tempest, especially a mother traveling with three children. But at that moment in summer 1875, Fanny Osbourne thought only of escape. She was restless, determined, and aching for excitement. The bridge was a challenge.

Fanny had slipped out of San Francisco like a whisper, fleeing her faithless husband and hustling her children and their governess onto a train bound east. There were no corks popped, no friendly hands waving them off at the station. After stopping to see her family in Clayton, Indiana, she and her children would catch a train to Indianapolis on the Terre Haute, Vandalia, and St. Louis railroad—what people here just called the "Vandalia 'road." In her bag were four train tickets from Indianapolis to New York.

But then the rain came. In the summer heat, the first drops that fell from a dim prairie sky may have seemed like a benediction. God knew she needed one—no one but her closest friend, Dora, supported Fanny's decision to leave her husband. The drops grew into streams and the streams into torrents. For eight days and nights, it poured. Meandering streams swelled into rushing rivers, and the wide White River began gushing over its banks as it cut its way down the state.

Sheets of rain fell like dark, heavy curtains, trapping Fanny in this brick house with all her dreams of escape. As she waited at the window and rechecked her trunks, she must have felt those dreams pried off and blown away, like the house shingles that bounced and skittered down the road. She could not go back to California, to the little doll's house where Sam had installed her, to waste what was left of her youth waiting for an uncertain future. A mail steamer, the *City of Brooklyn*, was in New York harbor, ready to take her and her children to Europe. She was going to be an artist. She was going to put an ocean between her and Sam.

The storm let up briefly but then let go full force—"as if all the water-spouts of heaven and all the mill-dams of earth had broken loose," in the view of the local newspaper, the *Danville Union*. With nearly fourteen inches of rain in Indianapolis—a record for July that would stand for the next 140 years—it was about to become the worst flood of the century in the state.

Water broke through the levees and swept wildly over fields of corn, wheat, and oats. A stable with three horses floated down one river, and then a corncrib with more than half a dozen chickens on top. The clock was ticking away not only the hours to Fanny's train but her possible escape routes to Indianapolis. Large sections of the Vandalia track washed away, traffic halted as roads went underwater, and bridges across the White River began to lurch and fall. The tide took down one end of the bridge at Pecksburg, then broke a span between Danville and Cartersburg into four pieces and dumped them in a cornfield.

Sparked by courage, impulsiveness, or madness—and she was touched by all three—Fanny decided to outrun the flood. She hired a driver and an old country omnibus pulled by two stout horses. The man likely balked when Fanny first approached him—this little lady in a prim traveling suit with its layers of flounces and ruffles. But for a tiny woman, Fanny had a command-ing presence. When she was full of determination, her powers of persuasion were impressive—especially with men.

Under a deceiving soft cloud of curls, her piercing eyes could pin you to a wall, people said. But she also knew when to play helpless. "The aggressive female is always worsted in traveling," she advised the children's governess. So while one of her small hands rested on the pistol she always carried in her bag, the other might dab her moist eyes with a handkerchief as she pleaded her predicament. By the time she finished talking to the driver that day, he had agreed to follow her orders.

The roads around Indianapolis were swampy even in the best weather; driving over them now would be like shooting the rapids. Fanny might have been riding up front with the driver or huddled in back with her children, with only oilcloth storm curtains to keep out the muck as they slid along the road and plummeted into ruts, churning up spumes of mud. Either way, her bustle would have been a serious liability, making it impossible for her to dig her feet into the floor and brace herself against the seat back. Though she could fold the bustle up like a fan behind her, she still had to perch, rather than sit, on the front of the seat leaning forward—an especially precarious position when a plunge into a deep hole could throw the passengers into a heap on the floor.

When the travel party came to a bridge that was still standing, men ran toward their vehicle trying to wave them off, shouting that it was unsafe to cross. But the driver lashed the horses to go ahead and they hurtled over it minutes before the bridge collapsed, Fanny later wrote. Nearly every bridge in the county would be wiped out before the flooding stopped.

By the time Fanny and her children reached Indianapolis, her story must have been written all over her—her traveling suit caked with mud, weeds, and silt. But the legend of this bold, even reckless woman had already gone before her. On the train, as one conductor relieved another, he introduced her as "the lady who drove over the Vandalia 'road."

After Fanny and her children had arrived safely in Europe, she described that part of their journey in a letter to Dora. She insisted that she would never risk her children's lives like that again. But her account of their narrow escape had more swagger than regret, as if she had started a journey from which there was no turning back. It was not just a test of the limits of her nerve—it was a test of the limits of being a woman in that era. It was the first of many times that Fanny would plunge into the unknown, heedless of the consequences, to pursue her dreams. It would make her a famous woman—and change the course of literary history.

⚜

NOTHING ABOUT THE BABY GIRL who entered the world during tornado season in Indiana, on March 10, 1840, was boring or predictable—that needs to be established from the start. Her parents—twenty-nine-year-old Esther and twenty-four-year-old Jacob Vandegrift—gave her the gentle, flowery name Frances Matilda. But even as a child, their daughter had no use for such sweetness and would abandon it for the sassier nickname "Fanny." (Later, in Europe, she also refashioned her maiden surname Van de Grift, in deference to her seventeenth-century Dutch ancestors.)

Even Fanny's baptism in the White River thirty three years before she crossed its raging waters was dramatic. At the time, the Vandegrifts lived in Indianapolis next door to the church of the young minister Henry Ward Beecher, abolitionist and brother of Harriet Beecher Stowe. The town, especially the female population, was intrigued by this upstart parson who preached about prison reform and wore open shirts instead of a white cravat. When a lock of his long, wavy hair fell onto his face during sermons, he swept it off with a dramatic brush of his hand.

Like the rest of the nation, Indiana was then caught up in a fiery debate about which Christian religion practiced the only valid method of baptism—sprinkling, pouring, or immersing—a dispute that bored the forward-thinking Beecher to tears. He and a few like-minded ministers announced they would hold a cross-denominational baptism, and Beecher pledged to baptize those who wished to join his congregation by any method they chose. With nearly the entire town watching, Esther Vandegrift stepped forward into the river with Fanny, and a cascade of water spilled through Beecher's fingers over the baby's head, glittering in the April sun like raindrops from heaven.

Though Indianapolis was by then the state capital, it might as well have still been a frontier town—largely isolated by a river that was too shallow for commerce and land too swampy for decent roads. The unpaved streets oozed with deep, sticky mud and were littered with tree stumps and weeds. Beecher's first services were held in a makeshift church upstairs in a building where a flock of sheep also congregated on Sundays. Many townspeople still lived in log cabins and nearly everyone kept pigs. With their skill in opening gates, the pigs were often out and about in the streets and were probably the only ones who luxuriated in the mire.

Fanny would recall her childhood life there and, later, on her family's farm in nearby Clayton as primitive. The women made clothing from coarse linsey-woolsey, which was woven on looms in nearby farmhouses. When the clothes were too worn to wear, they tore them into strips and wove them together into rag rugs. To her, the backwoods town's only connection with the outside world seemed to be the National Road. Every couple of weeks, she thrilled to watch a mud wagon lumber along it, heading for unimaginable places—though, in fact, it went only as far as Illinois. "Oh but that was romantic to me, leading as it did straight out to the wide, wide world!" she later wrote.

The town and the surrounding woods were a child's land of enchantment—of drinking sassafras tea and catching lightning bugs in a jar to read by at night. Purple cabbage and flint corn grew fat in the garden, wild turkeys and geese flew overhead, and healing herbs like snakeroot and slippery elm were within reach. "Laid up in the trunks of hollow trees were rich stores of wild honey," she later recalled. "And the forest, traversed by cool streams, where wild vines clambered from tree to tree, made bowers fit for any fairy queen."

Yet the thin, tough little girl was more tomboy than fairy queen. She refused to be left behind with the girls to sit quietly and play with dolls while the boys jumped out of trees and forded streams up to their necks. Instead, she roamed the woods with the boys, gathered dirt and gravel in her skirt to build forts and rivers, and once used a neighbor woman's best lace nightcap to catch minnows. She was a prototype for Jo March, years before Louisa May Alcott created the strong-minded, boyish sister in *Little Women*.

"Fanny was what the children called a 'tomboy,' and always preferred the boys' sports, the more daring the better," her younger sister Nellie Van de Grift Sanchez wrote in her fond biography, *The Life of Mrs. Robert Louis Stevenson*. "She was a high-spirited, daring creature, a little flashing firefly of a child, eagerly seeking for adventure, that might have brought upon her frequent punishment were it not that her parents held exceedingly liberal views in such matters."

Jacob Vandegrift, who had run away from home in Philadelphia to escape a cruel stepfather, believed that parents should withhold discipline and leave children to develop according to their intrinsic natures. Consequently, his children adored him. Jacob wanted his five daughters to feel that they could be independent and fearless. He raised Fanny, Josephine, Betty, Cora, and Nellie like his son, Jake—teaching them to ride, shoot, hammer nails, and hunt, though Fanny refused to kill an animal or bird.

Jacob was a builder who owned his own lumber and real estate businesses, though he "made money easily but spent it royally," according to Nellie, and would die poor. He had a deep chest, broad shoulders, blue eyes, and rosy skin. Fanny, a daddy's girl, loved to sit on a fence to watch him do circus tricks on horseback. She inherited his penetrating glance and mouth, which turned down slightly at the corners, as well as his fiery temperament.

"He had a hasty temper but a generous heart, and while his hand was always open to the poor and unhappy, it was a closed fist ready to strike straight from the shoulder to resent an insult or defend the oppressed," Nellie wrote. He was also fair-minded and loyal. Though Esther Keen reportedly confessed to him during their courtship that she had already been married and divorced, he wed her without further questions. And he stayed loyal to his onetime neighbor Henry Ward Beecher, during Beecher's 1875 trial for adultery.

Fanny never heard Esther speak an angry word to a child—an impressive feat for a mother of six, especially in an era when parents were free with the back of their hands. Aside from her gentleness and beauty, Esther would be most remembered for once holding a rabid dog's mouth shut to protect her children until help arrived. Fanny clearly got her physical fearlessness from her mother.

But Esther's daughter seemed to inherit her rebellious spirit from the more colorful women in the family—like Aunt Polly, who puffed on a corncob pipe when smoking was almost unheard of in women. Or Aunt Knodle, who sat in her window—"ready, like Dickens's heroine, Betsy [*sic*] Trotwood, to pounce out upon passing travelers," Fanny wrote. Anytime Aunt Knodle saw a horse she thought was being mistreated, she seized its bridle and lectured its driver.

Fanny never knew her maternal grandmother, a vivacious beauty named Kitty Weaver, but she knew the story of her vanity by heart from the hushed moment she was first shown Kitty's red satin slippers. According to the family story, on her way to a ball, Kitty walked to her carriage in the snow in the thin slippers and caught a cold that killed her. Later in her life, Fanny would be known for wearing red ballet slippers and other delicate shoes "often totally unsuited to the occasion," according to Nellie.

Fanny's paternal grandmother, Elizabeth Vandegrift, would sniff at Kitty's story and insist that she had worn much daintier slippers in her youth. "But when I looked at my grandmother and studied her features, her high hooked nose, her big, keen eyes, sharp like swords, the haughty outline of her curved lips, her massive shoulders and deep chest, and listened to her imperious voice, doubts assailed me," Fanny later wrote. "I could believe that she had led an army of Amazons in cuirass and buckler, but my imagination refused to picture her in a silken train smiling at gallants from behind her fan."

Elizabeth fed Fanny's imagination with wild and frightening bedtime stories about witch-fires, apparitions, and the Inquisition. But it was the whole aura of her grandmother's storytelling sessions that sent shivers down Fanny's spine. After she led Fanny in bedtime prayers about hell and damnation, the tiny child would mount Elizabeth's big mahogany four-poster bed, feather bed, and mattress "stuffed with the best curled hair." From there, she watched wide-eyed as Elizabeth dismantled her grandmotherly self one piece at a time—first her lace cap, then the false front of hair over her forehead (which looked to Fanny as if she were removing her scalp), and finally her black skullcap.

"With the skull-cap my grandmother, as I knew her, disappeared and a strange and awful man stood in her place," recalled Fanny, who would then bury her face until the lights went out. "Though my terror was excessive, I do not think I should have liked the stories, generally grim or tragic, so well in a different setting." Fanny developed a flair for Gothic melodrama from these sessions, where Elizabeth "told every incident as dramatically as though she had participated in it herself." It was a talent she passed down to her grand-daughter, and one that even Fanny's detractors would grudgingly admire.

When Fanny was in high school, neighborhood children gathered on the cellar door after supper to hear her tell ghoulish tales. Sixty years later, her schoolmate Ella Hale could vividly remember how they huddled closer as the evening sky grew as dark as Fanny's eyes. "Fanny was always the central figure," Ella recalled, "because she was the only one who could tell really interesting stories."

If Jacob Vandegrift's children were to develop as nature made them, Fanny concluded at an early age that it was her nature to be evil. "That heaven was not for a wicked child like me who could not always tell wrong from right, I was convinced," she later wrote. Her boldness and temper may have helped convince her of this, but the biggest influence seems to have been her olive complexion. Though it is not apparent in photos, it was con-sidered dark-skinned in a time and place that idealized a fair complexion. At school, children taunted her with a nasty rhyme: "N——, n——, never die, black face and shiny eye." Later, rumors reportedly surfaced suggesting that Esther's first husband might have been Fanny's Creole father.

At home, Fanny's complexion was "the despair" of her dark-skinned moth-er's life. Aunt Knodle embroidered shoulder-length nankeen mittens, which were sewn onto the girl's dress every day to keep her hands and arms from getting any darker. Grandma Elizabeth tried to bleach her skin with lotions and soaps, and sewed Fanny's gingham sunbonnet into her hair before she left the house. When all the rubbing and scrubbing failed to produce the requisite magnolia skin, however, Fanny's grandmother finally concluded, "She is that color by nature—God made her ugly."

BUT FANNY GREW up to be pretty—the most attractive of the Vandegrift sisters, Nellie wrote, with her "piquant prettiness and sparkling vivacity." As a teenager, she tamed her curly dark hair by pulling it into two long braids. This showed off her delicate mouth, straight nose, clear complexion, and eyes that were like black velvet.

Before long, gangly teenage boys were lurking around the Vandegrift house and carving Fanny's initials longingly into trees. With five lively girls in the family, the home became a social hub for dances and card parties, which scandalized their Quaker neighbors. Even George Marshall, Fanny's childhood buddy, started treating her like a girl. Marshall would seem to be a highly eligible suitor for a spirited girl like Fanny: Dark and attractive, with large melancholy eyes, he was a talented actor, dancer, and singer. But even he didn't have a chance when an eighteen-year-old named Samuel Stewart Osbourne came to town.

Fanny was sixteen years old and clattering in the garden on stilts when the young Kentuckian pushed open the front gate to make a social call. He was tall and handsome, with steady blue eyes, thick blond hair, and a Southern genteel manner. He also had an air of assurance that the local boys probably lacked: He was already private secretary to the governor of Indiana. And he was intriguing, if not a little dangerous: a free thinker, avowed atheist, and relentless charmer. The attraction was immediate. That night, Fanny is said to have told her sister Jo that she could have George Marshall because Fanny intended to marry Sam Osbourne. She did, a year later, on Christmas Eve 1857, in a house that her father gave her as a wedding gift.

Some guests were taken aback by how young the bride and groom were. "They looked like two children," one remarked. Still, they would have looked like children in dazzling dress-up. Fanny wore a heavy white satin gown trimmed in old lace, with a low-necked bodice. Her hair, pulled away from her bright black eyes, fell in curls around her neck. Sam wore tight, fawn-colored trousers strapped under varnished boots, a white brocade waistcoat sprigged with lavender flowers, and a lavender-blue coat that must have brought out his milky blue eyes.

Not much is known about the first few years of the Osbournes' marriage, except that a swift thirty-eight weeks after the wedding, eighteen-year-old Fanny gave birth to their first child, Isobel Stewart—"a honeymoon child," as Sam would later tell his daughter. Nellie wrote only that Fanny was happy and idolized her husband as she had her father. But four years into their marriage, by the time the Civil War broke out, Sam was ready for a change. He sold Fanny's house—now his property, though Fanny may have supported the idea—to purchase a farm with his father-in-law. Then he moved his wife and Isobel, commonly called Belle, in with the Vandegrifts, and he volunteered for the Union forces.

Sam's fighting spirit proved short-lived, however. In the kind of restlessness that would become a pattern, he resigned his post with the 46th Indiana Volunteer Regiment six months after he was called up, without seeing any action, and enrolled in the local guard. Within another year, Sam was two thousand miles away from his wife, in a dusty silver-mining camp in Nevada, having sold his share of the farm. With borrowed cash, he had embarked on another noble venture, to help George Marshall (now Jo's husband) get to the warmer climate of California in hopes of healing the tuberculosis he had contracted during the war. George died crossing the Isthmus of Panama, but Sam continued on. Once he reached the West, he got caught up in silver fever.

"PERHAPS, JO, WE ARE GOING to return to you very rich!" Fanny wrote to her sister from New York in spring 1864, on the first leg of a journey to join Sam in Nevada. She gleefully repeated what Sam had written to her about San Francisco: that the miners' shirts had diamond buttons and their women bathed in champagne, and their white marble houses were like sculptures. Under her joyful words, however, a grimmer motive for heading west might have lurked. Fanny was trying to hang on to her wayward husband.

The journey took forty-seven days. The transcontinental railroad would not be completed for another five years, so she and six-year-old Belle traveled by train to New York and by steamer past blockaded Confederate ports to Panama, where they visited Marshall's grave—the first time, Belle would say, that she saw her mother cry. Then they crossed the isthmus by rail and sailed to San Francisco. From there, it was another 450 miles in a jostling stagecoach to Austin, Nevada, where Sam was working his silver claim.

It took remarkable spirit and courage for a twenty-four-year-old woman who had never been more than twenty miles from home to embark on such an arduous journey unescorted. Slender, barely five feet tall, and looking like a teenager, Fanny must have seemed like easy prey for swindlers, and worse.

She braved ship rats and seasickness, stifling heat and filthy accommodations. She was cheated by railroad ticket takers—one went so far as to throw her and her baggage on the tracks—and accepted money that a gallant man collected from other passengers to help pay her and Belle's fare. Recounting this in a letter to her sister, she tried to head off any scolding from Jo about her scruples. "Believe me, I was quite proper," Fanny insisted. "I began by refusing." But she quickly added, "Do not tell this to our folks. It's useless to worry them."

Despite Fanny's brave front, she was clearly distressed. Even before reaching Panama, she was counting her pennies and stuffing Belle with pine nuts to curb her hunger. Yet like other women who headed to mining camps, Fanny was probably sustained through her journey in part by visions of greater status for women in the West. She was a voracious reader and no doubt familiar with the growing genre of stories, novels, and poems for women that portrayed the West as a place where they could gain influence and power.

Advice for women heading west could be found in such unlikely sources as *Godey's Lady's Book*, alongside sumptuous hand-colored engravings of nineteenth-century fashions. And *Godey's* stories such as "Beauty Out West: or How Three Fashionable Ladies Spent a Year in the Wilderness" suggested that women might even find life in the wilderness purer and nobler than in civilization.

Jacob Vandegrift was more skeptical about the promise that a genteel life awaited his daughter on the frontier. Into the envelope of a farewell letter, he had slipped a pocket derringer to protect her, he wrote, from "the riffraff." And while he commended Fanny for her courage, he also warned her to be careful: "The West is a promising country, but dangerous. I fear that you will find life there very different from what you have known."

THE DESOLATE NEVADA wilderness that Fanny saw from the stagecoach must have seemed almost unearthly, with its dry lakebeds and desert seas dotted by sagebrush and squat piñon pines. She had gone beyond the reach of the National Road that had seemed so exotic in Indiana, far from the comforting embrace of the flat green cornfields and flower-embroidered meadows she had known.

Located in a forbidding steep, narrow canyon in the Toiyabe Range, the Austin area had seen few white people beyond Pony Express riders until a worker at one of their stops discovered an outcrop of silver-bearing quartz in May 1862. By the following September, up to a hundred people arrived a day—a pace that startled even mining veterans—and hundreds of potentially rich mines were being worked. Then just as quickly, around the time Sam Osbourne arrived, the fever began cooling.

When Fanny and Belle stepped off the stagecoach, the slapped-together town was already in decline, as shaky as the tumbledown brush huts, tents, and canvas-roofed shacks that dotted the rocky landscape. Gusty winds off the mountains blew snow and ice through the camp in winter and clouds of dust in the scorching summer—and were a real hazard for women in wide skirts and crinolines. Drinking, gambling, and brawls were common, along with nighttime robberies at gunpoint on the unlit roads.

Unknown to Fanny when she left Indiana to join Sam, the couple was broke. He had borrowed money to buy a share in a mine that so far hadn't panned out. In a letter to her family, Sam had promised that Fanny would not have to cook or wash dishes in Austin, leaving her "plenty of time to read and draw [and] teach Belle." In fact, Fanny would not only have to haul water from the Reese River to wash dishes and make her own soap—she would have to leave Belle to roam the encampment largely on her own.

Yet there was a footloose spontaneity to camp life that must have cheered Fanny, at least at first. She had barely settled in when half a dozen women arrived at the Osbourne cabin one snowy evening and invited her to accompany them to a party at a camp a few miles away. There were no mirrors, so one of them held up a tin frying pan for her to look into while she arranged her hair. Then the group piled into a sleigh made of a large packing box on runners and sledded down the snowy hills. There was no shortage of dance partners at the party: Fanny was among a handful of women in a roomful of men.

In their tiny mountainside cabin, Fanny set about turning hardship into a calico-skirted adventure. She built the furniture herself and turned old dresses into curtains. For Belle, who slid down a dirt hill to their door from a trail above, she made panties out of flour sacks. Fanny's life as a camp wife was never idle. She chopped wood to heat the water she hauled for bathing. She set up a shooting range in her backyard and killed intruding rattlesnakes with a Colt revolver. To complete the picture of the frontier woman, she took up smoking and learned to roll her own cigarettes.

Fanny's cooking skills were pushed to the limit by the scarcity of ingredients that came out of the dry alkaline dirt. She later recalled, "Beef and bread . . . bread and beef was almost the sole diet at Reese River." She devised fifteen ways of preparing beef, no doubt shedding tears of frustration as she did, and cooked it as best as she could on a sagebrush fire. In the absence of yeast, she made soda bread. Her greatest triumph, according to her sister Nellie, was making imitation honey for griddle cakes out of boiled sugar with a lump of alum.

Fanny also kept a cool head about the dangers of frontier life. People in Austin were jumpy about the possibility of attacks by the local Paiute and Shoshone tribes. In 1860, a short but deadly burst of fighting had broken out between miners and Paiutes at Pyramid Lake, about 150 miles west of Austin, and tensions between the groups were kept vividly alive by the overblown reporting and prejudices of the local newspaper, the *Reese River Reveille*. So it was with some fear that Fanny noticed Paiute men beginning to gather outside her windows and watch as she did her chores. She didn't want to offend them by closing the curtains. Instead, sensing that they were hungry, she served them bread and tin cups of coffee—actually a hot concoction made with bran that passed for coffee. "They would divide the food carefully, eat it and go away silently," Belle later recalled in her autobiography, *This Life I've Loved*, "but never without adding to the stack of firewood by the side of the house."

While Sam was struggling in the mining camp, Fanny was thriving. It seemed that there was not much she could not handle. Like many frontier women, she was discovering that Victorian roles of men and women were blurred in the West. Single men darned their socks and washed their own dishes. And although women were still expected to soften the rough edges of the frontier with their gentleness, the kind of work required of them belied any notion of females as weak or delicate. In the West, women could be both masculine and feminine—a perfect fit for Fanny.

Other rules were different here too. There were about six thousand men and fewer than sixty "respectable" women in Austin. With the dearth of women and the transient nature of their lives, friendships between women were difficult to build and sustain. So women in the camps crossed class boundaries to become friends. And married women went out with and entertained both married and single men at home.

As it was in Indiana, Fanny's home became a center of social life in Austin. Men from different countries gathered there in the evenings to talk, play monte and charades, and sing songs that reminded them of home. For Queen Victoria's birthday, Fanny threw a dinner for some of the English miners, even attempting a plum pudding.

As much of a draw as her genial husband and cozy house were, many of the miners must have been there just to be near Fanny. She was a mesmerizing combination: tough but feminine, witty and fun but with a reticence that also made her mysterious. At twenty-four, her sexuality was beginning to mature. And she had decided to embrace her "exotic" beauty, defiantly wearing jewel tones that brought out her olive skin.

Despite their scruffy beards and flannel shirts, many of the miners who gathered at the Osbourne home were college-educated young men—

adventurous, living on the edge, and working in the most dangerous conditions. With her freshness and natural beauty, Fanny was like a soothing breeze blowing through the stifling heat of the mines. Many of them must have fallen in love with her. Sam's business partner, a curly-haired Welshman named John Lloyd, would fall the hardest.

IN AUSTIN, SIX-YEAR-OLD Belle Osbourne begged her father to take her where he went when he disappeared to work every day through a hole in the ground. So one day Sam put his daughter in a bucket hung by a rope over a deep mining shaft and casually stuck a burning candle into a lump of clay on her cap. Then he lowered her into the dark mouth of the mine, where little glimmers of candlelight on the caps of the workers below made her feel like she was floating above the stars.

This magical scene was one of the most vivid memories of Belle's childhood, made more so because she was received at the bottom into the arms of a miner named Johnny Crakroft. With the shortage of child playmates, Crakroft would become one of her best friends in Austin. On baking day, Belle was allowed to visit the reclusive miner in his cabin, where he shaped dog and elephant treats for her out of sweetened sourdough. When she was older, her father told her that Crakroft had fled Virginia City after he was suspected of killing a man.

In mining camps, children like Belle enjoyed the kind of freedom that would make modern parents giddy with fear. When the Osbournes moved to Virginia City, Belle's best friend was a barber and gambler named Billy Bird, who was of mixed black, white, and Cherokee blood. Unlike the miners, in their slouch hats and muddy boots, Bird wore the professional gambler's signature sweeping frock coat and a shining diamond in his shirt. He taught Belle not to be afraid of Native people and cut her hair in a "boyish bob" that he slicked down with bear's grease.

On the slopes of Mt. Davidson, 6,200 feet above sea level, "Virginia," as they called it then, was a city built on silver—literally. A vast network of tunnels and timbered shafts curved through the earth hundreds of feet below the bustling streets. According to Mark Twain—who developed his colorful style as well as his pen name at the local newspaper, the *Territorial Enterprise*—the city was also literally booming: "Often we felt our chairs jar, and heard the faint boom of a blast down in the bowels of the earth under the office," he wrote in *Roughing It*.

The mountain was so steep that the city slanted like a roof and was laid out in a cockeyed, crazy-quilt fashion. With about eighteen thousand residents, it had all the features one associates with a boomtown: enormous wealth, drunkenness, gambling, holdups (of women as well as men), opium dens, and loose morals. On summer nights, the city was like a great, dazzling street fair—a torch-lit parade of peddlers, showmen, and quack doctors selling apparatuses to test lung health.

The town was also home to a growing number of wealthy families who built fancy brick and stone houses and dressed in stylish clothes. The Osbournes would not be one of them; their home was a cardboard and canvas shanty. When the wind swept down the mountain, the cloth walls in these flimsy houses would flap back and forth, "literally alive with moving mirrors and pictures," one resident recalled. A gallery of family pictures floating about could make you feel as if you were being visited by ancestral ghosts. More alarming was the possibility of fire. Fanny stayed up nights watching nearby blazes to make sure the flames didn't swoop down on the wind and send her tiny tinderbox of a home up in smoke.

In Virginia City, Sam decided that he was not cut out for mining and got a job as a court clerk. It is understandable—miners there worked deep underground, in temperatures as high as 120 degrees and under threat of cave-ins and flooding. Less defensible, Sam borrowed more money to buy shares in a new mine. Though he wrote to Jacob that he was putting aside funds to pay off his debts, the Osbournes' finances were still tight enough that Fanny had to take on outside work.

Sam put a cheerful spin on this in his letter home. Fanny was "doing splendidly" sewing for the wealthy townswomen during the day and baby-sitting their children while the women socialized in the evenings, he wrote. She earned four dollars a night—"a day's earning for a miner." Even more lucrative was her skill at cards, where, he boasted, she could rake in forty dollars a day. Thinking better of this, he assured her father that "this shall be her last gambling." For his part, Sam thanked Jacob for not losing patience with him. "Most people in your fix would have blown a youngster up sky high who had filched a thousand dollars of their money into the sea." He assured Jacob that he would stay there "till Doomsday" working to pay him back.

Sam was shaping up to be a spotty, if good-natured, provider, but Fanny was loyal to him and believed he was to her. "I am sure I wouldn't change my sorrel-top for a man with a ton of gold," she wrote to Jo. But cracks were beginning to show in their marriage. In the same letter to Fanny's sister, Sam mentioned their arguing and brazenly urged Jo not to believe everything Fanny wrote, adding, "You know she is not accountable for what she says, for her mind is not exactly right—her head is not screwed on right exactly—and she is prone to take offence at everything."

Sam began to look for comfort elsewhere—and in Virginia City, he did not have to look far. Prostitution put down roots early there, so it was firmly entrenched by the time wives and other "respectable" women arrived. One of Fanny's contemporaries noted that many of the men "live after the Salt Lake style, only they are not as honorable as old Brigham was, for he married all his wives according to his religion. Here they marry but one, and the unmarried ones are always dressed the richest." Sam certainly made sure that his mistress's house was richly dressed, as Fanny discovered when she arrived home from a rare trip to San Francisco to a literally empty house. Sam had lent all their furniture to his new mistress.

Fanny carefully worded a letter home about it, leaving out the woman's line of work, though her rage was palpable. "You spoke of my nice furniture. Sam lent the most of it to a woman while I was gone and now she refuses to give it up," she huffed. Fanny planned to take the matter into her own hands. She would confront the woman herself, she wrote, and if Sam's mistress refused to give Fanny's furniture back, she would involve the police.

Fanny got her furniture back, but not her husband: Soon he was on the road again, fleeing his wife and debts, and wooed by the mirage of another silver strike that would finally pay. He set off with forty or so other prospectors to the Coeur d'Alene Mountains in Idaho, leaving Fanny and Belle to cope as best they could in Virginia City. This time, Fanny didn't hear from him for months.

It was an anxious time to be alone in the Comstock. Silver in the shallower ground appeared to be exhausted. Banks, which could finance the machinery needed to reach the deeper, richer deposits, were taking over silver mining, buying claims from individual miners for a song. Fanny stuck it out in Virginia City for several months, but when her friend John Lloyd decided to throw in the towel and head for San Francisco on Christmas Eve, she joined him, dressing Belle as a boy for the journey.

Almost as soon as they arrived in San Francisco, Fanny received word that Sam had been killed in an Indian attack on his prospecting party. Whatever was left of her righteous anger with him must have melted into grief and regret. Unlike many wives of her time, she had refused to ignore her husband's infidelity. One can imagine that she even felt a twinge of wickedness and guilt for driving him off. But she also had to look forward. She was a penniless widow in a strange city, with an eight-year-old child to support. At twenty-six years old, she dragged her weary body into a heavy black mourning dress and likely wound her country-girl braids around her head to look older. Then she went out to find a job.

Two

Fashion was big business in San Francisco when Fanny and Belle arrived. In a city founded on getting rich, what better way for a new millionaire to advertise his wealth than by parading his well-dressed wife? Yet the women who set the style in San Francisco were not the society wives but the city's prostitutes. While most prostitutes lived in poverty, many others, especially the madams who ran their own brothels, were regular patrons of small clothing shops, fueling more respectable economic opportunities for the women who owned and staffed them. For a short time, before male-dominated department stores and ready-made clothing took over toward the end of the century, female milliners and dress- and corset-makers did a thriving business. And in San Francisco, their shops provided one of the few places where women could enjoy an exclusively female culture.

Ironically, female dressmakers thrived as long as women wore fashions that were constrictive and uncomfortable. The decade's new emphasis on women's rears ushered in a crinoline called the "crinolette," which humped in back and encased women in a steel and cotton cage from the waist down. Soft, homemade corsets gave way to professionally made longer and tighter ones with whalebone or steel stays that compressed a woman's rib cage and squeezed her stomach bulk into her chest cavity—and required professionally constructed bodices that fit over them like skin. Yet forgoing a corset was not an attractive option to most women. It was seen as sloppy, while wearing a corset was a sign of self-control and self-respect.

Almost all American women could sew, but few could enter the dress-making trade with only home-sewing skills. Fanny decided she would be one of them. As a child, she had learned to do delicate needlework on the ruffles for her father's shirts, and she put elaborate trim on the dresses, petticoats, and panties she made for Belle. According to her sister Nellie, Fanny was hired as a fitter, who cut garment pieces from cloth—the highest position in a shop. It seems more likely that she was a lower-paid finisher, who did fine needlework and trim. For her to land either position was exceptional. It might have helped that, according to Belle, her mother also passed herself off as French without speaking a word of the language—a ploy that could only have worked because no one ever tried to converse with her in French.

It was just as well that Fanny didn't need to speak at work—she was too anxious, overworked, and depressed to want to talk much anyway. Belle claimed that period was so painful to her mother, she would not want to speak of it for the rest of her life. When their money ran low, Fanny took a room south of Market Street in the cheap boardinghouse where John Lloyd was taking up residence. On a "mean street" near a shot tower where molten lead was poured through a copper sieve to make bullets, it was a sketchy place for a single mother with a small daughter—a rough neighborhood populated mostly by sailors and single men.

Fanny worked day and night, hunched over a needle and thread, making dresses for ladies that she could not afford for herself. It was repetitious work that strained her back and eyes and left her fingers numb. During the day, she had no choice but to leave Belle in the care of the landlady and her son while she went to work. In the evenings, her lamp-lit fingers crocheted baby socks and bootees and embroidered pincushions and sachet bags, while her daughter slept in the room they shared. Fanny sold these through the Women's Exchange, a charity marketplace that sold goods made by poor women.

Dreary as their life was, Belle would recall, "There were bright spots even there, and the brightest of all was John Lloyd." Like Fanny, Lloyd was barely scraping by after his poor luck in the Nevada mines. But the young blond Welshman had not lost the ambition that brought him to the United States. During the day, he worked as a law clerk. In the evening, he studied law books he checked out from the library.

Lloyd devoted every Sunday, his only day off, to Belle—giving Fanny a much-needed break and opening up another adventurous world to her daughter. Starting off in the dim morning fog, they would row out in a hired boat among the ships in the bay. When they found one that Lloyd thought was friendly, they asked to climb aboard and a rope ladder was dangled over the side. One week, Belle recalled, they might be served break-fast by a sailor "with a bare chest and arms most fascinatingly adorned with ships and anchors and ladies with fish tails," which he obligingly displayed for her admiration. The next week, a South Seas islander might give her a carved coconut for a gift. From there, they took a paper bag of cream puffs to eat on a perch at Fort Point, at the narrows of the Golden Gate.

Thanks largely to Lloyd, Belle would remember a meager birthday in the boardinghouse as the happiest of her life. "My mother (at the cost of I dare not think how many stitches) bought the head of a china doll and made the body herself, stuffing it with rags," Belle later recalled. Out of bits of left-over silk and satin from the dresses she made for women, Fanny crafted a remarkable miniature wardrobe for the doll—"clothes that could be put on and off and most elegant underwear trimmed with lace and perfect in every detail, even to the tiny buttons and buttonholes."

Lloyd bought a miniature tea set and made a chair and table out of a cigar box for the doll. Using the Welshman's penknife, Belle cut her birthday cupcake into four pieces and served them on tiny tin plates. "My mother, in her black dress, did her best to smile," Belle later wrote. "John was very gay and looked happy and boyish with his pink cheeks and crisp curly hair. I imagine he was working as hard to distract my mother's attention as he was to entertain me."

In fact, the boyish, blushing Lloyd was hoping to do more than distract Fanny. As a mutual friend later said, Lloyd was "crazily in love" with her.

Sacrificing his Sundays to take care of her daughter was a pretty clear declaration of that, as was his suggestion that Fanny and Belle take a room in his boardinghouse, where he must have thought he could watch over them—and surely dreamed of romancing Fanny. Her black widow's dress might have even made her more alluring. For Victorian men, mourning gowns were quite tantalizing—a sign of a woman's bereavement but also a symbol of her sexual experience and new availability. On a young, pretty woman, it must have been a potent combination for a man in his twenties.

Whatever dreams Lloyd had about Fanny, however, they were soon shattered. One day, Belle was playing on the stairway in the boardinghouse when the front door opened. Standing in the doorway was a tall man with a wide hat and trousers stuffed into his boots. Sam Osbourne had returned to reclaim his wife.

SAM COULD EXPLAIN EVERYTHING. He and another miner, Sam Orr, had strayed from their prospecting party, avoiding the "Indian massacre." Then they had tramped, hungry and penniless, through deserts, small towns, and settlements, doing odd jobs to work their way home. Sam may not have picked up many useful skills in the Comstock, but he had learned how to tell tall tales. He told Belle he had escaped death four times in one day—by thirst, drowning, ambush, and rattlesnake bite.

Belle later seemed puzzled why Sam did not get word that he was alive to Fanny sooner. One can guess that it was because once back in civilization, he took time to sample some of its pleasures on the way to join his grieving wife. Fanny must have been skeptical of Sam's story, but she would have wanted to believe him. She was relieved that he was alive and hoped that they could make a fresh start.

Sam got a job as a law clerk. Fanny got pregnant. The family moved to a rented house on Fifth Street, where John Lloyd boarded with them. Fanny wrote home that their house had a bedroom for Lloyd, who paid them forty dollars a month for room and board and laundry. It was not an unusual arrangement in those days, though a little awkward given Lloyd's feelings for Sam's wife.

Sam wrote to tell his father-in-law he was considering investing in another mine. Apparently, this was the last straw for Jacob. "Your letter, containing the command to come home, was received a few days ago," Sam replied to Jacob in February 1867. "I need not tell you that I would be mighty glad if I could make the arrangements to go home right off—but I can't do it yet." He had debts to pay and no money for their tickets home, he wrote. In reality, though, Sam had no intention of going back to "the states," as people in California still called the eastern part of the country. After a blistering Methodist upbringing, he experienced San Francisco as a cool salve of tolerance and freedom.

Fanny could see that Sam, like other men who went west to make their fortunes, would also feel too humiliated to return home without one. But Fanny believed he should feel no shame, since he had done his best. "I am sure you will none of you think any the less of us now that we are poor—though I can assure you that we don't intend to remain so," she wrote to her brother, Jake.

Even with Sam back in town, the family was poor—to the point that Fanny avoided social calls out of shame for her threadbare clothing. She had traded her widow's weeds for a sturdy housedress that could take daily dirt and sweat. But the family was too strapped for her to retrieve her proper clothing—customary morning and evening gowns, walking suits and carriage dresses—out of storage in Virginia City. When the outdated clothing finally arrived, she tore out the seams and recut and retrimmed them so she could visit the relatives of her sister Jo's new fiancé, Ben Thomas. "I remember when I lived about as well and thought I was poor," she wrote to Jo after visiting their home. "I know what being poor is now."

When she finished her housework, Fanny crocheted puffy baby sweaters with ribbons and lace to sell through the Women's Exchange for one dollar apiece. "Someone is always wanting for a sack, so I am kept in a continual hurry," she wrote to Jo, "one is lying before me now unfinished that I had been working at all day, Sunday though it be." She was also learning to use watercolors to hand-tint photos. If she should need to do it for money, she wrote, "It is very showy, cheap, and can be done in a short time."

With Fanny's fingers flying to help keep her family afloat, Belle continued to enjoy an uncomfortable amount of freedom. Sam would take her to a matinee and see her "safely" to her seat. Then he would leave her alone in the dark theater while he moved on to other engagements, meeting her in the lobby after the play. "I am sure my father must have shocked the whole community by taking me, an innocent child of nine, to see *The Black Crook*," she recalled of one musical spectacle about black magic. "The depravity of that burlesque shook the world."

Though Sam had a carefree demeanor, he also had spells of deep depression. But Belle wrote that she never heard her father say a cross word. She fondly recalled that he would sneak her puffs of his cigarette over his shoulder when Fanny wasn't looking and take her on "glorious walks," where he told her, "Learn to enjoy the moment. Yesterday is gone, tomorrow hasn't come yet."

Signs of depression slipped into Fanny's letters home. She missed the companionship of her sisters but despaired of ever enjoying it again. "That I should seems too great a happiness for me," she wrote to Jo. It was a wisp of a line, thin as a shaving from her pencil, slipped between talk of her garden and her work. But it told much about the sadness welling inside her. She felt that she was not entitled to happiness or able to control her own destiny, and the two seemed as entangled as the threads she rolled between her fingers into a knot.

Fanny and Sam did not write much about each other in their letters home. Both wrote much more warmly about John Lloyd, who had graciously found Sam work at his own expense. "You don't know what a good fellow Lloyd is," Sam wrote to his father-in-law after Lloyd graciously withdrew from applying for a higher-paying job so that Sam could secure it instead. And Sam was clearly relieved when Lloyd passed up another job offer in Mexico. "If he had gone I would not know what to do, for he is our right bower,"

Sam wrote to Fanny's brother, Jake. "If we go back—or rather when we go back—we will certainly take him with us."

Lloyd's feelings for Fanny continued to spill out in quiet, poignant ways. Sam was cross with her when she brought up going home, but Lloyd tried, at least, to bring her family closer. He secretly took a picture of Jacob to be elegantly framed so that Fanny could mount it on the wall and feel that her father was looking down on her. "Wasn't that thoughtful and kind?" Fanny wrote delightedly to Jo. "He is always doing something of the kind."

While her husband's eyes were wandering, Lloyd's were glued on her. When Fanny had a photo of herself taken, he insisted on buying two. "I think it flatters me a great deal," she noted, basking in the attention. "I was never half as pretty in all my life." Lloyd seemed to have studied her from her head to her tiny size-four feet. For Christmas, he gave her a beautiful pair of French slippers "that fit exactly."

Could Sam have been blind to the steamy emotions clouding the windows of his home? He might have simply been too preoccupied to notice. Shortly into her pregnancy, Fanny discovered that he had another mistress.

Fanny kept Sam's infidelity, as well as her pregnancy, from her family—it must have been too painful and humiliating to write about them. But a teary letter to her newly married sister Jo said all that she could not put into words. Fanny reflected on the aspects of Jo's current life that ensured a secure and happy future as well: "Your little child with you in your own home, no anxious ponderings over tomorrow, a husband you can respect and believe in implicitly, and who loves you—there is much in your lot to be envied by any woman."

In April 1868, Fanny gave birth to the couple's first son. She planned to name him Lloyd Samuel, but Sam insisted that his own name come first. (Though Samuel Lloyd bore a strong resemblance to Sam, he went by "Lloyd" most of his life, and it is used here for clarity.) A month later, Fanny left her husband. Barely recovered from childbirth, she packed her trunks and gathered her children for the trying journey through Panama and New York to Indiana.

THE APPLE TREES in the orchard and the deep, shady porch welcomed Fanny, Belle, and baby Lloyd back to the Vandegrift home and kept them there through the following spring. For nine-year-old Belle, the visit would leave memories of warm ginger cookies and barrels of cider in the root cellar, pale gold cornfields in autumn and first snow in winter. For Fanny, the homecoming must have been bittersweet. Though the house was bulging with her siblings, they were all moving on with their lives. Jake was in business in Indianapolis. Jo, a Civil War widow, had remarried a banker, Ben Thomas. Betty was home awaiting the birth of her first child with James Patterson, an army officer.

For months, Sam begged and pleaded with Fanny to come back to San Francisco. He promised he would change his ways. Her family undoubtedly also encouraged her to do the respectable thing and return to her husband. Finally, after a year, she agreed. She brought along her younger sister Cora, who would go on to marry Sam Orr, the silver prospector who had tramped back from Idaho with Sam Osbourne. At least the return trip to San Francisco was easier. The rails forming the first national railroad, the Union Pacific, were connected the month before she left. This time it took only ten days to reach San Francisco.

Sam was now a man-about-town, earning a good living as a court stenographer. Otherwise, their life started to fall into an uncomfortably familiar pattern. Fanny got pregnant. Sam moved the family to a new home. This time, however, he bought a house at Eleventh Avenue and East Eighteenth Street in East Oakland, then known as Brooklyn, a town where cowboys from the valley still drove their herds down the main drag to cattle boats at the waterfront. It was a safe distance from Sam's social life in San Francisco, as well as from John Lloyd.

Fanny had a home, for the first time since her father had given her one as a wedding gift. It was a prefab cottage that had come around the Cape Horn in pieces, but it made her feel grounded. White, with a peaked green roof and a front porch curtained with climbing roses, it looked out on the estuary where the ferryboat would bring Sam home from San Francisco. Fanny threw every inch of her tiny body into the hopeless task of making the house—and herself—into something he would want to come home to. Inviting smells wafted out to the garden as she became a skilled and inventive cook. In her large yard, the "young and slender woman, wearing her hair in two long braids down her back" tended masses of flowers and fruit trees. "Of all the lovely gardens she left in her trail through life, I think the one at East Oakland was the most gorgeous," Belle later recalled.

Little paths led past Fanny's shooting range to her "secret garden," where she nurtured her growing artistic impulses. One path went to a studio where she painted still lifes of flowers. She also built a darkroom and tackled complicated "wet-plate" photography, though amateur photography was pretty much unheard of for another decade.

The Osbournes' second son, Hervey, born in March 1871, was a beautiful child. Unlike Belle, who was dark and curly haired like her mother, and Lloyd, who was fair and blond like his father, Hervey was a striking mix—with dark eyes and long golden curls that billowed around his shoulders. The harshness of Fanny's life had not given her much time to play with Belle and Lloyd when they were babies. With Hervey, that changed. Suddenly she was laughing and cooing, something that sounded foreign to her older children.

Belle recalled that Fanny also had more time for her. "My mother influenced me in those days in many ways that I shall never forget, especially in her hatred of anything that savored of snobbery," she later wrote. Fanny taught her to be considerate, to put herself in other people's shoes, and to consider her dark skin beautiful. She dressed Belle in crisp yellows and pale blues, "which made me look still darker, on the principle that Sarah Bernhardt followed in exaggerating her thinness when it was the fashion to have a rounded form."

Fanny loved children, but she was not a fussy mother or a gushy one, except in letters. A grand gesture was more her style of showing her love. When Belle wanted to give a party but knew their little cottage was too small, Fanny—who had "a real flair for the stage"—organized a musical entertainment. She made costumes and directed the cast, and remade the barn into a fairyland of colored lanterns, greenery, and bunting that thrilled Belle and dazzled her friends.

Underneath the happy times, though, even a child could see that Fanny and Sam were not happy together. When her father was away, Belle later wrote, "home was a pleasant place. My mother, busy with a dozen different things, painting flowers, shooting with a rifle at a mark, grafting roses, stuffing spiced cantaloupes for pickling, or making designs in clay, would let me help her and explain what she was doing." Being alone with her father was also nice, "but when my mother joined us there was often a tension, an atmosphere of suppressed feelings that chilled me."

Three children, a new house, and Fanny's near manic devotion to crafts and hobbies could not distract her from the central lie of her marriage. Sam *had* changed—but instead of reining in his affairs, he had become more flagrant. By the time Hervey was born, he was living openly with his new mistress in San Francisco. There was no need for Fanny to watch for his ferryboat—he came to East Oakland only on weekends. And his infidelity had become a subject of gossip on both sides of the bay. When snickers and whispers followed her, Fanny lifted her head and maintained a proud silence.

SOMETHING HAD TO CHANGE, but what? Divorce laws gave a woman about as much room to move as her corset. And in some ways, marriage and corsets served a similar restricting function: A woman who refused to stay put in either faced crude assumptions about her lifestyle and became an outcast. It did not matter whether a husband was an adulterer—women were the losers in most divorces. Alimony was often given in one small sum and not large enough to support children, for the woman who was lucky enough to get custody of hers. As Fanny's brief experience in the work world showed, she could hardly feed one child, let alone three. With poverty, disgrace, and the loss of her children likely outcomes for a woman who left her marriage, it is no wonder many wives ignored their husbands' philandering. But Fanny could not make herself do this.

According to a Vandegrift family story, the child Fanny once asked if she could change her name to Lily. Her mother had replied that she *was* a lily—"a little tiger lily!" That must have stung Fanny—a lily was white like the skin of pretty little girls, as well as a symbol of modesty. The hardy tiger lily, on the other hand, grew wild next to country roads and in ditches and was a symbol of passion. In her usual defiant way, though, Fanny came to embrace the hardy, flaming flower and planted it in all her gardens. She was a passionate woman: She had loved her husband fully and she could not accept that she should be happy with less in return. She could not change her nature any more than her skin color to fit Victorian standards.

During a long visit after Hervey's birth, Sam's mother pounded in Fanny's failures as a Victorian wife. Cynthia Osbourne already held Fanny responsible for Sam's atheism, though he had adopted it in college in rebellion against his parents' strict brand of Methodism. But Fanny had failed to be the moral angel in the house—her lack of interest in "spiritual things" had not guided Sam back to his faith. In fact, according to her mother-in-law, Fanny was responsible for Sam's infidelity. She later said, "Fanny's temper drove him to most of what he did."

Sam was now reveling in his freedom in San Francisco. Reflecting his new status, he had a trim Vandyke beard, was outfitted by the gentlemen's emporium Bullock and Jones, and carried himself, according to Belle, in "the grand manner of a Kentuckian." He became an early member of the all-male Bohemian Club, which held monthly entertainments called High Jinks and rowdy summer retreats in the redwoods. Founded by artists and writers in 1871, it quickly expanded to include businessmen and others who only needed to have an interest in the arts and deeper pockets than the art crowd. (Visiting the club in 1882, Oscar Wilde said, "I never saw so many well-dressed, well-fed, business-looking Bohemians in my life.")

While Sam had found his niche in the city, his daughter was struggling to fit in. Belle's childhood in mining towns with mostly grown men as friends made her seem odd to other children. Her lack of a formal education—or much of any education—made it difficult for her to settle down to rote classroom learning. By the time she reached Oakland High School at the age of fourteen, she recalled, "I never understood a word of any of my studies. . . . It is a wonder to me now how I ever managed to stay on as long as I did." As a teenager, she developed a rebellious streak. When her teacher discovered that one classmate did her algebra homework for her and another her French exercises, she was sent home in disgrace. Years later, she could not remember how the family handled this, but she could imagine. "My father of course would have taken my part and sympathized with me if I had burned the schoolhouse down," she wrote. Her mother probably "gave me a well-deserved scolding that made no impression."

Soon after, to Belle's delight, she was withdrawn from Oakland High. Based on the clever caricatures and sketches that filled her exam books— her teacher even asked to keep some—Fanny enrolled her in the new California School of Design (later the San Francisco Art Institute). Fanny also hired a governess, Kate Moss, to care for her two boys so she could join Belle there three days a week. For Belle, it was nice together time with her mother. For Fanny, it was also an attempt to carve out a separate life within the confines of her marriage.

JUST SAILING TO SCHOOL across San Francisco Bay on a side-wheel ferry was like the beginning of some great adventure. The bay was a moving picture. Some days, when the sun danced on the water, pinpricks of light glittered across the ripples like sparks off silver spurs. Other days, the fog lay thick on the water, muffling the calls of the seagulls overhead. It was like being propelled through a cloud until the city suddenly emerged out of the mist.

Once on shore, Fanny and Belle could follow their noses to the California Market, a bustling hall of produce stands and eateries. In the steamy seafood restaurants, they could get plump fried oysters in a hollowed-out loaf of French bread or a mound of shellfish, a steak, and a mug of coffee for twenty-five cents. Above the market's awnings were the windows of the Bohemian Club and a large domed cage of live owls, the club's mascot. In rooms let from the Bohemian Club, the School of Design offered classes for twelve dollars a month.

The art school's director, Virgil Macey Williams, was a talented figure and landscape painter who had studied art in Italy and was among the early white travelers to Yosemite Valley. During her time at the school, Fanny became part of a social circle of artists that included Virgil, the musician Oscar Weil, and the poet Charles Warren Stoddard. But Virgil's wife, Dora, became the intimate female friend she had been longing for since she left Indiana.

A Boston Yankee whose ancestors were among the original European settlers of Martha's Vineyard, Dora Norton Williams had spent most of her adult life as a single, working woman—unlike Fanny, whose movements had been dictated by her husband since she was a teenager. Dora was eleven years older and had been a schoolteacher during the Civil War in South Carolina, where she had not withheld her Yankee views. Later, she gave up teaching for the "rather pleasant and lucrative occupation" of coloring and finishing photographs at a Boston studio. She was studying freehand drawing at Harvard College when her teacher, Virgil Williams, asked her to marry him. She was forty-two. It was her first marriage and his second.

Slim and pretty, with dark hair and eyes, Dora was a charming eccentric. On the street or at the school, which she helped run, you could hear her before you saw her. Dangling from her belt on little chains were silver items— a mesh purse, pencil case, knife, and buttonhook—that tinkled like wind chimes when she walked. She moved decisively through the school and life, mouth firm and back straight, in homely hats, rustling silks and velvets, and noisy bracelets and necklaces.

Dora was a talented still life watercolorist and prided herself on "a frankness that was sometimes rather appalling," according to Belle. She and Fanny immediately bonded over that, along with their individuality, unconventional lives, and mutual interest in art. Through forty years of correspondence, they would gossip, discuss art, and confide their yearnings and frustrations, sometimes bolstering each other's confidence and sometimes stinging with their sharp tongues.

It was while traveling to and from school on the ferry that Belle began to notice how much attention her mother attracted, with her "features cut like a delicate cameo." By then, Fanny was copying French fashions to make the kind of clothes for herself that she had once made for other women. Like many girls, Belle remembered one of her mother's outfits especially well: a slightly bustled, dark-blue-and-green plaid skirt and basque that fit tight over her waist and hips, with white ruffling at the neck and wrists and gold buttons up the front. Peeking out from the basque were blue velvet leg-of-mutton sleeves that matched the blue velvet toque framing Fanny's curls. "Her figure was slender, with the hour-glass effect slightly accented," Belle wrote, "and with her nicely shod little feet and dainty gloves she well repaid the many glances cast her way."

One of the men who gave Fanny more than a passing glance was her husband's friend Timothy Rearden. A lawyer who had sailed into San Francisco Bay in 1863 aiming to get rich, Rearden was also fluent in ancient Greek and translated medieval German. Unassuming, with black Irish eyes and a dimpled smile behind a walrus mustache, he seemed temperamentally more suited to academia than to courtroom drama. Yet he would go on to become a superior court judge and be remembered by the writer Ambrose Bierce as very likely the foremost scholar in the western United States.

When Fanny met him, the thirty-five-year-old bachelor headed the library of the Mercantile Association and contributed poems and essays to the *Overland Monthly*, where he was an associate of Bret Harte. Fanny found him full of contradictions—shy but prickly, prejudiced despite being the target of anti-Irish slurs, and both suspicious and supportive of independent women. Rearden recognized Fanny's talent as a storyteller and encouraged her to try her hand at writing fiction. She did, giving him her short stories— likely fairy tales or fables—to review. Some were published in *Very Young Americans*, a children's magazine that sold for five cents in grocery stores.

Rearden also seems to have needled Fanny constantly—about her grammar and spelling, her looks, her advancing age, and her behavior. But she enjoyed pushing back. She admired his intellect and liked taking on his sexual and ethnic bigotries. She tried to poke holes in his cynicism, which she saw as a sham. "I know he is peculiar," she once wrote to Dora, "but then it is not his faults that I dislike but himself that I like and have liked all these years."

Rearden was a friend of John Lloyd, who was also a lawyer by then. In a letter to his mother, Rearden observed that Sam had no family instincts while Lloyd was so in love with Fanny, he would cry if teased too hard about it. Still, Rearden started his own flirtation with Fanny as well. Her letters to him show that the two sparred and flirted energetically. In a few, there are suggestions of rendezvous. "Come and see me at home or here," she wrote in one, probably from the School of Design. "Late in the afternoon is not so dangerous." In another, she teased, "When you marry allow your wife to act according to her own notions of propriety. Come to think of it—I suppose writing this note is another impropriety."

Fanny had decided to renounce the role of pitied, rejected wife and enjoy some of the freedom her husband felt entitled to in their marriage. She was trying to build a more independent life—learning how to paint, earning pocket money writing fiction, and traveling in an artistic urban circle. The attention of Rearden as well as John Lloyd—both educated, ambitious men on their way to success (Lloyd would become a wealthy bank president)—must have been especially flattering.

Whether Fanny chose either man as a lover is a matter of some debate. Most biographers have agreed that her passionate adventures probably did not go beyond flirtation. One Stevenson biographer speculated that Rearden may have been homosexual, though his daughter later insisted that he had no interest in Fanny because he was in love with a "beautiful cultured blonde" at the time. Pregnancy also would have been a concern for Fanny: It was one thing for her to defy convention and another to be cast out by society and lose her children—both real possibilities if she was caught having an affair.

If Fanny did have dalliances with either or both of the men, they clearly did not blossom into love affairs that tempted her to leave her husband for them. She seemed to value Lloyd primarily as a friend she could count on. But he and Rearden were clearly mesmerized by her. They did not quite know what to make of Fanny: She did not fit into either of the Victorian molds of seductress or wife. Instead, she dangled before them, with her smoldering eyes and brave heart, untamable.

Neither Rearden nor Lloyd would marry until later in life, and their wives would not approve of Fanny. When Fanny returned to San Francisco as a widow in her fifties, Lloyd's wife snubbed her. Despite his wife's disapproval, however, he remained a loyal friend and handled Fanny's financial affairs—taking care of her to the end, in his way. Rearden was dead by then—he died at fifty-three, four years into his only marriage. His widow also refused Fanny's social invitations. But her husband had saved Fanny's letters and story manuscripts until he died.

AMONG THE BLOWUPS and embarrassments that convinced Fanny to leave Sam, one stayed especially vivid in Belle's mind. She and her mother were sitting in the parlor of the East Oakland house with the front door open to take in the fragrant breeze from the trellised porch, when they heard the gate of the picket fence click. Coming up the rose path was a young woman in a flashy costume and saucy hat atop a huge chignon—all flounced, puffed, and fringed like a Victorian lampshade.

One can imagine Fanny's wrath at the sight of Sam's mistress brushing against her prized cloth-of-gold roses. She stepped outside and gave the visitor a fierce look that the woman simply ignored as she continued up onto the porch. Fanny demanded to know why she was there.

The woman stammered, briefly flustered, and then tossed her head. "I came to make a friendly call," she sniffed. "There is no reason why I shouldn't."

"There is a very good reason why you should not come into my house," Fanny said, going on to address the woman in words that were short in every way. Within minutes, the visitor sashayed fiercely back down the path, "her bustle wagging insolently behind her," Belle recalled.

In late spring of 1875, Fanny packed up her children—Belle, sixteen; Lloyd, seven; and Hervey, four. But this time, instead of running away with them, she was going to run toward something. Emboldened by Belle's progress in art school and her own first prize in drawing for the term, Fanny decided she and Belle should attend the Royal Academy of Fine Arts in Belgium. Daughters in stylish families often studied at European schools—and their mothers sometimes spent time abroad to avoid scandals at home. Sam could hardly have argued when Fanny pointed out that he was already supporting two households, so it would not be a heavy financial burden. At any rate, she managed to convince, or browbeat, him into financing her plan.

Fanny was packed and ready to go quickly, if not quite sure where she was going. This could be said of Fanny throughout her life. She did not even tell the children they were leaving until their trunks were full, according to Belle. And though the plan must have been brewing for a while (and was why, Belle later guessed, Miss Kate had been drilling her in French verbs for several months), it was not particularly well thought out. Did one year of art school in San Francisco qualify Fanny and Belle for the academy in Belgium? Since Fanny could not afford to take Miss Kate, who would care for the little boys while their mother was at school? But it was not in Fanny's nature to worry about the details or prepare for the worst. If she did, she might not have been able to do the extraordinary things she did.

Fanny had a particularly striking photo of herself taken before she left, when she was refashioning herself as an artist and independent woman. In its surprising simplicity, it captures how she was shrugging off the feminine ideal usually celebrated in Victorian portraits. It also reveals Fanny as a prototype for the "New Woman" nearly two decades before the term was coined and depicted in the popular press as a female who smoked cigarettes, wore neckties, carried a gun, and generally acted like a man.

In the photo, Fanny wears a white cravat and a jacket with a man's lapels—both symbols of strong-minded women. Her voluminous hair, usually slicked back and tamed, is loosely twisted into a thick and slightly messy knot, with a few escaped wisps curling at her temples. Fanny's smooth face looks untouched by the years and the harshness of her life. She is not leaning gracefully on a studio prop, but squarely faces the camera, though she gazes beyond it, as if toward a future she could only imagine—a future that would begin with the wildest ride of her life through the flood of the century in Indiana.

THREE

"After many moving adventures by field and by flood we are at length domiciled at the heart of the old city of Antwerp," Fanny wrote to Dora Williams in August 1875. Describing the daredevil ride she and her children took in Indiana, where they had stopped to visit her family, she could not resist adding, "We plunged over embankments into foaming torrents, at the risk of being swept away and drowned, half a dozen times." By then, Fanny habitually carried her small gun in her purse for her children's and her own protection. If she wanted the freedom to travel and engage with life on her own terms, it was less cumbersome than having to attach herself to a man.

Though she was traveling toward some notion of independence, Fanny still was not above using men to help her get there. She wrote to Dora about finally arriving in Antwerp late one rainy night on a crowded Channel steamer. The customs officers boarded only to announce they would not check baggage until the next morning, leaving the passengers stranded onboard without enough beds. "I watched for a chance to get near the best-natured-looking of the officials," Fanny wrote, "[and] tried to look as helpless as possible, it was very easy to do, I can assure you, I had only to look as I felt, and said, 'We are American ladies alone; you see how unpleasant it will be to remain here all night; I trust to your courtesy.'" Their trunks were lifted down and quickly opened and closed, and a carriage was hailed to take them to a hotel. According to Belle, her mother inspired this kind of solicitous attention over and over: "When in any difficulty, she only had to look helpless and bewildered, and gallant strangers leaped to her assistance."

Fanny had put all her energy into the hard work of getting her family to Europe. But that night, she let herself feel that she was on the brink of a great adventure when she heard the bells of Antwerp's Gothic cathedral from their hotel. Fanny listened with tears in her eyes, feeling that the chimes were a welcome to the Old World and a good omen.

There were other good omens. Miss Kate had surprised them by turning up on the deck of their ship after it embarked from the U.S. The governess had planned to go only as far as New York, where she had relatives. But she was devoted to Hervey and adored Fanny (though she thought Fanny's relationship with Belle was too sisterly), so she decided to pay her own way in steerage to join them instead. And once the travel party arrived in Antwerp, a Flemish family took them under their wing, helping them get a room and their bearings in Belgium.

Fanny found the old seaport city quaint and romantic—the candlelit shrines to the Madonna on street corners, the bell pulls so high she needed a stepladder to reach them, the men in enormous trousers and women in high headdresses. Sometimes she and Belle felt as if they were in an opera. "We hardly seem to feel real to ourselves," Fanny wrote to Dora. Oddly, the city seemed to crystallize what she saw in Rearden. In a letter, she likened him to Antwerp, "a city that might be changed in almost any way for the better, and yet in that change would lose all its attractions."

Setbacks also came rather quickly, though Fanny handled them with her usual efficiency. Old-world Antwerp did not welcome women in art school. And Fanny's golden-curled son, Hervey, came down with a fever that stumped the doctor. He recommended that the boy see a pediatric specialist in Paris. Within a week, without knowing the language or where she was going, Fanny packed up the family, resettled them in a modest, sunny apartment near Montmartre, and had Hervey under the care of a Parisian doctor.

Paris was still trying to regain its balance after war with Prussia in 1870 and the 1871 Paris Commune. The city had been shelled, toppled, and torched. The streets around the Osbournes' apartment on the rue de Naples were in ruins, though nearby the Basilique du Sacré-Coeur was just beginning to rise in Montmartre. Their apartment was on high ground, where the air was fresh and their water was brought in from artesian wells, instead of from the sewage-clogged Seine—both good for Hervey's health.

At first, Fanny was afraid to leave her son's side, but his health seemed to improve rapidly under his new doctor's care, and Miss Kate was there to dote on him as well. In November, she and Belle ventured out into the Parisian art scene at one of the most exciting times in its history. The art capital of the world was in ferment over the radical, loose-brushed paintings of a new movement known as Impressionism. Students were flocking from around the world to catch the latest developments in painting, lithography, and other decorative arts.

Fanny and Belle enrolled in the Académie Julian, founded by painter Rodolphe Julian. It was more accessible to foreigners than the prestigious École des Beaux-Artes and popular with Americans because it offered instruction from respected Beaux-Artes professors in a more informal setting. (Later alumni included Diego Rivera, Henri Matisse, Marcel Duchamp, and Robert Rauschenberg.) The school had branches all over Paris. "One of them, miraculously, is reserved for women," Fanny wrote to Dora. "Absolutely everyone comes, and it promises to be exciting."

Not only did Académie Julian welcome women—unlike the Beaux-Artes, which did not admit them for another twenty-two years—it also allowed women to draw from nude female models and male models who were bare except for a wisp of strategic draping, though the female students were still barred from painting in the same room as their male colleagues. The nearly nude male models did not seem to faze Fanny, but she had some reservations about the female models. "I must say that when the woman stands on the platform and jokes with [Monsieur] Julian, and, sitting on the edge of the platform puts on her drawers and chemise, still talking with him, she becomes to me no more a model but a woman, and I don't exactly like it," she wrote to Dora.

To get to the women's studio, Belle and Fanny climbed a narrow, winding stairway in Paris's first covered walkway. The Passage des Panoramas was unlike anything they had ever seen. Outside, the streets were muddy and littered with rubble, but the Passage held the fantasies and desires of Parisians under its peaked glass ceiling like a bell jar. Colored lamps and "flaring gas jets depicting giant watches and fans flickering in the air" lit the mosaic-tiled arcade, as Émile Zola described it in his novel *Nana*. Shop windows on either side displayed toys, stamps, cigar cases, tinseled jewelry, music boxes, and silks in primrose yellow and peacock blue. They led to the Théâtre des Variétés, where concerts and comedies were performed. Along the way, the sweet scent of vanilla from the chocolatier mingled with fragrant musk and Russian leather and wafted up to the second-story windows, which were pushed open, as if to let in fresh air on an outdoor street.

Inside the upstairs windows, however, the dirty female quarters of the Académie Julian were "crowded to suffocation with ladies from every quarter of the globe," Fanny wrote to Rearden. If she got there late, which she often did after tending to Hervey and getting Lloyd off to school, she could not even see the models.

Photos and paintings of the female atelier at that time show a lively menagerie of easels, canvasses, brushes, palettes, and intent women in smocks and bonnets. During the week, the ambience was pleasant, with an easy camaraderie between the students. But on Saturday morning, the acid-tongued artist Tony Robert-Fleury descended on the room to critique their work. "He is excessively significant and very disagreeable," Fanny wrote to Rearden, and he seemed to take the greatest pleasure in finding faults. Some students wept when he left. Robert-Fleury declared one of Fanny's paintings "innocent, natural, and truthful"—not a ringing endorsement but neither one to induce tears.

Belle was thrilled that the student assigned to help her get oriented in class was Abigail May Alcott, Louisa's sister and the model for the artistic Amy in *Little Women*—"a tall willowy creature with a chignon and one long curl that even then was old-fashioned," Belle later wrote. Alcott, who was Fanny's age, had done the illustrations for the first edition of *Little Women* and would go on to exhibit a painting at the Paris Salon of 1877. At the age of thirty-eight, she would marry a twenty-two-year-old Swiss tobacco merchant, Ernest Nieriker, and die the following year, seven weeks after giving birth to a daughter, whom she named after Louisa May.

May Alcott wrote a jaunty guide for American women artists, *Studying Art Abroad, and How to Do It Cheaply*. It offered advice for living in Paris on four francs a day, and included tips such as packing cheap underclothes that could be used later as paint rags. For Parisians, this new breed of independent American women took some getting used to. Fanny wrote humorously of being studied everywhere in the city. On an omnibus, people listened to her strange speech in fascination; when she yawned, she claimed, a man "rose up and looked down my throat with the greatest interest."

"I HAVE NEVER seen Paris so charming as on this last Christmas day," Henry James wrote in one of his dispatches to the *New York Tribune* at the end of 1875. At thirty-two, James was in Europe for the first time as an adult, wiring back sketches of the city to help pay the bills while he worked on his second novel, *The Americans*. One day Fanny and James would be friends, but in the winter of 1875 their worlds seemed thousands of miles apart.

In mid-December, only two months into Fanny's art studies, Hervey took a turn for the worse. The doctor told her he was "threatened with scrofulous consumption." How much she understood about this tuberculosis, which attacks the lymph glands of the neck, is unclear. But the word "consumption" would have been enough to terrify any parent in the days when the cause was unknown and the treatments could be horrific. "We have to paint his side every night for a month with some drug so powerful that everyone in the room is almost blinded by it," she confided to Rearden.

The snow fell heavily in December, and even two fires in one room could not keep the family warm. With doctor bills and Hervey's medicines, they were barely surviving. Then Sam, whose mistress was now triumphantly installed in his wife's East Oakland cottage, informed Fanny that he would not be able to send extra money for Christmas. She had just decided that she would have to forgo presents for the children when a check arrived from Rearden—the one bright spot in a miserable month. "I am sure you will not mind that I took most of the money for them instead of myself," she wrote in thanking him.

The boost to her spirits was short-lived; two months later, she anxiously wrote back to him that Hervey's doctor now advised her to take the boy out of the city every morning to drink fresh ox blood. She had worked so hard to get to Paris, she could hardly believe what was happening. She had built a magnificent canopy of dreams, like the Passage des Panoramas, but it was beginning to shatter. "I have given over going to the atelier for a month past, to my heartfelt sorrow," she added. "Such another opportunity I shall never have while I live again."

Fanny was even more forthcoming in a letter to Dora that month. "We are very poor," she wrote. "My children are always hungry, and I cannot manage to keep them fed properly." Fanny pawned trinkets to buy grapes and cakes to tempt Hervey to eat, but by then he could not swallow. "His eyes are bright and feverish and he trembles all the time."

Scrofula could tear through the small bodies of children quickly, and that was clearly what was happening with Hervey. But Fanny could not accept that he was dying. She ate little, slept less, and was, she said, almost only eyes. "The ladies at the art school asked me to pose for them as 'Sorrow,'" she wrote to Rearden. "If Mr. Julian pays me I will do it, I am so in need of money. It would certainly be the first time my troubles did me any good." To pass the long nights, she read John Forster's three-volume *Life of Charles Dickens* and wrote long, wandering letters to Rearden, likening herself to Dickens's muddleheaded Mrs. Nickleby. The sparring was still there—she and Rearden may have both needed it to hang on to a semblance of normality—but she was also starting to question whether she was wrong to have left Sam.

"It does not seem to me that there are three such children in the world as mine," she wrote wistfully. "Doesn't it seem that these children ought to be happiness enough for one woman's life? If I lose one of them I shall die."

Of course, Hervey might have contracted tuberculosis before they left the United States, and his care would have been no better there than in Paris. But she was guilt-ridden and frantic. She asked Rearden not to tell Sam about Hervey's illness. It was cruel to deprive him of being by his son's side, but she probably couldn't bear his recrimination too.

While Fanny and Miss Kate were consumed with Hervey's care, his siblings were also suffering. Poor Belle was again on her own, in a city where a girl of sixteen did not walk on the streets unchaperoned. But if anyone knew how to handle such freedom, it was Belle. It was harder on Lloyd, who was already having a tough time at school, where his classmates called him "Prussian" because of his blond hair and accent. "We were miserably poor," he later recalled, "it seems to me that I was always hungry; I can remember yet how I used to glue myself to the baker's windows and stare longingly at the bread within."

Finally even Fanny had to accept that Hervey was dying and she notified Sam. On March 25, he arrived in Liverpool to a chilling cable: "Still living. Fanny." Sam got to Paris for his son's last few days. On April 5, he wrote to Rearden, "Our poor little boy died this morning at five o'clock, and his mother is almost paralyzed with grief. I will remain with her until her condition will allow me to leave her and then will speed right home." Sam went on to say that when Fanny had read a letter from Rearden at the bedside of her dying child, it had "grated harshly on her feelings." It is likely that Rearden had scolded her for her selfishness in following her dream. But Fanny did not need Rearden to do that—other letters from home were critical of her too. With Hervey's death, it seemed that she and her children had paid dearly for her attempt to create an artistic, independent life.

Two weeks later, Fanny wrote a long letter to Rearden describing Hervey's hideous final days. She wrote of how Sam covered his face with his hands when he saw his son's tortured body, and of leaving Hervey's side only to buy some toys on his fifth birthday:

> *I did not dare leave him because every few hours he bled in a new place. I shall never forget the smell of blood. He would say, "Blood,*

> *mama, get the things; wait until I am ready." Then he would clasp*
> *one hand in the other, close his eyes, and say "now," would clench*
> *his teeth and wait, and not a moan or cry or tremble would be per-*
> *ceptible, though the pain made him deathly sick afterwards.*

No one in the family could bear to watch Fanny administer the treatment, but Hervey took it bravely—though Fanny sometimes wished he would fall unconscious. She recalled:

> *When in the most violent convulsions, his bones snapping in and*
> *out of joint like the crack of a whip, and covered with blood, he lay*
> *back in my arms, looking into my eyes and listening to my words*
> *through it all. I couldn't bear that he should suffer terror of mind as*
> *well as anguish of body, so I tried to speak encouraging, comforting*
> *words into his ear.*

Then one day Fanny smelled blood but could not find it, though she looked so closely down his throat, she singed the hair around her face. Finally, she realized why she could not find it:

> *He was bleeding internally. He asked that his father should sing a*
> *song that he had heard long ago. Something, he said, about goodbye*
> *to the old home and the young folks play round the little cabin door,*
> *once he woke and said, "Lie down beside me." After that he never*
> *spoke again.*

Such a lengthy, detailed passage about a child's death may seem morbid today, but Victorians commonly wrote them in their letters and diaries. Long death scenes usually took place at home and children who died were often photographed in their mothers' arms or in tiny coffins for keepsake mourning cards. But Fanny's account was more vivid and emotionally honest than most. Everything she describes—convulsions, bedsores (when Hervey's bones "cut through the skin and lay bare"), and internal bleeding—was consistent with the final stages of scrofula. Everything except Hervey's angelic stoicism through what had to be excruciating pain. That seems to be something Fanny had to believe to make her child's death at all bearable.

Belle would never be able to write about this time in her life. Lloyd conjured the terrible episode when he was forty-five years old: "Even after all these years the memory of that ebbing life recurs to me with an intolerable pathos—the wasted baby hands, the burning eyes, the untouched toys, the untasted hot-house grapes lying on the counterpane."

While Fanny's world was caving in, blocks away in Montmartre another American painter was living out Fanny's dream. Mary Cassatt was four years younger than Fanny and had been studying art for sixteen years. By the age of thirty-one, she had decided that to become a professional painter, she would need to forgo marriage and family. Yet Cassatt's most famous paintings would help perpetuate the fantasy of devoted, unselfish motherhood. As the mothers on her canvasses bathe, nurse, and caress their young, their gaze is always on their children, as if, as Fanny wrote, "that should be happiness enough for one woman's life." Fanny would never be the artist Cassatt was, nor the kind of mother Cassatt idealized in her paintings.

ON APRIL 8, Fanny dressed Hervey for the last time in clothing she had bought him with the money Rearden had sent for Christmas and cut off a lock of her son's golden curls. It was the first bright day of spring, and as she slipped his wasted body into the clothes, she remembered his last wish—to see the sky and grass again on the first sunny day. In her hysteria as she walked next to his little white coffin to the cemetery, she tried to tell him how beautiful the day was.

Hervey's death tore the family to shreds. Fanny and Sam seem to find no comfort in each other. He sped home as soon as he could and she stayed on with the children. Either Fanny wanted to give her daughter a chance at the substantial art education she herself would never have or she could not bear to return to East Oakland. She tried going back to art school with Belle, but she wrote to Dora that she could hardly hold a palette. "She grew paler and paler, seldom spoke, and it was like being with a ghost," Belle later wrote.

In Antwerp, when Hervey had first fallen ill, Fanny had written to Rearden of curious sensations that likely stemmed from her mind's attempt to separate from the profound trauma she was experiencing. She had hallucinations of vases and pitchers toppling from shelves, but when she jumped up to catch them, there was nothing there. Then, walking along the street, she wrote, "I felt so light that it seemed to be with the greatest difficulty that I could keep my feet down upon the earth; it seemed so much easier to float along than to walk."

Fanny was floating now—anchorless in a sea of grief and doubt. She relived Hervey's final hours over and over. Some days, she wrote to Rearden, she felt her child "must be tired lying so long on his back, and that I must dig him up and turn him over."

She would never be the same; she would never have that open trust in life she had carried with her from the Midwest across Panama through silver-mining towns and San Francisco to Europe. Fanny's remarkable courage and perseverance would reemerge, but so would the mental symptoms brought on by Hervey's death. She could never put her child to rest—his death continued to haunt her even as she later chose to dedicate her life to keeping her future husband from succumbing to tuberculosis as well.

Fanny was finally snapped out of her daze when the doctor who had cared for Hervey became alarmed about her other son's wan appearance. He told Fanny she must get Lloyd out of the city. A sculptor friend suggested an inexpensive artist colony in the countryside. As she had almost a decade before, Fanny crawled into a black mourning dress. Then she boarded a train with her two remaining children for the fresh air and quiet of a summer in Grez-sur-Loing, on the edge of the Fontainebleau Forest.

FOUR

On a chilly Edinburgh day in spring 1870, Robert Louis Stevenson was lurking in Greyfriars Kirkyard. A dark mist swept past the churchyard's sooty tombstones and crypts; it speckled his face and made his blond hair fall in straggles about his shoulders. He was nineteen years old. Louis was not attending a funeral; he had come there to be morbid. "From the morning I was gone," he wrote to his cousin and confidant, Bob Stevenson, that evening, "[I] tried to find out where I could get Haschish, half-determined to get drunk and ended (as usual) by going to a graveyard."

Today we might regard young Louis as a "goth"—or just another gloomy youth looking to score something to lift his mood. His response to the "hot fits of youth" that often pulled him down was to hang out in cemeteries, where his spirits sank to even lower depths.

Greyfriars was especially accommodating to Louis's mood that day. Brooded over by the dark, immutable Edinburgh Castle on its rocky volcano crag, the churchyard was already a favorite setting for Gothic expression in the early photography of David Octavius Hill. Skeletons danced on ledgers and plaques among the fancy mausoleums that sheltered the remains of aristocrats. In one, a life-sized effigy of a caped seventeenth-century laird stood in a grim greeting. In another, a figure lounging on a tabletop tombstone peered out with sightless eyes, his gnarled face propped upon a hand, as if just aroused from sleep. The churchyard's high, crumbling walls enclosed Louis in his gloom.

He wandered among the vaults and mausoleums, his boots leaving soft imprints in the wet grass. Louis knew that he was walking in the sinister steps of the "resurrection men" who had come there to rob graves in the early 1800s. Edinburgh was then renowned for medical research and eager to fortify its reputation in the new field of anatomy, but religious beliefs and legal restrictions limited the supply of cadavers to dissect. So grave robbers watched for new burials and then snuck into the churchyard and dragged fresh corpses out of graves to sell to the University of Edinburgh for dissection.

Doctors hungry for knowledge, and bodies, did not ask questions. But horrified families took action according to their means—the rich cemented in their dead with stone walls and vaults, while people of humbler means installed iron cages called "mortsafes" over graves. Then two enterprising Irish laborers in the city, William Hare and William Burke, came up with an easier method of meeting the demand for fresh bodies. Instead of waiting for people to die of natural causes, they murdered them. They sold the remains of at least sixteen recently terminated victims to anatomist Robert Knox before they were caught. Hare escaped death by turning King's evidence; Burke was convicted and hanged—and his body dissected, his ultimate contribution to medical research. Not surprisingly, that bit of local history had nestled deep into Louis's feverish imagination. One day he would weave it into his short story "The Body Snatcher."

Other remnants of Scotland's brutal past that Louis knew only too well rested uncomfortably under his boots. Instead of taking him to play in the park, his darkly religious childhood nanny, Alison Cunningham, had taken him to cemeteries to view the graves of religious martyrs, especially those of the Covenanters. In that churchyard in 1638, the zealot group had signed a pact to defend the Scottish Church against intervention by the British Crown, sparking a half century of violent religious conflict. More than a thousand Covenanters ended up imprisoned in the churchyard, and many of them were executed or died there. The remains of Sir George Mackenzie, the Scottish Lord Advocate known as "Bluidy Mackenzie" for sending so many of them to their slaughter, was shrouded behind heavy black doors in a domed mausoleum not far from the trench where the bodies of dozens of Covenanters had been thrown.

Still, Louis's funereal haunts had a certain creepy charm. He was struck by the way the old stone houses of Candlemaker Row butted up against the cemetery, so life and death literally carried on there side by side. Walking among the graves, he could hear the sounds of people washing dishes, singing, or crying. "Only a few inches separate the living from the dead," he would later write. On another visit to a cemetery next to a hotel, a beautiful housemaid flirted with him from a window and eventually was persuaded to descend from her post. "Her hair came down, and in the shelter of the tomb my trembling fingers helped her repair the braid," he would recall.

But on this day in March 1870, Louis was pondering his future. Sickly most of his life, he did not have a young person's sense of invincibility. He believed he was forever living "a few inches" from death. And he felt that his father, Thomas Stevenson, was pressuring him into a career in civil engineering that he was neither suited for nor desired. He was convinced that he would die young and spend most of his short life in an office buried under pages of tables and formulas.

It was not just the career his father intended for him that depressed Louis. It was the specter of a life of lockstep conformity and narrow Victorian morality that middle-class Edinburgh represented to him. Except for his cousin Bob, he felt he had no kindred spirits among men, let alone women. As a student at the University of Edinburgh, he would describe himself as "lean, ugly, idle, unpopular." Above all, he was lonely. After dark, he escaped to streets that "decent" people did not speak of, much less venture to, and hung out with prostitutes and lowlifes.

Louis stayed at Greyfriars for about two hours, immersed in melancholy. He felt desperate to make something of his life—to leave behind more than just another of the "severe, monotonous, and lying epitaphs" he read on the tombstones. "To believe in immortality is one thing," he would later write, "but it is first needful to believe in life."

TWELVE YEARS EARLIER, from a third-story window in a neat row of identical Georgian houses in New Town, Edinburgh, a young boy looked out on life. From the day and night nurseries in the front of the house, he could see across the street into the leafy Queen Street Gardens, where other children ran under the watchful eyes of their nannies. In the distance, the climbing tenements of Old Town and the romantic turrets and battlements of the medieval castle were etched against the sky. From the back windows of the nursery floor, in his nanny's room, he could peer into the windows and square backyards of other New Town houses like his. On a fair day, he could see the wide mouth of the River Forth, known as the Firth of Forth, and beyond that, Fife, the onetime kingdom of Scottish monarchs.

For years, the views from those windows would be Robert Louis Stevenson's most consistent connection with the outside world. The author whose name would one day be synonymous with boyhood adventure spent much of his childhood in his nursery, here at 17 Heriot Row and in two previous family homes, confined by illness and his parents' fears. "Many winters, I never crossed the threshold; but used to lie on my face on the nursery floor, chalking or painting in water-colours the pictures in the illustrated newspapers; or sit up in bed, with a little shawl pinned about my shoulders, to play with bricks, or dolls, or what not," he later wrote. His future wife had a livelier "boyhood" than he could have hoped for.

It was not unusual for young children in upper-middle-class Victorian households to eat, play, and sleep in their nurseries. The arrangement kept children's messes and disruptions, as well as children themselves, neatly contained. But Louis's nursery days were longer and darker than those of many of his peers. As a toddler, he suffered a serious case of what was then diagnosed as croup. It turned him from robust to scrawny and pale—what the Scottish call "shilpit." This was followed by more scary illnesses than a child could count on one hand: chicken pox, bronchitis, scarlet fever, whooping cough, and gastric fever, among others. Sometimes the treatments were equally scary, if not damaging, to his health. His croup was treated in part with leeches on his feet, and antimonial wine was a staple medicine throughout his childhood.

Louis's parents and doctors seemed most concerned about a hacking cough that nagged him—it seemed he had inherited a "weak chest" from his mother and maternal grandfather. Deemed too fragile to attend school regularly or go out in Edinburgh's cold sea fogs, heavy rains, and fierce winds, he was largely a shut-in—an only child whose only regular playmate was his adult nanny.

LOUIS'S PARENTS, Thomas Stevenson and Margaret Isabella Balfour, had met in 1847 on a train to Glasgow. He was an established twenty-nine-year-old lighthouse engineer and she was the buoyant eighteen-year-old daughter of a minister in nearby Colinton. They were married a year later. Their son was born in the middle of the century, on November 13, 1850. His name, Robert Lewis Balfour Stevenson, was a blend of those of his grandfathers, Robert Stevenson and Lewis Balfour. (In his teens, Lewis altered his name, keeping the Scottish pronunciation but adopting the French spelling "Louis," and it is used here to avoid confusion.) At home his parents called him Louis or Lou, possibly because his cousin was also named Robert. Louis was an only child, which was especially unusual in the fertile Victorian era—he had fifty-four first cousins.

As a father, Thomas was a strange mix of soft and despotic. He invented silly names for his son—Smout (from the Scottish word for small salmon), Signor Sprucki, and Baron Broadnose. Among Thomas's charming eccentricities was a fondness for stray dogs, especially a spaniel he named Bob. He sometimes bought lunch for Bob at a confectioner's and worried about where Bob was sleeping or whether Bob had had the foresight to bury a bone in the churchyard for Sunday night, when food scraps were scarce.

Thomas also had a quirky contempt for book learning, a legacy of his own strappings in school. He often said the best lesson a boy could learn in school was how to sit on his "bum."

Louis's father was also prone to melancholy and given to fierce mood swings, from "freakish gaiety" to gloom and anger. Despite his manly broad shoulders and a square jaw framed by muttonchop sideburns, he had a rather wobbly foothold in life. The youngest of thirteen children, only five of whom survived infancy, Thomas had written stories in his youth but was coerced by his father to join the "family calling" of lighthouse engineering. His career brought him wealth and prestige, but his storytelling was relegated to tales that he told himself to fall asleep at night. Thomas was also morbidly religious—tormented by harsh Calvinist dogma and an obsession with his own sins. He became a fanatic about the idea that art should always teach a moral principle. All of this set him up for a difficult relationship with his creative son.

Margaret Stevenson was as sunny and sweet as her husband was dark and pessimistic. She too was the youngest of thirteen children, nine of whom lived into adulthood. Her ancestors had been genteel landowners, the Balfours of Pilrig, unlike Thomas's, who were largely tenant farmers, millers, and maltsters. Blond, attractive, and girlish, Margaret was intelligent but determined to ignore the ugly or painful realities of life—including, apparently, her husband's rages. She was subservient and almost childlike in her relationship with him. She and Thomas were so wrapped up in each other, Louis complained that "the children of lovers are orphans."

Because of her own bronchial ailments, Margaret was a semi-invalid during Louis's childhood. When he was young, she stayed in bed until noon and did not go out with him often. Thomas encouraged this, treating her like a delicate glass figurine, and seemed to develop phantom illnesses in sympathy with his sickly wife and son. But when Louis's health improved in adolescence, so did hers. After her husband's death, when she was fifty-nine, she made the rigorous trek to the South Seas with Louis, and she learned to ride a bicycle at nearly seventy. She outlived both her husband and her son. It is tempting to question whether Margaret's ill health was tied to fears of another childbirth or her husband's rages, or a wish to avoid the responsibilities, traumas, or tedium of parenting. Still, it was common for even healthy affluent parents to turn over their children's care to nurses and nannies, for better or for worse. And in the case of Louis's nanny, Alison Cunningham, it's difficult to say whether it was for his good or not.

"CUMMY," AS THE STEVENSONS called her, was a weaver's daughter, thirty years old when she took charge of eighteen-month-old Louis. Aside from her strict Calvinism—which was more rigid and narrow than the Stevensons'—she could be playful and curious. She sang and danced for Louis, and when she read him Bible and Covenant stories, her voice swelled with drama. Cummy reportedly turned down at least one proposal to marry and have children of her own, choosing instead to give her life to caring for Louis. After his death, this story was often repeated as testimony to Cummy's saintly devotion to him. Today it seems rather odd. Still, it earned her Louis's weird dedication to "my second mother, my first wife" in his famous book of poems, *A Child's Garden of Verses*. (A short poem to his "first mother" near the end of the book recalls that she also read him rhymes.)

It might have been better had Cummy been a little less devoted to Louis. Among her dour convictions, she considered pleasures such as theater, novels, and card games the work of the devil. This made little Louis tremble for the souls of his whist-playing parents, who also gave dinner parties. Her dramatic tales about damnation made him terrified of hell and preoccupied with sin. He was a little bundle of worries—even before he turned six, he fretted that he would not play the harp well enough for heaven, that he had forgotten to pray for his father's safe return from a trip, and that the fuses in Thomas's travel bag would catch fire and make his sherry so hot it would burn his mouth. "I was sentimental, sniveling, goody, morbidly religious," he would recall. Childhood photos reveal a serious, skinny boy with a big head and tired eyes.

Not surprisingly, Louis's fears reached a fever pitch at night, in the inky shadows and creaky corners of his nursery. In *A Child's Garden of Verses*, he would imagine a world where glittering stars packed a little boy into bed and "went round in his head," or where his bed became a boat that sailed smoothly through his dreams until morning. But in his own childhood, the night nursery was often a disturbing place, where he navigated the streams and "the mountainsides of dreams" in a kind of terror.

When he had fevers, the world around him swelled and shrank. His clothes, hanging on a nail, blew up as large as a church and then shrank to a small, distant dot. The nursery walls heaved and collapsed—he must have felt that they could crush him. His cough kept him awake at night, but he was terrified of sleep in case he should fall into eternal damnation before he woke. As an adult, he recalled repeatedly "waking from a dream of Hell, clinging to the horizontal bar of the bed, with my knees and chin together, my soul shaken, my body convulsed with agony." It was worst on stormy nights, when the wind "going about the town like a bedlamite" whipped his vivid and overburdened imagination into a frenzy. He heard the wind as the thundering gallop of a horseman "riding furiously past the bottom of the street and away up the hill into town," he would recall. "I think even now that I hear the terrible *howl* of his passage and the clinking that I used to attribute to his bit and stirrups."

Apparently Margaret was not summoned to comfort Louis on these stormy nights in the nursery, but Thomas sometimes sat by the child's bed and calmed him by holding aimless conversations with imaginary mail-coach drivers or told him stories from outside the nursery door. For the most part, though, it was Cummy who appeared out of the darkness and scooped up the frightened boy.

As an adult, Louis was aware that Cummy's care was not always enlightened. But she was always *there*. He kept a tender memory of her gathering him in a blanket on feverish nights and showing him the lit windows of houses where, she said, other children were up sick too. Some of Cummy's other nighttime remedies were less benign. She served Louis strong cups of coffee, prayed with him for his parents' souls, or told him more tales of the

Covenant "Killing Time." Cummy may have had no idea she was traumatizing Louis, but one wishes his parents had popped their heads into the nursery more often to see that she was.

THE FERTILE MIND that made fears monstrous could also turn the tedious and humdrum into adventure. Louis would celebrate this in his legendary poem "The Land of Counterpane," in which a sick child's bed becomes a kingdom where he sends "ships in fleets / all up and down among the sheets" and marches lead soldiers "with different uniforms and drills / among the bedclothes, through the hills." As he grew, fantasy was the greatcoat he could wrap around himself to make life bearable when he was sick and interesting when it was dull. "An opera is far more *real* than real life to me," he wrote to his mother when he was twenty-one. "I should like to *live* in one."

The gift of a pasteboard theater on Louis's sixth birthday lifted the curtain on new daydreams. The little box offered a world that was bigger and wider, brighter and more terrible, than the one outside his windows. Through Skelt's Juvenile Dramas, plays, and miniature theater kits to assemble at home, Louis could disappear into palaces and dungeons, gulp salty sea air and gallop through dark forests, duel with villains and rescue damsels in distress. The adventure began with Saturday excursions to the stationer's to purchase scenery and characters, which sold for "a penny plain and twopence coloured." Savvy boys did not buy colored sheets because painting them to life was an experience to be savored. But by the time the last scene was painted, the thrill was gone. The dramas themselves and the directions for staging them were uninspiring, so Louis created his own. "The world was plain before I knew him; a poor penny world," he wrote of Skelt, "but soon it was all coloured with romance."

Also that year, Louis's cousin Robert Alan Mowbray Stevenson, or Bob, came for an extended visit. At eight years old, Bob too needed an escape—from the gloomy family home where his invalid father, Alan Stevenson, had been deteriorating since his nervous breakdown a few years before. "We lived together in a purely visionary state," Louis would recall of Bob's visit. The dreamy cousins made up their own countries, where they ruled and made wars, and they didn't leave them even at meals. Bob ate his porridge with sugar because his country was buried under snow; Louis ate his with milk because his country was flooded.

But the happiest memories of Louis's childhood were of visits to Colinton Manse, the home of his grandfather Lewis Balfour. Located at the foot of the Pentland Hills, about a five-mile walk southwest of Edinburgh, the manse was heaven for Louis and his cousins. Inside, the house seemed exotic, filled with books and relics that Margaret's brother John brought back from India, where he had served as a doctor. Outside was a lawn bordered by a holly-lined hedge and a giant yew tree with a swing. The wheel of a paper mill upstream sent the Water of Leith foaming through the estate; the smell of rushing water and the sound of birdsong and children's voices would always flow through Louis's memories of the place.

Louis could be a rowdy boy there, playing in the sunshine with his cousins, though he usually insisted on taking the lead and ended up in bed with a fever for a couple of days after. He claimed he was a master at hide-and-seek, not because he ran fast, but because he could hide under a carrot plant and crawl noiselessly through leaves. But he would never enjoy—or be skilled at—competitive sports. He could rouse his spirits for football only by pretending the ball was a missile being passed between Arabian nations at war. And he was utterly indifferent to the pleasures of golf, the game Scotland gave to the world. As he grew and his health improved, he preferred walking, riding, swimming, skating, and canoeing.

Despite, or because of, his deeply religious upbringing, Louis discovered that he liked sin, blasphemy, and lying. "It is good for boys to be violent and unruly, and to hate all constituted authority; for it is of such boys that good citizens are made," he wrote later to his mother. And sometimes sin paid off. He once broke into an empty house, though he became so panicked about being found out that his parents sensed something was amiss when he returned home. Their concern heightened his guilt and sent him into hysteria, to which he was already prone. That evening, he heard someone say that he must have been studying his books too hard, and he was sent to the country on holiday the next day.

His mother's chest ailments, and presumably his own, provided Louis with one happy benefit—sunny trips abroad. In the 1860s the Stevensons became part of a health fad that was sweeping Britain. "Climatotherapy" called for decamping to exotic locales in search of relief from illnesses that had no medical cures. A steady stream of consumptives and other health-seekers from the north headed toward the French and Italian Riviera. Whatever the journeys might have done for their physical health, living in sun-drenched Mediterranean fishing villages surely boosted their emotional health.

When Louis was twelve, the Stevensons, accompanied by Cummy, took a lengthy tour to Marseille, Nice, and Menton, and down through Genoa and Naples. Louis returned with his mother to Menton the following winter. The tonic of sunshine, orange groves, and sea air worked some magic on his mind. He became a confirmed Francophile and would learn to speak and read French fluently.

This and other travels with his parents also gave Louis a feeling that life was somewhere else—outside the nursery, Edinburgh, even Scotland. Once he was back home, he would stand near Waverley Station, on the North Bridge that joins Old Town and New Town, looking down at the trains "vanishing into the tunnel on a voyage to brighter skies," and long to go with them. Wanderlust would become the cure for whatever ailed him in life. As a young man, he would write to his mother, "You must understand . . . that I shall be a nomad, more or less, until my days be done."

WHEN LOUIS WAS FOUR, Margaret recorded in his baby book that he dreamed "he heard the noise of pens writing." When he was six, before he could read or write, he dictated to his mother his first piece of literature, a history of Moses, which won him the prize in a family writing contest. From then on, Louis dictated stories whenever he could find someone with a pen to write them down.

For a boy who liked to tell stories, however, he was in no rush to learn to read them—in part, because he liked having them read to him instead. He learned to read when he wanted to, at the age of seven. His formal education limped along in this vein, with Louis generally avoiding schoolwork and spending as many years out of school as in. Illness, his parents' hypochondria, his father's unconventional views on education, and his own short attention span were his allies in this endeavor.

At six, Louis began mornings at Mr. Henderson's Preparatory School but was pulled out after a few weeks because of poor health and did not return for two years. At ten, he started at Edinburgh Academy but was plucked out by his parents after fifteen months to travel in Europe. After a term at Burlington Lodge Academy in England and stints with various tutors, he ended up at Robert Thomson's, a private day school in Edinburgh for frail and "backward" children. Possibly because the school did not assign homework, Louis managed to remain there from the age of fourteen until he entered college at seventeen. Though hardly "backward," he never distinguished himself academically. His cousin and first biographer, Graham Balfour, observed that "if he was bright and ready when he was interested, his attention was often short-lived, and to many of the subjects in his curriculum it never was given at all."

Socially, Louis did not find school pleasant. He was teased from the start, when Cummy changed his wet shoes for him in front of his classmates at Mr. Henderson's. His long stretches of time solely in the doting company of adults may have kept his individuality intact, but it also made it difficult for him to fit in. Though kind and sensitive, he was also precocious, high-strung, and gawky—the "butt of the school," according to one schoolmate. "In body, Stevenson was assuredly badly set up," H. Ballyse Baildon, a classmate at Mr. Thomson's, wrote of Louis at fourteen. "His limbs were long and lean and spidery, and his chest flat, so as almost to suggest some malnutrition, such sharp angles and corners did his joints make under his clothes." Thomas Stevenson, every bit the image of the manly captain of industry, did little to boost his son's self-confidence.

Though Louis would recall that he was often held up as an example of an "idler," he was actually engaged in the hard work of teaching himself to write. During his short stay at Burlington Lodge, when he was twelve, he founded and wrote the only issue of the *School Boys Magazine*, which included stories of heroes left in lit boilers, hidden under floors, and about to be burned alive. The next year he wrote a libretto for an opera called *The Baneful Potato*. In his teens, he started to try his hand at writing novels.

Louis's idyllic visits to Colinton Manse ended when he was ten, with the death of his grandfather. Later his father leased a cottage in Swanston, in the Pentland Hills, which would become the family's holiday home for several years. For Louis as a teenager and young man, it was what the manse had been for him as a child. The vast, rolling hills were his soul's home, where he could take long, rigorous treks with his dog, Coolin. They must have made a striking silhouette: the shaggy Skye terrier and the sticklike man walking with long, loose-limbed strides over the crest of the hills.

From this vantage point, Louis could see how fast Scotland was changing, and he gathered material for later sketches that would capture the dying characters and speech of the countryside. One essay began "In a pleasant, airy, uphill country, it was my fortune . . . to make the acquaintance of a certain beggar. I call him a beggar, though he usually allowed his coat and his shoes (which were open-mouthed indeed) to beg for him." When the beggar opened his own mouth, he preferred to discuss the poems of John Keats and Percy Shelley.

Another sketch immortalized the shepherd John Todd, who had grit and dash, smelled of "windy brae," and stalked the hills with his yellow staff under his arm and his plaid thrown loosely over his shoulder. At a time when many Scots were "refining" their speech to sound more English, Todd spoke a rich dialect of Scots with a "honied, friendly whine." But his voice could also shake the hills when he was angry. "He touched on nothing at least, but he adorned it," Louis wrote. "When he narrated, the scene was before you." Walking with Todd gave direction to his writing. As Todd made a rugged part of history come alive for him, Louis believed writing should do that for readers. "Novels begin to touch not the fine *dilettanti* but the gross mass of mankind," he wrote, "when they leave off to speak of parlours and shades of manner and still-born niceties of motive, and begin to deal with fighting, sailoring, adventure, death, or childbirth."

At home, Thomas was increasingly alarmed and irritated by his son's budding interest in writing fiction. As far as he was concerned, Louis was on course to take up engineering studies at the University of Edinburgh and join the family firm. It must have been in part a desire to crush his son's literary aspirations that explains Thomas's bizarre reaction to Louis's first publication, *The Pentland Rising: A Page of History*.

Thomas and Margaret had actually suggested that Louis write a pamphlet-sized history of the Covenanter uprising of 1666, which culminated in a battle on Rullion Green in the Pentland Hills. The Stevensons offered to pay for one hundred copies to be printed on the bicentennial of the Covenanters' defeat. But rather than writing it as straight history, Louis had composed a gripping narrative. Though it was suitably pious and grounded in fact, Thomas was not happy. Louis's aunt Jane Balfour was at the house on Heriot Row while the sixteen-year-old madly tried to alter the work to please his father. "He had made a story of it, and by so doing, had, in his father's opinion, spoiled it," she recalled. "It was printed not long after in a small edition, and Mr. Stevenson very soon bought all the copies in, as far as was possible."

Thomas purchased all the copies so they would never be seen, not even by family and friends. It must have been a crushing blow to his teenage son, who was trying to assert himself as an artist and a young man, as well as make his father proud. And it wasn't the last time Thomas would try to break the wings of his son's creative aspirations.

A career in engineering beckoned. But Louis would do everything he could to avoid his preordained future.

AT THE UNIVERSITY OF EDINBURGH, Louis embarked on an education that was quite different from the one his father had intended for him. It usually occurred outside the university gate, where crumbling Old Town and its temptations glimmered like a great, sordid tapestry. To a university professor whose classes he dodged, Louis later admitted that he had viewed the man as "part of a mangle through which I was being slowly and unwillingly dragged—part of a course which I had not chosen—part, in a word, of an organized boredom."

He threw himself into developing "an extensive and highly rational system of truantry, which cost me a great deal of trouble to put into exercise." Part of the trouble was that he needed to get signed certificates of attendance from professors who had seen his face so seldom they would not know him on the street. Some obliged, but engineering professor Fleeming Jenkin said, "It's quite useless for *you* to come to me, Mr. Stevenson. There may be doubtful cases; there is no doubt about yours. You have simply *not* attended my class."

The small allowance Thomas Stevenson allotted his son during these years was likely meant to keep Louis out of trouble. Instead, it confined his wanderings to some of the seedier venues of both Old Town and New Town. Louis hung out in "howffs" (public houses) or their illicit counterparts, "shebeens," when he could afford to drink and on the street when he could not. He lost his virginity in a brothel when he was a teenager.

Near the university, Louis explored Old Town's stone alleys and winding passages, called "closes" and "wynds"—some "so narrow that you can lay a hand on either wall; so steep that, in greasy winter weather, the pavement is almost as treacherous as ice." He was fascinated by the "lands," the smoky, decaying tenements whose jumbled stories jutted to the sky like human beehives. A century before, rich and poor had lived together in lands up to fourteen stories high, but Edinburgh's aristocrats and professionals had happily fled Old Town for the spacious elegance of New Town in the late eighteenth and early nineteenth centuries, abandoning the poor to fend for themselves. Destitute families crammed into squalid Old Town tenements, some sleeping on straw in windowless and decrepit dwellings. On one of his late-night outings, Louis stood looking up at one of the buildings and imagined that he could hear all the people snoring and clocks ticking inside, "family after family contributing its quota to the general hum, and the whole pile beating in tune to its timepieces, like a great disordered heart." His own heart was wrenched at the thought of how fragile life there was: In the wee hours in 1861, a 250-year-old land had given way, crushing half the residents.

Louis's teenage ventures into Old Town wynds and lands were not just a kind of picturesque slumming. They fostered a growing sense of social injustice that was modern and especially unusual among privileged young men. Edinburgh was no longer the hotbed of genius it had been during the Enlightenment; as he began to see it, hypocritical piety and grubby acquisitiveness had displaced intellectual ferment. Louis objected to the moral duplicity and complacency of the rising new bourgeois class. New Town's spreading blocks of airy homes and well-ordered streets—the "wilderness of square-cut stone" that John Ruskin called "graves of the soul"—were a symbol of that.

Though Louis still lived at home, he adopted a shabby style that would proclaim his independence. He grew his hair down to his shoulders and sprouted a mustache. He eschewed the frock-coat-and-top-hat uniform of respectability for the cloak of the artistically inclined—a bohemian velvet jacket. It was a look that suited him most of his life, and the one the world would come to know him by. It was not of its time—long hair, for example, was not fashionable for Victorian men. But it was strangely timeless, so that even today Louis looks almost contemporary in photos (especially after he added a "soul patch" to his chin in his thirties in France).

His appearance often drew jeers. Besides being unorthodox, it was slightly, provocatively effeminate at a time when beards were the roaring emblem of masculinity. But Louis did not shy away from embellishing his already odd looks. He was out to wave his freak flag in the face of smug and prosperous Edinburgh.

Partly in rebellion and partly for adventure, he hung out with seamen, chimney sweeps, thieves, and "threepenny whores"—a transient social circle "continually changed by the action of the police magistrate." There was a refreshing honesty and frankness (as well as color) in dives that he believed was missing in New Town drawing rooms. But he also found psychological refuge there. Among social outcasts, he felt accepted without mockery. His affinity for offbeat characters and colorful places would blossom in his fiction years later.

One of Louis's hangouts was a brothel, where he wrote in the kitchen. He was respectful and affectionate with the women, who called him "Velvet Coat." At the time, he didn't care much for girls of his class; he preferred prostitutes like the "great-haunched, blue-eyed" Mary H., whom he wrote of in an autobiographical fragment not published until well after his death.

His tender handling of Mary's feelings, which unfurl like a delicate fern, reads more like a recollection of puppy love than of a business transaction. He remembered that when Mary occasionally took factory work, he would see her on her way home, but she did not want him to recognize her, and her eyes did not meet his. "It never occurred to me that she thought of me except in the way of business, though I now remember her attempts to waken my jealousy which, being very simple, I took at the time for gospel," he wrote. Years later, he met her on the street, about to emigrate to the United States. They spent a few hours in a pub and realized that they had been dear friends though neither knew it at the time. "I still can feel her good honest loving hand as we said good-bye," he recalled.

Louis inherited some of his softness toward prostitutes from his father, who had founded a rescue mission for "fallen women." But unlike Thomas, Louis was more opposed to the disgrace and hypocrisy that surrounded prostitution than to the institution itself. He had a strong sexual appetite and he readily sated it. He was "beset by fleshly frailties," as his friend Sidney Colvin would officially word it after Louis's death. Off the record, Colvin noted that the young Louis "was a loose fish in regard to women."

Laughed at by other students at the university for his airs and clothes, Louis was seen as offensive and arrogant by some. In Scotland, unlike

England, a university education was open to the sons of farmers as well as bankers. Louis's cavalier attitude toward school was not appreciated by boys of humble origin, who tended to take their education very seriously, well aware of their parents' sacrifices to make it possible. And while Louis may have been open-minded about prostitution, he was at that time hardly a feminist. When male university students rose up against the Edinburgh Seven—the first female medical students, led by Sophia Jex-Blake—he wrote in a letter to a female cousin, "I give her posterity; but I won't marry either her or her fellows. Let posterity marry them if posterity likes—I won't."

ROSALINE MASSON, an Edinburgh writer who met Louis at about that time, would remember him then as "precocious, interesting, affected, and egregiously egotistic." But years later, after he was famous, Louis would recall aching hopelessness as his overriding feeling then: "how I feared I should make a mere shipwreck, and yet timidly hoped not; how I feared I should never have a friend far less a wife, and yet passionately hoped I might; how I hoped (if I did not take to drink) I should possibly write one little book."

Through the charade of his engineering studies, he continued to teach himself to write. He always kept two books in his pocket—one to read, one to write in. He made up dialogues as he walked the hills and wrote down what he saw and heard. "Thus I lived with words," he observed. "Description was the principal field of my exercise; for to any one with senses there is always something worth describing." He read widely, and when he came to a passage he particularly liked, he sat down immediately and tried to copy it. As he later said famously, "I have thus played the sedulous ape to Hazlitt, to Lamb, to Wordsworth, to Sir Thomas Browne, to Defoe, to Hawthorne, to Montaigne, to Baudelaire, and to Obermann." He knew that he failed to capture their style, but it gave him practice in rhythm and construction.

It is poignant to think of Louis at twenty, carrying his work between smoky brothel kitchens and his former day nursery at Heriot Row (now his study), scribbling fervently in order to leave behind a scrap of immortality. He was alone with his thoughts too much, as he had been as a child. The activity of his mind sometimes scared him—the way it galloped and thundered like the night wind. And he was still haunted by vivid nightmares that lingered in his psyche all day. His doctor prescribed an unspecified drug that helped control them, and eventually he would learn how to harness his dreams into the raw material for stories, but at the time they made him fear that he was losing his mind.

In Louis's childhood nursery, there stood a cabinet made by an infamous Edinburgh criminal, Deacon William Brodie—a respected alderman by day and thief by night. Fueled by his dreams and nighttime excursions into the underbelly of Edinburgh, Louis became haunted by the idea that, like Brodie, he was living a double life. Despite his defiance and newfound hedonism, he felt guilty and sinful. He confided to his cousin Bob, now a student in Cambridge, that he felt he should do some kind of rescue work in the seamier parts of town, "but *I cannot trust myself* in such places." Masquerading as an engineering student was also taking a toll. He must have felt like a ticking time bomb. "My daily life is one repression from beginning to end," he wrote to Bob, "and my letters to you are the safety valve."

FIVE

In the eighteenth century, the Scottish coast was a sailor's nightmare—beaten by the opposing North Sea and Atlantic Ocean, and riddled with conflicting tides and currents, uncharted reefs, and invisible rocks. It was worst at night, when the darkness seemed to have no end. Scotland's ferocious rains and winds snuffed out primitive beacons, such as a coal fire on a hill or burning candles in a tower, which were used in milder climates to guide mariners to safety. In 1799 one three-day storm alone wrecked more than seventy ships and sent hundreds of men to their deaths.

Louis's grandfather Robert Stevenson saw it as his duty to God and Scotland to bring light to that darkness, and he wanted his sons to carry on that mission. He created a family enterprise that spanned generations and produced ninety-seven lighthouses, bathing the coast of Scotland in a horseshoe of light. His monumental achievement, Bell Rock—the oldest working sea-washed lighthouse in the world, on a granite reef off the coast of Arbroath—was captured by J. M. W. Turner in his signature epic style, during a storm: a luminous tower against a gray sky, uncowed by the angry waves crashing over it.

Lighthouse construction in those early days was less a business than an adventure. Engineers needed to invent and improvise—and be physically hearty enough to clamor up slippery rocks with tools and supplies, lay foundations, and spend whole days wet. And in the end the sea could still outwit them and destroy years of work in seconds. But Robert "had in him a reserve of romance which carried him delightedly over these hardships and perils," his grandson Louis later wrote in *Records of a Family of Engineers*, an unfinished history of the family who came to be known as the "lighthouse Stevensons."

Robert could be altruistic—he refused to take out a patent on his design, optic, or architectural inventions, believing that they were for the public good, not private gain. But he was also a shrewd businessman and an intimidating father. He thought he could tame his sons into becoming engineers the way he tamed the sea, by sheer force of will. He demanded that any interests that might distract them—especially writing—be stamped out.

Robert successfully bullied his sickly and sensitive son Alan into being an engineer instead of a classical scholar. But when he found that Alan was writing poetry, he pushed him harder. Alan suffered a mental breakdown (and possibly developed multiple sclerosis) in his midforties and retired. Robert did not have to cajole his son David into engineering, but his youngest, Thomas, revived his fears about Alan. Enraged when he came across some fiction Thomas had written when rifling through his son's belongings, he implored Thomas to give up writing and tend to business.

Louis's father did tend to business. In partnership with David after Alan's resignation, he oversaw the construction of twenty-seven onshore and twenty-five offshore lights, and built harbors and docks. But engineering was never a smooth fit for Robert's quirky and volatile son. Unlike his brothers, Thomas took storms as a personal insult, especially when they demolished his work. Still, like his father, Thomas expected his son to follow in his path, however unsuited Louis was to the physical demands of the work. And like Robert, Thomas came to deride literature as devious and harmful.

LOUIS'S ENGINEERING APPRENTICESHIP began after his first year at the University of Edinburgh, when he was shipped off to study the harbor works at Anstruther in July 1868. Though he was less than fifty miles from home, on the coast of Fife, to him it seemed like the end of the earth. "I am utterly sick of this grey, grim, sea-beaten hole," the seventeen-year-old wrote to his mother after a month. Unmoved by his whining, his parents sent him a month later to Wick, where he again found little in his engineering work to interest him. Instead, he became absorbed with the idea of underwater diving.

One gray day, Louis found himself on a diving platform, in a Captain Nemo–style copper diving helmet and thick layers of woolen underwear, with twenty pounds of lead on each foot. More weights were thrown on him and he lumbered down the ladder into a new world:

> Some twenty rounds below the platform, twilight fell. Looking up, I saw a low green heaven mottled with vanishing bells of white; looking around, except for the weedy spokes and shafts of the ladder, nothing but a green gloaming, somewhat opaque but very restful and delicious.

When his underwater guide, a diver named Bob Bain, gestured to him to leap onto a stone, Louis was incredulous. How could that be possible in his heavily weighted gear? But he gave a little push with his toes and found himself soaring through the sea like a bird in flight. When Bob laid his hands on Louis's shoulders to check his rise, Louis's feet kept climbing, and Bob had to haul them back down and prop Louis on his feet "like an intoxicated sparrow." The experience, Louis would later say, was one of the best of his engineering education.

In the summer of 1870, Louis undertook his third apprenticeship, on the islet of Earraid, where Thomas had established the shore station for construction on Dhu Heartach, the main rock of the ten-mile-long Torran reef. Though the practical aspects of engineering continued to be a struggle, by then his apprenticeships were supplying Louis with stories about smuggling and shipwrecks, and he was developing a love affair with sailing and salty air that would last the rest of his life.

Unlike Anstruther and Wick, Earraid captivated Louis's imagination from the time he first saw it "framed in the round bull's-eye of a cabin port," with the "sweet smoke of peats which came to me over the bay, and the bare-legged daughters of the cotter . . . wading by the pier." Beyond the lighthouse workmen's settlement, the tiny islet off the southwestern island of Mull was remote and wild. Exploring land that had changed almost as little as the stars in the night sky, Louis steeped himself in "past ages."

Louis's time on Earraid deepened his feel for what was inside him—and it wasn't a passion for surveying and leveling. He was there only two weeks, but he left filled with images that would electrify his work for years to come. His knowledge of the island (renamed "Aros" in his fiction) would fuel a pivotal turning point in *Kidnapped*. And in his short story "The Merry Men," Earraid was again Aros and "merry men" the nickname for the "dance" and almost mirthful sound of the big breakers crashing off its shore. In the tale, an island wrecker who plunders crashed vessels goes mad and watches men and ships meet their doom in gleeful anticipation of his haul.

Louis's summer apprenticeships exposed a chasm between father and son that was deeper than the difference in how they pondered a stream or a swell. Thomas saw life as he saw the ocean—as something to be feared and controlled. With his somewhat fragile hold on life, he braced himself against the uncertainties and complexities it hurled at him, finding comfort and answers in religion. Though a man of science, he struggled to reconcile it with his faith. In an essay on the laws of nature, Thomas concluded that a stone falls partly because of gravity, but partly because God willed gravity into existence. Men of science and literature should refrain from writing anything that would shake the faith of others, he wrote.

Thomas's son lusted after experience and truth rather than reassurance. He was a diver by nature—one of those whom Herman Melville called the "thought divers, that have been diving and coming up again with bloodshot eyes since the world began." Louis would use his writing to plumb the human condition. It would sometimes be a lonely journey—into a darkness where he might shout and never be heard, where comforting myths were just a vanishing haze of light above, but where he could also soar like a bird.

IN SPRING 1871, Louis presented a paper, "Notice of a New Form of Intermittent Light for Lighthouses," before the Royal Scottish Society of Arts. Though it earned him a silver medal, it was scant on technical knowledge. Soon after, Thomas interrogated him about his studies. "I owned I cared for nothing but literature," Louis wrote later to a friend. "My father said that was no profession." A compromise that was bound to satisfy neither of them was reached: In fall Louis would switch his studies to law. Thomas believed that his son could write in his spare time, like Walter Scott, who had also had to support himself and his family as a barrister.

"Tom wonderfully resigned," Margaret cheerily insisted in her diary. It is to Thomas's credit that, unlike his father, he stopped pushing his son into an engineering career. But he would not stop voicing his disappointment for the rest of his life. Louis's failure to become an engineer left a scar on him as well. In some way, he saw it as cowardly: "Real men" to Louis were men of action. Literature could never serve humanity as well as the work of his ancestors. After he was a successful author, he felt guilty that his books made him more famous than the lighthouse Stevensons.

Thomas's disappointment in Louis would be amplified when his brother and partner, David, retired from the family firm and was replaced by his sons. Charles and David Alan Stevenson proved to be talented engineers. But Thomas's working relationship with his nephews was strained, perhaps because he was reminded daily that they had followed in the footsteps of their father and grandfather, unlike their wild and troublesome cousins, Louis and Bob Stevenson.

BOB STEVENSON'S RETURN to Edinburgh from Cambridge in 1871 was nothing short of life support for his cousin. "I was at last able to breathe," Louis said in describing his feelings that summer. "The miserable isolation in which I had languished was no more in season, and I began to be happy." The twenty-four-year-old had come home to study painting at the Edinburgh College of Art. The death of his father, Alan, in 1865 after a long, dark decline had given Bob an independence that Louis envied. He had freely chosen a creative life and traveled through France on summer breaks while Louis was slogging through his engineering apprenticeships.

Bob was his cousin's idol and confidant from the time they created play kingdoms in their porridge bowls. As a young man, he was also a fellow rebel who would help Louis break free from the repression he felt in Edinburgh. Bob was handsome, athletic, brilliant, and irresistible to women. But men also found him dazzling. Walter Raleigh dedicated his book *Milton* to Bob, for his "radiant and soaring intelligence." William Butler Yeats called him a better talker than Oscar Wilde, whose charm was "a mask which he wore only when it pleased him, while the charm of Stevenson belonged to him like the colour of his hair." Though Bob's ambition was to paint, it seems that his great genius was for talk. In describing his cousin's verbal flights of fancy, Louis wrote that he "changed like the patterns in a kaleidoscope, transmigrated (it is the only word) from one point of view to another with a swiftness and completeness that left a stupid and merely logical mind panting in the rear."

Bob was more flamboyant than Louis in his dress, talk, and rebellion, but he lacked his cousin's ambition and determination. His life plan in his early twenties was to divide his patrimony into ten parts and spend one each year. When it ran out, he would commit suicide. In the meantime, he and Louis dedicated much of their time to a kind of performance art they called "jinks," or "absurd acts for the sake of their absurdity and the consequent laughter."

The most elaborate jinks were in the service of "Libbelism," inspired by an alias, "John Libbel," which Bob had given a pawnbroker when he had to pawn his trousers for railroad fare home from Wales. The cousins were determined to make the imaginary Libbel an Edinburgh phenomenon. They flooded the city with calling cards that they had printed for him, corresponded with eminent citizens in his name, had empty parcels delivered "with Mr. Libbel's compliments," spent whole days inquiring anxiously at lodging houses if Mr. Libbel had arrived, and eventually "let slip" that they were searching for the heir to the great Libbel fortune. Still, they did not realize how much Libbelism had taken hold until one day when they were trying to pull off a prank on a jewelry store clerk. "Suddenly the man's eye took fire, and he started back," Louis later recalled. "'I know who you are,' he cried; 'you're the two Stevensons.'" His colleague, a big fan of their pranks, would be so irked to have missed them, the man added, and he invited them back for tea.

With laughter now Louis's "principal affair," his law studies at the University of Edinburgh took a back seat. "We did not look for Louis at law lectures, except when the weather was bad," a classmate recalled. He was more likely to show up at meetings of the Speculative Society, the university's exclusive literary and debating club. Though Louis was remembered as a weak, nervous speaker, he took bold positions. He opened one debate by advocating the abolition of capital punishment, and he expressed the heretical view that contemporary American literature ranked with that of Britain.

At the Spec, Louis was friends with Walter Simpson, son of the famous Edinburgh obstetrician James Young Simpson, who introduced chloroform to ease childbirth, defying other male doctors and clergy who believed that labor pains were God's will. James Simpson had died by the time Louis met his son, who lived with his siblings in a small New Town house where Louis was welcome at any hour. Unlike Bob, Walter did not have a genius for talk, but he was thoughtful and pleasant and would become Louis's travel companion for the next few years.

Louis's closest friend at the Spec was Charles Baxter—a legal apprentice, practical joker, and dependable drinking companion at the pubs on Lothian Road. Baxter would become Louis's lawyer, financial agent, and close friend for life. He was the burly opposite of his waiflike friend, inspiring their classmate John Geddie to say that together the two resembled "a slim and graceful spaniel with a big bull-dog, jowled and 'pop-eyed,' trotting in its wake." According to Geddie, they often came late to lectures, interrupting the speaker, and once the lecture resumed, they would abruptly bolt, leaving behind "a spirit of unrest that made concentration on legal quiddities impossible."

One might imagine the elder Stevensons' nerves fairly frayed by this time, as some of polite Edinburgh began to pity them their wayward and disheveled son. Though they surely did not know, or want to know, the extent of Louis's extracurricular activities while he was at school, at home he was the source of growing confusion and exasperation. Edinburgh writer Flora Masson recalled a dinner party at Heriot Row, where her end of the table was "almost uncomfortably brilliant" as father and son disagreed on almost everything:

> *Mr. Stevenson seemed to me, on that evening, to be the type of the kindly, orthodox Edinburgh father. We chatted of nice, concrete, comfortable things, such as the Scottish Highlands in autumn. . . . But Louis Stevenson, on my other side, was on that evening in one of his most recklessly brilliant moods. His talk was almost incessant. I remember feeling quite dazed at the amount of intellection he expended on each subject, however trivial. . . . The father's face at certain moments was a study—an indescribable mixture of vexation, fatherly pride and admiration, and sheer bewilderment at the boy's brilliant flippancies.*

Yet underneath his flippant demeanor, and that of his friends', Louis later wrote, "There kept growing up and strengthening a serious, angry, and at length a downright hostile criticism of the life around us." In politics, needless to say, father and son were miles apart. Conservative Thomas called himself a Tory while Louis was a self-described "red-hot socialist."

In trying to develop his own values and spiritualism, Louis found guidance from two surprising sources. One was Fleeming Jenkin, the University of Edinburgh engineering professor whose refusal to cover up for Louis's truancy had impressed him. In their midthirties, Jenkin and his wife, Anne, were fun, open-minded, and creative. Their lively home, where both Louis and Charles Baxter participated in elaborate theatricals, was a refuge from the tension at 17 Heriot Row. And Jenkin—an independent thinker on religion and early enthusiast of evolution—was a mentor and alternate father figure to Louis.

The second was a father figure in absentia, Walt Whitman. Louis was among the early readers of *Leaves of Grass* when it appeared in Britain in 1868, in *Poems of Walt Whitman*. The British version was heavily censored, omitting the homoerotic "Calamus" section and the signature "Song of Myself," but Louis still had to keep his copy at a tobacco shop instead of at home, where Thomas would have considered it blasphemous. Louis later credited Whitman's expansive spirit of love and equality with guiding him in creating his own moral code. In the essay "Books Which Have Influenced Me," he wrote that *Leaves of Grass* "tumbled the world upside down for me, blew into space a thousand cobwebs of genteel and ethical illusion, and, having thus shaken my tabernacle of lies, set me back again upon the strong foundation of all the original and manly virtues."

With his new friends and Bob, Louis formed a society called LJR, an initialism for Liberty, Justice, and Reverence. Club meetings at a pub in Advocate's Close consisted of hours of drinking, discussion, and planning practical jokes. What the "reverence" in the title referred to is unclear. The LJR constitution advocated abolishing the House of Lords and liberation from the doctrines of the established church, and began with a call to "ignore everything that our parents have taught us."

Unfortunately, the constitution fell into the hands of one of their parents, Thomas Stevenson, who failed to see the humor in it. Thomas must have been prowling surreptitiously among Louis's papers when he discovered it— an act painfully reminiscent of his own father, Robert, finding Thomas's writing when he snooped among his belongings. And Thomas was as incensed as his father had been by what he found. His blowup was just a skirmish in the escalating war over Louis's soul. It was heading toward an explosive confrontation—one that would push Louis to a nervous breakdown.

IN JANUARY 1873, Louis had just come out of a serious case of diphtheria with a newfound longing for honesty. So when Thomas questioned him about his religious beliefs one evening, he answered candidly that he did not believe in Christianity or the church instead of lying "as I have done so often before." He might as well have confessed to murder. Margaret whimpered that it was the worst thing that had ever happened to her. Thomas wailed that his whole life was a failure. Once again, at the age of twenty-two, Louis was torn between being true to himself and lying to preserve his parents' vision of what he should be, between developing as a man and remaining emotionally a child.

An undercurrent of bitterness and hysteria dragged down the household for months, and Louis's health along with it. Like one of his future fictional characters, he would come home from a night of drinking and high-flying talk, "my heart stirred to all its depths and my brain sparkling like wine and starlight," to find the house all lit up and his parents waiting for him in dour respectability. Finally, the family agreed that he should visit Margaret's niece Maud and her husband, Professor Churchill Babington, the vicar of Cockfield parish in Suffolk. No doubt the Stevensons were hoping for a religious miracle.

Arriving at Cockfield Rectory in his worn velvet jacket and a straw hat, Louis did not know quite what would greet him. He did not expect it to be an attractive woman who was not the vicar's wife lying before him on a sofa. Frances Fetherstonhaugh Sitwell was also fleeing an unhappy home to visit her friend Maud Babington. At the age of thirty-four, she was mourning the recent death of her twelve-year-old son and contemplating leaving her husband, Reverend Albert Sitwell, "a man of unfortunate temperament and uncongenial habits." Louis must have been struck by her immediately because he turned shy and was relieved to be pulled away by her ten-year-old son, Bertie. But once he and Sitwell started talking later that day, they couldn't stop. They laughed and cried together until late into the night.

Louis was just one of many younger men to be attracted to Frances Sitwell—or Fanny Sitwell, as she was more commonly called. A friend later claimed that more men fell in love with her than with any other woman he knew. "Worshipped" seems a more accurate description of the feelings she inspired, since men tended to describe her in lofty terms such as "deity" and "angel." (None remarked upon the more earthly humor in her name.) Irish born, with almond eyes and an aquiline nose, she was intelligent, warm, understanding, and generous with her heart and sympathy (despite her own considerable troubles), especially to needy young men.

Sitwell and her friend Sidney Colvin became known for championing talented budding writers (including, in later years, Joseph Conrad). She recalled that she immediately thought Louis was an "unmistakable young genius" and suggested that Colvin come from London to meet him. Colvin too was dazzled. At the age of twenty-eight, he was an established art critic and a professor of fine arts at Cambridge, well traveled in artistic and literary circles in London. "But this new Scottish youth, his first shyness past, beat everything I had ever known," he later recalled. "Genius shone from him, he held and drew you by the radiance of his eye and smile no less than by the enthralling quality of his conversation."

Colvin was in a position to make a difference in Louis's career, and he set out to do so immediately. He advised Louis that the best way into a literary career was by publishing essays in journals, and he discussed possible projects and publishers with him. Louis immediately began work on an essay called "Roads."

Louis spent a rosy month at Cockfield Rectory reading poetry and walking with Sitwell, and playing with her son. By the end, she recalled that she had become his "fast friend," though that hardly describes Louis's feelings. He had fallen in love, probably for the first time in his life, and he would pour out his feelings in long letters to Sitwell over the next several months. But he seemed to have little understanding of what she was feeling—or of the nature of her relationship with Sidney Colvin.

LOUIS RETURNED HOME TO TURMOIL. While he was gone, a dying cousin, Lewis Balfour, had decided he must warn Louis's father about Bob Stevenson's evil influence on Louis. Thomas humiliated Bob by confronting him on the street, accusing him of ruining his household and his son with his depraved atheistic beliefs. (In fact, Louis was an agnostic, but that was apparently no comfort to a man with Thomas's black-and-white view of life.) Thomas banned Bob from his home and his life and said that he and Margaret were ceasing to care for their son and believed he cared little for them.

Barring Bob's ungodly views from his home did not silence them in Thomas's mind. Less than two weeks later, he fumed to his son that he would rather see him dead than an atheist. "He said tonight, 'He wished he had never married,' and I could only echo what he said," Louis, obviously shaken, reported to Sitwell. The gist of his father's speech, he wrote, was: "I would ten times sooner have seen you lying in your grave than that you should be shaking the faith of other young men and bringing such ruin on other houses, as you have brought already upon this."

Margaret Stevenson was out that evening, but it is unlikely that she would have openly contradicted her husband had she been home. She seemed to see it as her wifely duty to present a united front with Thomas against Louis, though their rows usually drove her to hysteria, according to her son. Years later, she claimed that neither she nor Thomas knew that he was in such distress during this period.

But Louis's distress was profound. He felt trapped—reminded every day that he was a deep disappointment to his parents but dependent on them financially until he could launch a writing career. He wrote to Sitwell that he thought he would lose his mind under the stress. His health deteriorated and, at five foot ten, his weight plummeted to 118 pounds. He developed a facial tic. His cousin urged him to leave home. "[Bob] said if I were to lose my health here my father should hear some language from him about his religion that he was not capable of thinking possible," Louis related to Sitwell.

In October 1873, Louis slipped out of Edinburgh, turning up on Sitwell's London doorstep. By this time, she and Sidney Colvin had also become alarmed about Louis's mental and physical state. Colvin had quickly sensed that under Louis's gaiety, he was troubled and frail, "already heavily over-strained, from self-distrust and uncertainty as to his own powers and purposes, and above all from the misery of bitter, heart- and soul-rending dis-agreements with a father to whom he was devotedly attached."

The two arranged for Louis to see Andrew Clark, a London specialist in lung disease. Clark pronounced Louis's lungs delicate but his nervous system shattered. He insisted that Louis recuperate in Menton, the French mecca for the prosperous sick, and that neither of his parents accompany him. The Stevensons were suspicious about what part Colvin and Sitwell may have played in Clark's diagnosis, but the next day Louis was headed for the warm embrace of France.

THE "MEDITERRANEAN CURE" did not alleviate Louis's symptoms initially; in Menton, they seemed to get worse. He was exhausted and nervous, unable to read or write. His mind felt detached from his body—"like an enthusiast leading about with him a stolid, indifferent tourist," as he described it in "Ordered South," his essay about the experience. Still, there were some euphoric moments. In December, he began a letter to Sitwell: "The first violet. There is more secret trouble for the heart in the breath of this small flower, than in all the wines of all the vineyards of Europe." The flower's scent intoxicated his brain and sent tremors through his soul, he waxed on, and its "singing" was one of those "delicate penetrating sensations that passes, like a two edged sword, through your heart."

Even for a man with Louis's hyperconscious sensibility, it was an exceptional passage. And the next day he related that he had been on opium when he wrote it:

> *I had a day of extraordinary happiness; and when I went to bed,*
> *there was something almost terrifying in the pleasures that besieged*
> *me in the darkness. Wonderful tremors filled me; my head swam*
> *in the most delirious but enjoyable manner; and the bed softly*

oscillated with me, like a boat in a very gentle ripple. It does not make me write a good style apparently, which is just as well lest I should be tempted to renew the experiment.

It was not Louis's first experience with opium, nor his last. He smoked it often in Menton, perhaps prescribed by his doctor for depression or his cough. But opium was easily available over the counter in Britain, as were heroin and cocaine. *Mrs. Beeton's Book of Household Management*, the bible for middle-class Victorian homemakers, included powdered opium, along with the mysterious "blue pill" and laudanum (a mixture of opiates and alcohol) in its list of twenty-six drugs that every housewife should stock in her home. Louis was well aware of the drug's uplifting as well as addictive qualities. He once wrote to Bob that he was so miserable, he had to "struggle to keep from liquor and opium and things of that sort."

Early in his convalescence, Louis managed to write a long letter to his parents declaring his moral independence from them. They wrote back accepting his position. The exchange of letters must have been therapeutic for him at the time, but later he discovered that his parents thought he was out of his mind and were trying to calm him. It is a telling incident: On some level, the Stevensons seemed to equate their son's independent thinking with insanity.

Sidney Colvin's long visit was another tonic. Colvin couldn't have been more different from Louis: He was cautious and fussy, with a trim pointed Shakespeare goatee. Rather staid for a young man, Colvin described Louis at twenty-three as a "youngster," though he was only five years older. Louis's relationship with Colvin had none of the rowdy camaraderie of his other male friendships, but Colvin would always be encouraging, generous, and steady—a rock that grounded his fluttering friend.

After a long and costly convalescence on the Riviera at his father's expense, Louis returned home in April 1874 to resume his life and law studies in Edinburgh. Though his nervous symptoms had reappeared on the way home, he found his parents much warmer to him, even when he arrived in his latest eccentric garb, a Tyrolean hat and long blue cloak. Within two months, however, he was headed south again, this time to England, where Colvin was arranging his introduction to the London literati.

Sponsored by Colvin, Louis was elected to the Savile Club, one of the newer private gentlemen's clubs, which welcomed young and established writers and editors. In London, he met Leslie Stephen, the editor of the popular *Cornhill Magazine* and the father of Virginia Woolf. Stephen would encourage Louis's writing, along with that of other Savile Club members such as Henry James and Thomas Hardy.

The visit was a chance for Louis to enjoy fellowship with other aspiring writers in one of the world's literary centers. But even in the relatively casual atmosphere of the Savile, he stood out in his worn cloak and frayed embroidered smoking cap. Henry James would later be a close friend, but when they met that summer, James dismissed him as a *"poseur."* (Louis, in turn, called James "a mere club fizzle.") Andrew Lang—a Scottish folklorist best remembered for his Color Fairy Book series—described Louis on first sight as "more like a lass than a lad." (Louis called the British-educated Lang a "la-de-dady Oxford kind of Scot.")

Such unfavorable first impressions seemed to melt after spending time in Louis's presence, however, and Lang was later to say hotly that the shabby young Scot "possessed more than any man I ever met, the power of making other men fall in love with him." In his element around fellow writers, Louis seemed to blossom into a man of almost unearthly charm. Something about him "at first sight struck you as freakish, rare, fantastic, a touch of the elfin and unearthly, a sprite, an Ariel," Colvin wrote. "[He] would flash on you in the course of a single afternoon, all the different ages and half the different characters of man, the unfaded freshness of a child, the ardent outlook and adventurous day-dreams of a boy, the steadfast courage of manhood, the quick sympathetic tenderness of a woman."

The Savile Club became Louis's London headquarters for the next five years. The young critic and historian Edmund Gosse remembered being enthralled by Louis immediately. Gosse, whose book *Father and Son* would chronicle his own struggle with a puritanical father and escape into literature, found Louis's gaiety his "cardinal quality" at that time. "He was simply bubbling with quips and jests," Gosse later recalled, "his inherent earnestness or passion about abstract things was incessantly relieved by jocosity; and when he had built one of his intellectual castles in the sand, a wave of humour was certain to sweep in and destroy it."

From about this time on, people often commented on the light in Louis's wide-set eyes, describing them as luminous, gleaming, and penetrating; lit up by his smile, they turned from soft brown to violet blue. Louis's constant motion was another signature characteristic. While he talked, he always paced the room, twirling his cigarette. At Gosse's home, Louis never sat normally in a chair or settee but "with his legs thrown sideways over the arms of them, or the head of a sofa treated as a perch." In particular, Gosse wrote, a certain shelf was "worn with the person of Stevenson," who would leap onto it sideways and stretch his legs out the length of it.

It was as if Louis's body was as febrile as his mind. Gosse wrote that even as their friends became saddled with houses and jobs, like once-dancing deep-sea creatures who had become adhered to rocks with their tentacles, "he alone kept dancing in the free element, unattached."

LOUIS'S WIT AND CHARM may have been on dazzling display that summer, but inside he was depressed—possibly because he was unsure where he stood with Fanny Sitwell. Ever since he had met her, Louis had been deluging Sitwell with long, windy letters. Often touching, sometimes sophomoric, they chronicled his daily life and thoughts, from his problems with his parents to his hopes and fears for his writing. She was like a therapist to him, someone to whom he believed he could reveal himself "in all my humours and not think always that I have committed an indiscretion." Yet it's striking how unnatural those letters often feel, as if he was not truly being himself.

In part, Louis was drawn to Sitwell because she was eleven years older.

Though he had had a few crushes on younger women, he was more often only partly smitten. Perhaps after his years of social awkwardness with his peers, he was not quite comfortable with women his age. His letters to Sitwell sometimes read as if he was trying to figure out what a lover should be like and he overcompensated for his inexperience with bold declarations. "I would not give up my love of you for eternity," he proclaimed in one. "I would not go back for God." He was a romantic young man but also a very needy one, who grew hysterical when Sitwell's response did not arrive promptly at the Spec, where she discreetly sent them.

What Sitwell felt about his letters—and how intimate the two were—can only be guessed at because she asked him to burn her half of their correspondence. Her request suggests that she returned some of his feelings, though her future husband, Sidney Colvin, claimed that she was adept at gently converting misplaced "masculine combustions" into "the lifelong loyalty of grateful and contented friendship." Still, Sitwell would have been a very naïve thirty-four-year-old not to have felt the heat from a young man who declared, "I can think of nothing but of how much I love you." She must have enjoyed Louis's passionate outpourings; at the very least, for more than a year, there is no evidence that she discouraged them, although she was becoming romantically involved with Sidney Colvin.

Compared to the sex-charged, high-strung Scot, who was like a ride on a runaway horse, Colvin was a Sunday trot on a country lane—perhaps what Sitwell was looking for after her son's death and her difficult marriage. At any rate, she did not need to worry about impulsive moves from him. After her formal separation from her husband in 1874, she and Colvin became quietly recognized as a couple but continued to live apart until they married in 1903, when he was fifty-eight and she was sixty-four.

At some point in 1874, Sitwell decided to level with Louis and give him the brush-off. He tried to accept it graciously and fall into step with her other male adorers. He surrendered the field to Colvin, without evidence of jealousy, and the friendship between the two men continued to flourish. Still, Louis could not easily convert his "masculine combustions" into "contented friendship." Again, he seemed unsure of how a lover—or now a spurned lover—should act, and he made the perplexing choice to try to act as a dutiful son. In letters, he began to address her as "mother" and "Madonna," though his definition of a mother as "some one from whom I shall have no secrets; some one whom I shall love with a love as great as a lover's and yet more" was confused at best. If this was a son's love for his mother, it was decidedly Oedipal.

WITH TENSION AT HOME and his nervous symptoms flaring again ("Louis breaks down and is giddy," Margaret wrote in her diary), he now looked for escapes from Edinburgh as often as he could. Holidays in France became his self-prescribed treatment, especially now that Bob was in Paris studying under the dashing painter Charles-Émile-Auguste Durand, better known as Carolus-Duran. Like his fellow student John Singer Sargent, Bob must have been drawn to Carolus-Duran's atelier because of its international atmosphere and looser curriculum than that of the École des Beaux-Arts.

If London was where Louis made his professional debut, Paris was the stage for his personal liberation—particularly the bohemian Latin Quarter, where Bob had an apartment. Among the gypsy artists, writers, and intellectuals in colorful, threadbare clothing, he was no longer a freak—just another refugee from conformity and respectability. American painter Will Low, who would become a lifelong friend, recalled that when he met Louis, he had heard that he was "'going in' for literature, but this had not interested me particularly, for in those days we were all 'going in' for one thing or the other; and so long as it was not banking, commerce, politics, or other unworthy or material pursuits it merely seemed the normal and proper function of life."

Louis tagged along with Low, Bob, and other artists when they fled their cramped Paris studios forty miles southeast to Barbizon to paint *en plein air* in spring and summer. In the footsteps of the Barbizon school a generation before them, most notably Théodore Rousseau and Jean-François Millet, the painters were drawn to the rich landscape of marshes, woods, and meadows of the Fontainebleau Forest, as well as to the cheap accommodations and camaraderie.

Several years later, in his 1892 novel *The Wrecker*—cowritten with his stepson, Lloyd Osbourne—Louis would capture his and Bob's footloose style of travel in the characters Stennis *aîné* and Stennis *frère*, "a pair of hare-brained Scots":

> They had come from London, it appeared, a week before with nothing but greatcoats and toothbrushes. No baggage—there was the secret of existence. It was expensive, to be sure; for every time you had to comb your hair, a barber must be paid, and every time you changed your linen, one shirt must be bought and another thrown away; but anything was better (argued these young gentlemen) than to be the slaves of haversacks. "A fellow has to get rid gradually of all material attachments; that was manhood" (said they); "and as long as you were bound down to anything,—house, umbrella, or portmanteau,—you were still tethered by the umbilical cord."

The search for freedom, self-discovery, and a new definition of manhood—it reads like a Victorian version of Jack Kerouac's *On the Road*. But the weightlessness Louis felt on the road always ground to a halt when he stepped back under his parents' roof.

WRITING WAS NOT bringing Louis any closer to leaving the family home. Though Sidney Colvin had proposed that he write at the pace of an essay every few months, he shrank from the idea, responding that he had to let each one gestate in its own time. And Louis also had difficulty completing writing projects. He tended to become intoxicated with new ideas but was less enthusiastic about carrying them through. When he died, he would leave behind a trail of unfinished manuscripts and concepts that never materialized.

His first essay, "Roads," was rejected by the *Saturday Review* but published in *The Portfolio* (where Colvin was the main art critic) on December 4, 1873. A light reflection on hiking in the English countryside, it earned him three pounds, eight shillings. More important, it was the first time he saw his words in print, though not his name—he had chosen to publish it under the pseudonym L. S. Stoneven. In 1874 he published some reviews and more essays, but he was insecure about his early efforts; from his letters, it is clear how important the encouragement of Colvin and Sitwell was as he developed his writing voice. He wrote to Sitwell that he was "aghast" at the "feebleness" of "Roads," but when he saw it in print, he believed it would be the pinnacle of his writing career. He anticipated a future career as a hack in a memorable comment to Bob, who was equally uncertain about his future in art. "Stick in;" he teased, "we shall never be swells, but we can be cheesy sort of shits, with a push."

Louis was working on other projects that never saw print, including collections of short stories and essays, and a novel. But he was also unsure that he would ever be up to the feat of "physical and moral endurance" that writing a novel entailed.

In February 1875 Louis met a man who would inspire him to create one of the most famous characters in literature. At twenty-five years old, William Ernest Henley was at the Edinburgh Royal Infirmary to get treatment for tuberculosis of the bone. Stricken with TB at the age of twelve, Henley had his left leg amputated below the knee at sixteen and had just been told he would lose the other foot as well. Instead of accepting his diagnosis, he sought treatment from Joseph Lister, whose experiments with hand washing, sterilization, and antiseptics in surgery and on wounds had earned the infirmary a reputation as one of the most progressive hospitals in Britain. Lister's pioneering treatments to reduce infection would save Henley's foot but would also require extensive surgery and bed rest.

When *Cornhill* editor Leslie Stephen took Louis to meet him, Henley had been confined to the infirmary for eighteen months—a long time for anyone, much less a rambunctious young man, to be flat on his back. But Henley, the son of a Gloucester bookseller who had died in poverty, was determined to make a literary career regardless of his circumstances. He had been using the time to write and submit verse about his hospital experience to *Cornhill*. Published together later as "In Hospital," the sequence of twenty-eight poems was a shockingly frank and gritty account of Henley's emotions and observations of staff, visitors, patients, and death.

Henley's dire situation could only have made Louis's health and depression problems pale by comparison. Yet Henley's vitality seemed to glow against the gray walls of the infirmary. Everything about him was larger than life—his wit, his laughter, his courage, his wild red beard. Louis visited Henley often, hauling his burly friend up and down the stairs for carriage rides in spring that Henley would remember warmly the rest of his life. The two shared a longing for adventure and experience; they bantered about women and booze and literature. Henley grew to love Louis (whom he insisted on calling "Lewis," viewing "Louis" as an affectation), but he did not coddle him. He described his friend in a poem as "All eloquence & balls & brains; / Heroic—also infantile." Louis seemed to admire Henley's tough outspokenness, though his jealousy and combativeness would eventually leave their friendship in shreds.

Henley is best remembered for the poem that became known as "Invictus," written during his lonely, painful months in the Royal Infirmary. A defiant affirmation of courage and refusal to give in to despair, it began:

> Out of the night that covers me,
> Black as the Pit from pole to pole,
> I thank whatever gods may be
> For my unconquerable soul.

Over the next generations, the poem would travel the globe to become a source of inspiration to many people, including Nelson Mandela, who credited it with giving him the courage to continue during the darkest hours of his twenty-seven years in prison. It ended with the familiar but stirring words:

> It matters not how strait the gate,
> How charged with punishments the scroll.
> I am the master of my fate:
> I am the captain of my soul.

ONE CAN'T HELP but wonder how those words struck Louis, who was among the first to read them in 1875. At twenty-four, he was hardly the captain of his soul. His health was shaky, and the sluggish start of his writing career meant that he had no choice but to continue studying law and sponging off his parents. Frustrated in love, he had never experienced both sexual and emotional intimacy with a woman. He had set the age of twenty-five as the official end of youth—he could not have known it then, but his life was more than half over.

The last term of Louis's law studies made the Edinburgh winter of 1875 even chillier, try as he might to warm himself with thoughts of the forest at Fontainebleau. His desperate parents offered him a bribe of £1,000 (equivalent to nearly $145,000 today) if he passed the bar.

Somehow, in July, he did pass his final examination and was admitted to the Scottish bar. He and his parents rode through Edinburgh in their fashionable barouche, Louis sitting up on the collapsible hood, waving his hat to those he passed "like a man gone quite mad," according to his cousin Etta Balfour.

The traditional brass plate, "R.L. Stevenson, Advocate," was mounted on the front door at 17 Heriot Row, and his mother insisted that he sit for a photo in his wig and gown. But Fleeming Jenkin seemed to have a better sense of what the milestone meant to Margaret's son. "Accept my hearty congratulations on being done with it," he wrote to Louis. "I believe that is the view you like to take of the beginning you have just made." Louis began and ended his legal career with a short, weak effort to secure briefs.

He had slipped the leash of parental control once again, but it did not feel like freedom. Though Louis's passion for Sitwell was on the wane, he doubted he would ever love another woman. "I don't know but that a good dull marriage with a dull good girl would be a good move," he sniffed to her the following January. He had published more essays and reviews, but he reported that his life was at a standstill. "If you were to ask a squirrel in a mechanical cage, for his autobiography, it would not be very gay," he wrote. "Every spin may be amusing in itself, but is mighty like the last." Honoring morality, virtue, and love could be difficult and even painful, "but they string your life together; now mine's all in rags."

Walking and canoeing remained his escape. In the summer of 1876, he and Walter Simpson embarked on a canoe trip that Louis hoped to chronicle in a book. Beginning in Antwerp, they paddled through Belgium and then France, along canals and the Oise River. In September Louis headed for the artist colony in Grez-sur-Loing, where he would meet an American woman who was mourning the death of her young son.

The river tour was an apt metaphor for Louis's life at that time. Before he met Fanny Osbourne, he was floating, as he once wrote, like "a leaf on a river with no volition and no aim." With her, he would become one of the most famous writers in the world.

SIX

Grez-sur-Loing looked the same when Louis arrived at dusk on an evening in late summer. The same as the summer before, when he, Bob, Will Low, and others had gone there seeking a venue for a new artist colony because Barbizon was "played out," Bob said, choked in the summer with the old-school artists. And it probably looked pretty much the same three hundred years before that, when an eighteen-year-old widow, Mary, Queen of Scots, had gone there to mourn the death of her sixteen-year-old husband. The castle where she stayed was now a romantic ruin, but the picturesque medieval bridge still arched over the Loing. Peasants in wooden shoes clopped over it on their way to and from the wheat fields, and shepherds still herded their flocks home through the cobbled streets. Louis had found the town a little too sleepy and melancholy for his taste, but the quaintness and light were precisely what attracted his friends. The gray, shadowless days lent themselves to landscapes bathed in a hazy atmosphere that became a trademark of the "Grez school" of painters.

Louis arrived on foot with his rucksack. Though he still took to the open road "afoot and light-hearted," like Whitman, he was acutely aware that other men his age were heading down a different path—one that dead-ended into marriage. This had inspired him to pose as a sage on marriage in his essay "Virginibus Puerisque," published the previous month in *Cornhill*. Editor Leslie Stephen allowed some writers to sign with their initials, and

Louis would become known throughout the world by the ones he signed his essay with: "R.L.S."

Louis contended that bourgeois marriage was mundane and unromantic, a perilous remedy to the inevitable breakup of male friendships and fear of aging alone. He imagined that most people simply picked a mate by checking off a list of desired qualities—a "pleasing voice, moderate good looks, unimpeachable internal accomplishments after the style of the copy-book" being chief among those a man looked for in a wife. "You have only to look these happy couples in the face, to see they have never been in love, or in hate, or in any other high passion, in all their days," he declaimed. In fact, love was probably "too violent a passion" to bring to wedlock, which he characterized as "a sort of friendship recognized by the police." Still, he urged men to jump into the fray; matrimony was comfortable and pleasant, if not easy. "For marriage is like life . . . ," he concluded, "it is a field of battle, and not a bed of roses."

Now, as he walked through the ancient streets to join his friends, even the green pastures where male friendships thrived seemed threatened. Grez may have *looked* the same, but Hôtel Chevillon, the inn they had claimed as their summer clubhouse, was not. Their female-free zone had been shaken by the arrival of two American women painters, a rare event in the area's art colonies, where *en plein air* landscape painting was still almost exclusively male terrain. In France, just being a woman artist was potentially compromising, and social beliefs dictated that women painters could not go out into nature unchaperoned and lacked the strength to carry their equipment. As a result, they were largely restricted to domestic subjects and outdoor scenes viewed from a window.

The artist friends who awaited Louis's arrival in Grez were no doubt less concerned that the female invasion would compromise the women's virtue than that it would inhibit their own horseplay and bawdy freedom of speech. So Bob had gone down ahead to rid the inn of them. Instead, curiously, he had sent back word that Fanny and Belle Osbourne were "of the right sort."

Bob met the Osbournes in a novel way. As Fanny described the meeting to Timothy Rearden, "I was helping [Lloyd] fish and I caught the gentleman as he was rowing by in a little boat, by the back of his collar in such a way that he had to land and ask me to disengage him." Belle captured it in a sketch that she sent home to her father. Perhaps it was their comical introduction that made Bob decide mother and daughter were "of the right sort." Or maybe he learned that they had already lived among miners and gamblers.

A more traditional American woman—the Osbournes' nanny, Kate Moss, for example—was quite definitely of the wrong sort. Miss Kate was appalled at the inn's primitive sleeping arrangements: spartan male and female bedrooms on an upstairs floor, separated only by a narrow hallway. At the end of the hall, like a monument to vulgarity, was a single shared bathroom. After two days, she fled to a fashionable French resort as a paid companion to a wealthy aunt. "Though she shed a few tears on leaving, it was a very happy face that looked back at us from the window of the diligence," Belle recalled.

Miss Kate's eyes would have popped out had she seen the inn when the Osbournes returned in summer. Cigarette butts, matches, and broken paintbrushes littered the staircase and courtyard. Men's bathing costumes dried in the sun at the foot of the garden, and easels dotted the meadows and forest. The male painters had arrived, in linen smocks and velveteen shirts, sporting fezzes, sombreros, Phrygian caps, and berets, splattered with paint. Mostly British and American, they brought with them a freedom of conduct "that escapes geographical definition," in the words of Will Low. Elsewhere in France men might wear ascot ties to country outings, but in Grez, "the view of a stalwart gentleman clad in a straw hat, bathing trunks and bathing sandals as his only wear, traversing the streets on his way to the *bureau de tabac* was not unusual."

Laconic Walter Simpson, whose Grez conduct included drinking absinthe with his pet monkey, arrived a few days ahead of Louis from their canoeing trip. He prepared the female newcomers for his friend's arrival with stories of their exploits together, as did Bob Stevenson. Even in her somber mood, Fanny could appreciate a charming man. She deemed Bob the most colorful and attractive of the lot (and later called him the hand-somest man she ever saw)—with his black mustache and hat, loosely knot-ted neckerchief, bright striped socks, and luminous talk.

Eight-year-old Lloyd had a different take on Bob on first sight. "He smiled pleasantly, hat in hand, with a mocking expression that I learned afterwards was habitual with him, and which reminded me of the wolf in *Little Red Riding Hood*," he later wrote. Bob was certainly licking his lips over Lloyd's sister, Belle, now a bewitching mix of wholesome and naughty. With enormous brown eyes and ebony hair that cascaded in waves down her back, the seventeen-year-old caused quite a stir among the new arrivals. But Belle's heart was stolen by Frank O'Meara, a twenty-three-year old col-league of Bob's at Carolus-Duran's atelier who sang Irish ballads with a voice that "melted the heart."

Before long, the Osbourne women were calling their male colleagues by their last names, like the guys, while the men were luring them into private walks to chat about the others. ("Talk about women being gossips, I never saw any like men," Fanny wrote to Rearden.) Fanny and Belle joined in some of their activities and avoided others, and were treated with respect because, as Bob observed, "where the greatest latitude prevails, the utmost nicety of conduct must be observed."

Fanny was touched by how the artists watched over Lloyd, and they spoiled her and empathized with her grief in a way she had not experienced before from men. No doubt Rearden would think it weak and silly for her to go on grieving for her dead child, she wrote to him, adding, "They don't think so here, but they are only mad artists who are not ashamed to laugh or cry as it pleases them . . . though of course, as you have hinted so generously, they will soon forget me, it will be long before I shall forget them."

Yet Fanny always made a striking impression, one not easily forgotten. The villagers called her "the beautiful American" and her fellow artists sketched her mouth and nose and modeled her arms in clay. To the Phila-delphia painter Birge Harrison, she had a profound character that could have made her "the leader of a great movement" had she been born in an-other century. Fanny was "a grave and remarkable type of womanhood," he recalled of her at Grez, "with eyes of a depth and somber beauty which I have never seen equaled—eyes, nevertheless, that upon occasion could sparkle with humor and brim over with laughter."

LOUIS FIRST SAW her through a milky haze of cigarette smoke and firelight. He had ducked under the stone archway into the courtyard of the inn, where he could hear the raucous, wine-fueled conversation after dinner from the open windows of the salle à manger. It was clear that any objections to the Osbournes had been all but forgotten by the jovial group inside. Louis paused to study the party, gazing through the top of the Dutch door, which was open to let in the evening breeze. The women were certainly a picturesque addition—Fanny, with her dark eyes and curls, and Belle, perhaps in her bright red beret and stockings, like a precocious poppy.

Louis's eye could have been caught by Belle, as his cousin's was. Instead he was drawn to her mother, a woman ten years his senior, though that was not apparent from the way she looked and acted. As usual, Fanny was a vision of unconventionality. She might have been entertaining the spellbound group as she often did, with one of her stories about life in a mining camp or the time she traveled on the trail of the Pony Express—exotic tales that made his own exploits seem like child's play. She took unladylike drags on a cigarette and waved her hands in the air while she talked, sending silvery ribbons of smoke spiraling around her. Her tiny feet rested on the rung of a man's chair next to hers. It was enough for Louis to see that she was unlike any woman he had ever met.

Possibly aware that she was being watched, Fanny looked up and was struck by the sight of this stranger staring at her with "a sort of surprised admiration," according to Belle. Framed like a Rembrandt portrait in the half-open door, Louis's pale face, flushed cheeks, and flowing hair were illuminated against the night by a lantern hung above. Another woman of her era might have cast her eyes downward out of modesty or social convention, but Fanny held his gaze, and in that moment, he must have taken in the full force of her beauty: the mysterious shadow of a smile, the rich, dark glow of her skin in the lamplight, the "eyes of gold and bramble-dew," as he would immortalize them.

"Her face startled him. It was a face he wanted; and he took it in at once like breathing." Louis used those words to describe one of his fictional heroes, but they might well recall his feelings that night. He had tumbled into love at first sight—something that would repeatedly happen to his dumbfounded heroes in the years to come. "It had never taken me like that before," another character says, "but the want of her took and shook all through me, like the wind in the luff of a sail."

As the story was often told, Louis then leapt into the room like he was hopping a fence, received a hero's reception, and took a seat at Fanny's side. Some Stevenson biographers have dismissed the idea that he vaulted over the half-open door as sentimental nonsense created by Fanny's children and others to embellish the Stevenson legend after his death. Maybe that was not exactly how it happened, but such a dramatic entrance was certainly true to his style—and it makes a tantalizing detail, given that Fanny was assuredly half-open to a sexual affair. Others have doubted Louis's claim that he was lovestruck the moment he saw his future wife in the flickering lamplight. Yet he believed he was, and twelve years later, he would recall "the day when I looked through the window" as a red-letter memory in his heart. "Her eyes took hold upon mine and clung there, and bound us together like the joining of hands," the narrator of yet another short story says, "and the moments we thus stood face to face, drinking each other in, were sacramental and the wedding of souls."

"WE HAVE BEEN LIVING a charming lotus eating, Brook farm, sort of life," Fanny wrote to Rearden that summer. Her words captured the spirit of the art colony well: It was a more sensuous and playful version of the

American utopian communal settlements that had sprung up in the States earlier in the century. Fanny and Belle were part of the first contingent of artists who would establish Grez as one of the most popular art colonies in France for several years. Far from home, in their self-contained community, the artists could forget the cares and rules of the world beyond. Their recollections of summers there left a ribbon of dreamy images and sensations: the spicy smells of the forest at dawn; red poppies spattered like brilliant paint strokes across the green fields; tall glasses of steamy French drip coffee and *petits vins* from grapes on the nearby hills; village girls moving through the meadows at night like fairies, with crowns of glowworms in their hair.

"Art and life were such synonymous terms with us, in those days," Low wrote, describing that time. They practically lived outdoors. They ate most meals at a table in the arbor or had baskets delivered to them in the field and ate at their easels so they did not lose any of the mellow light. Large canvasses were often left out in the woods at night, protected only by oilcloth, until completion. It was unthinkable that passersby would damage or take the *paysages intimes*.

The artists hung their smaller works in the *salle à manger* in the evening for the group's comments. During the exuberant after-dinner conversations, they critiqued art and literature and ranted about politics and "the respectable and well-to-do," according to Lloyd. As a boy listening to the grown-up talk, he developed the idea that philistines were a race of people to be kept at a distance. One of Louis's favorite expressions was "a common banker," used as a form of derision. When he added that he hoped to die in a ditch, the wide-eyed boy envisioned common bankers jingling by his crumpled body, "oblivious and scornful."

Despite Louis's smoldering exchange of looks with Fanny that first night, in the light of day he was no doubt a little unsure how to approach this exotic creature who had entered his life like a Midwestern tornado. First, there was the awkwardness of her marital status. He must have learned rather quickly (if not before he arrived) that she was unhappily married, but it was still something of a hurdle. And he had never met an American woman. Aside from the male painters he knew through Bob, his sense of

Americans had been shaped mostly by literature, beginning with *Uncle Tom's Cabin*, the book from which most Europeans developed their first impression of the U.S. His main American reading—James Fenimore Cooper, Nathaniel Hawthorne, Edgar Allan Poe, Henry David Thoreau, and Walt Whitman—may not have given him much insight into "new" American women such as Fanny and her daughter.

"There is a young Scotchman here, a Mr. Stevenson, who . . . never saw a real American girl before, and he says I act and talk as though I came out of a book," Belle wrote in a letter home. (Louis later clarified that she seemed to be out of a Bret Harte story.) Both Stevenson cousins found Americanness a source of wonder that summer. They were tickled by California painter Hiram Bloomer's observation, "These parts don't seem much settled, hey?" Louis told Belle he had "laughed for an hour at the idea of such an old place not being much settled."

Meanwhile, Louis began courting Fanny partly through her surviving son. He told him stories, read to him, and made him feel protected. He took Lloyd for canoe voyages on the river that included imaginary naval battles and moonlight explorations of the castle ruins with lanterns. "R L S always paid children the compliment of being serious, no matter what mocking light might dance in his brilliant brown eyes," Lloyd would recall, "and I instantly elected him to a high place in my esteem."

When the weather was too sunny to paint, the group splashed in the river and played games that included splitting into teams to sink one another's canoes. Louis led the games with the zeal and high spirits he put into everything he did, according to Belle. Reckless and always game, Fanny joined in even the rowdiest play, though she couldn't swim and wore a wool bathing costume that had sleeves and reached below her knees. Yet even in the dowdy beachwear of the day, she managed to look stylish. With her red espadrilles, her waist tied with one scarlet bandanna and her curls tucked under another, Belle noted that her mother looked like a little girl. For Fanny, it was a wistful escape to a more carefree time, when she was a tomboy in Indiana running with the boys. "I can manage a canoe perfectly just as I would ride a horse, and am sunburned and blackened and bruised until you would hardly know me," she boasted to Rearden. Like their male colleagues, the Osbournes sometimes went barefoot to meals and compared the sunburn on their legs, shocking one female visitor who came down to dinner in full dress.

When the sky was gray, Louis carried Fanny's painter's equipment—a folding stool, parasol, portable easel, and paint box—on his back, bounding across the meadows on his grasshopper legs while she bounced along behind in her petticoats. Fanny was not an especially talented painter, but she was a quick study and certainly skilled enough to justify her presence among the art students in Paris. She adopted the Barbizon style in her Grez paintings, and her sketch of Louis, in an embroidered Indian smoking cap, captures his sparkling eyes and long, tapering fingers.

While Fanny drew or painted, Louis no doubt contemplated what it was about her that so possessed him. Her hourglass figure was slender, her cascading curls untamed. Her skin had the golden sheen of sunny days, unlike that of the girls he had known. And then there were her penetrating eyes— eyes that he would later describe as "insane." One minute, they were like dark pools of rainwater in the woods, glittering in a shaft of sunlight; the next, like "the sighting of a pistol." They were eyes you could not walk away from. He could not, anyway. Warm, mournful, mischievous, seductive, vulnerable, sharp, uncanny—they were all the things he feared and longed for in a woman.

Louis had been hooked from the moment Fanny's eyes had announced her frank sexuality as well as her sorrow. And he admired her candor and strong opinions; the nakedness of her thoughts and emotions excited him. He liked big personalities—and hers was as big as the American frontier, with a blend of female sensuality and masculine swagger that he found intoxicating. For Louis, Fanny was the woman of a bad boy's dreams—a fellow outsider, rebel, and adventurer, with whom he could truly be himself.

Sometimes he coaxed Fanny to stay behind at the inn, where they fell into deep conversations that her son remembered as interminably long. And he monopolized her at meals. Lloyd and Belle began to think of Louis and Fanny as always together. "[Louis] has turned out a charming fellow and he is perfectly charmed with Mamma," Belle wrote to a friend. "They can't get him to go off boating or canoeing or anything, he just sits by the stove and smokes cigarettes and talks to her." Fanny had begun to cast off her sadness. Though one artist had lamented that she was losing her tragic look, Belle wrote to the Vandegrifts that Fanny was "ever so much better and is getting prettier every day."

Fanny was dazzled by Louis's intellect but taken aback by his childish behavior and paroxysms of emotion. Even in her circumspect letters to Rearden, she wrote that she very much liked Louis, who was "the wittiest man I ever met; only I do wish he wouldn't burst into tears in such an unexpected way; it is so embarrassing." Yet she saw past Louis's social awkwardness to his kindness and generosity, and felt his vulnerability was a sign of strength. Despite her usual brave front, Fanny had been tiptoeing through an emotional minefield since Hervey's death. She had memory lapses and was so nervous that her hands shook when she held a pen or paintbrush. Louis slipped his hand into hers and steadied her through her sadness and fear. And his attention helped her believe in herself again. As Sidney Colvin once noted: "As long as [Louis] was there, you kept discovering with delight unexpected powers in yourself."

Physically, Fanny realized, he did not have much to recommend him. He was a sliver of a man, with straggly hair, bad teeth, and eyes set too far apart. And other men she knew had lived much fuller lives. But she had met none who lived life so fully, whose talk alone could take her to places she could not find by herself. He talked like he walked—always one step ahead of her. Sometimes that made her feel small and slow, and she doubled her step to go faster. He never eased his pace, just smiled over his shoulder, beckoning her to keep up—and when she was really lucky, she almost could.

As their desire for each other heated up, one can't help but imagine that it was somehow entangled with their surroundings. "The air penetrates through your clothes, and nestles to your living body," Louis had written about Fontainebleau in "Forest Notes," published in May 1876. "You forget all your scruples and live a while in peace and freedom, and for the moment only." For Fanny especially, that time must have been something to savor for the moment, like the fleeting beauty of a summer day. It was a chance, perhaps her last, to feel a man's love again, so far from home that no one there need ever know. And there were Louis's words, nestling into her body, lulling her into release: "All the puling sorrows, all the carking repentance, all this talk of duty that is no duty, in the great peace, in the pure daylight of these woods, fall away from you like a garment."

IT APPEARS THAT LOUIS and Fanny first made love in the embrace of nature: in a canoe on the Loing. The river may simply have been the most private place they could find, but it was still the kind of romantic setting both would have chosen—a serene river that twisted along the woodlands and slipped out of sight beyond an old mill.

"The love I hold was borne by her," Louis later wrote of the Loing in one poem. In another, which begins, "Mine eyes were swift to know thee, and my heart / As swift to love," he wrote:

> On the stream,
> Deep, swift and clear, the lilies floated; fish
> Through its shadows ran. There, thou and I
> Read Kindness in our eyes and closed the match.

In yet another poem, two lovers row home in the evening after lovemaking in a boat filled with flowers.

When Fanny and Louis first made love is unknown. They did not leave behind a cache of love letters to enlighten literary historians. Possibly, they destroyed their correspondence, so the progression of their early relationship is now something of a puzzle. Louis's feelings after his three-week visit to Grez are easier to ascertain. In November, the month after he left Fanny, he wrote to his friend Charles Baxter that he was "damnably in love." And he began writing an essay on falling in love, which he described as "the one illogical adventure, the one thing of which we are tempted to think as supernatural, in our trite and reasonable world."

Fanny's correspondence is less revealing. Only her letters to Rearden survive, and in these she was actively evasive and misleading. Her writing is disjointed, hyperbolic, and a bit frantic, no doubt reflecting her state of mind but also making it difficult for anyone who reads them to know what she was really feeling. The memoirs of Belle and Lloyd also offer little help. They slip lightly over this time and, no doubt to protect their mother's reputation even after her death, both would retain a childlike insistence that she was not sexually intimate with Louis until she married him.

Some of the couple's biographers have theorized that Fanny was more interested in Bob that first summer, based on her effusive early praise of him and her account to Rearden of a walk the two took during which Bob advised her about the Grez artists she should not associate with when she returned to Paris. He singled out the American Walter Palmer and added, "You must have nothing to say to *me* for I am only a vulgar cad. But Louis is a gentleman, and you can trust him and depend upon him."

Some have interpreted this as evidence that Fanny was interested in Bob until this moment, when she shifted her feelings toward his cousin. But this theory rests on the premise that a woman will simply redirect her intimate feelings as instructed to by a man—or at least that Fanny would. There is no evidence that Fanny's praise for Bob's handsomeness equated to love, and she and Louis already seemed to be inseparable. And Louis's essay "On Falling in Love," written soon after, suggests that their feelings were mutual. "The ideal story is that of two people who go into love step for step, with a fluttered consciousness, like a pair of children venturing together into a dark room," he wrote. "From the first moment when they see each other, with a pang of curiosity, through stage after stage of growing pleasure and embarrassment, they can read the expression of their own trouble in each other's eyes."

However deep her feelings for Louis were, Fanny likely saw their affair as something that could not last. For him, though, sexual intimacy with Fanny was not simply a romp with an older woman. It cemented his emotional commitment to her—a kind of role reversal that is striking for a Victorian man. As he wrote in his love poem, he immediately became hers "wholly . . . unalterably . . . in honourable service, pure intent . . ." Making love to Fanny reset the course of his life. Like the river flowing behind and ahead of them, she would carry him to his future.

THERE WAS NOTHING casual about the couple's reunion in fall in her tiny fourth-floor apartment in Paris. "The day when I came to see you in Paris after the first absence" would become a love anniversary for them as cherished as "the day when I looked through the window." Once he was in Paris, 5 rue de Douai became Louis's forwarding address. For male companionship, Low recalled, he and Bob were left alone.

Fanny and Louis had landed on the soft shoulder of bohemian Paris, where they could continue their affair nearly as freely as in Grez. It was still a drastic step for Fanny, who risked losing what little security she had. But both she and Louis were suffocating under the weight of social propriety, and he hated hypocrisy as strongly as he loved her. Her willingness to take that risk for him only strengthened his feelings for her. "Bob and I both recognized how serious a passion held him, all impossible of realization as it then appeared to be," Low wrote.

It's likely that Louis and Fanny were among the crowds that gathered around the window of the art dealer Giroux et Cie to see Édouard Manet's scandalous *Nana*. Depicting the fleshy actress Henriette Hauser getting dressed while a man in a top hat and evening dress peers at her derrière, it was rejected from the 1877 Salon as an "outrage to morality." Again, it was the subject's cheeky manner that caused the outcry. The painting was not a stolen glimpse at a woman dressing; "Nana" flaunted her frilly chemise and satin corset of blue instead of plain white, the acceptable color for virtuous women. It did not help that faintly outlined under her chemise were drawers, which were still considered too masculine by some. (Bettering Nana,

Fanny would later don a pair of Louis's silk drawers, which she found rejected and unworn in his bedroom closet at Heriot Row.)

Corsets and lingerie had a tremendous appeal to Victorian men, for whom the image of stay laces being pushed through corset holes conjured visions of intercourse. Louis was no exception. After he and Fanny were married, he would send Henley a playful poem that prompted his friend to remark to Baxter, "Louis has confessed that female underclothing—smocks, hose, garters, drawers—are his fate, and that the noblest sight in the world is washing." As much as Louis appreciated lingerie on a woman, however, he preferred to see it come off. His poem "Now bare to the beholder's eye" waxes on the thrill of exposure as liberation, when a lady's "be-ribboned battlements" lie like soldiers "scattered as they fell," freeing her to be a "living woman" again.

Louis drew on Fanny's Paris milieu to dash off some slight articles for the fledgling magazine *London*, a Conservative weekly founded by his Spec chum Robert Glasgow Brown. A thinly disguised Académie Julian was the subject of "A Studio of Ladies," a small gem of awakening feminism no doubt influenced by Fanny. Louis began the article by noting some of the ways men exercise financial tyranny over women, such as charging female art students a higher fee than men, a practice embraced by "M. Concert" (a pseudonym for Rodolphe Julian). Men know they must hang on to the purse, Louis wrote, "for we are fonder of women than they are of us; we must bribe them to come to us." At M. Concert's studio, however, the women made a point of getting their money's worth, and a bit more, out of their male models. They rearranged the men's hair, poked them with their maul-sticks, stretched measuring tape over their bodies from limb to limb, and even made one man fetch coal during his break. They kneaded another "splendid brawny Hercules of a fellow" into the thankless pose of a dying gladiator, which he was ordered to hold for sixty minutes. (Female models were allowed a break every thirty minutes.) "An hour on end in the attitude of the Dying Gladiator is no joke," Louis observed, and the bruiser sweated, quivered, and was generally "the spectacle of an agony" as the minutes ticked away. Some of the women began to take pity on him, but one painter insisted that he tough it out the full hour. "Don't you see that the man is suffering?" the others implored her. Without missing a beat, she laid a glob of paint on her canvas. "I just love to see him suffer," she replied.

Fanny was not mentioned in Louis's more serious essay "On Falling in Love," but she must have been secretly thrilled to read it in *Cornhill* in February. The man whose heart had more often been only "somewhat engaged" by lovers now wrote hotly that "passionate love" was "kindness, so to speak, run mad and become importunate and violent." Belle remembered the shabby apartment at 5 rue de Douai lit up with excitement the evening Louis came bounding up four flights of stairs waving a magazine with a glowing review. The review urged readers to keep their eye on "one Stevenson"—a phrase that became his nickname for months afterward.

Fanny may have been invisible in Louis's work, but she was already influencing his career. He started writing fiction again and finishing it. He went back at a short story he had set aside three years before; "An Old Song" was published anonymously in *London* in March. By that time, he had also begun writing "A Lodging for the Night," about the poet and thief François Villon. He would complete two more short stories before that ran, also unsigned, in fall in *Temple Bar*, a monthly magazine founded by Dickens protégé George Augustus Sala.

It seems hardly coincidental that Louis's career took this critical turn just as his personal life did. Fanny was his muse, the wild spark that ignited his literary imagination. Unlike his parents, she believed in his talent and urged him to devote himself to the kind of writing he loved; unlike Colvin, she thought he was more likely to have financial success with fiction than with essays. Without Fanny's influence, Louis might now be a forgotten man of letters instead of one of the greatest voices in Scottish literature.

By early spring 1877, it appeared that their future was about to come to a halt. Sam notified her that he was coming to France in May, presumably to collect the family after his mistress vacated their Oakland home. Fanny was still attending art classes, but in the fall she had written to Rearden with disarming honesty, "I don't expect to become a great painter. I never did. I haven't the talent. I only paint and study because it pleases me to. I know just what there is in me." Perhaps Rearden had conveyed this to her cash-strapped husband. Whatever prompted the visit, the prospect of it sent Fanny's nervous symptoms flaring. In April she sent Rearden her wildest letter to date.

The marvelously inaccurate letter is a study of a mind in turmoil. This time Fanny grossly exaggerated her artistic success, probably to convince both Rearden and herself that she and Belle were justified in continuing at the atelier. While Belle chimed in to insist that they were not leading a "gay, rollicking, dissipated life," Fanny methodically described their Paris associates in a way to make each seem more charmless and safer than the last. It was impossible to paint the Stevenson cousins as anything but gay and rollicking, of course, though she did manage to claim that they had ruined their health from "over-education and dissipation," were threatened with insanity, and had reformed their wild ways. But when she went on to praise Louis's writing and acts of generosity, her fighting spirit shriveled like a leaky balloon and she reclaimed her genuine voice and feelings. Those "despised Bohemians" were the truest gentlemen she had ever met—"born gentlemen" in the American sense, whom she had not known to do an unkind or dishonorable thing. She would miss them terribly when she returned home, she reflected: "The two mad Stevensons who with all their sufferings are men out of spirits, but so filled with the joyousness of mere living that their presence is exhilarating, I shall never see again."

BACK IN HIS PARENTS' HOME, Louis was in the throes of one of the downsides of falling in love: jealousy. He wrote to Charles Baxter to tell him of Sam's imminent arrival, adding that it made him sick to even write of it. Sam arrived in Paris, paid an overdue bill to Fanny's landlord, and accompanied the family to Grez but left abruptly soon after. Apparently, he had no reservations about leaving his wife and daughter unchaperoned in a group of men.

Sam allegedly departed because he received bad news about the stock market, where he had investments. But anger might have been as big a factor. Fanny must have overruled his doubts about Belle's progress by insisting that she needed another year to complete her art studies. His daughter was there for the opportunities a European art education could open to her, and for once, Sam could not count on her to side with him against her mother, now that her heart was entangled with O'Meara's. But it was clear to Sam that Fanny was not eager to return to their previous life. After spending time at the casino in Boulogne and attending theater and vaudeville shows in London, he returned to San Francisco, leaving behind an unpaid bill for his stay at Hôtel Chevillon. It appears that he also curtailed or even cut off the allowance for his wife and children.

Fanny's lover was in such a rush to get back to her, he arrived in London from Edinburgh as Sam was leaving London for home. The second summer was not as idyllic in the artists' little Shangri-la. Hard up for cash, Fanny picked up her writing again with characteristic aplomb, as if it were a piece of embroidery she had set aside and forgotten. She asked Rearden to send her a story she had left with him, "Too Many Birthdays," to give to the young American artist Walter Francis Brown, who was looking for a children's story to illustrate. (Brown later illustrated Mark Twain's *A Tramp Abroad*.) A simple morality tale about problems that occur when a princess is granted her wish of having birthdays on demand, it was published in July in *St. Nicholas*, a popular American children's magazine. The story includes the kind of striking imagery that would become a staple of Fanny's fiction: To fulfill her wish, the princess must take pills that are each a tiny replica of her in a casket-shaped box; the miniature girl is slightly aged in each successive pill. Suitors reject the princess because they believe she is older—an interesting plot twist, given Fanny's current situation, though she wrote the story before she met Louis.

That summer, Lloyd decided he wanted to be a writer too, and later he sent Louis a fanciful article about their summer, complete with a photo of himself in a naval uniform. Louis's response was telling of both his ardor for Fanny and the magical way he related to children. "Your account of the life and adventures at Grez is deliriously exciting, full of intrigue and incident," he wrote. "I have been reading Robinson Crusoe again. He was a fool to you. He could not fish worth a cent and was afraid in a boat. . . . I am dere Sam ures til deth Lord Stevenson."

Over this year and the next, Louis and Fanny were getting a good sense of each other's eccentricities and emotional volatility. Fanny still had trouble "guiding her pen" and found that her letters sometimes contained "the most contradictory nonsense." She continued to have problems remembering—perhaps a consequence of trying to block painful recollections of her married life and son's death. Fanny's Paris doctor said her memory would soon recover, but when she left the apartment, O'Meara made a note of her clothing and cab number in case she did not return when expected. Fanny was also getting well acquainted with Louis's temper, which frothed up at a Paris restaurant after he sent back a bottle of burgundy that he decided was "corked," or contaminated with cork taint. When the waiter returned with another corked bottle, Louis hurled it against the wall into pieces.

Extravagant mood swings—from gaiety to utter gloom—were something the lovers could share. The man who had once considered escape from his depression in brandy, laudanum, or death would write of his sweetheart, "One day I find her in heaven, the next in hell." Fanny believed they were both suffering from one of those vague Victorian maladies, a "nervous crisis." Her description of Louis's bizarre behavior was certainly convincing evidence:

> When he begins to laugh, if he is not stopped in time, he goes into hysterics, and has to have his fingers bent back to bring him to himself again; and when his feelings are touched he throws himself headlong on the floor and bursts into tears; and you never know when either thing is going to happen. I like him very much but

there are times when it is a little embarrassing to be in his com-
pany; and sometimes, I imagine, not altogether safe.

When Louis could not stop laughing on a cab ride in Paris, Fanny refused his request to press on his fingers. This made him laugh harder and insist that if she didn't, "he would bend my fingers back and break every bone in them, which he proceeded to do, and I only saved them by suddenly biting his hand till it bled." With all the mood swerving and finger biting and bottle smashing, it is striking that neither of them showed any desire to flee. Perhaps this is what Louis meant when he wrote in "On Falling in Love" that lovers "can read the expression of their own trouble in each other's eyes."

By the end of that second summer, more American women had begun dropping in at Grez. Among them was a New Englander who would cause trouble for Fanny. Margaret B. Wright arrived with her children—Marian, a colleague of Belle's at Académie Julian, and Charles, who went to school with Lloyd in Paris. While her daughter studied art, the twice-widowed Wright wrote clever, satirical articles about their life in France that were published widely in the United States. Fanny considered her a friend, and the Osbournes were going to move in with the Wrights in Montmartre to cut expenses when they returned to Paris in October. Yet Wright was taking notes that she would later use to humiliate Fanny.

IN NOVEMBER 1877, Fanny was pleasantly surprised to read that a woman she believed she knew had escaped the hardscrabble mining life to Paris, where she had taken the city by storm. Fanny remembered Louise Mackay as one of the women who had whisked her off to a party on a makeshift sleigh when she arrived at the Nevada mining camp. "I wonder if she remembers when she held a tin pan for me to do my hair," Fanny mused to Belle.

In Austin, the widowed seamstress had been barely supporting herself, her mother, and her daughter until she met and married John Mackay on his way to becoming a Virginia City millionaire. Yet Louise Mackay would not have been able to forget her bleak Nevada days had she tried. When she attempted to enter New York blueblood society, she was snubbed and humiliated, as if the soot of the mines still clung to her taffeta gowns. So instead she fled to France, where she hosted a lavish dinner and grand ball for former U.S. president Ulysses Grant and his wife, Julia. The glass courtyard of the Mackays' four-story mansion fronting the Arc de Triomphe was strewn with hothouse flowers from Nice and the dinner tables set with jewels from the 1,250-piece silver service John Mackay commissioned Tiffany to make from his Nevada ore. Hundreds of guests, including French president Patrice de Mac Mahon, danced in the ballroom until dawn.

Mackay's victory was something of a vicarious triumph for Fanny. That same month she had made her own disheartening debut among a snobby group she hoped would accept her, the London literati. She had gone to the city when Louis developed an eye infection that, by his account, left him unable to read or write for nearly a month. Alarmed and unable to reach Bob, Fanny took him across the Channel for treatment. While there, she also got surgery for an injured foot, and Frances Sitwell invited her to stay at her home while she was recovering.

Louis's colleagues were no doubt eager to peruse his married mistress, who had trampled on Victorian etiquette by openly taking him into her apartment to nurse him and then to London unchaperoned. And they got a shocking eyeful when they did see her: the wild mane of curls, the unladylike brown skin (at the very least, the mark of a woman who had to work outdoors), the rough beauty and even rougher tongue. Fanny's untutored and uncensored speech must have grated like fingernails on a chalkboard to Louis's verbally fastidious friends. It was as if she had been plucked barefoot from the muddy, swine-trodden streets of Indiana and dropped into the literary center of the world.

From the beginning, Louis's colleagues kept a polite distance from her. Colvin and Sitwell called her by her first name but did not offer theirs. "I was so out of place in their house that a corner was arranged, or disarranged for me," Fanny wrote in a comical letter to Rearden. Amid the tasteful pale greens and blues of Sitwell's drawing room, they wrapped her in yellow shawls and spread tiger skins around her. She felt like Pocahontas. Then solemn Colvin and stately Sitwell sat by her, discussing literature and the arts, literally over Fanny's head. "But occasionally [they] came down to my level and petted me as one would stroke a kitten," she noted.

Fanny's greatest faux pas was to smoke in Sitwell's home. In Victorian England, only working-class and "fast" women smoked, and it was considered offensive for anyone to do so in the company of a woman of Sitwell's stature. Louis had warned Fanny against it, but when Leslie Stephen and William Henley came to visit, she was so engrossed in their conversation (or perhaps, so nervous), she pulled a cigarette out of her pocket and lit up without thinking. No one said a word. After the guests left, however, Colvin went out for tobacco and papers and asked Fanny to demonstrate to him and Sitwell the art of rolling a cigarette. "Now I call that real politeness," the frontier gal drawled to Rearden.

Though Fanny made light of her awkward encounter with Louis's friends, she sincerely hoped they would like her. Louis wrote to Sitwell that she had made "a very enthusiastic friend." But Fanny would never truly be comfortable in a literary circle that felt she did not belong there. At least her courage and forthrightness in London won admiration from the person who mattered most to her: her lover.

Back in his parents' home after returning from London, Louis admitted to Henley that he was "a miserable widower" and lonely going to bed "where there is no dear head upon the pillow." When he joined Fanny in Paris on Christmas Day, he was weary and exhausted from work. But that year he had taken steps as a fiction writer with "A Lodging for the Night." The short story was published with a byline in *Temple Bar* in October 1877 and without one the following month in the *New York Times*.

This remarkable early effort featured a frank dialogue about relative morality and class privilege between an aristocratic military man and a poet who is also a scoundrel and thief. Its opening image of the city, hushed

under a blanket of snow in November 1456, announced the arrival of a fresh
and rare talent:

> The snow fell over Paris with rigorous, relentless persistence;
> sometimes the wind made a sally and scattered it in flying
> vortices; sometimes there was a lull, and flake after flake de-
> scended out of the black night air, silent, circuitous, intermi-
> nable. To poor people, looking up under moist eyebrows, it
> seemed a wonder where it all came from.

IN JANUARY 1878, *Temple Bar* published Louis's short story "The Sire de
Maletroit's Door," about a young "cavalier" who finds himself dangerously
lost in the dark one night in Burgundy during the Hundred Years' War.
Chased by a hostile crowd, he stumbles through a trick door into a surprising confrontation with his fate.

Belle knew nothing of the story when one evening, she and Louis were
sitting on a rug in the Osbournes' apartment, looking for images in the
flames of the coal fire stove while Louis waited for Fanny to dress for dinner. At first he lazily conjured castles, clouds, and animals, but when some
of the coals fell and the light shifted, he perked up. Like a magician, he
drew Belle in as he began to invoke a tense chase from glowing embers. Did
she see the doorway, nearly hidden in the shadows? And the young man
running down the street? Could she hear the shouts of the men chasing him
and see the glint of their swords? The desperate young man pressed into
the doorway, but the others were gaining on him—they would be there any
second.

"He cannot escape!" cried Belle, who could now see it all as clearly as
Louis. "They are killing him!"

But wait, Louis continued: As the young man flattened himself against
the door, it swung open behind him and swung shut again, leaving him in a

pitch-dark room. He had evaded his pursuers, but where was he? Frantically, he slid his hands over the smooth surface of the door, but he could feel no knobs or handles—he was trapped. He saw only a thin line of light deep in the shadows. Should he stay where he was or go farther into the darkness?

Just then, Fanny came into the room, and she and Louis headed out to a restaurant, leaving her teenage daughter dismayed. When Belle later discovered that the chase figured in a story Louis was writing, she begged him to divulge the young man's fate, but he laughed off her questions. Then one evening he ambled into the apartment and tossed a copy of *Temple Bar* in Belle's lap. "Here's your story!" she recalled him saying. "It was like Louis to have turned that half hour of waiting by the fire with me into one of the red-letter memories of my life."

Louis was also hurrying to rework his journal from his 1876 canoe trip with Walter Simpson into a book manuscript because, he wrote to Colvin, "I want coin so badly"—presumably to help support Fanny and her children. In his hands, *An Inland Voyage* became as much an inward voyage to find meaning outside of a conventional life as it was a book of travel. He was paid only £20 for the book, which sold a scant 485 copies the first year. However, in a glowing review, Savile Club member P. G. Hamerton called Louis "one of the most perfect writers living," and ironically, "one of the very few who may yet do something that will become classical." In Paris, Fanny must have been especially thrilled by the book's final words:

> You may paddle all day long; but it is when you come back at
> nightfall, and look in at the familiar room, that you find Love
> or Death awaiting you beside the stove; and the most beauti-
> ful adventures are not those we go to seek.

Fanny and Louis's beautiful adventure was about to slam up against Victorian reality, however. A blackmailer had been sending Louis anonymous letters, apparently threatening to reveal their love affair to Sam. Then Margaret Wright's scathing article about the Grez art colony, "Bohemian Days," appeared in the popular American periodical *Scribner's Monthly*—and it reached a much larger audience than the one for Louis's book. Wright had arrived in Grez with an antagonism for bohemians, and she was apparently a disgruntled outsider during her stay. She poked fun at the artists' grandiose egos and ideas and assigned them silly nicknames. But her elaborate attack on Fanny, the "Queen of Bohemia," was more about racism and sexual jealousy than providing journalistic color. Wright noted the "swarthy stain upon her complexion" and her "barbaric taste for splendor." Naïve European men might see something regal in Fanny's Moorish looks, but an American woman could see through her:

> Before New World eyes, looking from nearer into barbarism,
> there is none of the glamour which sees romance and poetry
> in simply dusky skins, wild, free motions and turbulent lives,
> so that real, unromantic barrenness and poverty of nature is
> as visible to them in a deposed daughter of the Incas or Mex-
> ican dancer as in the pale factory girl who toils and spins and
> knows nothing else.

Sparing her own daughter any mention, Wright found no artist in the group to praise except Bob, who painted "the tenderest, dreamiest landscapes that go from Bohemia to exhibitions." Here Wright seems to have conflated charm with talent. Though competent, Bob never distinguished himself as a painter. His friend Will Low was more talented and had several paintings accepted into the prestigious Paris Salons. But in a later article, Wright would viciously slander Low and his French wife, Berthe, who translated *Treasure Island* into French, calling her "ugly and coarse in appearance, and with barely education enough to spell out the words of such novels as came in her way." Wright concluded the Grez article by implying that Fanny and Belle were among the male and female artists who coupled off and wandered into the secluded forest at dusk, allegedly to search for "motives" but in reality to make love.

Why did Wright feel such animosity toward Fanny and her daughter? In a letter to Rearden in November, Fanny had fondly recounted their two families celebrating a painting commission Marian had won with oysters and champagne in teacups. But soon after, the Osbournes abruptly moved out. Belle described Wright in her memoir as the kind of woman who "spared no trouble in arranging other people's affairs." She and Fanny were undoubtedly two bossy, oversized personalities living in a space that could not contain them, but Wright's rank social prejudices appear to have fueled her portrait of Fanny.

One also senses Wright's discomfort with Fanny's freedom. Fanny did not play by the rules. She skipped between the prescribed male and female domains—acting with the liberties of a man and the sexual power of a woman. Her "female side" embroidered, cooked, devotedly tended to her children, and sometimes acted coy; her "male side" capsized canoes, carried a gun, ventured to Europe alone, and somewhat openly kept a lover. Many women of her era would have considered Fanny's behavior unnatural and even subversive. Of course, Wright could have confronted her onetime friend about cheating on her husband in a quieter way. Instead, she ensured that Fanny would be publicly exposed in one of the most widely circulated periodicals in the United States. Rearden saw it. It is safe to assume that Sam and most of San Francisco did too.

WRIGHT'S ARTICLE, along with the blackmailer's threats, likely prompted Fanny's sudden decision to return to California that summer. (Stevenson biographer Claire Harman has suggested that Wright actually might have been the blackmailer.) Belle claimed she never asked why the family was suddenly leaving, but this seems disingenuous, given how close she and her mother were. There might have been a complicating factor that Belle did not wish to recall. In June, Louis sent Charles Baxter a mysterious query: "Can a man, a British subject of age, marry an American girl (of age, *if necessary*) in Scotland? . . . Would this be easier managed in England by special license?" Did Belle think she was pregnant? Whatever the circumstances, they passed. Belle's relationship with O'Meara ended, and she left France brokenhearted. Possibly she had been hoping for a marriage proposal from him that never materialized. As parting gifts, O'Meara gave her a pug and a portrait of himself by his studio mate John Singer Sargent. Belle would not see him again. After finishing his art studies, he retreated to Grez and died of malaria at the age of thirty-five.

Louis's cousin Graham Balfour later wrote that although Fanny had known the possibility of divorce was open to her, she needed to consider others and "was not free to follow her inclination." This seems at least partly true. To the romantic Louis, propriety might mean little next to love, but Fanny had to be more practical. The scandal of a divorce could estrange both of them from their families. And the disgrace might be worse now that Sam could use her adultery as grounds for divorce and to seize custody of their two remaining children. That prospect must have seemed especially frightening to her after losing Hervey.

Fanny might also have been wary about putting her life into another man's hands. Louis was young, and his passion for an older woman could cool when she was five thousand miles away. And even if she married him and received custody of her children, how would he support them when he could not support himself? He was penniless, and they would surely be headed toward destitution as well as disgrace. Fanny had learned the grim realities of poverty in Paris, where two of her children had gone hungry while she used most of their meager funds to try to save the life of the third. Like most unhappily married American women of her era, she could well have decided to sacrifice her own desires for the well-being and security of her children. For all but the wealthiest women, separation was simply a much more viable solution than divorce.

Louis saw his future happiness slipping away with her. "This is the last 20 days of my passion," he wrote to Baxter. "'Twill then be over for good." In London, where the Osbournes were staying for a few weeks, he took work churning out copy for Henley, who was now editing *London*. Fanny recalled that Louis and Henley often wrote an entire weekly issue to keep the magazine afloat, dashing off poetry when needed because it filled up more space:

"'Hurry, my lad,' Mr. Henley would shout; 'only six more lines now!' My husband would scratch off six lines, hand them to the printer's devil, who stood waiting with outstretched hand, and the situation was saved for another week."

To ten-year-old Lloyd, the journalist Louis seemed suddenly more mature and important. He wore a double-breasted blue suit and a stiff felt hat tipped to one side. He talked about filling up space and going to press and dashed up in cabs and dashed away again. Lloyd was particularly impressed with Louis's new cane, which he invested with romance and adventure for the boy. "He said that in a tight place there was nothing to equal it, and somehow the impression was conveyed that journalism often took a man into very dangerous places."

When the day for the Osbournes' departure arrived in August, a miserable party headed for Euston Station, where the family would catch the boat train to Liverpool. Fanny and Louis had given each other their hearts, which was really the only thing they had to give. But that might not be enough to bring them back together. Whatever hopes they might have shared, they knew that they might very well never see each other again.

One imagines a romantic scene at the station: Fanny's arms stretched out to Louis from the train window, he grasping her hands tight as the train starts to roll, until her fingers finally slip from his. But that was not how it happened. Louis was too hurt or angry for a long, painful goodbye. He did not even wait for the train to leave before he turned and silently strode away down the long platform under the wrought-iron roof. "My eyes followed him, hoping that he would look back," Lloyd recalled. But Louis never did, and the boy watched him get smaller and smaller until he vanished in a blur of steam and bustling travelers, disappearing as quickly as he had once dropped into their lives.

SEVEN

Fanny Osbourne stepped across the threshold of her old Oakland house in a daze. It had been more than three years since she had lived there, and much longer since she had plotted her escape from there. Garden plants now climbed in the windows and tumbled onto the porch, so that the house appeared to have risen from the dirt with them. In the garden, she had grafted tender rose stalks onto hardier bushes to help them thrive and nurtured hopes of a creative life in her art studio. Now the flowers were as limp as the waning days of summer, and there was no clear path to the studio.

On the porch, she had taken her last stand to protect the primacy of her family, blocking Sam's lover from entering her home. Since then, the woman had been mistress of the house, rearranging Fanny's belongings to suit her own taste and sleeping in Fanny's bed. More painful, memories of Hervey as a healthy toddler echoed through the still rooms. There were days ahead that must have shaken Fanny's sanity, when she would sense Hervey moving just outside her vision, just beyond her reach. Nearly a decade later, she would write a story about a mother who feels her dead child's spirit return to her, describing it as "not so much as a breath, a movement in the air" and a "faint reflection, something almost luminous." In France she and Sam could not afford to give Hervey a permanent resting place; instead, his body had been buried in a temporary plot in Saint-Germain Cemetery, to be thrown into a common grave if it was not moved in ten years. The thought of her child's unsettled body unmoored Fanny as well.

Love and loss—she had lived with them so long, they must have seemed inseparable to her. For the time being, she probably felt she would need to keep the love for Louis that had been flowering in her heart locked inside her head. A visit to her family in Indiana on the way back had shaken any hope she had of smoothly reuniting with him. Fanny's high-spirited father—who had married her mother, Esther, when she was a divorcée—might have been an ally, but Jacob had died while Fanny was in France. Public opinion had turned against divorce in the postwar climate of anxiety over the nation's moral decline, and Indiana was among the states that had tightened divorce laws. Fanny's siblings stood firmly against her ending her marriage, largely because of the stigma it would attach to them thousands of miles away. Frantic letters of protest chased her home.

There had been a bright spot on the visit: Fanny's youngest sister, Nellie, joined her, Belle, and Lloyd for the final leg of their journey. Blond, blue-eyed Nellie was prim and serious, a grammar school principal at the age of twenty-two. She was a voracious reader, though her parents had largely confined her home reading, like Fanny's, to the Bible and *Webster's Dictionary*, which Nellie "read to rags." A brother-in-law's Christmas gift of Charles Dickens's works was a highlight of her youth.

Fanny hoped Nellie would provide companionship for brokenhearted Belle. And she wanted to expand her sister's world beyond the plains. Arriving in California in fall 1879, Nellie would always remember feeling as if she had landed in paradise. Fanny, heading back to a future she did not want, could not share her sister's enthusiasm.

Belle blissfully resumed her morning walks with her father, and Lloyd would recall how he enjoyed Sam's amiable nature and "universal popularity." Fanny's plainspoken San Francisco friend Dora Williams cast Sam's charm in a different light, however. He was "a noted story-teller, and had always a pleasant way about him that made him quite generally liked," she wrote later, "but finally, people in San Francisco found out that he was far from pleasant at home—as I know very well myself." Dora added that Sam's substantial salary was spent "on anybody's family but his own."

Biographers often assume that Fanny and Sam resumed sexual relations on her return, but there is no evidence of this—and some suggestion that instead Sam took the children away from Fanny and threatened to turn her out on the street. According to one report, Lloyd was sent to boarding school and Nellie and Belle to a boardinghouse. Sidney Colvin's comment in a letter to Charles Baxter that Fanny was "away from the enemy, but with access to the children" suggests that this may have been the case. Fanny's letters to Timothy Rearden hint at fears of Sam cutting off her support. Sam was likely either punishing her for the insinuations of adultery in Margaret Wright's article or warning her not to seek a divorce.

The couple's relationship was soon in enough turmoil that Fanny sought help, possibly of a legal nature, from Rearden. She also composed an amusing semi-autobiographical fable, "The Story of the Ravening Sheep," to explain her side of the story to him. Fanny appeared in it as a sheep barely subsisting with her lamb (Hervey) on a small spot of clover until a she-wolf (Sam's mistress)—who had passed as a sheepdog to the blind and foolish shepherd (Sam)—destroyed their shelter and devoured their clover. The sheep had to watch helplessly as her lamb died and his dead body was dumped in a hole in the ground. She often wished she too would die.

Later, when the sheep spied the she-wolf's own sleek and fat little cub, her "weak brain" gave way and she chased him back to his mother, her eyes "the size of dinner plates, from which shot blue and green flames." At least that is how the she-wolf described it to the shepherd, who then confronted the sheep. But she could not remember all the details and wanted only to go to a quiet place where she could ponder whether she was truly a ravening sheep. On the way, she was warned that the only thing worse than her discovering she was mad would be for other animals to find out. Deemed too dangerous to roam about freely by the shepherd, she was carried off to a small paddock by the sea.

With so little information about Fanny's personal life available from this time, her wry tale is the closest thing we have to a sense of her feelings and the state of her marriage after her return. It is most striking for its suggestion that Sam may have had a child with his mistress or supported the woman and her child at the expense of his own starving children in France. The story also illustrates how well the Victorian obsession with appearances served men like Sam. He could use the ugly spectacle of Fanny's confrontation with his mistress years before to accuse his wife of hysteria, the catchall term for Victorian women who behaved badly, while evading responsibility for his own actions. Yet Fanny was behaving rather generously by this point. Later hearing that Sam's lover was now dying of tuberculosis in Los Angeles, she wrote to Rearden that she would like to send the woman "the first money I can get, anonymously I suppose, for it wouldn't be 'respectable' that's your word, is it not? to do it openly."

Sam seemed to feel himself freer than ever to roam and began indulging his baser desires in seedy Chinatown brothels and drunken debaucheries. Still, he adamantly opposed divorce because it would scandalize his strict Methodist mother. (Visiting Fanny in Indiana, Cynthia Osbourne had professed shock that Sam's wife "didn't seem at *all glad* at the thought of seeing him again—after the long separation.") In essence, both his family and Fanny's formed an oddly united front against her. It is no wonder that her headaches and other mental symptoms flared.

Soon after her return, Fanny did something that symbolically defied the notion of preserving appearances: At the age of thirty-eight, she chopped off her long, luxurious tresses of hair. A woman's long hair was like a jewel to Victorians—indeed, snippets of it were often curled into lockets or fashioned into jewelry. And because women rarely cut their hair, except in cases of illness, it was a connection to their past. But hair was also one of the few means of expression available to women. One can imagine what Fanny wanted to say—that with each ringlet that snaked onto the floor, she was severing another remnant of her life with Sam.

IN SUMMER, when Fanny had left England, *London* magazine was running a series of Louis's stories collectively entitled "Latter-Day Arabian Nights." They chronicled the adventures of dashing young Prince Florizel of Bohemia—who, despite his royal blood and fabulous wealth, shared with his creator "a taste for ways of life more adventurous and eccentric than that to which he was destined by his birth"—and his loyal companion, Colonel Geraldine. The series kicked off with three sensational stories together named "The Suicide Club."

The concept for a suicide club had started with an imaginary train ride cooked up by Louis's cousin Bob Stevenson: a lavish final send-off for people who had wearied of life. Leaving Charing Cross Station at midnight, stocked with champagne and other delicacies, the locomotive would plunge off the cliffs of Dover, carrying the grim revelers to their deaths. Louis reimagined the train as a secret club where disaffected gentlemen could pay to orchestrate their own deaths. Each man's fate is literally determined by the hand he is dealt in a macabre nightly card game: Whoever receives the ace of clubs must kill the man who receives the ace of spades, thus concealing the suicide as an accident to preserve the doomed gentleman's honor. Posing in disguise as new members of the club, Florizel and Geraldine set out to stop its profiteering president. Bob Stevenson makes a memorable appearance as a young man giving away cream tarts, one of his last absurd acts before joining the club—a gesture reminiscent of Bob's youthful "jinks" and plan to commit suicide when his patrimony ran out.

Louis's idea to set the suicide stories in a gentleman's club brilliantly tapped into an uneasy class transformation in Britain: the eroding status of a Victorian "gentleman" in the ascendant capitalist economy. As Sarah Ames, a National Library of Scotland librarian, has written, the leisured gentleman, born into social position by his genetic good fortune, was becoming an anachronism as entrepreneurs and self-made men rose through the sweat of their brow. Louis's satirical club provided a respectable way out for these gentlemen—though ironically this "latest convenience" was through the enterprise of a modern businessman.

Four years after its magazine debut, the "Suicide Club" stories would be gathered with "The Rajah's Diamond" (the further adventures of Florizel and Geraldine, which completed the *London* series) and four other Stevenson tales into *New Arabian Nights*—a book that was to have a considerable impact. Literary historian Barry Menikoff has credited it with establishing the short story in Britain, replacing the elaborate three-volume novel. Drawing on his familiarity with French and American short story writers such as Edgar Allan Poe, Nathaniel Hawthorne, and Théophile Gautier, Louis crafted complex but lean, tightly focused tales that fit better with the faster pace of the times. "The Suicide Club" also introduced a fantastic and durable literary setting: a gaslit cosmopolitan underworld of intrigue and adventure. This "fairy London," as the Argentine writer Jorge Luis Borges called it, would be the scene of many future fictional crimes—most notably those created by Arthur Conan Doyle, whose Sherlock Holmes and Dr. Watson are themselves reminiscent of the brilliant "Suicide Club" hero and his loyal sidekick.

When the *Arabian Nights* stories debuted in 1878, however, there was no hint of the influence they would exert. They did not suit the subdued subscribers to *London* and may have hastened the magazine's collapse the following year. And Louis earned a slender £44 for seventeen installments. Writing the stories did nothing to ease his emotional suffering that autumn, either. Within a month of Fanny's departure, he was in Le Monastier, a village in the Cévenol hills of France, where he struggled to be done with them. "I think I shall die of Arabians," he wrote to William Henley. "How I hate them, words cannot tell."

No one knows what agreement Fanny and Louis had made when they parted, but it seems clear that he, at least, expected her to attempt to dissolve her marriage, while he could only wait helplessly for that to happen. He was anxious and depressed and wanted to find a tranquil place where he felt free to wander, hope, and love. But as a struggling writer, he always felt financial pressure to make his escapes pay—whether he was merrily canoeing down a river or fleeing a nervous collapse.

He decided on a walking tour of the Cévennes, a mountain range that is part of the Massif Central in southern France. The rugged cliffs, moors, and history of religious persecution—of Calvinist Protestants by the Catholic monarchy—gave the area a familiar Highland feel. It was also one of the most wild and remote areas in France and he chose to traverse it alone. A homemade sleeping bag, tins of sausage, a leg of mutton, a bottle of Beaujolais, books, a revolver, and a whisk were among the supplies he packed.

To carry his hefty load, he purchased a donkey "the color of an ideal mouse, and inimitably small" for sixty-five francs and a glass of brandy. Hiking in his country velveteen jacket and knitted spencer, he prodded, coaxed, and reluctantly flogged Modestine, as he named her, for twelve days over the rocky terrain, sometimes resorting to carrying his own supplies. Along the way, he met colorful characters, was drenched by rain, slept under stars "shaken together like a diamond dust upon the sky," and sometimes breakfasted on chocolate, brandy, and tobacco. He recorded his experiences, along with a history of the struggle of the Protestant Camisards, in *Travels with a Donkey in the Cévennes*. His evolving relationship with Modestine was threaded through the journey in a way that would grate on some reviewers but charmed readers. Today Louis's trail and rental donkeys are part of the local tourist industry.

In his dedication to Sidney Colvin, Louis noted that every book is essentially a letter from the author to his friends. To Bob, he wrote more explicitly of his book's coded allusions: "Lots of it is mere protestations to F., most of which I think you will understand." Fanny was there humorously in his relationship with tiny Modestine, with her kind eyes, "determined under-jaw," and frustrating refusal to move as fast as he wanted her to. She was there most beautifully in a mystical night Louis spent on Mont Lozère, the highest peak in the Cévennes.

Louis set up camp in a green dell so thickly encircled with pines, it was like a private room under a canopy of open sky. He fell asleep with the setting sun, hearing nature "breathing deeply and freely," and awoke before dawn at an hour he claimed is known only to those who slumber in the open air—a time when all the outdoor world suddenly stirs at once. He woke thirsty, drank some water from his tin, and lay back to smoke. Except for a hazy strip of the Milky Way, the stars were clear and jewellike against a deep indigo sky. Gazing at them, he felt almost perfect contentment, but not quite. As he lay "between content and longing," his thoughts were drawn

back to earth by a silver ring he wore on his wedding band finger, glinting
against the night.

Fanny was thousands of miles away, but her presence seemed to fill the air
between him and the stars. In the book, Louis wrote:

> I became aware of a strange lack. I wished a companion to lie
> near me in the starlight, silent and not moving, but ever with-
> in touch. For there is a fellowship more quiet even than soli-
> tude, and which, rightly understood, is solitude made perfect.
> And to live out of doors with the woman a man loves is of all
> lives the most complete and free.

Fanny was clearly part of him now, essential to all he dreamed of doing. The night sky stretched over him like a vast unwritten page, the stars
blinked with possibilities, and the shimmering band on his finger connected
him to them.

A FEW MONTHS after Fanny's return, she and Sam suddenly left together
on a trip, and a week later they sent for Belle, Nellie, and Lloyd to join them
in Monterey. At the time, the girls interpreted this as a thaw in the obvious
chill between Sam and Fanny, but in reality, Sam was simply resettling
his ravening wife farther away, in a "paddock by the sea" about a hundred
miles down the coast. Perhaps by then Fanny accepted his accusations of
madness as her only escape route.

Fanny had an infallible gift for landing in the center of history being
made—whether it was in the Nevada silver fields or Impressionist ateliers in
Paris. This time she chose Monterey, a future artists' mecca that had begun
taking form three years before when French painter Jules Tavernier settled
there after a transcontinental trek to sketch scenes of life in the West for
Harper's Weekly. Once the capital of Alta California under both Spain and

Mexico but largely abandoned in the rush for gold, the sleepy town seemed to the newcomers to be untouched by hectic modern life, like Grez-sur-Loing. It was steeped in Spanish culture and the sea. Cool, secluded gardens nestled behind high adobe walls, gnarled cypress tumbled down the windswept headlands, silver ornaments tinkled on saddles and spurs, and Spanish echoed in the streets. There was a picturesque topsy-turviness that inspired the artists: High wooden sidewalks fell off abruptly into sand dunes and an inverted whale jawbone might serve as a garden archway. It was said that you could walk down the main drag, Alvarado Street, in broad daylight without meeting a soul, yet, as Lloyd recalled, it was always a point of honor to gallop down that same street "at breakneck speed, no matter how trifling your business."

Sam installed his wife at Maria Ygnacio Bonifacio's boardinghouse on Alvarado Street. When Belle first glimpsed her mother there, Fanny was making furniture with an ax and hammer: "A smile was on her lips, and for the first time in months she seemed alive." In an old, familiar pattern, Sam's initial weekly visits to his children quickly stretched into absences of several weeks, and those he did make were spent largely behind closed doors in heated conversation with Fanny—by this time about divorce, Belle later realized. In her seaside escape, Fanny's health improved, and she started to gain back the weight she had lost. She was often seen galloping sidesaddle on her mustang, Clavel, her riding skirts lifted on the wind.

Belle and Nellie slipped easily into the local social life, aided by weekly cascaron balls at the town's public hall. (The name came from the old practice of breaking eggshells filled with gold dust on the heads of dancers so that the floor and everyone on it glittered by midnight.) One of the most popular men on the dance floor was Adulfo Sanchez, the handsome son of an old local family and co-proprietor of the Bohemian Saloon, a favorite haunt of artists despite a sign at the door that warned "*No Rowdyism Allowed.*" "There were no class distinctions in Monterey; we danced with the butcher, the baker, and—the saloon keeper," Belle wrote in her memoirs. "Particularly with the saloon keeper," she added, referring to Nellie, not herself. The gregarious barman fell in love with Belle's studious aunt and crooned his feelings under her bedroom window in moonlight serenades that were still a custom in the town.

Belle's grief over the artist she left behind in France, Frank O'Meara, lifted considerably at first sight of a painter in Monterey. Joseph Dwight Strong, a rising star in the California art scene, was among a group of horsemen gathered near her train when she alighted onto the dusty road. Blond, with close-cropped hair and a twisted mustache, he jumped down from his horse to greet the newcomers. Like Belle, he had studied painting with Virgil Williams and returned recently from Europe, where wealthy San Francisco friends had sent him to further his art education.

Belle had met Joe years before on a ferry in San Francisco Bay, and there was something about the charming artist that must have reminded her of her father. A fellow Bohemian Club member, Joe was known for concocting a grossly excessive punch that impressed even that notoriously bibulous group, and he announced his arrival in Monterey with invitations to a "Bohemian Blowout." Despite his considerable talent, he would be remembered in Monterey for spending more energy "fraternizing with male friends and entertaining ladies" than working. By summer 1879, both of the young couples would be engaged—Nellie and Adulfo officially, and Belle and Joe secretly.

In Monterey, Fanny and Belle shifted toward decorative artwork well suited to their talents. Fanny painted miniature portraits that yielded "amazing likenesses," according to her daughter, though Belle found those of herself unflattering. Belle dipped into a growing decorative art trend, painting folding screens. Fanny was also writing—very likely inspired by Louis, and probably encouraged by him too. Before she returned to the U.S., they had begun cowriting a sensational novel to be titled *What Was on the Slate*.

From Monterey, Fanny reported to Rearden that she'd sold two stories and a painting, using the earnings to buy horses for Belle and Nellie. It was not the wisest financial decision in her circumstances, but she was ecstatic to be able to spoil her daughter and sister with money she had earned herself: "You'll never believe it; I hardly could myself, but in [one] month, I made 325 dollars!" she wrote. "I begin to believe that I am not such a poor creature after all, when the last check came I burst into tears, to the surprise of everyone."

In summer, she submitted more pieces for publication. These might have included a children's story and two reported articles that appeared in print during the next two years.

Two of the pieces had Chinese subjects, a provocative choice in an era of unparalleled bigotry against Chinese immigrants. Chinese men—once welcomed into the U.S. to work in the gold mines and on railroads for substandard pay—were increasingly viewed as a threat to jobs and wages during the postwar economic downturn of the 1870s. Unlike European immigrants, the Chinese were also considered unassimilable, with their long queues and Eastern dress and cuisine. San Francisco became a hotbed of anti-Asian sentiment, where demagogue Denis Kearney provoked the unemployed to vent their anger by burning and looting Chinatown businesses.

"A Funeral in a Chinese Fishing-Camp" appeared in *Lippincott's* in January 1879 under the byline "F. M. Osbourne." It began with a somewhat bold political commentary on Chinese life, and death, in San Francisco:

> The Chinese who are among us, and so strikingly not of us,
> bury their dead usually with maimed rites. The terrorism of
> the hoodlum, the unfeigned hostility of the Irish newcomer,
> oblige them to make little of these last offices and hurry their
> dead unceremoniously to earth.

In the poor fishing camps of Monterey, however, "under the soft mists of the Pacific, they may be as Chinese as they desire," Fanny wrote. The article went on to describe a day when she and a group of artist friends were invited to witness and sketch a traditional Chinese funeral by one of the mourners.

Fanny was a good reporter and writer, deftly evoking the pageantry of the ancient ritual. But she lost the courage of her empathetic opening convictions. She wrote of her disdain for female mourners beating their heads on the ground until they bled and her revulsion at the odor of dried fish and other foods that were emptied into the coffin, without providing any cultural context for them. She resorted to quoting the Chinese people who spoke to her party in stereotypical broken English. The article deflated the prevailing notion of Chinese immigrants as a threatening, shadowy mass, but they still felt like the exotic "other."

Fanny did break through cultural barriers briefly when she observed an old woman and a young mother speaking softly near the coffin. She could not understand their words, but from their tone and gestures, she imagined their conversation and pain, and she felt a connection to them. "The young woman's patient sorrow and the old woman's kindly sympathy made them seem nearer to the humanity which I know, and less related to the remote and strange civilization of the East," she observed. This longing to connect with women across cultural divides would grow stronger in her as she continued to travel the world.

The cultural insensitivity in Fanny's article is more puzzling because it was not a feature of her children's story "Chy Lung, The Chinese Fisherman," which ran in *St. Nicholas* the following year. Perhaps *Lippincott's* editors had wanted the nation's racist mood to color her account of the funeral. Even Mark Twain and Bret Harte had played to anti-Asian stereotypes in their 1877 play *Ah Sin*. And *St. Nicholas* chose to illustrate "Chy Lung" with ugly Asian caricatures. The children's magazine misspelled Fanny's name "Osborne," though it was the second time her byline appeared there.

In Fanny's story, a fisherman in China named Chy Lung is faced with starvation when his nets repeatedly return empty. Egged on by an evil Sorcerer of the Sea, he resorts to greedy and selfish acts. When he entangles two mermaid sisters in his net, he lets one of them go. But fearing a beheading if he does not provide food for the banquet of a great mandarin, he offers the other mermaid to the chef. Ultimately, her sister appeals to his sense of morality, and Chy Lung rescues the mermaid and is forgiven.

Many cultures have variations on this folktale, in which a fisherman meets a mermaid, talking fish, genie, or other magical creature who presents him with a moral choice. Fanny's version grew out of a very rough short story she had left with Rearden before she went to France. She added themes that reflected the issues she was grappling with after her return: sudden impoverishment, the threat of homelessness, forgiveness for selfish acts (perhaps her culpability in her son's death). Other changes reflected Fanny's evolving consciousness about women. She added the two mermaid sisters to the final version, making them the moral center of the story. And she changed the name she had originally given her male hero, Ah Choon, to that of a woman who was at the center of a notorious trial in San Francisco during the 1870s.

Chy Lung was one of twenty-two immigrant women barred entry to San Francisco for being "lewd," part of California's efforts to seal its borders to the Chinese. At their local trial, the women were deemed prostitutes because they were traveling without husbands and wore colorful, loose clothing—prompting the judge to declare that there would be "no indelicacy or impropriety in gazing down their sleeves." But the women pressed on, and when *Chy Lung v. Freeman* reached the U.S. Supreme Court, they were triumphant. (Justice for Chinese immigrants would not prevail for long. In 1882 Congress passed the Chinese Exclusion Act, the first federal law barring a specific ethnic group.)

Perhaps it was just a coincidence that Fanny named her character Chy Lung, though she certainly would have empathized with the plight of women who were subject to base assumptions because they were traveling alone and wore colorful clothing. Or she might have deliberately attached the name to the story, as she had created the characters of the mermaid sisters, to pay tribute to female strength and solidarity.

"Sargent's Rodeo," by F. M. Osbourne, appeared in the same issue of *Lippincott's* as "A Funeral in a Chinese Fishing-Camp," but Fanny seemed on much more comfortable ground in this retelling of a cattle drive with vaqueros in the Carmel Valley. Again looking beyond some language that is considered racist today, it is an exuberant piece of memoir writing. Fanny's cowgirl heart and soul are evident in her depiction of life on the range, and the article gives voice to many other aspects of her identity: mother, sexual being, adventurer, writer.

Fanny used her venture into a male domain to play with Victorian definitions of gender and propriety. Her opening line, "The ladies will have to rough it" (issued by the trail boss Sargent), is both an invitation and a challenge. "Roughing it" means riding horseback along the edge of cliffs, sleeping on hay, and being alert to trail dangers such as bucking horses and cattle stampedes. Penknives are the only eating utensils; after-meal cleanup consists of wiping them on the grass. Fanny, Nellie, and Belle are among the women who accept the trail boss's challenge. As the party sets off, Fanny records their shyness about parading through downtown Monterey, such as it was, dressed in short skirts and trousers for camp life. Yet she is not shy at all about jumping into a man's saddle the next day when she is advised to by a vaquero. "The hitherto undivulged desire of my heart was placed before me in the light of necessity," she writes. "I was to ride a man's saddle 'leg aside.'" In the relative freedom outdoors, Fanny was renegotiating concepts of womanhood and equality.

Fanny's freewheeling writing style in "Sargent's Rodeo" is refreshing for a female writer of her time, but it was no doubt jarring, even unseemly, to the readers who preferred more verbal inhibition from women. One moment she is delicately evoking the "cool violet odors" of wildflowers in the early dawn or a breeze that is "warm like the breath of an oven." The next she unflinchingly describes cowboys tearing the small intestines, still smoking from the body heat of a newly killed heifer, to prepare a dish they called "marrow guts" for their dinner. Nor is Fanny prim when lustily describing a handsome, free-spirited handyman named Bob stretched out before the campfire one evening. "Bob looked a fine creature, and never showed to better advantage than at that moment," she wrote, "lithe and strong and shaggy, he lay there like a wild animal taking its rest."

Across the ocean, winter and spring did nothing to ease Louis's melancholy. He crisscrossed the Channel with his usual restlessness, holing up at the Savile Club for afternoons at a time and often sleeping at the homes of friends. Fanny's letters to Louis, none of which have survived, were apparently as erratic as her mood and health. His own health and spirits seesawed according to when, and more often if, he received one.

Still, as always, Louis worked. A group of sketches of his hometown, *Edinburgh: Picturesque Notes*, was published in December 1878. But his lovingly ambivalent portrait rankled some. *The Scotsman* noted that the author's affection and admiration for the city were buried under cynical humor and sniffed, "It is not, we believe, 'good form' now-a-days for youths to be earnest or enthusiastic about anything under the sun." Worse, the unidentified reviewer branded Louis "a well-bred lounger, a *flaneur*, not deeply interested in anything."

The irritation of his countrymen fanned into anger the following year when Louis's essay "Some Aspects of Robert Burns" ran in *Cornhill*. Burns was a national treasure, the "ploughman poet" and songwriter whose oeuvre includes "Auld Lang Syne." Louis paid tribute to Burns's brilliance, but he chose to focus on less flattering aspects of the man's character, specifically his callous and wanton womanizing, which Louis felt accounted in part for his downward spiral and death at age thirty-seven. The essay would have repercussions even many years later. By some accounts, early efforts to erect a monument to Louis after his death were stifled partly because of residual anger over his criticism of Burns.

Louis's efforts to prove himself financially independent continued to fall short. When not borrowing money, he gave what little he had away. After his short story "Providence and the Guitar" ran in *London*, he sent his fee to the couple who'd inspired it—impoverished strolling actors he and Fanny had met in Grez. He directed a monthly retainer to his friend William Henley, another struggling writer, who often acted as Louis's literary agent. He came to the aid of his cousin Katharine de Mattos, Bob's sister, who was attempting to establish herself as a writer after a divorce from her husband of four years. And when a cabby robbed Colvin of some valuable art prints he was transporting, Louis gave his friend a whopping £400 to help defray the cost of repayment.

Perhaps it was a similar generosity of spirit (and hope that playwriting would be more lucrative than churning out essays and stories) that inspired Louis to collaborate with Henley on a play about Deacon William Brodie, the eighteenth-century Edinburgh cabinetmaker by day and criminal by night. Brodie's double life had haunted Louis since his childhood, and he had written a melodrama about Brodie when he was nineteen and embarking on his own double life in seamy Edinburgh haunts. Henley was convinced they could rework the play into a financial and critical hit. The two worked on it separately and together, setting out to hole up for a week at Swanston, the Stevensons' country home, with Louis wearing a donkey driver's suit that looked so strange, his dog barked at him. Though the collaboration cemented the friendship between Louis and Henley, and the play would eventually be staged, it was essentially a failure. It also presaged three more ill-fated collaborations between the two men.

Louis's health woes—lethargy, difficulty focusing, headaches—took a more alarming turn in April. He informed Colvin that he had collapsed from "weakness, languor, loss of appetite, [and] causeless swelled testicle just appearing for the sake of fun you would say, and irritation of the spermatic cord." Louis traced his symptoms and "causeless" swollen testicle to his anguish during a dry spell in letters from Fanny, although the cause may have been a sexually transmitted disease. Thomas and Margaret Stevenson convinced their son to accompany them to Shandon Hydropathic Establishment, yet the visit did little to ease his symptoms or his ever-tense relationship with his parents. He wrote to his friend Fanny Sitwell that he was never as lonely as when he spent extended time with them.

By this time, Thomas and Margaret knew about Louis's relationship with Fanny. In February 1878, when he was living with her in Paris, Louis had invited Thomas there to tell him about it. Thomas had taken it well, presumably reasoning that the liaison with an older, married woman was not dangerous as long as it stayed in Paris. Yet now, with Fanny gone, Louis's parents and friends hoped they could simply will his feelings for Fanny away with her, despite all signs to the contrary. His friend Edmund Gosse was incredulous that Louis—his "emblem of life," the "General Exhilarator"—should feel depressed without her, prompting this reply from Louis:

I envy you your wife, your home, your child—I was going to say
your cat. There would be cats in my home, too, if I could but get it!
not for me, but for the person who should share it with me. I may
seem to you "the impersonation of life" . . . but my life is the imper-
sonation of waiting.

The waiting was finally about to end, however. According to legend, Louis received alarming news about Fanny's health from someone in the United States in July 1879. Perhaps it was this or the prospect of another dreary spa excursion with his parents that gave him the final push he needed. Two days after his letter to Gosse, he met Thomas and Margaret at the train station in Edinburgh, where they were to embark together, to tell them that he had been called away on business. A week later, he was sailing to America, with the hope of bringing Fanny Osbourne back with him as his wife.

He would nearly die trying to get to her.

LOUIS'S FRIENDS TRIED to dissuade him nearly until the moment he set sail from Glasgow. To make the trip pay, he planned to write a book about the emigrant experience. It was a grand canvas. Nineteenth-century globalism was in full swing: Technological advances such as the steamship, train, and telegraph were shrinking the world. Fueled by the Long Depression, European immigration was surging, especially to the United States. But colleagues such as Gosse still considered the trip the "maddest of enterprises." Coexistent with the idea of the U.S. as a land of opportunity was the darker view that it was an uncivilized intellectual wasteland—a view Louis's Anglocentric literary friends tended to embrace. They believed that his career ascent would be crippled without his contacts at the Savile Club, and it was impossible to write anything of merit so far from London.

Apart from their concerns about Louis's career, his friends considered the enterprise truly mad—or maddening—because he was chasing after Fanny Osbourne. Henley wrote of it to Charles Baxter in terms more suggestive of a child's first excursion to the park alone. Though he and Colvin "couldn't say no to his going," Henley wrote, Louis had "promised" them he wouldn't venture farther than New York—a claim that is almost certainly false. Louis merely intended to do the honorable thing by Fanny, Henley insisted, and if she were worthy of him, she would have put "herself out of his way for ever." Of course, Fanny *had* put herself five thousand miles out of Louis's way and returned to her husband, but that was not enough for Louis's possessive friend, who seemed to see the trip as a personal abandonment. "If it come to the worst . . . ," Henley lamented, "we shall lose the best friend a man ever had."

Henley and the others refused to see that for Louis, wooing Fanny back was nearly a matter of life and death. Should he fail in that "great purpose," he would write to Colvin after he set sail, "I don't yet know if I have the courage to stick to life without it. Man, I was sick, sick, sick of this last year." Louis seemed to believe the trip was necessary to bring resolution to their tortured situation. Though Fanny and Sam were living separately, she had stalled in moving any further toward divorce. He probably rightly sensed that she needed a dramatic show of his love and commitment to make the final break—and pursuing her across the world certainly was that. But Louis also needed to make his own dramatic break—with his parents, in order to end his prolonged youth. "No man is of any use until he has dared everything," he wrote to Colvin in August, "I feel just now as if I had, and so might become a man."

The quest for freedom and self-discovery that Fanny and Louis had each started alone had led them to each other, and now they needed each other to see it through. Louis's transatlantic voyage was another leg of a journey that had begun when Fanny sailed in the opposite direction toward an uncertain future, and him. She had "dared everything" and her courage must have inspired Louis to do the same. She was the first woman to challenge his identity, and she would become the connection between his past and future, childhood and manhood, the old and new worlds. It was as if he needed her to show him the way, and she needed him to help her finish what she had started—as if their whole lives had been leading to this.

FANNY MAY NOT HAVE GRASPED how daunting the transatlantic journey was for Louis—after all, she had traveled longer and farther in a corset and with children in tow. For Louis, however, leaving his comfort zone in Europe for the first time was so traumatic, he went numb. "I seem to have died last night," he wrote to Colvin on the eve of his departure, "all I carry on from my past life is the blue pill." His stomach was uneasy already, which may have necessitated packing the "miracle" pill—a purported remedy for cholera, liver ailments, rheumatism, and syphilis, though in reality it was merely a strong laxative laced with mercury. He signed his letter "the husk which once contained R.L.S."

Louis was used to slipping in and out of himself when he traveled, but this time he was crossing class as well as national borders. The twenty-eight-year-old adopted a new name and social rank, identifying himself for the ship's records as "Robert Stephenson, clerk, aged 20." He considered buying a steerage ticket partly for financial reasons, partly so he could write of the "worst of emigrant life" up close. But to write, he needed a writing desk, so he opted to go second cabin instead. It was still just a partition away from steerage, and he shared the squalor, sickness, crying, arguing, and other aspects of life below deck. Traveling in the bowels of a ship would be a far cry from his forays into the underbelly of Edinburgh, where he could return at night to the downy comfort of Heriot Row, and the experience would change his writing.

His account of ten brutal days on the steamship *Devonia* makes up *The Emigrant Ship* (later retitled *From the Clyde to Sandy Hook*), the first half of his book *The Amateur Emigrant*. Before he left, Louis had seen the U.S. as a "promised land," where, as Walt Whitman suggested, an open society was emerging in the aftermath of the Civil War. In the book, Louis asked

American readers to imagine a young man, reared to follow rigid traditions and distrust his instincts, who hears of "a family of cousins, all about his own age, who keep house together by themselves and live far from restraint and traditions; let him imagine this, and he will have some imperfect notion of the sentiment with which spirited English youths turn to the thought of the American Republic."

His corresponding image of his fellow emigrants as young, bright-eyed, and industrious was quickly dashed when he met them. They were "family men broken by adversity, elderly youths who had failed to place themselves in life, and people who had seen better days." Suddenly he saw in sharp focus the effects of economic depression and dislocation that had existed at the periphery of his vision in Scotland—the homeless men in Glasgow, the cellar doors broken and stolen for firewood, the "closed factories, useless strikes, and starving girls." He had never taken their plight "home"; now that he was living among them, he had no choice. Louis would ultimately conclude that most emigrants were drunks, idlers, and incompetents who were fleeing failure but destined to carry their failure with them. But his critique of industrial capitalism was radical at the time, especially in a book of travel, and his vibrant sketches of fellow travelers humanized a group more often considered a faceless mass.

More radical was his choice to mix with the working class—a breach in the class hierarchy that defined Victorians. (Steerage passengers were labeled "men" and "women," while those in second cabin and saloon were "gentlemen" and "ladies.") He joined in the amusements, ate much of the same food (which sometimes included scrapings from the saloon passengers' plates), and got to know and like many of the steerage passengers. He also found himself sharing some of their ways of thinking. Surprised at first when some turned up their noses at steerage fare, he too grew "greedier for small delicacies" day by day and noticed that his own mood rose and fell according to the teatime offerings.

Louis always had disdain for his own class, but viewing the high-born passengers literally from down below, he saw their condescension in a stronger light. He detested the poverty tourists who went sightseeing in the steerage section, "picking their way with little, gracious titters of indulgence . . . ," he wrote. "It was astonishing what insults these people managed to convey by their presence." He asserted that some of his new acquaintances were "grand gentlemen" with about the same intellects and natural capacities as "the bankers and barristers of what is called society."

Louis's narrative was not without his signature playful, offbeat flourishes. He gleaned tips on traveling illegally from the ship's stowaways. Similarly, in the second part of his journey, by train, he would be drawn to the hoboes who rode the rails, though they took to their heels at train stops too fast for him to solicit their travel advice. "These land stowaways play a great part over here in America, and I should have liked dearly to become acquainted with them," he later wrote.

For the most part, however, the posed distance, picturesque elements, and breezy style that characterized his earlier travel essays were missing. An emigrant ship did not inspire lyricism, as he wrote. And it was impossible to be detached when you knelt in vomit trying to help a sick passenger whom the ship crew had all but ignored, or when descending to the lower quarters where the air got so rancid, "each respiration tasted in the throat like some horrible kind of cheese." He was developing a stronger and more muscular voice, fueled by a political consciousness and fierce humanity that would find its way into his fiction as well. In following Fanny, he was finding himself.

LOUIS'S FIRST VIEW of the New World was dim and wet. He disembarked in New York in pouring August rain and remained soaked until he departed the following evening. "One sees it is a new country, they are so free with their water," he quipped in a letter to Colvin.

New York's first view of Robert Louis Stevenson was also dim and wet. Ten days at sea had not improved his usual rumpled looks. An itchy rash had spread across his body (probably scabies, contracted on the ship), and he had lost fourteen pounds—astonishingly, because even with the blue pill, he wrote to Henley, "I could not sh-hush!—the whole way." In his wet clothes, he made the rounds of booksellers to promote his work, but they were unimpressed.

Louis had hoped to give his weakening body time to dry out and recuperate from the sea voyage before slogging on by rail to California. But a disappointing report about Fanny's mental distress convinced him to press on. He quickly dispatched "The Story of a Lie," a short story he had finished on board the ship, to Henley for publication in the *New Quarterly Magazine.* Then, on the eve of his three-thousand-mile rail trip to meet his lover, he sat on the floor of his room and scratched himself from ten at night until seven in the morning. The next day, like a snake shedding its skin to make way for new growth, he wriggled out of his wet clothes, left them on the kitchen floor of his lodging, and set out on the second part of his journey.

INTERNATIONAL IMMIGRATION WAS big business in the U.S. by the time Louis began his cross-country trek. Western railroads, which needed immigrant passengers to stay financially solvent, bought up land to sell them and hyped the opportunities in the West to Europeans in leaflets and colorful magic lantern slideshows. As desperate as they were to turn a quick buck, however, the railroads weren't looking to populate the states with scrawny scribblers like Louis or even his travel alter ego, Robert Stephenson. Writers, clerks, doctors, lawyers, architects, teachers, and clergymen were told to stay home. The U.S. already had a glut of intellectuals; brawn was valued over brains in prospective new American citizens.

Castle Garden immigration center in Manhattan advertised the smooth efficiency and hearty welcome that awaited immigrants when they arrived there. Instead, Robert Louis Stevenson found mayhem. Passengers from four newly arrived ships were being funneled through the rain onto a single riverboat to Jersey City, where they would disembark in another surging crush to the train. Barking porters charged among the crowds; open carts of bedding stood in the rain; panicked passengers pushed, elbowed, and ran. "Children fell, and were picked up to be rewarded by a blow," Louis observed. He caught a tower of heavy boxes before it toppled over onto one child; in the stampede, neither the porter nor the child's mother took any notice.

Such was the chaotic beginning of *America: The Emigrant Train* (later renamed *Across the Plains*), Louis's remarkable travelogue of his twelve-day journey across the U.S., which makes up the second part of *The Amateur Emigrant*. Had Louis been traveling on his parents' money, he could have gone first class and paid extra to ride in a Pullman car, with its plush bedding, lamps, mirrors, and tables. Instead, he paid about a quarter of the price for the "immigrant" fare, which was essentially third class. This usually meant riding in stuffy, springless old day-coaches with backless wooden benches. Passengers often slept on the floor, and food was expensive and sometimes unavailable. The cars were too cramped to write in, so sometimes he crouched on the platform between them to work.

Once moving, images rolled past Louis's vision like pages in a picture book of America at the end of the frontier period: cornfields and sunflowers stretching in a ribbon along the track; fences painted with ads for tobacco and ague cures; broken wagon wheels, tumbleweeds, and ox bones. Dots ahead on the horizon grew into buildings or grazing cattle and withered again into dots behind him. In Pennsylvania Dutch Country, Louis recorded "pleasant villages, carts upon the highways and fishers by the stream"; in Iowa, garden townships that "spoke of country fare and pleasant summer evenings on the stoop." The poetic names of states and rivers—Minnesota, Dakota, Susquehanna, Ticonderoga—lilted through his ears like music.

At a station restaurant in Pittsburgh, he was waited on by a "coloured gentleman"—the first black person he had ever encountered. Despite Louis's relatively enlightened social attitudes, it should be noted that he was not entirely free of the prejudices and insensitivities of his day. Even though he disparaged American bigotry against Chinese immigrants in the book, for example, he also played into the common myth that Chinese men were effeminate because of their dress. But his honesty and self-deprecating humor rescued him from some embarrassing displays of racial condescension. In Pittsburgh, Louis was stunned to find the black waiter's manner "patronisingly superior." (One imagines the waiter was equally stunned by his customer's shabby appearance.) Louis wrote:

> He was indeed strikingly unlike the negroes of Mrs. Beecher Stowe, or the Christy Minstrels of my youth. . . . I had come prepared to pity the poor negro, to put him at his ease, to prove in a thousand condescensions that I was no sharer in the prejudice of race; but I assure you I put my patronage away for another occasion, and had the grace to be pleased with that result.

The meal was his first in thirty hours, and sleep deprivation was also beginning to take a toll. His ordeal was about to get worse, however. Through Iowa, Louis had been traveling on "mixed trains" that combined immigrant cars with those of higher-paying passengers. At Council Bluffs, Iowa, on the eastern bank of the Missouri River, he transferred to a Union Pacific "immigrant train." He and the other passengers were "sorted" and "boxed" for transport: women and children in one car, single men in another, and Chinese in the third. With another man, he purchased a board and straw-filled cushion to place across their seats for sleep; he went in with two others on a communal washing dish, towel, and bar of soap.

"Equality, though conceived very largely in America, does not extend so low down as to an emigrant," Louis wrote. Conductors were surly and noncommunicative, so passengers were often at the mercy of newsboys, who could also be bullying and contemptuous. One rudely kicked aside Louis's foot when he was propping open a broken door for air. "Though I myself apologized, as if to show him the way, he answered me never a word," he wrote. But later he felt a touch on his shoulder and a large, juicy pear was placed in his hand. It was the same newsboy, who had observed that Louis looked ill and afterward coddled him and sat by him to cheer him up. It was an example of what Louis called the "uncivil kindness of the American."

Things got a little hallucinatory crossing the plains of Nebraska. For Louis, ill and reeling from the opiate-and-alcohol "remedy" laudanum, the endless plains must have seemed a reflection of his own hollowed-out self. He perched on top of a fruit wagon in his unbuttoned shirt and trousers, searching the horizon for something different, but there was nothing for his thoughts to hold on to. It felt as if they were not moving at all, and movement was essential to Robert Louis Stevenson. Adding to the surreality, his train was sometimes passed by others packed with immigrants heading east. Had they made their fortunes? he wondered. "Were they all bound for Paris, and to be in Rome by Easter?" It didn't seem so, because whenever they crossed paths, the eastbound immigrants wailed "Come back!" to them through the open windows. Still, their train steamed on, following the "hope that moves ever westward."

At Ogden, Utah, there was a much-needed transfer to the better cars of the Central Pacific line. With the passengers cooped up for ninety hours, Louis's car had begun to stink abominably. "I do my best to keep my head the other way, and look for the human rather than the bestial in this Yahoo-like business of the Emigrant train," he wrote. But there was plenty of bestial behavior to observe, which he laid out in a chapter called "Despised Races."

The passengers in his car now were mostly American immigrants moving west—"lumpish" and loud, with little curiosity about others and a cruel sense of humor. Of all their ignorant attitudes, he found those toward the Chinese passengers to be the worst. "They seemed never to have looked at them, listened to them, or thought of them, but hated them *a priori*," he wrote. Louis's most eloquent anger was reserved for the treatment of Native Americans, "over whose own hereditary continent we had been steaming all these days." By the time of his journey, many Native people had been slaughtered or pushed onto reservations, and those left behind were often forced to beg for food. Louis wrote:

> Now and again at way-stations, a husband and wife and a few
> children, disgracefully dressed out with the sweepings of ci-

vilisation, came forth and stared upon the emigrants. The silent stoicism of their conduct, and the pathetic degradation of
their appearance, would have touched any thinking creature;
but my fellow-passengers danced and jested round them with
a truly Cockney baseness. I was ashamed for the thing we call
civilisation.

Finally, more than three weeks after he left Scotland, Louis woke one
morning to the bracing scent of pine and a glimpse of foaming river near the
old California Gold Rush town of Dutch Flat. "It was like meeting one's
wife," he wrote. They were descending from the summit of the Sierra Nevada to Sacramento, nearly seven thousand feet over 105 miles. By the next
day, Louis was on a ferry crossing San Francisco Bay when daylight broke.

Louis had no time to relish the gates of gold. He hurriedly made his way
down the coast to Monterey. He had survived, but his body was nearly broken. He was malnourished and covered with a burning rash and would soon
be diagnosed with malaria, contracted on the train ride, and pleurisy. He
spent his last dollars on a room in a boardinghouse and stowed his valise.
Then he set out through the sand dunes to the adobe where Fanny and her
children were staying. But he was so ill and weak, he had to stop first for a
stiff drink at the Bohemian Saloon to stave off collapse.

FANNY AND LOUIS stood face-to-face and miles apart. Lost time, uncertainty, and the opposition of family and friends to their union filled the
space between them. Was the hothouse passion they had felt in France
hardy enough to survive all that they would be up against now?

The year had changed them. Louis would have noticed how Fanny's
scandalously short hair became her, the curls licking her cheekbones and
neck and framing her deep black eyes. But he must have also seen in her

eyes the way he looked to her—gaunt and ragged, with angry red blotches on his face and hands. This could not be the young man who had bounded up four flights of stairs to her apartment in Paris with a glowing review of his work. His ever-brilliant eyes, which had mesmerized her in Grez, popped like glass doll's eyes above his pale, hollow cheeks.

"He looked ill, even in my childish gaze . . . ," Lloyd would recall. "His clothes, no longer picturesque but merely shabby, hung loosely on his shrunken body; and there was about him an indescribable lessening of his alertness and self-confidence."

However much Fanny had longed for Louis, his sudden appearance must have made her even more anxious about the fragile life she had constructed, and what lay ahead. She was already a subject of gossip in old-world Monterey for wearing short hair, smoking cigarettes, and living separately from her husband. Sam was due for a visit, and Louis's presence in her living quarters could only damage her reputation further.

Like meeting one's wife, Louis had written when California had opened its arms to him. But Belle would recall that neither he nor Fanny acted like a romantic lover. They were "gay and full of banter," but "almost coldly casual" toward each other. And when the visit ended, Louis had no idea if he was any closer to Fanny in California than he had been in Scotland.

"This is not a letter, for I am too perturbed . . . ," he confessed to Baxter. "I know nothing. I go out camping, that is all I know." In dire financial straits, Louis left, with a horse and wagon, to camp in the mountains above Carmel Valley. Biographer Claire Harman has suggested that he was suicidal by this point. Several miles into the unfamiliar wilderness, he collapsed. For the next three days, he lay in a feverish stupor, just able to drag himself far enough to get water for himself and his horse. He kept alive on coffee.

Lying awake under the stars, Louis must have been reminded of that night in the mountains of France when, with Fanny's scent still on his clothing, he had written of longing for a companion ever "within touch." What a cruel turn it would be if he should now die alone under the stars, with Fanny finally nearby but out of reach. Lines from a poem he had written on the train, a premonition of death, most certainly spun in his head:

Bury me low and let me lie
Under the wide and starry sky,
Joying to live, I joyed to die
Bury me low and let me lie.

It was the closest Louis had come to death, and it would be the first of many times he would cheat it. Like a fantastic plot twist in one of his future novels, he was rescued by a bear hunter and a former lighthouse keeper. Anson Smith and Jonathan Wright, partners in an Angora goat ranch, took him home, smothered him with goose grease, and nursed him roughly. His London friends must have thought he had really gone native when he wrote to them that he was living with the rancheros:

> *I am lying in an upper chamber nearly naked with flies crawling all over me, and a clinking of goat bells in my ears, which proves to me that the goats are come home. . . . The old bear hunter is doubtless now infusing tea; and Tom the Indian will come in with his gun in a few minutes.*

A later letter from Joe Strong, meant to assure Colvin that Louis was in good hands, instead must have confirmed his worst fears about the intellectual barrenness of the States. The "climet" agreed with Louis, Joe wrote, and he was "in exelent health and actualy growing fat."

When Louis was well enough to hold the reins, he returned to Monterey. In letters to his friends, he admitted that his presence had made Fanny's situation even more complicated, though he also hinted that, like the donkey Modestine, she needed him to prod her along.

LLOYD OSBOURNE WAS APPREHENSIVE. The eleven-year-old did not see as much of his father as he wished to, especially in Monterey. He must have wondered if Sam understood the strains of his life. He was the only male in a household of women who were always fussing and ordering him about. Even the old Bonifacio sisters, usually invisible and silent on the top floor, chimed in if sheer boredom drove him to some natural boy behavior like lassoing the calf in the backyard.

Lloyd had been eagerly anticipating his father's latest visit, but he was crestfallen when Sam arrived. The boy was no doubt used to searching the faces of adults for clues to what was going to happen next in his rather unpredictable life, and he could see that his father's was clouded behind his pointed golden beard. Sam seemed preoccupied, with precious little time for his son. Instead, he and Fanny told Lloyd to do his homework while they talked in the adjoining room. But their subdued voices had a "strangely disturbing quality," Lloyd would remember. He could make out Fanny reproaching Sam for Hervey's death and Sam pleading his financial straits at the time. Then suddenly his mother blurted out, "Oh, Sam, forgive me!" The intensity of her voice tore through her son "like a knife."

A short time later, Lloyd was looking forward to another visit—this time from Louis. Lloyd worried about his older friend since he had arrived in Monterey. Though Louis seemed as gay as ever, he looked thinner and shabbier to the boy with each passing day. Fanny assured her son that "experience" was important to a writer, and Louis's experience in Monterey was even a "gold mine." If that was so, Lloyd puzzled, why did he still look so poor?

An outing with the Scotsman was usually highly imaginative, with Lloyd spontaneously cast as a pirate or smuggler or other romantic figure. Yet this time Louis hopped along on his long strides, nearly heedless of the boy trying to keep up with him. The two stayed, disappointingly, themselves. And when Louis finally began to speak, that same intonation Lloyd remembered from his parents' talk—"so colorless and yet so troubling"—crept into his voice.

"I want to tell you something," Louis said. "You may not like it, but I hope you will. I am going to marry your mother." Lloyd was dumbstruck. He thought he would cry but didn't; he felt he should say something but couldn't. "All I know is that at last my hand crept into [Louis's], and in that mutual pressure a rapturous sense of tenderness and contentment came flooding over me."

In October, Louis related to Baxter that Sam had agreed to a divorce and would support Fanny financially as long as she and Louis lived separately and waited until "a decent interval" had passed before marrying. "The only question is whether I shall be alive for the ceremony," he added. To further keep up appearances, Fanny would return to Oakland and Louis would continue recovering in Monterey before moving to San Francisco. "So you see he doesn't wish to be foolish in the way I imagine you thought he would;" Fanny boasted in a letter to Rearden, finally able to gush a little about her lover, "indeed I think him the only really wise person in the world."

Objectively, Louis was no better—and perhaps even worse—a marriage prospect for Fanny than he had been when she left him in France. He was still young and penniless, and now he was also frail and sick. But the scare of losing him after he had risked everything to be with her must have given her the courage to risk everything for him. Louis could not offer her the comforts and consistency many Victorian women sought in a marriage. With his health in ruins, he could not even promise her a future together. But he could give her the security of his love and devotion, for however long it might last.

EIGHT

An icy wind was heaving down Bush Street when Mary Carson answered the knock at her boardinghouse door a few days before Christmas 1879. A stranger who looked half wasted away was standing on the doorstep. His brogues and ulster gave him away as a foreigner; their shabby condition suggested he had fallen on hard times. The young man's fingers fluttered nervously as he inquired about a room, and she could see that one of his front teeth was missing and others were spotted like water stains on marble. Carson gave Robert Louis Stevenson the most searching look he would ever remember—and he was used to searching looks. She contemplated whether to shut the door on him. But when she gazed into the depths of his eyes—eyes, she would recall, that "could look right through you"—she decided to take a chance. "He had such a big heart—," she said years later, "too big for his means."

On the streets nearby, San Francisco was dressing up for Victorian Christmas, a relatively new phenomenon in California. Christmas tree lots dotted the street corners, some boasting cuttings from virgin redwood forests in Marin. Blown-glass ornaments from Germany glistened on the shelves of department stores and holiday displays capitalized on the new trend of window-shopping.

Carson's new lodger did not seem to take much solace in the holiday cheer. The record low temperatures that had blanketed the Napa Valley in snow and frozen creeks in the East Bay kept him largely in his room. Louis spent most of his time under the bedcovers writing, breaking up coal and chopping kindling with a hatchet on his windowsill to keep the fire in his room burning longer. On Christmas Day, he slipped out for a meal alone.

Louis had happily fled Monterey for San Francisco just days after Fanny's divorce finally came through that month. His time there had been trying. In November, he and Fanny learned that Belle had been secretly wed to Joe Strong for three months, setting off a new round of gossip about the Osbourne family. Louis's persistent cough and growling stomach had made it difficult to focus on work. He spent solitary hours walking on the shore or lying in the sand in his overcoat. A fisherman who remembered him later as the thinnest man he ever saw asked Louis what he did for a living. Louis replied, "I sling ink." He worried incessantly that he was not slinging it fast enough to shoulder the responsibilities of an instant family.

Louis could not have known then how prescient Fanny had been when she told her son that Louis's experience in Monterey was a "gold mine" for a writer. The pine woods south of town, the rippled sands spotted with twisted cypresses, the clouds of birds keening overhead, and the pounding surf would inspire the setting for his most famous novel. In *Treasure Island*, Louis would recast the area as wild, uncharted territory where a youth who had sailed across the sea could perish or earn his manhood, defying the wisdom of the adults who charged themselves with his safety. It was the perfect backdrop for a swashbuckling version of the late coming-of-age story he was living in California.

Moving to San Francisco had brought him nearer to Fanny but no closer to easing his money worries. For all Louis knew, his parents had cast him off. Within days of Fanny's divorce, Sam Osbourne had lost his job with the district court and had to renege on his promise to support her in return for delaying her marriage to Louis. Relief might have come from her entitlement to the Oakland house, which had been purchased with funds she brought into the marriage, but Sam hung on to the deed for another two years. The responsibility of supporting Fanny, her sister Nellie, Lloyd (in boarding school), five cats, a dog, and two horses had suddenly fallen on Louis's scrawny shoulders.

The day after Christmas, he sat in a café composing a note to Sidney Colvin that was as much ledger as letter. It is an image out of Dickens—the frayed, bone-thin man hunched over his figures, tallying expenses against projected earnings, amid a crowd of people still sated from the festivities of the day before. Louis's work had been beset by the usual starts and stalls. He had lost valuable time trying his hand at a novel, to be called *A Vendetta in the West* or *A Chapter in the Experience of Arizona Breckenridge* (a title sparked from Fanny's recollection of a man who named each of his many daughters after a different state). He had given up the novel halfway through and was struggling to write the second part of *The Amateur Emigrant*. He was banking on the first part, about his experience on the emigrant ship, being picked up for publication or, he wrote to Colvin, "by God, I'll starve here."

BY JANUARY, Louis did indeed appear to be on the path to starvation. He made light of his plight in a letter to Colvin describing his formula for living in San Francisco on seventy cents a day. Breakfast at a café consisted of coffee, a roll, and butter for ten cents. "R.L.S. used to find the supply of butter insufficient; but he has now learned the art to exactitude, and butter and roll expire at the same moment," Louis quipped. He had also learned to confine himself to half of the full bottle of wine placed before him with his midday meal. This kept lunch—a full meal, wine, coffee, and brandy—to fifty cents. In the evening, he repeated the ten-cent roll and coffee of the morning. Between meals he walked, "engaged darkly with an inkbottle," or met Fanny at the Ferry House a few times a week for a tryst. Whenever he returned to his lodging, Carson's youngest child announced, "Dere's de author," prompting Louis to observe that he was at least "poor enough to belong to that honourable craft."

When Louis did not go out at all, Mary Carson suspected he was too weak and brought him a tray of food. She liked to chat with him when she made his fire while he wrote in bed, though she would stop short if he seemed intent on his work. "Go on, Mrs. Carson," he would say, without breaking his stride. "I can write and talk at the same time."

His health was still far from hardy. The pleurisy he had suffered from in Monterey concerned him—chest pain and cough seemed unusual while living a quiet life in a mild climate. He and Fanny had discussed marrying as soon as her divorce came through so she could care for him. But they were still trying to squeeze into the narrow mold of Victorian propriety that seemed essential for both of their families to welcome their union. Ironically, as if to comment on the futility of this effort, Louis received anonymous letters claiming he was the father of an infant born to a servant at the home of his old mentor, Fleeming Jenkin. Louis knew the woman, coincidentally named Margaret Stevenson, and referred to her in a letter to William Henley as "an enchanting young lady whom you have seen." But he did not give credence to the charge. After his death, when a Robert Stevenson, gamely dressed like the author, claimed to be the love child, the story was shown to be false.

Fanny's divorce might have been cause for celebration. One would like to think it was intoxicating for her to taste freedom for the first time in her adult life, to break free of a twenty-two-year marriage to a man who was reliably unfaithful throughout. Instead, she and Louis seemed busy fending off near universal condemnation of her divorce and their union. Fanny kept the divorce from her family in Indiana, who already blamed her for supporting her sister Nellie's engagement to a Hispanic man, Adulfo Sanchez. Strangely, instead of returning the favor, even Nellie fretted that Fanny's immoral behavior would scandalize the Sanchez family's sense of honor. For Fanny, getting Nellie wed without disgrace was one more reason to delay her own wedding.

Fanny's relationship with Belle was also strained since she had discovered her daughter's secret marriage. In a letter home, Nellie surmised that the couple—who had been dating for about six months—had decided to marry on impulse after Fanny asked them to get to know each other better first. In the midst of trying to disentangle herself from Belle's father, Fanny was probably especially fearful that her twenty-one-year-old daughter might be repeating her own mistakes. Joe was talented and good-natured, but he had a shaky work ethic and a strong taste for alcohol. Belle's father, however, had no misgivings about the marriage or qualms about concealing it from Fanny. Sam readily gave the couple his blessing.

Years later, Belle wrote that Joe had begged her to marry him quickly after Fanny told him she was hoping for a more financially stable match for her daughter. Given her mother's relentless economic insecurity, that would not be surprising. Elsewhere Belle claimed she eloped because she resented Louis. However chic Fanny's affair with him may have seemed in France, back in her family's social circle, Belle was angry that her mother would leave her father for "this penniless foreigner"—a man who was also only a few years older than her own beau.

Meanwhile Fanny was at the center of a tempest brewing on the other side of the Atlantic. Of Louis's close chums, only his cousin Bob had not condemned his romantic quest to America. In fact, Bob envied Louis and begged for any news about Belle, no matter how dull. With his usual disregard for punctuation, Bob chided his cousin for moaning that he did not see Fanny enough: "To see a person in 'cachette' once in a week or two weeks seems nothing to you why man it is life." Though Bob was seeing a blond *bébé* in Paris who was "a burning fiery furnace really," he was still so enamored with Belle that he knew he would give himself up to her even if it meant no more to her than fleeting sexual gratification.

Louis's mentor, Fleeming Jenkin, also encouraged him to disregard people's disapproval if he wanted to marry Fanny. But after witnessing his distress without his lover the previous spring, his other friends were concerned about his distress now that he had reached her. In the emerging pattern that would last until Louis's death, they appointed themselves guardians of his career and sometimes even his personal life. Though Louis continued to assure them that he did not intend to leave California without Fanny, they were determined to get him back, preferably alone. Colvin and Henley still insisted Louis was motivated by chivalry, which he had carried too far to retract. He had gushed himself into a heroic stance and "burdened himself with a divorced invalid," Colvin fumed to Charles Baxter.

Their concern would be more sympathetic had it not been tinged with condescension, self-interest, and outright jealousy of Fanny's claim on Louis's affection. "It is absolutely necessary that he should be brought to see that England and a quiet life are what he wants and must have if he means to make—I won't say reputation—but money by literature," Henley spluttered to Colvin. A quiet life would also serve Henley's desire to make money collaborating with Louis on plays, which he continued to press for despite Louis's exasperated pleas that he needed faster and more dependable income. And it would be more conducive to Colvin's efforts to groom Louis as a conventional man of letters in Britain—something that was impossible as long as he lived away from his "equals."

"Of course there is always the chance of his settling to some cadging second-rate literary work out there, and if I am not mistaken Mrs. O would not at all object to that result," Colvin wrote to Baxter. Their hostility toward Fanny blinded Louis's friends to the fact that under trying circumstances in Monterey, he had completed a brilliant Gothic thriller and love story, "The Pavilion on the Links," which Leslie Stephen had accepted for *Cornhill*. Arthur Conan Doyle would later call it "the high-water mark of [Stevenson's] genius" for the vividness of its characters against the stark, windswept coastal terrain, as well as its tight construction and the precision and eloquence of Louis's language.

The *New Quarterly Magazine* had also snatched up the tale that Louis had written at sea, the heavily autobiographical "Story of a Lie." It features a headstrong, self-righteous father, "the Squire," and his alienated son, Dick Naseby, who loves his father but feels so misunderstood by him, he grows to nearly hate the sight of him. There is also the woman Dick wishes to marry, Esther, whose black dress "took possession of his mind" the moment he first saw her. (Esther was a dead ringer for Fanny, with "her strong black brows [that] spoke of temper easily aroused and hard to quiet" and "something dangerous and sulky underlying, in her nature, much that was honest, compassionate, and even noble.") In the story, tensions between father and son reach a breaking point when the Squire accuses Dick of taking Esther as his mistress and scandalizing the family.

Louis's feelings toward his real father had softened during his harrowing journey across the Atlantic. He now felt that he loved Thomas more than anyone but Fanny. But his communication with his shocked and hurt parents was vague and largely through intermediaries. For all they knew, their destitute son was in a lawless country shacking up with a married woman. Worked into a frenzy over the scandal they anticipated it would bring on the family name, they were considering fleeing Scotland. Not surprisingly, Thomas blamed Louis's immorality on his rejection of Calvinism—and even held one of Britain's foremost evolutionists accountable. "I lay all this at the door of Herbert Spencer," he thundered to Colvin. "Unsettling a man's faith is indeed a *very* serious matter."

Louis could have predicted this melodrama—in fact, he did in "The Story of a Lie." In the tale, which had hit British newsstands in October, the Squire calls his son's love affair "the death of me." A month later, Thomas howled at Colvin, "Is it fair that we should be half murdered by his conduct?" Like Louis's fictional parent, Thomas demanded his son choose between him and the woman he loved. He tried to lure Louis into abandoning Fanny—first with £20 for a single ticket home, and later with a fake plea from the family doctor that Thomas was urgently ill and needed his son. But Louis did not take the bait: He wrote to Henley that Fanny was also ill and, in his habit of speaking as if he were already wed, "I won't desert my wife."

LOUIS AND FANNY desperately needed friends, and they found them in Fanny's eccentric pal Dora Williams and her husband, Virgil. The couple welcomed Louis without judgment: Virgil had been unhappily married and divorced when Dora met him and she had wed him with her usual forthright composure. Like everyone else, at first the couple was taken aback by

Fanny's threadbare suitor, especially after Sam's polished good looks. Arriving home one day to find this peculiar stranger talking to his wife, Virgil thought Louis was a tramp whom Dora could not get out of the house. But they were soon won over by Louis's charm and earnestness.

Virgil talked literature, art, and travel with Louis and took him to the Bohemian Club, where he could use the library. But attempts to interest him in the club's boozy pastimes were wasted. "Drink is more the order of the day than wit," Louis wrote to Colvin. He was more content to drop in at the Williams home to visit Dora, who was confined to an invalid chair recovering from illness. Ostensibly, he came to cheer her up, but Dora recognized that he was also looking for any chance to wax on about Fanny and marriage. When their conversations veered into politics, she found his views refreshing for a British man. On one occasion, Louis paced the floor rapidly as he bewailed Britain's "stupendous blunder" in mistreating the colonies. If Great Britain and America had stayed united, he felt, they could have led the world in noble causes. "His point of view struck me at once as being new—broader and more finely humane," she recalled.

Fanny and Louis also spent time with Belle and Joe after Fanny's fury over their elopement had died down. The young couple was now part of San Francisco's bohemian set, living in an artist studio tucked between Montgomery Street offices. When Joe was not painting portraits, he took any work he could get. Once asked by a client to camouflage a black eye the man had gotten in a fight, Joe seated the man behind a gold frame and applied makeup to his face as if he were painting his portrait.

Belle did clever illustrations for greeting cards and fashion advertisements. The couple's housekeeping was "of the sketchiest," she would recall. So were meals: Dinner might consist of oysters roasted on a shovel and a jug of mulled claret, heated with a poker off the fire. Sometimes Belle and Joe met Fanny and Louis for dinner at one of the city's many cheap restaurants and afterward talked by the fire in their studio.

Louis lived in San Francisco only five months, but the city's influence could be felt in his work years later. He found it the most interesting and least American city in the U.S., with its cosmopolitan "airs of Marseilles and of Pekin [*sic*]." As an international seaport, it was also a gateway to adventure. In his sprawling detective story *The Wrecker*, coauthored with his stepson, it would figure prominently as the city where a plot is hatched to retrieve and sell opium trapped in a shipwreck in the Pacific.

In Louis's essay "A Modern Cosmopolis," the city appeared to be a reflection of the instability of his life while staying there. Surrounded on three sides by water, it felt exposed and jittery, battered by the booming Pacific and "shaken to the heart" by earthquakes. The fog contributed to his disorientation: Pouring in off the ocean in the afternoon, it wiped away all the familiar signs of his surroundings. "One brief impression follows another," he wrote, "and the city leaves upon the mind no general and stable picture, but a profusion of airy and incongruous images of the sea and shore, the East and West, the summer and the winter."

No doubt influenced by Fanny's views, Louis expanded the critique of American notions of equality that he had begun on the immigrant train. (As Fanny once noted to Dora, Americans were proudest of what they did not possess: freedom.) San Francisco telescoped the jarring contrasts of the Gilded Age that he had seen elsewhere in the States—splendor and suffering, civilization and mob vengeance. In Monterey, Louis had observed the powerful lure of the American Dream and those cultures, primarily Mexican and Native American, that were perishing under the onslaught of the "millionaire vulgarians of the Big Bonanza." In San Francisco, he drew an evocative image of the rich vying for stature in their palatial Nob Hill mansions above the Stock Exchange—"the heart of San Francisco: a great pump we might call it, continually pumping up the savings of the lower quarters into the pockets of the millionaires up the hill."

For a student of human nature and budding adventure writer, the romantic remnants of the city's outlaw past were another gold mine. At the *San Francisco Chronicle* building just a few blocks from Louis's boardinghouse, Mayor Isaac Kalloch's son gunned down editor Charles de Young after the newspaperman shot the mayor in a political feud. Seamen were shanghaied in the streets, and one night Louis came upon a man poised for vengeance at a street corner, "a long Smith-and-Wesson glittering in his hand behind his back." This was a bigger, seamier canvas than the one he had found so irresistible as a young man in Edinburgh—a throng of gambling houses, secret societies, and dangerous dives, as Loudon Dodd, his lead character in *The Wrecker*, would describe it.

Italian fishermen, Dutch merchants, Mexican vaqueros, New England schooner captains, South Seas traders—they all rubbed shoulders on the rowdy streets. "From what I had once called myself, the Amateur Parisian, I grew (or declined) into a waterside prowler, a lingerer on wharves, a frequenter of shy neighbourhoods, a scraper of acquaintance with eccentric characters," *The Wrecker*'s Loudon Dodd would recall. "My delight was much in slums." Like Louis, his fictional character was especially fascinated by Chinatown: "I could never have enough of its ambiguous, interracial atmosphere, as of a vitalised museum." A few blocks from Louis's doorstep, the Chinese settlement was a collage of textures and colors—from the kites tangled in telegraph wires overhead to the smoky opium dens underground, and in between, crowded living quarters and markets of curious vegetables.

Another colorful haunt was the apartment of an eccentric friend of Fanny's and the Strongs', Charles Warren Stoddard, a gay poet and restless author of popular Pacific travel books. Blue-eyed, curly haired, and genial, Stoddard had moved to San Francisco with his family at the age of eleven and was instantly smitten. Like most gay men, Stoddard publicly lived a closeted life in the States; traveling to the South Seas, he found sexual attitudes franker and more tolerant. Barely veiled accounts of his amorous adventures with men in his books *South-Sea Idyls* and *Summer Cruising in the South Seas* drew crude remarks from his fellow writer and Bohemian Club "brother" Ambrose Bierce. But close friends like Joe Strong were more accepting. Stoddard once asserted to Joe that "girls are well enough in their own way, but not to go to bed with," to which Joe casually responded that bed was where he found women *"perfectly charming."*

While his friendship with Bierce was deteriorating, Stoddard found a new friend in Louis, who visited his apartment in a crumbling Gothic mansion where ivy creeping through a window spread across the ceiling. Entering the "aerie," which seemed to float midair on Rincon Hill, must have felt like stepping out of bone-chilling fog into the tropics—an exotic nest filled with coconut bowls and plumes, baskets and shells, war clubs and spears from Stoddard's travels.

Louis left his first visit with copies of Stoddard's *Idyls* and Melville's *Typee* and *Omoo*. He had longed to travel to the Pacific ever since he was a law student, when a visitor to Heriot Row had praised the Navigator Islands, now Samoa, as a "balm for the weary"—an even more seductive image in his reduced circumstances in San Francisco. Louis returned to visit Stoddard, the poet visited Louis in his room, and the two roamed San Francisco while Stoddard filled Louis's head with visions of the natural beauty, intriguing island cultures, and casual and inexpensive lifestyle of the South Seas.

Twelve years later, Stoddard and his eccentric dwelling would turn up in *The Wrecker*, as would Mary Carson and her husband (as hapless stock gamblers Mr. and Mrs. Speedy). They were among the many eccentric people and places that Louis collected and tucked away in his mind, to be reanimated later, like magic lantern slides, by the light of his imagination.

AS WINTER SET IN, Louis's financial situation was grave. Sam had still not resumed supporting the family and was snooping into Louis's finances, presumably hoping he would not have to. Money and letters from the Stevensons had not reached their son and he took the silence for disinheritance, though he bravely insisted it was for the best because he had moral doubts about inherited money. But he reduced his one substantial meal a day to bring his daily budget down to forty-five cents.

Not surprisingly, the ordeal of Louis's sea and rail travel and his poverty in California would further weaken his health, yet it is worth noting that he saw it as one further sign that his health had been deteriorating before he left for the States. From Monterey, he had written to Gosse:

> *I am going for 30 now, and unless I can snatch a little rest before*
> *long, I have, I may tell you in confidence, no hope of seeing 31. . . .*
> *It is a pity in one sense, for I believe the class of work I might yet*
> *give out, is better and more real and solid than people fancy.*

This was a bittersweet consolation—his writing was improving, if not his health. Louis and Fanny believed that the realism and critical commentary he was integrating into his work made it stronger. To Henley, he wrote, "I am only beginning to see my true method." Louis thought that *The Amateur Emigrant* was not his most eloquent book but would be the most sought-after, with its big, popular canvas. But he was so broke, he had asked Colvin to try to place the first half, "The Emigrant Ship," with a publisher before he finished the second.

Again, the view from Britain was myopic. Colvin wrote that Louis's painfully honest depiction of steerage travel was distasteful and dull and would harm his half-formed reputation. "Fortunately dulness is not a fault the public hates," Louis protested, "perhaps they may like this vein of dulness." Henley was even more blunt, and cruel. He argued that the book was both weak and pretentious. Still, through a friend, Henley placed it in February with *Good Words*, where editor Donald MacLeod, a Scottish clergyman, praised it as "full of force and character and fine feeling." MacLeod would not pay for it until he could run it the following year, however, and Louis could not afford to wait. So Henley and Colvin withdrew it and sent it to the publisher C. Kegan Paul.

Louis was brimming with other American-themed topics, including essays on Thoreau (which would appear, along with an earlier essay on Whitman, in *Familiar Studies of Men and Books*), Benjamin Franklin, and William Penn, and one on the vitriolic San Francisco populist Denis Kearney and his sandlot followers. But his colleagues were getting fed up with American subjects and the Americanisms creeping into his letters. "Louis Stevenson is a vile Yankee now, I suppose—," his college chum James Walter Ferrier sneered to his sister Elizabeth Ann, who went by the nickname "Coggie." "He doesn't talk about being 'ill,' but says 'I have been very *sick*'—can you vomit?"

Broke, hungry, and *sick*, Louis felt crushed under the weight of disapproval from all sides. He begged his friends for no more sermons on his personal life. He asked Colvin to ease up on his lavish and "eloquent dispraise" of the first half of *The Amateur Emigrant*, his most promising source of income, while he was trying to plunge ahead with the second half. "You rolled such a lot of polysyllables over me that a better man than I might have been disheartened," he wrote wearily. Yet Louis *was* disheartened and began to have doubts about his new direction.

In her biography of Fanny, Nellie Van de Grift Sanchez wrote that her sister's "profound faith in [Louis's] genius before the rest of the world had come to recognize it had a great deal to do with keeping up his faith in himself." Though Nellie overstated Fanny's role in recognizing Louis's genius, her assessment was otherwise accurate. Fanny was the only person close to Louis who encouraged him to trust his instincts as a fiction writer at the lowest point in his career, and he began submitting his work to her for criticism. "He has a line that belongs to him alone and would be an idiot to leave it for money and flattery," she had written earlier to her friend Timothy Rearden. "Later on if he works and lives he will get both fame and money, I am sure."

If he lives had become a refrain in their lives—one that reveals how precarious Fanny's own situation was after her divorce. If Louis should die before they wed, she would be financially and socially worse off than if she had stayed married to Sam. Louis worried about this and sometimes urged her to marry him sooner to legalize her claim to his inheritance (should he still have one) if he died. But she held out. Louis was born into respectability and could disregard it at whim. But she did not have that luxury. Now both an adulteress and a divorcée, she might also be seen as a gold digger. Her position was fragile and untenable. Only Louis's love for her remained steadfast—the one rock she could cling to in an era that did not consider divorced women entitled to a second chance at happiness.

To Gosse, Louis announced his engagement to the woman he had loved for four and a half trying years and boasted, "I do not think many wives are better loved than mine will be." It was not an easy way into a marriage, but the bond forged between Louis and Fanny at this time would hold them together through the difficult challenges ahead. Was he reminded of their embattled love when he climbed the steep footpaths up Telegraph Hill, with its shacks and cottages dangling on the edge of the cliffs? Nellie would recall Louis gazing up at them with wonder, marveling at the confidence, or simple trust in God, that gave people the courage to build their lives on such a perilous perch, knowing that at any moment the earth below could open up and swallow them.

THE FIRST BLOOD came in spring. Feverish and coughing profusely, Louis believed his pleurisy had relapsed. Yet he dragged himself to the finish of *The Amateur Emigrant* and sent it to Colvin. "The second part was written in a circle of hell unknown to Dante; that of the penniless and dying author . . . ," Louis wrote in an accompanying note. "I feel sick even to think of it."

Fanny immediately moved him to a hotel in East Oakland so she could take better care of him. She brought in her own doctor, William Bamford, whose familiarity with pulmonary ailments had begun when he tended to miners in the California foothills. Fanny and Louis were surely again tempted to marry so that she could take him into her home. But by now his parents had joined the family chorus pushing them to wait.

The Stevensons had been frantic about their son's health since early January, when the *Glasgow Herald* reported alarming accounts that Louis was "lying seriously ill in the United States." By then, Colvin had resigned himself to the idea that no amount of condemnation from Louis's friends would dissuade him from "starving with [Fanny] and her boy." He intervened with Thomas, telling him that Fanny had gotten a divorce and she and Louis were to marry. The new, respectable spin on the situation was the salvation the Stevensons had been praying for. Thomas sent his son £50 and a gruff apology of sorts. He also pledged to help the couple if they honored his wish to delay their marriage as long as possible.

Then suddenly, the din of voices screeching for social decorum was silenced by more resounding concerns. Louis's coughing attacks got longer and more violent until blood frothed up his throat and filled his mouth. A hemorrhage was a new and alarming health milestone—one that suggested classic consumption, or pulmonary tuberculosis.

Now he suffered cold sweats, burning fevers, and deep fits during which he could not speak. Bamford was not optimistic. With death staring him in the face, Louis began to succumb to the fatalism that always lay just under his cheerful demeanor. He wavered between fighting for his life when he finally had a chance of happiness and caving in.

But Fanny was not ready to give up on Louis's life. Instead, she flew into action. She determined to move Louis into her home, where she could nurse him properly, feed him, keep him warm, and boost his spirits. Of course, she could be courting disaster. Sam had just resumed providing support, but now he would be justified in cutting it off and throwing them out. It could irretrievably damage the fragile beginnings of a truce between Louis and his parents. And she might be helpless to save his life, as she had been with her son Hervey.

April was the fourth anniversary of her child's death. Fanny's mind must have gone back to that other April day—to the dank Paris apartment, her frantic candlelight search for blood she could smell but not find, her boy's stiff body when the last breath left him—an image preserved in her mind like a Victorian postmortem photo. Then a young man's face had appeared out of the darkness in Grez. He had been awkward and nervous, so thin she felt a strong wind might knock him down. But his strength had lifted her from the emptiness that must have felt like it would last a lifetime. She could not let him die now. She was guided not only by love but by her firm belief that the world had not seen all that Robert Louis Stevenson had to give.

At times, Fanny could be interminably slow to move, mulling over a course of action for months or more. But she could also make life-changing decisions breathtakingly fast. As soon as Bamford said it was medically safe, she moved her young lover into her family home, for all the world to see. It was a brash, reckless, and courageous thing to do, and it very likely saved his life.

UNDER BAMFORD'S GUIDANCE, Fanny plunged herself into Louis's care, calling on nursing skills she had learned while tending to her son. She spent sleepless nights monitoring Louis's breathing and nurtured him with soups and custards. His health turned a corner. Bamford would credit Fanny's care with pulling Louis from the brink of death.

Gossip surrounded the Oakland house—including from Bamford's wife, Cornelia. Among those who had taken sides in the Osbourne divorce, she had stood with Sam, whom she viewed as a long-suffering victim of Fanny's "infatuation for a young writer." Inside Fanny's house, it was left to Nellie, the third member of the household, to face the wrath of the Vandegrifts when word of the divorce seeped to Indiana. In a letter to her sister Betty, Nellie revealed that the worst of the trouble was not the divorce but Fanny's impending remarriage. Her morbidly realistic reason for not reporting on the planned nuptials sooner, she wrote, was that she "was sure that Mr. Stevenson was dying and that thus the matter would be settled." Still, she admitted that Louis was otherwise a good man and she could not speak ill of Fanny. "She has always heaped every kindness upon me," Nellie reflected. "And I must say that I am sure that she is a good woman—no better ever lived—but she is weak, and had had an unhappy life."

Sam Osbourne's response to the new living arrangement was a happy surprise. He continued to support the household, which was both a relief and an embarrassment to Louis. It seems that once Sam had given up the battle to hang on to his wife, he assumed his characteristic affability—though he did remark to a coworker that if he ever wed again, it would be to "the ugliest woman he could find so that no other man would want her." There is no record of how two of the other men who had sorely wanted his wife—lawyers John Lloyd and Timothy Rearden—greeted the news of her engagement. Rearden, on his way to becoming a superior court judge, grumblingly handled her divorce. His later wedding gift to Fanny, an antique funeral urn, suggested condolences more than congratulations on her new marriage.

The Stevensons were kept blessedly vague about their son's living arrangements and knew only that he was being cared for by friends. In "The Story of a Lie," reconciliation comes only when the son, Dick, falls seriously ill. Then the Squire nurses him and asks for his forgiveness. In real life, reconciliation was not quite as neat. When Thomas learned that Louis had become ill after caring for his landlady's son, his concern took the form of a rebuke. "What an idiot you were to act as a nurse," he wrote in a curt note. "When will you learn to take care of yourself."

Then Thomas heard of his son's hemorrhage from Baxter. He also learned, possibly via a letter from Fanny to Sitwell intended for that purpose, that money was needed immediately to get Louis to the higher and drier climate his doctor insisted on. By mid-April, Thomas wired his son, "Count on £250 annually." Louis was ecstatic. His parents could not change overnight—Margaret still fretted about how to put the best public face on the situation—but their touching effort to finally accept his unorthodox life choices showed how desperately they loved their son and did not want to lose ties with him.

The Stevensons' gesture of support provided practical, as well as psychological, relief. Louis could afford to have his painful, rotting teeth removed and replaced with dentures. He could get a vital break from the enormous pressure to produce that had pushed him to the point of collapse. On sunny days, he could lounge in the warmth of Fanny's garden, where the blossoming fruit trees and roses were dazzling.

Despite Nellie's fury about Fanny's marriage in her letter home (which she may have exaggerated to stay in the family's good graces), she would warmly remember Louis during his recovery at the Oakland house. He was surprised by the "mechanical cleverness of American women" and watched as she and Fanny cut, fit, and sewed their own clothes. Other times he amused them by talking in broad Scots with a Highland nasal twang "until we cried for mercy." With Nellie sometimes acting as amanuensis, Louis wrote the first part of his book *Prince Otto* and dedicated it to her when it was published in 1885. Nellie would later name her son Louis.

Finally, after several weeks, Louis was just well enough to take a ferry across the bay to San Francisco to be wed. He and Fanny had not held out for the full year their families had pressed them to wait before marrying, but they refused to wait any longer.

FOR A ROMANTIC, Louis was grimly honest when he later described his wedding day, May 19, 1880, to a friend:

> *It was not my bliss that I was interested in when I was married; it was a sort of marriage in* extremis; *and if I am where I am, it is thanks to the care of that lady who married me when I was a mere complication of cough and bones, much fitter for an emblem of mortality than a bridegroom.*

To save money, the couple took a cable car instead of a hansom cab from the Ferry House up Nob Hill to the Williams home. Virgil was out of town, but Dora walked with them from there to the home of Reverend William Anderson Scott. They must have seemed an odd couple to him: the stick-thin boy-man, his face ghostly but for his burning brown eyes, and the dark woman with equally piercing eyes and a graying mane of curls, who came up no higher than his heart. The couple fudged the facts they gave Scott for the marriage record. Fanny was boldly honest about her age, forty, but shamelessly declared herself a widow. Louis claimed to be thirty years old, narrowing the age gap between them by a year. With Dora acting as both best man and bridesmaid, they exchanged vows and plain silver rings. Then the threesome went to a Viennese bakery for a "grand blow out of ices."

Fanny and Louis were now officially respectable. And they spent their wedding night at the appropriately fashionable Palace Hotel, the largest and grandest hotel in the western United States. They arrived by carriage, stepping down under the spectacular soaring glass roof onto the marble-tiled promenade. They strolled along the balustraded balconies overlooking the courtyard, the place to see and be seen in San Francisco. Anyone might think that they had left their odd, bohemian ways behind. But it was the last luxury they would enjoy for a while. A few days later, pockets drained, they left for their eccentric honeymoon. They would spend it squatting on an abandoned silver mine.

FANNY, LOUIS, LLOYD, and Chuchu, their dog, headed to the Napa Valley, where a number of consumptives had fled for the supposed healing powers of the fresh air and spring water on Mount St. Helena. Hearing of an abandoned mining camp up the mountain where they might stay rent free, they managed the steep, stony ascent in a double buggy until they had to climb a wooden ladder mounted on the hillside to get to their future lodgings.

The Silverado Mine had been bored into the earth just eight years earlier. But the venture went bust without ever managing to boom, short-circuiting starry-eyed plans for a prosperous city with street names like Ruby, Gold, and Garnet. On a triangular platform covered with rubble, three wooden sheds were wedged up the canyon wall like steps under an overhang of red rock. The first building had been the assayer's office. Now a single door panel, smashed and splintered, twisted there in the breeze. Branches of bay leaves clambered in through the empty window frames and a spray of poison oak was thriving through a hole in the floor. The second and third sheds contained three-tiered miners' bunks—eighteen beds in all—and more litter. For the duration of their stay, the honeymooners, and Lloyd, would need to walk outside and climb a plank to an open doorway suspended in midair to get to their shared bedroom.

With scraps of lumber and iron strewn around the buildings, the place was a dump, literally. In his memoir of the experience, *The Silverado Squatters*, Louis would admit that his vision of a mining ghost town had been a bit more romantic—"a clique of neighbourly houses on a village green, we shall say, all empty to be sure, but swept and varnished; a trout stream brawling by; great elms or chestnuts, humming with bees and nested in by song-birds."

A veteran of slapdash silver mining camps, Fanny's expectations were more grounded. After Louis ceremoniously cut away the poison oak growing through the floor, she took over. She made doors and windows out of light frames and cotton, using leather from discarded boots for door hinges. Out of scraps of wood and packing crates, she nailed together furniture. The mouth of the mine became her cooler for dried peaches, wine, and the fresh milk she had brought up the mountain daily. She hung pigeons, wild ducks, and other game bought from local hunters there. A stove and hay for the bunks were also hauled up the mountain.

When it was livable—"the beds made, the plates on the rack, the pail of bright water behind the door, the stove crackling in a corner"—Louis called it a fine example of "man's order, the little clean spots that he creates to dwell in." But it was a woman's ingenuity that created this "little clean spot." Louis was what the Scots call a "handless" man. When he wrote, "We had repaired the worst of the damages," we can assume it was Fanny who wielded the hammer and saw. This was to become the way they worked together. Whenever the irrepressible Louis felt an urge to move—for his health, to follow a dream, or out of simple boredom—Fanny made it happen. In this case, her imagination transformed an abandoned mine into a homey lodging; his imagination infused it with a mythic quality in *The Silverado Squatters*.

In their private castle in the air, Fanny and Louis could play with the strict gender roles of their day. Fanny, on her knees as she pounded a nail into place, might look up to see Louis lounging in the sunlight, draped in her shawl and wearing her mushroom hat backward with the feather drooping over his nose. Though her handyman skills gave Fanny an unusual domestic stature, this was not always to her benefit as a creative person. Louis's writing talent gave him the loftiest role in their family. But he wore his crown with ease and style, never imposing his domestic authority in a heavy-handed or entitled manner.

Fanny appreciated that Louis was not a typical husband, bellowing orders and expecting them to be instantly obeyed. She noticed his lax sense of authority early in their marriage, even in his whimsical relations with the family dog. In a letter to Dora, almost her only correspondence to survive from this period, Fanny described how Louis fruitlessly scolded Chuchu when the pooch scattered his slippers everywhere: "The difference between Louis' severity of discipline in theory, and shameless indulgence in practice in regard to Chuchu's education is amusing. Let us hope it will be the same with his wife."

Louis had been unnerved by the specter of earthquakes in San Francisco, but in Silverado he and his new family were truly living on shifting ground. They could hardly walk outside without sinking and sliding or tearing their shoes on the sharp rocks. Tunnels and mine shafts wound through the ground under them. At any moment, their makeshift quarters could collapse into a shaft or give way and carry them tumbling down the hill. At night, the yowls of coyotes and foxes sounded ominously close through the cracks in the walls and cloth doors. During the day, rattlesnakes whirred "like spinning wheels" on every side. But for two months, Fanny could give Louis the rest he had been longing for.

After a few morning chores, Louis was free to rest, wander, and write. Apparently, his recuperation did not forbid cigarettes, even as he had to be hauled halfway up a mountain to breathe crystal pure mountain air. Drinking alcohol was also routine. Fanny served frothy rum punch, sprinkled with cinnamon, midmorning and midafternoon every day. And at Schramsberg Winery, he tasted eighteen wines in one sitting—an impressive feat even for a man in robust health.

SHELTERING IN A PLACE where life went "rustically forward" appealed to Louis. One of the liveliest character sketches of his Silverado neighbors featured a quintessentially American character, the country rube. Irvine Lovelands, one of a local clan of squatters, was beautiful, brawny, and brutish. He seemed incapable of reading or reflection, Louis wrote, "and yet you were conscious that he was one of your own race, that his mind was cumbrously at work, revolving the problem of existence like a quid of gum." Hired by Louis to do odd jobs, he would work only as long as Fanny stood over him praising his strength. "I do not think I ever appreciated the meaning of two words until I knew Irvine," he went on, "—the verb, loaf, and the noun, oaf; between them, they complete his portrait."

Another sketch of a Russian Jewish merchant and his family, who helped Fanny and Louis find the mine where they would stay, is jarring for a modern reader because of its casual use of ethnic stereotypes. Using the pseudonym Kelmar, Louis painted Morris Friedberg as a somewhat scheming usurer. Kelmar's wife and children also had a "chink of money" in their speech. Yet Louis intended it as an affectionate portrait. "Few people have done my heart more good;" he wrote of the family, "they seemed so thoroughly entitled to happiness and to enjoy it in so large measure and so free from after-thought; almost they persuaded me to be a Jew." Louis's caricature and language were not unusual for a writer of his time, and he was shocked when a friend later charged him with anti-Semitism. Still, the sketch is surprising considering the enlightenment he usually expressed in his New World writing.

AFTER NEARLY TWO MONTHS, the squatters abandoned their perch, before the seasonal wet evening fog began settling into gullies and mountain crevices and Louis's lungs. His health was strong enough for an ocean voyage, and he longed to see Scotland and his parents. With Fanny's help, his relations with them were improving. Undoubtedly it was she who had seen that they had photos taken after their wedding to give Margaret something tangible to show at dinner parties.

The photo of Fanny could not be more different from the one she had taken the previous decade, before she walked out on her first husband to study art in France. The open face, messy hair, and man's cravat were gone. In place of the New Woman was a coiffed, dignified specimen of the San Francisco bourgeoisie. A hat suppressed her unruly curls and a string of beads at her neck reinforced the modesty of her high-collared frock. A large cross hung prominently—and, one feels, rather heavily—on her chest. This Fanny was calculated to please—and she did. The photo helped Margaret to sweep her worst imaginings under the rug. "I hope you both understand that I don't care for ancient history at all—know nothing about it," Margaret could write cheerily to the newlyweds by summer. From then on, she wanted only to hear of their future.

Before leaving the U.S., Louis and Fanny sent letters to their respective new in-laws. Intended to smooth relations, the letters also reveal the newlyweds' separate anxieties about what lay ahead. Fanny knew she was on trial and desperately wanted Louis's parents and friends to approve of her. Tactfully and painstakingly, she assured Margaret that she had no interest in trying to usurp the special bond between mother and son. She empathized with the Stevensons' emotional ordeal the previous year and suggested that they would take comfort in the fact that Louis had emerged from his journey and illness a better man.

Attentive to even the smallest details, Fanny corrected Margaret's mistaken impression that her new daughter-in-law was financially more sensible than her son, adding that Louis's genius outweighed his ineptitude in money matters. Fanny also insisted that the photo of her was flattering. "I do so earnestly hope that you will like me," she wrote with disarming honesty, "but that can only be for what I am to you after you know me, and I do not want you to be disappointed in the beginning in anything about me; even in so small a thing as my looks."

Louis's letter to Fanny's brother, Jake Vandegrift, was a sober assessment of their situation—and a poignant assurance that Fanny's future was secure whatever should happen to him. Louis feared that Fanny had not been fully truthful with her family about the gravity of his condition, he wrote, perhaps because she did not recognize it herself. But he felt his brother-in-law had a right to know. "If I can keep well next winter I have every reason to hope the best; but on the other hand, I may very well never see next spring," Louis wrote. He was taking his wife and stepson to Scotland because he was anxious for his parents to meet them. His father, a world-respected lighthouse engineer, would take care of Fanny and her son should he die. He closed with a wish: "I feel very ready to like you, if you will let me."

IN LATE JULY, Louis, Fanny, and Lloyd set out by train for New York and then by ship to Britain. They traveled first class all the way, courtesy of Thomas Stevenson. They would arrive in Liverpool on August 17, 1880, a year to the day after Louis had reached New York. He departed San Francisco a husband, a stepfather, and, Nellie wrote, "a citizen of the world."

Louis's friends—and many Stevenson scholars—would blame Fanny for the damage that his pursuit of her had wreaked on his health, but with her he had also become more serious about his work. Two years after his wedding, he wrote to the painter Trevor Haddon about fate as it relates to marriage or the kind of love that comes on suddenly and overturns your life: "I call that your fate, because then, if not before, you can no longer hang back, but must stride out into life and act." Louis equated his love for Fanny with liberation and action. It challenged him to take risks in his personal life that, on some level, both he and Fanny seemed to sense would enrich his work. Their intimations were correct.

As they sailed for Scotland, Louis was going home, but Fanny was heading into an uncertain future, away from her home, her friends, and her daughter. She would have to adapt to a new culture and way of life and face a social circle that was undoubtedly suspicious, if not hostile, toward her. As Henley had already written to Louis, "If she doesn't make you happy, I shall think her ungrateful and care but little for her." Fanny had no illusions that her new life would be easy. In some ways, sailing to Britain as Louis's wife was her bravest journey yet.

It would be eight years before Fanny and Louis would return to San Francisco, but it was inevitable that they would. The city was a "port of entry to another world"—to the distant island paradises that now filled Louis's head with dreams. The waves that rolled beyond the Golden Gate could carry them to a life that he could envision only in his most teeming imagination. "I stood there on the extreme shore of the West," *The Wrecker*'s Loudon Dodd says as he looks out from the Cliff House over the vast reach of the Pacific. One day Louis and Fanny would leave the West behind and set sail for those wilder shores.

NINE

eriot Row, a line of identical mansion facades of polished ashlar, loomed like a palace, or fortress, before Fanny when she arrived in Edinburgh. Everything about it—the restrained ironwork trim, the ornate lampposts, the sunburst fanlights framing the entryways—exuded elegance and authority. It was a long way from the sagging wooden cottage in Oakland, where the walls heaved in and out in a strong wind. The closest Fanny had ever come to such affluence was when she sewed for the nouveau riche in San Francisco and Virginia City.

From the moment she had met the elder Stevensons when the *City of Chester* landed in Liverpool, they were accommodating. Lloyd, now twelve and curiously looking more like Louis, had helped break the ice. Rambunctious after ten days at sea, he had made a ruckus at the hotel where the family was staying, but Margaret melted when the maid chasing him assumed he was Louis's son by birth. At dinner, Lloyd entertained everyone by marveling that the fish was served "with their skins off" and ordering a lemonade. "A lemonade!" Thomas Stevenson bellowed. "What is a lemonade?" The family patriarch then explained that "in this barbarous country," a lemonade was unknown, but he asked for a lemon so Lloyd could make his own.

Fanny knew that Louis's gentle strong-arming from California had helped smooth the way for her with his parents. "If you can love my wife," he had written to them, "it will, I believe, make me love both her and you the better." How his friends would greet her was a different matter. Sidney Colvin had been cordial when he came to meet their ship in Liverpool, but Fanny found it difficult to read people's true feelings in a country that seemed to wear politeness like a mask. Fortunately, she did not see Colvin's chilling, racist-tinged report to William Henley later that day. Louis might be happy enough with his new wife, Colvin wrote, but "whether you and I will ever get reconciled to the little determined brown face and white teeth and grizzling (for that's what it's up to) grizzling hair, which we are to see beside him in the future—that is another matter."

At 17 Heriot Row, under the lofty ceilings and soaring oval skylight above the spiral staircase, Fanny seemed even smaller and darker—or, as another of Louis's friends would obliquely put it, "darker than one would expect for a woman of Dutch heritage." The downstairs staff whispered about her. When two maids were gossiping about a Scot who had recently married a black woman from Africa, one saw Fanny approaching and quickly hushed the other, glancing pointedly at Louis's wife. Another commented that Fanny "spoke English very well for a foreigner."

By the time the Stevensons threw a dinner party to celebrate their son's marriage and welcome his new wife, her nerves must have been on edge. Fanny knew as well as anyone that the evening would be a chance for friends and relatives to study Louis's pistol-packing, olive-skinned American bride and assess whether he had made as big a mistake in marrying her as they believed.

The house was at its finest. Silver gleamed on the large mahogany dinner table and candlelight bounced off the stately paned-glass windows. As the guests gathered for dinner, however, Fanny and Thomas Stevenson became acquainted with each other's tempers. When the roast was served, Thomas fumed that it was overdone. Then he turned his wrath on the wilting maids in front of the dinner guests. Fanny looked to someone to defend the women, but the party fell silent. (Among the well-to-do, apologizing to household staff was considered so "ridiculous," in Louis's words, he had once wrestled with the idea for days before asking a servant he had treated harshly to pardon him.) When no one intervened, Fanny jumped to her feet and scolded Thomas for bullying someone who was not in a position to answer back. If he did so again, she added, she would leave his home. Shocked and chagrined, Thomas regained his composure and gently bid her to sit down.

The story of this confrontation became legendary in the Vandegrift family, emblematic of how the stern and daunting patriarch met his match in his son's tiny fireball of a mate. Like most family legends, it was likely embellished as it was handed down, but it is not difficult to believe some version of it happened. Fanny hated injustice and loved an underdog. She was as headstrong as Thomas and even more likely to lash out with anger that she usually regretted. There is no record of how the party guests responded, but Louis's maternal uncle, George Balfour, meeting Fanny for the first time, was amused by his nephew's cheeky bride. Evoking the Scottish slang for a woman who is a handful (literally, the term for a broom), he chuckled to Louis, "I married a *besom* myself and I have never regretted it."

For the most part, however, Fanny found Thomas charming. "The father is a most lovely old person" who is "hustled about, according to the humors of his wife and son, in the most amusing way" was her novel assessment of him to Dora Williams. "Occasionally he comes in with twinkling eyes and reports a comic verse of his own making with infinite gusto." Fanny met Thomas when he was an older man, and she could be freer and more generous with him than his son, who never quite broke away from his father's ironhanded control. And Thomas was not put off that Fanny spoke her mind—he liked her saucy independence. Soon they bonded over their love for dogs, their forceful characters, and even their mood swings. He called her "the Vandergrifter" and "Cassandra" when she made gloomy prophecies, and she called him "Uncle Tom" or "Master Tommy." Within a few weeks, Louis could tell Bob Stevenson that his wife was getting along with his parents better than he had even dared hope.

Fanny was shrewdly aware that Louis's mental and physical health hinged on a smoother relationship with his father. She became an essential bridge between the two men—easing the emotional stress on Louis and his mother as well. Margaret soon felt that Fanny fit well into the household. "It was quite amusing how entirely she agreed with my husband on all subjects, even to looking on the dark side of most things, while Louis and I were more inclined to take the cheery view," she wrote in her diary.

Fanny's assessment of Margaret was equally adroit. "She is adored by her husband who spoils her like a baby; both I can see, have spoiled Louis," she wrote to Dora. Fanny noted that Margaret differed from her son in one respect: She was usually well-dressed and clean, while he was rarely either. For Margaret, fashion was second to religion, and she insisted on attiring the whole family in wedding garments—"what my mother significantly calls 'getting a few things in the meantime,'" Louis groaned to a friend. She immediately set about lavishing gowns and jewelry on her daughter-in-law.

She "plays dolls with me," Fanny reported to Dora. "She buys everything she can find in the shops for me, and is continually searching in drawers and boxes for things of her own to give me. When everything is exhausted she puts on her dressing gown and has a good time trying her own things upon me." Even Lloyd was aghast at the plunder from one of Margaret's shopping sprees for Fanny, which he enumerated in a letter to his sister: a dinner dress and walking dress, a walking cape, three pairs of gloves, a lace collar and cuffs, a black lace tie, a bonnet with yellow flowers, ruffling, and artificial red berries.

Margaret may have had another motive for showering Fanny with clothes: She felt her daughter-in-law's wardrobe was somewhat lacking in female frippery. "I have to dress properly and wear fallals and things, which is something of a cross to me, though not so much," Fanny confessed to her American friend. For the most part, though, she was thrilled and grateful. She wrote to Belle that she was dressing as her daughter had always wished her to, like a lady. More important, Fanny was overcome by the Stevensons' warmth and generosity in welcoming her and her son into the family. "They are the best and noblest people in the world, both of them," she later gushed to Belle, "and I can hardly write about them now without tears in my eyes. Every day, almost, I come upon fresh proofs of their thought for our comfort or pleasure."

Fanny tried to please her new in-laws up to a point—she held off on wearing black stockings when they came into fashion because Thomas found white stockings more modest, for example. But she also needed to be accepted for herself. She boldly skipped Sunday services when the rest of the family, including Lloyd, dutifully trooped off to church. ("Religion seems a thing to be serious about, but not to do monkey tricks over," she once wrote brazenly to her devout mother-in-law.) Instead, amusing herself by rummaging through Louis's wardrobe, she was shocked to find it "filled with every manner of garment that a man could possibly wear under any circumstances, and some too gorgeous to wear at all." She marveled at the selection of elegant men's underwear of silk cord "that just fit me, and which I at once appropriated, having one on at this identical moment." She suggested that her equally unconventional pal try to find some for herself in San Francisco.

While Louis dozed off during the Sunday sermon, Fanny, prancing around at home in his underwear, had a divine revelation: She could upgrade her husband's slovenly look. "This was the creature that Mr. Williams took for a tramp," she joked. "The tramp days are over, and this poor boy is now, for the rest of his life to be dressed like a gentleman." But her grand plan quickly fizzled. Louis was already cross that he had to be "brushed every morning"— a routine more suggestive of dog grooming. When Fanny set about playing dolls with *him*, dressing him up in smoking jackets and dressing gowns, he swiftly grew bored and barricaded himself behind a book. Rich or poor, Louis would always be wedded to his strange and singular style. His wife would have to content herself with ordering the same cut of velvet jacket from the same tailor every few years for the rest of their married life.

FOR LOUIS, the return to Edinburgh was not entirely a success. He arrived with a new appreciation for his parents and his hometown—"He was a citizen of the world, but a native of Edinburgh," a friend noted. But his lungs did not thrive in his native climate. His physician uncle, George Balfour, advised Louis and Fanny to hasten to a costly new tuberculosis sanatorium in

Davos, Switzerland, for the "Alpine cure." Balfour's opinion was seconded by Andrew Clark, the London doctor who had sent Louis to Menton for the "Mediterranean cure" for his nervous breakdown years before. Since the death of the poet John Keats at the age of twenty-five in 1821, consumption and creative genius were often linked. Until the bacillus that caused tuberculosis was discovered in 1882, delicate, overwrought young men like Louis, who were believed to spend too much time indoors reading or in deep thought, were considered ripe for "the decline."

The return home was also a stark reminder that Thomas was not ready to soften his grip on his son's career. He insisted that Louis's American travelogue, *The Amateur Emigrant,* be withdrawn on the eve of its publication. This was reminiscent of his attempt to quash Louis's first literary effort, *The Pentland Rising*, when his son was a teenager. But now Louis was a man and the book was ready to go to press.

The road to publication had never been easy. Louis disliked the publisher, C. Kegan Paul, who he felt continually underpaid him and had rejected his "Suicide Club" stories for book publication. In letters, Louis referred to the journal Paul edited, the *New Quarterly*, as the "New Tarterly" and "Paul's withered babe." In Silverado, when Louis had received galley proofs of the first half of the book, about his sea voyage on the *Devonia*, he could see Paul shared Colvin's view that he had strained the boundaries of decency with his gritty account of travel conditions for lower-class emigrants. Colvin and Paul had heavily marked out graphic journalistic depictions of degradation and squalor—such as Louis's characterization of the steerage living quarters as "pens" where passengers were corralled like "human animals"—allegedly because they might harm Louis's literary reputation.

According to Stevenson expert Julia Reid, "the breaching of bodily boundaries between classes" was particularly problematic. Louis had made his "itch" a symbol of common suffering, linking him to the working-class passengers, heedless of Britain's carefully structured social order. This challenged the prevailing belief that conditions such as scabies were exclusive to the "great unwashed" lower classes. Louis's vignette about inadvertently kneeling in a steerage passenger's vomit as he stooped to help him was also marked "*Intolerably* nasty" and the man's gentlemanly offer of his handkerchief to clean it off was "pompous and feeble" and "Must Come out at all costs." It was bad enough that the steerage passengers "stewed together in their own exhalations" (also marked for deletion); the idea that a man of Louis's social stature was stewing with them was unacceptable.

Weary of the whole project by then, Louis had accepted most of their changes. But now, Thomas Stevenson was determined to block even the bowdlerized version of the book. Thomas was an associate of partners in the Anchor Line, which owned the *Devonia*. Not only had Louis criticized the crew's treatment of steerage passengers, he had noted that the steamship line was preferred by stowaways and offered some of their tips for free passage. Louis did not name the ship or the parent company, and he would propose further modifying any possible connection to the Anchor Line in the text, but Thomas was adamant. It was Louis's worst piece of writing to date, he insisted. Indebted to his father, Louis had little choice but to acquiesce, and Thomas paid off Kegan Paul to withdraw it.

The first half of *The Amateur Emigrant* would not be published in Louis's lifetime. A censored version was included in a collection of his work a year after his death, but it was decades before his honest depiction of British class society at sea appeared in print as he wrote it. However well-intentioned, the attempts by colleagues and publishers to control his style and reputation were in essence an attempt to inhibit his growth as a writer—to keep him in a safely picturesque world of donkey treks and canoe trips. His contemporaries did not understand that Louis had moved beyond them; they had not traveled outside themselves as he had. Provocative social commentary and realism would not fully reemerge in his writing until his father was dead and Louis had turned his back on the oppressive respectability of Britain for the last time.

THOMAS STEVENSON'S LATEST assault on Louis's creativity made his son even more desperate to socialize with his friends in London on the way to wintering in the Alps. Arriving at the luxurious Grosvenor Hotel with a fragile husband, a rambunctious boy, a puppy, and a kitten, his exhausted wife wanted nothing more than to settle into their room to rest. But before Fanny could ease the hat off her aching head, Colvin, Henley, and Bob burst through the door. Louis would be in London less than two weeks, and they were not going to lose a minute of time with him. His mates left by midnight, but it was just the beginning of a procession of Savile Club members and friends who filled their room "from early morning until all hours of the night," Fanny wrote to Margaret—almost as if Louis were still a single man. The couple's stay there was an excuse for his friends to celebrate Louis's narrow escape from death and tempt him into a few more boozy flings before he submitted to the invalid regimen in Davos.

A handful of women dropped by, but Louis was thirsting for male camaraderie. This was not the time for polite drawing room conversation where, he would write in his two-part essay "Talk and Talkers," dangerous topics were smuggled out of the room until they could be "reintroduced with safety in an altered shape" and discussion between the sexes smoldered at exactly the point where it caught fire among men. In his essay, Louis did not blame this phenomenon on women but on their subjection—their conditioning from birth to please and tolerate the "infantile vanity" of men. The female social arts, he wrote in surprisingly feminist rhetoric, were "the arts of a civilised slave among good-natured barbarians." Outside the drawing room, and especially in marriage, men had much to learn from women.

Still, there was something in the infantile vanity, the flush-cheeked bluster, the amicable combativeness, the "racy flesh-pots" of conversation between men that was hard to beat. His friends were, after all, some of the most dazzling talkers in a golden age of talk. There was Bob Stevenson, who could "create for you a view you never held, and then furiously fall on you for holding it." There was burly William Henley, who roared you down and then flooded you with admiration. (Oscar Wilde, whom Henley once knocked over with his crutch, observed that conversing with him was "a physical no less than an intellectual recreation.") And there was Edmund Gosse, who dropped crystals of wit "so polished that the dull do not perceive it, but so right that the sensitive are silenced." The best talk—talk between spiritual brothers—was "as deep as love in the constitution of our being." And the man at the center of the weeklong bromance orgy was Louis. Men came alive in the glow of his company. To his friend Andrew Lang, Louis's personal magnetism "excited a passionate admiration and affection, so much so that I verily believe some men were jealous of other men's place in his liking."

For Fanny, it was a week of torture—and a glimpse at the future contours of her life as his wife. She certainly was not uncomfortable in groups of men, from silver miners to the artists at Grez, where she alluringly combined a kind of feminine coyness with tomboy fellowship. But among those men, she was treated as an equal and even adored; here she was an intrusion. Much as Yoko Ono would be blamed for the Beatles' breakup nearly a century later, Fanny would be seen as ruining the boys' club, the circle of men who would compete even with her for prominence in Louis's life—an awkward situation that the beloved man in the center would do little to assuage. Fanny sat smiling like a "hypocritical Cheshire Cat," she wrote to Margaret Stevenson, "talking stiff nothings with one and another in order to let Louis have a chance with the one he cares the most for."

It is easy to understand Louis's starvation for the particular pleasures of male camaraderie, however unwise the carousing that accompanied it may have been for a man about to check into a sanatorium. But one can also sympathize with Fanny. Just five months into her marriage—and after staying for two months with her new in-laws—she rarely had a moment to herself or alone with her husband. She desperately missed female companionship but felt snubbed by some of the wives in Louis's circle and even his cousin Katharine de Mattos. A longing for female camaraderie would haunt her throughout her marriage, as Louis's medical problems and the couple's nomadic search for a salubrious climate would make it difficult for her to build or sustain friendships with women.

Just months after nursing Louis toward some degree of health in California, Fanny was also trying to make sure he stayed well. Watching the clock as the men pounded down another round, she found herself "thirsting for their life's blood," she wrote to her mother-in-law. "I am sure they will find me out; that after the clock strikes ten, I begin to hate them." But they had already found her out, or believed they had: Her reputation as a grumpy party pooper was established on this trip. It was a thankless role she resented but would feel forced to assume for her husband's sake.

As Fanny feared, the whirlwind visit soon took a toll: Louis's health broke down. And the bill for their stay at the opulent hotel was so exorbitant, he needed to wire his parents for more funds to get them to the Swiss Alps before winter closed in.

WEEKS LATER, ROBERT LOUIS STEVENSON stood at the crest of a hill, contemplating the steep drop below. He was a mile high—about as close as you could get to the stars—and everywhere crescents of snow light sparkled back at the moon. Taking a deep gulp of frosty Alpine air, he sat down on his toboggan and pushed off. The long wooden sled slipped out from under the trees, then gathered speed until it plunged into a mad downhill flight, whirling around corners and racing blindly through shadows. Below him, the lights of the invalid community flickered in the valley, but for a few exhilarating moments of "joyful horror," that world vanished.

Since he arrived at Davos, tobogganing had become Louis's latest mania. And sledding alone at night added to the thrill. Louis said he'd prefer to die of anything but illness, and making the icy run in darkness was certainly one way to tempt fate. But for him, right then, tobogganing was also a way to control fate. On the days when he and Fanny took the headlong plunge together, he might pretend for a few moments that they were on an adventure.

Among the consumptive clientele at the Hotel Belvedere, the Stevensons had quickly become a hot topic of gossip: the chain-smoking divorcée who carried herself like Napoleon, the quivering long-haired husband, the boy who called his stepfather "Louis" and was allowed to read anything he wanted, and the ill-tempered black Skye terrier, Walter (most often referred to by his nickname "Woggs"). But the moonlight tobogganing was appalling. "He stayed in bed when he should have been out of doors and when he should have been in bed he played the fool with the toboggan," a fellow patient grumbled.

For the thirty-year-old writer in the winter of 1880, tobogganing was an affirmation of life. Tuberculosis was continuing its bloody rampage through Britain, killing four million people there between 1850 and 1910. The cool, clean air and bright sunshine of the high Alps were touted as effective treatments. Whatever the benefits of fresh air, about half the people who entered sanatoriums at the time died within five years.

Though Davos pulmonologist Carl Rüedi stopped short of diagnosing consumption, he put Louis on a strict regimen of mental and physical retraining. Cigarettes were banned, wine restricted to a local variety high in tannins, and his diet fueled by large quantities of beef broth and milk. There were set hours for fresh air, writing, and walking on a single straight path.

Louis's preferred approach to illness was to walk away from it until it hobbled him. But in Davos he couldn't walk away—sickness blanketed the mountain like the falling snow. Nearly everyone in the town had TB, and the graves that dusted the slopes on all sides were vivid reminders of how near death hovered. "People you had not seen for some time could usually be found in the cemetery," Lloyd later recalled, "though their intervening travels had been marvelously screened from notice." There was a frantic, desperate edge to the place—love affairs, cliques, and gossip were rampant, though Louis and Fanny tried to keep their heads above the fray.

As hard as it was for Louis to be there, it was no easier for his stepson or wife. Louis tried tutoring Lloyd himself at first, then hired tubercular tutors. One, a former Prussian officer, insisted on sticking a pocketknife down Lloyd's throat to enhance his German accent. The adolescent became lazy about his schoolwork. Though this would seem in keeping with Stevenson family tradition, Louis raised the possibility of a Swiss boarding school if he did not buckle down. Eventually, Fanny and Louis decided that it was healthier for Lloyd to be with a tutor (and later in a boarding school) in

England than in an isolated community of invalids. It may have been the best option under the circumstances, but the specter of yet another family separation in yet another new country must have shaken Lloyd's fragile sense of security.

Meanwhile, to Fanny's surprise, Rüedi cast a critical eye on her health as well. He diagnosed her overweight, in part due to an unnamed stomach disease, and put her on a diet. He also prescribed arsenic. Strangely, both Fanny and Louis thought the arsenic improved her stamina, though it could only have aggravated the heart and stomach problems she was developing.

Fanny had always been thin and was dismayed about the extra flesh accumulating on her five-foot frame. "It seems the fashion to be fat, and that's an advantage; I am quite in the Parisien [sic] style with my high shoulders and my stumpy fatness," she would write to Margaret. "All the same I hate it, and hate to see it in others." Her ever-skinny husband did not seem to mind and perhaps even envied and took pride in her plumpness, though he was surprisingly insensitive to her feelings, sometimes almost to the point of cruelty. "Her legs caved in owing to being no longer equal to the carriage of her fat body," he joked to Belle and Nellie Sanchez in one letter, describing Fanny elsewhere as a "barrel of butter." Fanny buried her pride and was as good-natured about his merciless teasing as she was about her new diet.

Louis's bride tried to make the best of her life among the sick and dying. She wrote in letters about the "little kindnesses going on that warm the heart" and encouraged Louis to take flowers to a girl near death on her nineteenth birthday. She busied herself sewing berets and painting pictures for the church bazaar and good-naturedly accepted being cast as an American "Indian squaw" in a theatrical. But sometimes her isolation and claustrophobia made her feel as if she might suffocate.

One of the few pleasures, for Louis especially, was a new male friendship. Violent hemorrhaging had sent the British Renaissance historian John Addington Symonds to the town, where he had settled permanently with his wife, Catherine, and their daughters. Symonds was a rigorous scholar who was appalled by the gaps in Louis's classical education and what he saw as his intellectual shallowness; Louis found Symonds more interesting as a companion than as a writer. But in their Alpine prison, a friendship flourished. Symonds was one of the few friends who liked Fanny and found the couple's story admirable; he would correspond with her later and remember her as Louis's "eager, gifted wife."

At the age of twenty-four, Symonds had been advised to marry to "cure" his desire for men; he had realized on his wedding night it did not. When he read Whitman's "Calamus" poems a year later, the justification of male love he saw in them changed his life. He quietly began to have sexual relationships with men, an amusement to which his wife reluctantly consented. By the time Louis and Fanny met him, the forty-year-old had written a study of Greek poets that defended homosexuality and published a translation of Michelangelo's sonnets to Tommaso dei Cavalieri with the male pronouns restored.

Symonds was part of a network of late-nineteenth-century queer male British and American writers that included Louis's friend Edmund Gosse, who had provided him with the introduction to Symonds. At the time, Gosse was happily married and claimed to remain so for fifty years. But he had also fallen in love with the sculptor William Hamo Thornycroft and would feel stubborn desires for men his whole life.

While the correspondence between these writers reveals their tacit understanding, their lives show how utterly alone each of them was in deciding how far to push homosexuality into the public eye. When Symonds urged Whitman to be more explicit about the homoeroticism in "Calamus," the poet acted shocked, issuing his famous disclaimer that his six illegitimate children proved he was "normal." (Perhaps he was unaware that Symonds had fathered four children.) At the time of his death from tuberculosis at fifty-two, Symonds was writing a bold account of his own sexual awakening, often hailed as the first self-conscious gay memoir, though it was not published until 1984. Gosse understandably chose to stay in the shadows. But he also helped strip the homoerotic content from a posthumous biography of Symonds and burned papers allegedly to protect his friend's reputation, something Symonds would have abhorred. Symonds had hoped his own story would help a generation of Victorian men who felt guilty, isolated, and tormented by their sexuality—ironically, men like Gosse, who confessed to Symonds that repressing his desires had made him feel like "a man buried alive and conscious, but deprived of speech."

It is intriguing to imagine whether the double lives of friends such as Gosse, Symonds, and Stoddard were fodder for the creator of Henry Jekyll and Edward Hyde. How much Fanny and Louis knew about that side of their queer friends' lives is unknown, but neither of them seemed to be uncomfortable or judgmental about homosexuality at a time when Victorian mores cast it as vile and degrading.

Winter in Davos seemed to help Louis in spite of himself. "I feel pretty sure that he never did any systematic open-air cure, or systematic anything," Symonds's frequent visitor Horatio Brown recalled. "He lived a far from invalid life, except when he broke down and retired to bed." Louis did not hemorrhage while they were there, possibly because he cut back on cigarettes, but he did not write much either. He felt crippled by the defeated consumptive mentality—one that novelist Thomas Mann would describe years later in his tragic portrayal of a Davos sanatorium, *The Magic Mountain*.

Newly conscious of the "wolverine on my own shoulders," Louis became obsessed with the deaths of young people. A teenage tobogganing mate found dead in his bed. Two small girls dying together, leaving their mother to return home alone. Then, in early 1881, Frances Sitwell, Colvin's companion and Louis's first muse, arrived in Davos with her surviving son, Bertie, who had become ill suddenly at the age of eighteen. For Louis, Bertie brought to mind fond memories of summer days and piggyback rides. Yet Louis found himself numb, uncharacteristically paralyzed between callous indifference and a horror that woke him at night.

Fanny helped tend to Bertie, though it conjured nightmares of her own son's death. Comforts were sought to strengthen his fragile hold on life—a puppet theater, a toboggan—and briefly his health rallied. But the teenager had "galloping consumption," the most malignant form of the disease, which could kill in weeks. By April he was dead, his body strapped onto a bobsled and whisked away to take its place among the community of the dead on the mountain.

❧

AGAINST HIS DOCTOR'S ORDERS, Louis—accompanied by Fanny and Woggs—hurried down from the mountain soon after. The couple ran out of cash en route to Scotland and were forced to extend their stay in a hotel in St. Germain, France, until they received money from Thomas to pay the bill. Five professionally barren months in Davos—"like a violin hung up"— had left Louis unsure what music was left within him. He was more nervous and excitable than ever, and in Paris he spit blood. Fanny's spirits dipped when she saw that the small health gains her husband had made in the Swiss mountains might already be lost on lower ground. She blamed herself for his setback, as well as for his nervous state, though she knew it was common among sanatorium residents. "There is no denying it, I am too soft," she wrote to Margaret. "I am fit for nothing but a kind of cheap nurse, to insist upon dry boots and shoes, and to look after draughts and things."

Perhaps Fanny sensed the new gossip about her being traded among Louis's friends. Even before she and Louis arrived in London, Henley was campaigning for Louis to part (at least temporarily) from the "schoolgirl of 40," insinuating in a letter to Charles Baxter that their friend's association with Fanny was causing "degeneration in his moral fiber." Henley apparently had expected Louis's wife to introduce order into his life. A later letter was warmer toward Fanny, but Henley could still not help adding that she was lazy, weak, and incompetent, and calling the marriage a mistake. (Perhaps Henley's opinion was colored by the contemporary rage among the British public against another Fanny—John Keats's lover, Fanny Brawne. At the time, Brawne's reputation as shallow and flirtatious—charges also aimed at Fanny Stevenson—was blamed for contributing to Keats's decline and death from consumption.)

Henley's letters set the tone for the way Louis's male friends would perceive Fanny, and many of his biographers seem to have simply adopted their view. Though his circle would offer Fanny varying degrees of acceptance, from grudging tolerance to wary friendship, there would always be an underlying strain of resentment and faultfinding. Nearly everything about her would annoy Louis's brotherhood. As unconventional as some of them might have been, they still had genteel expectations. Penny Fielding, general editor of the *New Edinburgh Edition of the Works of Robert Louis Stevenson*, sums up the strikes against Louis's bride in their eyes: "She was American, ten years older than him, a divorced woman with two children, and an independent, outspoken character who had led a tough life. She had a strong temper and she knew how to shoot a gun."

In other words, Fanny was everything that an orthodox female spouse was not—she did not have "anything in her of my wife, or yours," as Henley reminded Baxter. His friends could not seem to accept that Louis did not want a conventional marriage to a more refined, compliant, and, it must be added, fairer-skinned woman who would have been easier for conventional white Victorian men to bear. Perhaps most offensive, Fanny seemed to have little interest in altering her character to please them. In her way, she resembled one of Henry James's frank and brash American heroines, like Bessie Alden in the novella *An International Episode*. Disillusioned with British society, Alden scoffs, "I don't see why I should regard what's done here. Why should I suffer the restrictions of a society of which I enjoy none of the privileges?"

THE BENEFITS OF FANNY'S creative imagination and steadfast belief in her husband's talent were soon to become quite unmistakable. She had been perplexed by the disparagement of his colleagues, who did not seem to understand that he was professionally in transition. While Louis's colleagues nearly convinced him that his latest work lacked grace, Fanny countered that his voice was getting stronger—"so much fuller of thought, and so much more manly," as she wrote to Margaret. She was convinced that once he joined his old and new styles, "he will do better work than he dreams of now." As his primary and most outspoken critic, Fanny would push for more global context and political engagement in his work.

In the Highland village of Pitlochry, where the couple joined Margaret in June 1881, Louis's artistic juices began to flow again. Shut in by rainy weather, he and Fanny collaborated on a collection of ghoulish "crawlers" that Louis hoped to publish first in periodicals and then gather into a book. With their mutual fondness for stories of witchcraft and the supernatural, Louis and Fanny worked themselves into a frenzy reading their work aloud to each other into the wee hours. Aroused one night by screams from above her bedroom, their hostess, Mrs. Sim, called up her concern from the bottom of the stairs. "It's only Louis and I reading ghost stories to each other, and that last one was too terrible," Fanny called down. "It got on our nerves."

Their two-month joint venture yielded two of Louis's most highly re-garded short stories. "The Merry Men" was about the wreckers who eked out a living looting the carcasses of ships that crashed on Scotland's rocky shores. Wreckers stood only to lose if the seas were safer, so many opposed lighthouse construction, rationalizing that God put the rocks that fractured ships in the sea, so He must have willed the cargo for them. Still, a few were not above nudging God's hand by leaving shipwreck survivors to die or even luring ships to disaster. Louis's family of lighthouse engineers had all faced hostility from wreckers. In his haunting tale, a wrecker driven mad by alco-hol and religious mania internalizes the malevolence of the sea, delighting so much in watching sailors drown that he becomes complicit in one of their deaths.

The creative frisson in the Highland cottage also helped Louis bring to fruition "Thrawn Janet," a Hawthornesque tale that touched on Scotland's witch hunts in the sixteenth and seventeenth centuries. In the story, a cleric begins his ministry in a moorland village where the parishioners are con-vinced that Janet is possessed by the devil after her neck becomes thrawn, or twisted, though in reality she has suffered a stroke. The young, liberal min-ister believes he can use reason to drive the devil out of the people's minds; instead, his own mind is ultimately overwhelmed and destroyed by the hold of hell and damnation on their imaginations. Henry James would call the story, which Louis enriched with Scots dialect, "a masterpiece in 13 pages."

Years later, Fanny vividly evoked the couple's terror when Louis read the story to her:

> That evening is as clear in my memory as though it were yesterday—the dim light of our one candle, with the acrid smell of the wick that we forgot to snuff, the shadows in the corners of the "lang, laigh, mirk chamber, perishing cauld," the driving rain on the roof close above our heads, and the gusts of wind that shook our windows. . . . By the time the tale was finished my husband had fairly frightened himself, and we crept down the stairs clinging hand in hand like two scared children.

Fanny wrote a Western Gothic story of sorcery and folklore among people of Mexican, Spanish, Native American, and mixed descent in the Monterey area. It is a regional, or local color, narrative—a popular magazine genre in the U.S. and one of the most accessible to female writers. Following the typical format of these stories, Fanny's protagonist, a young white woman traveling west to Monterey, finds herself in an unfamiliar community that she must come to rely on for help. In this case, the woman must testify against a murderer who is also a warlock, or sorcerer, and wills her to die when he is hanged. Fanny's tale had a political edge that the genre often lacked: Monterey appears not just as a picturesque or quaint setting but as an ethnically diverse culture under assault by white expansionism—like the surrounding landscape that was, as one character notes, "denuded of so much forest growth by the rapacity of the Americans." In another departure, Fanny's heroine does not return to mainstream culture largely unchanged by her experience; instead, she absorbs the local folkways and beliefs she initially scoffed at and weds a man of Mexican descent, a marriage of two cultures.

"Thrawn Janet" easily found placement in *Cornhill*, despite the Scots dialect, as did "The Merry Men." Louis sent Fanny's story to Henley, who praised it and was certain he could sell it—a "great lift" for her because she knew he would be brutally honest. But the tale was rejected by the British magazines *Cornhill*, *Longman's*, and *Blackwood's*, where the editor noted that "the heroine would be more apt to stir up the prejudices than the sympathies of my readers." As Lena Wånggren, a scholar of Scottish and feminist literature, has noted, Fanny's California story more likely would have found a home in an American periodical. The story was eventually published as "The Warlock's Shadow" in *Belgravia*, a British magazine once known for sensationalism but by then a serious literary journal.

The Stevensons' joint collection of crawlers never materialized into a book. This was no doubt both a disappointment and a relief to Fanny, who knew that her talent was much more modest than her husband's but was still trying to establish her own identity as a magazine writer. "The only thing I fear is that my work will not be good enough to go into the same book with Louis's upon which he has set his heart," she asserted to Henley. "Mine alone would not be noticed much, but would be brought into such prominence by appearing with Louis's that I feel doubtful whether it is not foolish."

The creative synergy in the Stevenson marriage would continue, as the couple stimulated each other's imagination and mingled ideas. Stevenson scholar Hilary Beattie has noted that elements from Fanny's stories are echoed in Louis's fiction; there are hints of her Western Gothic in his short story "Olalla" and in *Dr Jekyll and Mr Hyde*. "These could be coincidences," Beattie wrote, "but perhaps too are evidence of the ways Stevenson's own work might have gestated in the fertile medium of his and Fanny's mutual storytelling."

As summer wore on, Louis got caught up in a doomed bid for the Chair of History and Constitutional Law at Edinburgh University—a position being vacated by a professor whose only recollection of Louis as a student was his absence from constitutional law lectures. Thomas had suggested the idea to keep his son nearby, but Fanny knew that it would not suit her husband's temperament or his health. And when Louis went to Edinburgh for a couple of days to apply for the position, she found herself "just dying" without him. Waking alone in bed, she wrote to her husband, "My heart beat as though it would break loose." To compensate for his absence, she painted, ate cake, drank too much sherry, and baked a gooseberry tart. But it was to no avail. Though Margaret suggested that a tidy room was one consolation for Louis's absence, Fanny sighed, "I find none myself."

Louis paid for the trip with a heavy cold and a hemorrhage, and the party, joined now by Lloyd and Thomas, moved to Braemar, near Balmoral Castle. The new location brought new nightmares, however. The rain was relentless and the cold bitter even by Highland standards.

For Fanny, who liked to be active and outdoors, being shut inside was difficult. Seeing her restlessness, Margaret bought her a piano cover to decorate with roses. Fanny deftly applied her needle skills and piecework speed to the activity, completing the task within days. "Oh Fanny, how could you?" her mother-in-law exclaimed. "That piece should have lasted you all summer!"

Still, fancywork seemed to placate Margaret's concerns about her daughter-in-law's lack of feminine taste, so Fanny busied herself with it whenever they were together. "I am not allowed to do any useful work," she drolly observed to Dora in the midst of embellishing a tea gown. "A change from old times, that, is it not? A maid darns my stockings while I do high art embroidery in a silk gown. Well there's nothing like change, especially a change for the better."

Despite their differences, Margaret enjoyed Fanny's company. When Fanny attempted to teach her mother-in-law how to swim, Margaret gushed to Cummy, "We have such fun together." Fanny enjoyed Margaret too, but she longed for a friend to whom she could speak more openly. She sorely missed Dora, but it was difficult to share confidences with five thousand miles between them. Still, when Dora sought her advice about a marital problem, Fanny was there to offer counsel. "I am a woman, and always take the woman's part," she wrote. "Much as I like and admire Mr. [Williams], I should not hesitate a moment to advise you to sacrifice him if it were for your own good."

Louis was always made restless by the trappings of conventional domesticity, and never more so than on those long, wet days in the house glumly known as "the late Miss M'Gregor's cottage." The little stone lodging was bursting with oversized personalities. Gosse, visiting on his way to see Hamo

Thornycroft, wrote to his wife, "This is a most entertaining household. All the persons in it are full of character and force: they use fearful language towards one another and no quarrel ensues." Louis felt desperate to escape. As happened so often, the only way out was through his head.

⚓

TREASURE ISLAND FLOWED out of a watercolor—a fantasy of far away painted on a gloomy day in Scotland. Had the downpour in the Highlands let up sooner in the summer of 1881, and had the Stevensons not had a restless boy to entertain, the classic adventure tale might never have been created.

As usual, Fanny had been carrying watercolors with her so that she could paint when she had a chance. During the spongy summer in Braemar, Lloyd had used her paints to turn a room into a watercolor gallery. It is unclear whether Lloyd or Louis painted the map that inspired the famous book. In their separate, embellished recollections, each claims credit, so it seems likely that Lloyd began the drawing and Louis filled it in. As he studied the map, something shimmered here or there through the translucent brushstrokes. Suddenly shiny weapons glinted in the sun, Louis would write in his essay "My First Book." Faces peeped out at him from the imaginary woods. Sun-browned old seamen darted in and out of the shadows. He scribbled in evocative names here and there on the map—Spy-glass Hill, Skeleton Island. In the top right-hand corner, he wrote "Treasure Island." Then, according to his stepson, Louis popped the map into his pocket and disappeared.

"I can recall the little feeling of disappointment I had at losing it," Lloyd later wrote. "After all, it was my map, and had already become very precious owing to its association with pirates."

But very soon Lloyd was to be repaid: From the fertile soil of the map, Louis had begun to write a bare-knuckle adventure, told from a boy's perspective, to amuse his stepson. The family assembled for a reading, and Lloyd was brought in as chief critic. As rain pelted the windows, Louis's rich voice began to tell the story of the fatherless boy Jim Hawkins and the high seas odyssey that would turn him into a man. He acted out each part, twisting his voice and gesturing as the sinister Billy Bones when he tells Jim he sailed with the notorious pirate Captain Flint and knows where his treasure is buried. (In fact, Louis once said he *lived* his characters, and if he ever discovered they were only paper and ink, he wouldn't be able to go on with them.)

Louis reported to Henley that the first two chapters had been a great success with Lloyd, adding that the only challenge was to keep the pirates' language clean. Otherwise, the words just flowed out of him. "No trouble. No strain. . . . No writing," he said, describing the creation of one of the most famous adventure stories of all time, "just drive along as the words come and the pen will scratch!" Although the new venture had begun simply as a playful diversion for Lloyd, Louis already imagined it could pay off as a book. "If this don't fetch the kids, why, they have gone rotten since my day," he boasted to Henley.

For the next several days, the family carried on as if marooned on their own island, surrounded by a watery world of constant rain. But Louis continued to write a chapter a day, so every evening brought a new adventure in the story of Jim's voyage with three British gentlemen and a dubious ship's crew in search of the buried treasure.

In the afternoons, Louis, Lloyd, and Thomas brainstormed about plot twists and island gear. Louis had slipped one outspoken and gutsy female character into the story in the beginning: Jim's mother chastises the "big, hulking, chicken-hearted" townsmen who are too meek to help defend her and her son against pirates coming to ransack her inn. Then she stomps home, sits down next to Billy Bones's corpse, and calmly counts out the money he owed her for his lodging from the dead man's chest of belongings. Otherwise, Lloyd was a stickler on two points: that the story contain no other women and that it consist of one exciting episode after another. Based on an incident from his father's childhood, Louis made Jim fall asleep in an apple barrel on the ship's deck, where he then overhears enough conversation to realize that the crew are pirates planning a mutiny. This colorful note became a turning point, one of the first exciting moments in Jim's journey to manhood, when he realizes "the lives of all the honest men aboard depended on me alone."

In fifteen days, Louis wrote an astonishing fifteen chapters of *The Sea Cook, or Treasure Island: A Story for Boys*. Forbidden to speak or get out of bed in the morning to avert hemorrhages, he was not much more than eyes flashing under a thicket of ruffled hair, Gosse noted. But Louis's head was charged with imaginative energy. As he wrote, he regularly consulted the map, discovering "obvious though unsuspected shortcuts." He used memories of Monterey to create a wild, melancholy island landscape and gave the pirates a catchy sea song:

> *Fifteen men on the dead man's chest—*
> *Yo-ho-ho, and a bottle of rum!*
> *Drink and the devil had done for the rest—*
> *Yo-ho-ho, and a bottle of rum!*

Louis's greatest triumph was the pirate Long John Silver—a complex, gigantic personality who is by turns charming and bloodthirsty. A self-described gentleman of fortune, Silver has "a face as big as a ham" and is "as agile as a monkey" on his wooden leg and crutch. "I thought I knew what a buccaneer was like," Jim says upon seeing him for the first time, "a very different creature, according to me, from this clean and pleasant-tempered landlord." Louis's inspiration for the pirate's finer side (if not his double-sidedness) was his friend William Henley—"a great, glowing, massive-shouldered fellow with a big red beard" and "unimaginable fire and vitality," as Lloyd later described him.

Every day in Braemar, a new installment of *The Sea Cook* blew a warm sea breeze through the family's claustrophobic quarters. Looking around at the assembled faces at one reading, Fanny was stunned by Thomas Stevenson's.

She had always suspected a freer spirit underneath the man's iron exterior despite his best efforts to snuff it out. At his father's demand, Thomas had stopped writing his own creative "nonsense" as a young man and buried his imagination, except on those feverish nights when he had spun tales colored with sailing ships and robbers to calm his own son's anxieties. And now the tale Louis was writing for Fanny's son was reawakening the child in his own father. Watching Thomas drink in Louis's words, "his noble head bent forward, his great glowing eyes fixed on his son's face," Fanny wrote, "one could almost see the creature of cramped hereditary conventions and environment, and the man nature had intended him to be." The reconciliation she had hoped for between father and son was beginning to flower.

When the journalist and author Alexander Japp came to visit Louis, he too was brought into the readings and became swept up in the story. He left with several chapters of the manuscript in his portmanteau and an offer to try to sell it as a serial to a juvenile magazine, where he believed it could bring in a fee of about £100. Japp found a ready home for the story in *Young Folks*, a penny weekly for adolescents who could not afford the upmarket sixpenny periodicals. (Bucking the contemporary trend toward gendered magazines, *Young Folks* claimed to serve girls as well as boys by including at least one domestic drama per issue. Some of these were written by the wives of regular male contributors, but the magazine also ran stories by American writers such as Louisa May Alcott, who was flagrantly pirated in Britain's juvenile press after the success of *Little Women*. However, swashbuckling adventure stories for boys got the most ink.)

The weekly's Scottish publisher, James Henderson, offered Louis only its minimum rate, about £30. But the writer readily accepted the fee as long as he could keep the copyright. "Louis is just now in the midst of a boys story; a story of pirates and a buried treasure, and a mutiny on board ship, and various things of that nature . . . ," Fanny wrote excitedly to Dora in September. "It seems to all of us to be very good indeed, and is not the least effort to him to produce it, and withal he gets pretty well paid for it in a boys paper, with the privilege of republishing it."

⚜

THERE WAS JUST ONE PROBLEM: Louis had never finished a novel. As with many of his projects, once his early creative burst waned, he had trouble sustaining his interest to see it through to the end. He felt paralyzed at the thought of how much writing he still had ahead. "Anybody can write a short story—a bad one, I mean—who has industry and paper and time enough;" he later reflected, "but not everyone may hope to write even a bad novel. It is the length that kills."

Soon Louis's health also took a turn for the worse. Arriving in Braemar for a visit, George Balfour immediately ordered a pine oil respirator for his nephew. The family tried to lighten the situation by ribbing Louis about the hideous contraption, which he was required to wear around the clock. "It has a snout like a pig's, with comical valves on each side that flap in and out as he breathes," Fanny wrote to Dora. "He is quite the pig-faced gentleman in it." But by the end of the month, it was dismally clear that Fanny, Louis, Lloyd, and Woggs were going to have to make the grueling trek back to Magic Mountain.

The one bright spot for Louis would be his visit to the *Young Folks* office in London on his way to the Alps. When he showed up in his usual threadbare wardrobe and disheveled hair, however, the clerks thought he was an imposter. They tried to order him out of the office, until Henderson intervened. Louis agreed to publish the story with Henderson's stronger title, *Treasure Island; or, The Mutiny of the Hispaniola*, under the pseudonym Captain George North. He also discovered that the first of what would be seventeen installments was about to hit newsstands, though he had several chapters yet to write.

Louis now had no choice but to finish the story fast. (Had he not, Fanny believed he never would have finished it.) The pressure to churn out installments was familiar to Victorian authors—Dickens famously wrote under the gun. But he had not been forced to deal with Louis's afflictions. Arriving to visit the Stevensons' chalet soon after their return to Davos, Symonds found the author "lying, ghastly, in bed—purple cheek-bones, yellow cheeks, bloodless lips—fever all over him—without appetite—and all about him so utterly forlorn. 'Woggs' squealing. Mrs. Stevenson doing her best to make things comfortable." Though Louis continued his pine oil therapy, his cough was so violent at night, he slept with hashish and a flask of chloral hydrate at his bedside to bring on sleep.

Treasure Island did not "fetch the kids" at *Young Folks* as much as Louis had hoped. According to one editor, the story did not raise circulation at all, rendering it a relative failure. And by the time Louis had finished writing it, the family's depleted finances necessitated an embarrassing request of Henderson. "I have never asked you on what principle you pay," Louis wrote to the publisher, "but if your payments are other than half yearly, I should be obliged for an early cheque, as I have somewhat outrun the constable."

It was a difficult winter for Fanny. She suffered heart palpitations in the high altitude and had to go to Bern for treatment for gallstones. Louis turned to other work, completing several magazine articles and *The Silverado Squatters*, and he collected some of his essays and stories into *Familiar Studies of Men and Books* and *New Arabian Nights*. But Louis's real passion that winter was playing with Lloyd.

When the boy received a fancy toy theater, Louis helped him give performances, patting his thighs to make the sound of galloping horses or screaming like a damsel in distress. "My mother, usually the sole audience, would laugh till she had to be patted on the back, while I held back the play with much impatience for her recovery," Lloyd recalled. Their favorite pastime was war games. Louis and Lloyd turned the entire floor of the chalet's freezing attic into a chalk map covered with mountains, rivers, swamps, "good" and "bad" roads, towns, and bridges. Over several snowy weeks, six hundred lead soldiers strategized their way across the floor, dodging fire from pellets (shot from small popguns) or deadlier marbles and cuff links. The opposing forces were well matched: Louis was a better strategist but Lloyd a better marksman. Louis wrote dispatches from the front for two imaginary newspapers and Lloyd churned them out on his hand-operated miniature printing press.

Fanny accepted this as she accepted Louis's other eccentricities, mentioning it as casually as the weather in a letter to her mother-in-law. "It is snowing heavily and I am very tired," she wrote on "Davos Printing Office" stationery printed by Lloyd. "Sam and Louis are quarreling loudly over a game of soldiers as they always do when they play." A more proper Victorian wife might have been exasperated by a husband who spent weeks on end on his hands and knees, waging mock battles with tiny tin soldiers and arguing about warfare with her child.

IN EARLY 1882, Louis began revising *Treasure Island* for book publication. At the same time, Fanny was having reservations about the serial being turned into a book. She confided to Gosse's wife, Ellen, that she did not consider it Louis's best work; she preferred his more artful writing in "The Merry Men." Fanny also felt that the life went out of the story midway. (*Treasure Island* does indeed lag halfway through, when Dr. Livesey, the most sympathetic adult character, takes over the narration from Jim for several chapters.) But Fanny also asked for Gosse's opinion, admitting that she might be too critical. Louis certainly considered her a tough but important reader. When she finally gave the book her blessing, he quipped to Henley that "the pert and hypercritical Fanny Van de Grift" had "eaten much of her venom; thinks the end quite good, and only wants a chapter or so re-written in the midst,—six chapters, I think it is, in point of fact—but you see me greatly relieved that it is so little, and greatly pleased to find someone bear me out about the end."

Fanny was not the only one who had doubts about the venture. Some of Louis's colleagues accused him of debasing himself in writing a children's book. This wasn't the serious literary work they had been expecting from him. "Let them write their own dam [*sic*] masterpieces for themselves and let me alone," he fumed to Henley. Long John Silver's alter ego had no reservations about publication, however, and as Louis's informal agent, he became the driving force to see that it happened. Then working at the British publishing house Cassell and Company, Henley clattered into the chief editor's office on his wooden leg and threw the *Young Folks* clippings on the man's desk, roaring, "There's a book for you!"

Cassell offered Louis £100 plus royalties. Characteristically, the fiscally challenged author had estimated by then that £50 would be "a Bloody Sight more than *Treasure Island* is worth." But he happily accepted. "A hundred jingling, tingling, golden, minted quid," he gushed to his parents. "Is not this wonderful?" The novel arrived in bookstores on November 14, 1883, in time for Christmas shopping. It was released three months later in the United States by Roberts Brothers, which had made its name with the publication of *Little Women*. Its popularity built slowly, but by the end of the decade, it would be one of the most widely read books of its time. In the years before international copyright, however, Americans read mostly pirated editions and Louis's initial overseas earnings were small.

"Boys who have lived since 'Treasure Island' was published . . . have a right to look back on all previous boyhoods with compassion, as boyhoods sunk in comparative darkness," a critic for *The Spectator* wrote, confirming its place as a classic. Louis's friends also wrote glowing reviews, a practice that would be considered ethically dubious now but was common at the time. Even Henley saw no conflict of interest in singing the praises of a book he had helped shepherd to publication. His anonymous review was the author's favorite, even before Louis discovered who had written it. Perhaps not surprisingly, Henley named Silver the book's "real hero," adding that "you feel, when the story is done, that the right name of it is not 'Treasure Island,' but 'John Silver, Pirate.'"

Published the day after his thirty-third birthday, Robert Louis Stevenson's first full-length piece of fiction became his most famous book, breathing danger and excitement into the prissy world of Victorian children's literature. Remarkably, while surrounded by suffering and dying children, he invented boyhood as an exhilarating adventure. But *Treasure Island* also struck a chord with Victorian men who shared Louis's nostalgia for a time when personal freedom and heroism seemed more possible. The Industrial

Revolution had eaten away at that idea, but *Treasure Island* celebrated it. Over time, Long John Silver—with his peg leg and his pet parrot, Captain Flint, on his shoulder—would become as famous as any real pirate.

Louis raised the standard boys' swashbuckling action tale to a new level partly by subverting some of its standard elements. Jim's first words suggest that the story will adhere to the usual comforting formula: An ordinary boy sets off on a daring adventure and returns home safely. But there is nothing soft or safe in the anarchic world Jim must navigate on his journey. The most dramatic moment—when he kills the mutinous pirate Israel Hands—is still a shocking test of courage for a children's book. In the scene, the plucky adolescent finds himself alone on the *Hispaniola* with the pirate, who intends to kill him. Locked in hand-to-hand combat, Jim retreats up the ship's rigging with two pistols. Hands hurls the knife at Jim, lancing his shoulder and pinning him to the mast, and Jim's gun releases two shots that send Hands plunging headfirst into the water. The boy coolly observes:

> He rose once to the surface in a lather of foam and blood, and then sank again for good. . . . Sometimes, by the quivering of the water, he appeared to move a little, as if he were trying to rise. But he was dead enough, for all that, being both shot and drowned, and was food for fish in the very place where he had designed my slaughter.

Also bucking the standard, Jim's tests of manhood are not just physical. His journey is also internal—he must learn about duplicity of character. His complex relationship with Long John Silver animates the book. The pirate is by turns charismatic con man, ruthless murderer, courageous leader, and sometimes even surrogate father to Jim. Once betrayed by him, Jim is not seduced again by his silver tongue. But he cannot help but respect the pirate as "twice the man the rest were," a brilliant strategist who could talk his way out of one scrape after another. By the end of the story, he and Silver owe each other their lives.

The moral ambiguity Louis injected throughout the story remains startling for a Victorian boys' adventure saga. The pirates are not the usual cardboard villains but have human dimensions that make them even scarier. The pillars of British genteel society who lure Jim on their treasure hunt are not that different from the pirates—they are manipulative, bumbling, and not above resorting to violence to satisfy their lust for gold. When the treasure is finally found—piles of glittering coins stolen from nations all over the world—only Jim does not rejoice. Instead, he reflects on the human carnage caused by the pursuit of that wealth. There were the seventeen men killed during the fateful journey of the *Hispaniola*, as well as the violence and suffering that had gone into amassing the treasure before Jim and his crewmates ever reached the island: "What blood and sorrow, what good ships scuttled on the deep, what brave men walking the plank blindfold, what shot of the cannon, what shame and lies and cruelty, perhaps no man alive could tell."

In the age of the British Empire, the book also refused to support notions of white superiority. When the ragtag survivors stop at a port town of "negroes, and Mexican-Indians, and half-bloods," Jim notes that the Caribbean settlement is alive with color and good cheer—"a most charming contrast to our dark and bloody sojourn on the island"—and clearly in no need of civilizing. In a final rebellious gesture, Louis lets Silver escape here with some of the booty—perhaps, Jim hopes, to rejoin his "negress" wife and live out his life in comfort. Some critics, then and now, find the pirate's escape from justice inappropriate for a youthful audience.

Louis dedicated the book to Lloyd. At a time when his stepson was approaching manhood, issues of honesty and male character were clearly on Louis's mind. In Davos, a visitor had criticized him for not censoring adult conversation or literature around Lloyd. Louis had replied that he had no patience with "this fairy-tale training that makes ignorance a virtue," something that had cost him "bitter misery." He believed that young people should get some idea of what the world is really like—"its baseness, its treacheries, its thinly veneered brutalities." Louis did not intend for the book to glorify the rewards of British imperialism for a new generation. Under the veneer of an adventure tale, he quietly urged young readers: *Learn to think for yourself. Don't accept what adults tell you as the truth.* A century later, John Lennon would credit the book with "[opening] my whole being."

Written under such trying circumstances, *Treasure Island* was not only a creative triumph, but a triumph of art over life. For Fanny, it was also a quiet personal victory: She had succeeded in her vow to safeguard Louis's health until the world could see his talent. Marriage to Fanny gave Louis a new maturity without destroying the buoyant youthfulness that made him unique. He took his family responsibilities seriously, but Fanny's unconventionality and equally adventurous spirit helped keep alive in him the "unfading boyishness of hope" that fueled the book. He called her his "teacher, tender, comrade, wife."

TEN

Three years into her marriage, Fanny was finding that it both broadened and narrowed her world. To friends and family back home, her life tripping through Europe as the wife of a rising young author must have been tinged with romance. The couple's letters arrived in the post with colorful stamps and exotic return addresses—in just over one year alone, from Ballachulish, Kingussie, Lochearnhead, Oban, and Peebles in Scotland; Montpellier, Marseille, St. Marcel, Nice, and Hyères in France. "I don't suppose our address will surprise you," Fanny wrote to Dora Williams from a hotel in Marseille, as if it were all a footloose adventure. "Nothing, I fancy about Louis and me will or can surprise anybody." But Fanny was also beginning to realize that Louis's invalidism would be dictating her life from then on, as the couple searched for better health for him closer to the sea or farther south or just beyond the next mountain.

For Fanny, each move to a new location meant another foreign city to navigate, another house "full of stories and but little else," she wrote to John Addington Symonds. She was always trying to reduce costs—on shipping, customs duties, silverware, furniture—and even went without anesthesia when she had a tooth pulled to cut the £40 fee in half. Invitations to stay with the Stevensons might include a request that visitors bring their own blankets or carry some petticoats Fanny had ordered. Margaret sent linens, plates, and money, and for Christmas Stilton cheese and bacon.

Yet no matter how broke they were, the couple always required good wine. Louis made occasional attempts to quit cigarettes or booze, but he turned them into such riotous entertainment for his friends, one wonders if even *he* took them seriously. Such bouts of abstemiousness were usually brief, and not all doctors encouraged teetotaling. One told him and Fanny that a good red wine would do more for Louis than all the medicine in the world and gave them two bottles from his own cellar to carry them until they could get a shipment from Margaret.

The Stevensons spent nearly two years in France, mostly in Hyères, an old winter health resort on the Riviera where they landed in February 1883. Their new residence, Chalet La Solitude, was like a doll's house—a tiny chalet built for the 1878 Paris Exposition and reconstructed on a sloping drive, with castle ruins above and views of the hills of Toulon and the sea. They hoped to settle there for years.

Fanny immediately set about making their new home healthier for Louis. Now that the link between bacteria and illness had been established, Victorian housewives were charged with eradicating the germs that lurked everywhere in their homes. Fanny insisted that cesspools be filled in, garbage hauled away, wastewater funneled into gutters. She also brought her usual quirky creativity to her mission: In Hyères, she arranged for fresh milk from cows in the zoo to be delivered to the chalet.

Like its new tenants, La Solitude was eccentric and somewhat impractical. The dining room was so small that plates of food had to be passed over the heads of dinner guests and the kitchen so narrow that when Fanny cooked, she was "in continual danger of being scorched by the range on one side, and at the same time impaled by the saucepan hooks on the other." But the garden was wild and spacious, with meandering paths through a grove of olive trees where nightingales nested—"a garden like a fairy story," Louis wrote to Frances Sitwell. It was the kind of setting to inspire the children's verses he had begun writing two years before, during the wet summer holiday in Braemar that had launched *Treasure Island*.

Louis had decided to try his hand at poetry for young people after seeing *Kate Greenaway's Birthday Book for Children*, which Margaret had brought with her on holiday. Greenaway's wildly popular illustrations of old-fashioned children in giant bonnets and smocked frocks drew on the Aesthetic style and sensibility then in vogue, which iconicized children as pure and innocent, untouched by the vulgarity and materialism of the modern industrial age.

"These are rather nice rhymes and I don't think they would be difficult to do," Louis had remarked as he leafed through the poems by Lucy Sale-Barker. When he felt too ill to summon the more sustained energy required for prose, Louis commonly wrote adult verse, which he described to *Atlantic Monthly* editor William Dean Howells as "children of the sickroom." That description was never truer than of the collection of poems he wrote specifically *for* children. His doctors' assurances that he could safely summer in Scotland and winter in France had collapsed into more blood spitting, high fevers, and an eye infection that appeared to threaten his sight. Rather than soaking up inspiration in his idyllic garden, he was confined to a darkened room for ophthalmia. And after his worst hemorrhaging to date, he was also undergoing pulmonary collapse therapy, a treatment that sometimes involved splinting sandbags to one side of a patient's chest to "rest" a diseased lung. Lying in the dark with his right arm strapped to his chest, Louis completed *A Child's Garden of Verses* writing with his left hand on papers pinned to a board laid over him.

It is easy to glimpse these grim circumstances throughout the poems in the final book. The child in one verse states:

> When at home alone I sit
> And am very tired of it,
> I have just to shut my eyes
> To go sailing through the skies—

The adult Louis's mind sailed back through his childhood nursery and garden and Colinton Manse, his family's beloved country refuge, to call up dimpled rivers, sweet-smelling haylofts, and playtime ships built with sofa cushions. Less idyllic childhood memories also haunt the pages of the book.

One section is titled "The Child Alone," and illness is a springboard for imagination in what is probably the collection's most famous poem, "The Land of Counterpane." In it, a feverish boy envisions himself a giant watching over the kingdom of his bed, where dolls and toy ships hum with activity on the billowing blankets and bedclothes.

Fanny believed that childhood games held special magic for Louis because he had been so rarely well enough to join in them. "There were brilliant episodes of play that remained clearer in my husband's memory than almost any other part of his life," she wrote. Louis's unusual ability to wriggle inside a child's sensibility also allowed him to bring a fresh conversational, even intimate, tone to the endeavor. He treated children as equals and fellow conspirators, and many of the poems read as one child writing to another.

The scope of the book is at once as small as a nursery and as big as a child's imagination. Within its comforting circular rhythms—the sun rises and sets, summers come and go and come again—the world is full of little surprises and connections to the larger world and other children. A tin soldier buried under snow in the garden sees myriad natural wonders before he is discovered again in spring; boys and girls on the other side of the earth dress for their day when you undress for bed; the paper boats you launch downriver float from your hands into those of children you will never meet. You might be confined within a garden wall, but an exhilarating ride on a swing makes you feel as if you are touching the clouds.

Adults exist on the periphery of this world, represented by a swishing skirt or a disembodied voice calling a child to tea. They are benign but boring, and the children in the poems are usually too fascinated with their own smaller world to look up to them. One child wants to shrink enough to fire the penny cannon on the bow of the toy ship commandeered by his doll, who has come to life; another closes her eyes to enter a tiny world where she meets insects and sails on leaves on rain puddle seas. When she opens her eyes again, it is to a jarring gray reality:

> High bare walls, great bare floor;
> Great big knobs on drawer and door;

Great big people perched on chairs,
Stitching tucks and mending tears.

Though Louis's book reflected the contemporary romantic view of white, middle-class British childhood, it is not all sticky sentimentality. Children's anxieties are there too, in the spidery shadows that creep upstairs with them to the bedroom, and in the sick child who lies awake waiting for the reassuring morning sounds that signal the night is ending. The deliciously nasty "Good and Bad Children" begins with the warning "Children, you are very little, / And your bones are very brittle" and ends with:

Cruel children, crying babies,
All grow up as geese and gabies,
Hated, as their age increases,
By their nephews and their nieces.

Some of the rhymes hopscotch lightly across Louis's antibourgeois sentiments. The famous poem "The Lamplighter" derides one of his favorite targets, bankers. To the child in the verse, no profession could be more exciting than lighting up the night sky—certainly not being a money changer like his father. "Foreign Children" is a satire on imperialism so sly, it is often interpreted as imperial propaganda. The speaker, a white British child, boasts that children in other countries must envy his superior life, but the poem paints their lives as much more enviable. They see lions, eat ostrich eggs, and play with turtles while the British child is "fed on proper meat" and stays "safe" in his home. Louis's illustration notes seem to have been aimed at enhancing the verse as a critique of smug British self-satisfaction. He called for the foreign children to be dancing out of a picture book, "showing each other marvels," while the English child was "at the leeside of a roast of beef."

Louis dedicated the volume to his childhood nurse, Alison Cunningham. She was "the only person who will really understand it," he wrote to her. (Cummy was perhaps also the most appropriate person, having filled his

youth with the combination of comfort and anxiety that the collection ex-
udes.) Margaret was hurt at being passed over for the honor and protested
that she or even Louis's aunt Jane Balfour deserved it more than Cummy.
Though Louis ended up dedicating individual poems to both his mother
and his aunt, he did not budge on the book's dedication. He felt that nannies did not receive enough gratitude or recognition for their work and that
he had not shown Cummy enough appreciation for hers.

Fanny declared the verses "lovely" in a letter to Dora and looked forward
to their publication. Yet in Louis's literary circle, there were the usual fears
that his venture into new territory would bruise his professional reputation.
They were "as timid as hens about this new experiment of their duckling's,"
Edmund Gosse recalled, "they hesitated and doubted to the last." Colvin
advised cutting what would become two of the most enduringly popular
poems. He called "The Swing" "commonplace" and fretted that a lamplighter was an "extinct animal" to children in the new electric era.

Nevertheless, with help from Andrew Lang, whose book of fairy tales was
enjoying immense popularity, Henley negotiated a contract with Longmans,
Green and Company on Louis's behalf, and *A Child's Garden of Verses* went
on sale in Britain for five shillings in March 1885. None of the top illustra-
tors were available, so it was released without artwork—a serious disappointment when Greenaway, Randolph Caldecott, and Walter Crane were
creating the late Victorian "golden age" of children's book illustration. Louis's
artist friend Will Low negotiated on Louis's behalf with Charles Scribner's
Sons for a U.S. edition, but Low was concerned that it would be pirated before he was available to illustrate it and urged Louis to rush it into print without art. The book did not appear with drawings until after Louis's death.

Reviews of the first edition were respectable if not glowing. A week after
the book appeared in Britain, Louis renamed it *The Complete Proof of Mr.
R.L. Stevenson's Incapacity to Write Verse* in a letter to Gosse and suggested
that a school exercise accompany the volume: "State Mr Stevenson's faults of
taste in regard to the measure. What reasons can you gather from this example for your belief that Mr S is unable to write any other measure?" The
poems looked "ghastly in the cold light of print," he winced. But the public

disagreed. *A Child's Garden of Verses* went on to become one of Louis's top three bestsellers and, along with *Treasure Island*, among the top ten sellers in any book category in the United States for nearly two decades. Widely imitated, it continues to be reissued and its verses are routinely set to music.

Peppered as it is with anachronisms like nursery nooks and water wells, the book's enduring popularity is somewhat surprising. Modern publishers sometimes exclude poems like "Foreign Children," which features wording now widely recognized as racist, such as "little frosty Eskimo" and "Japanee." Critics are still divided on whether the poem is imperialistic, and even if it is not, small children cannot be expected to understand its irony without guidance. But young people continue to feel the child in other poems speaking to them, far across time. More than a century after the book first appeared, rock stars Bruce Springsteen and Patti Smith read "The Land of Nod" for audiences and talked about its significance in their lives. When Smith took the stage in Edinburgh to read a number of poems from the book, the punk goddess explained that as a child, she had practically lived between the covers of *A Child's Garden of Verses*, reading Louis's rhymes over and over through a girlhood plagued by illness. "His poems were my companions, my friends," she said. "Robert Louis Stevenson was also a sickly child who knew what it was like to hear other children playing outside his window."

WHILE THE STEVENSONS were drifting in Europe, Fanny's daughter, Belle, was firmly rooted in the heart of bohemian San Francisco. Belle and Joe Strong had moved into a converted courthouse on Montgomery Street, where Joe shared a studio with the painter Jules Tavernier. The charming and immensely talented Tavernier was then the highest-paid artist in the city and possibly the most careless with money. Artists and writers—and occasionally the sheriff or a debt collector—streamed through the studio, which the two men had decorated with treasures from Chinatown and western mementos from Tavernier's cross-country travels.

The toddler Louis posed in a boy's dress.

Louis and his father, Thomas Stevenson. A distinguished lighthouse engineer, Thomas expected his son to be one too.

"Like a pic-nic on a volcano" was Louis's description of his troubled relationship with his parents, Thomas and Margaret Stevenson, shown here with their son on an outing in Wales.

Louis's cousin and confidant, Robert Alan Mowbray Stevenson

Fanny swept up her long braids for this photo of her as a young woman in Indiana.

Dora Norton Williams, Fanny's close friend

Samuel Osbourne, Fanny's first husband

Fanny looking like an independent "New Woman" twenty years before the term was coined

Russian prodigy Marie Bashkirtseff's painting *In the Studio* captured the atmosphere at Académie Julian, the Paris art school Fanny and Belle attended. Classes were segregated by gender, but women were allowed to paint from nearly nude male models.

An etching made from Fanny's drawing of the aspiring young author in a smoking cap

John Singer Sargent's strange portrait, *Robert Louis Stevenson and His Wife*, which the painter described as "the caged animal lecturing about the foreign specimen in the corner."

Fanny at forty, the bride to be, in a photo taken to calm the elder Stevensons' fears about her suitability as Louis's wife

Louis at twenty-nine, about to inherit a family when he married Fanny

Skerryvore, the Stevensons' home in Bournemouth,
a coastal health resort in England

The celebrated author in New York in 1887, after writing the three books that made him famous: *Treasure Island, Strange Case of Dr Jekyll and Mr Hyde*, and *Kidnapped*

Louis's friend William Ernest Henley. The poet wrote "Invictus" and was the model for the one-leggerd pirate Long John Silver.

A poster for the 1912 silent film *Dr. Jekyll and Mr. Hyde*, directed by Lucius Henderson and starring James Cruze

Lloyd caught his stepfather deep in thought in this photo taken at Skerryvore. Louis's intense eyes "could look right through you," one admirer said.

Jim Hawkins draws guns on Israel Hands in N. C.
Wyeth's stunning realist illustration for *Treasure Island*, the
book that launched the Scribner's Illustrated Classics
for Younger Readers series in 1911.

Spearing fish from the bowsprit of
the *Equator*. Louis is on the far right.

Fanny, shown here in a straw hat, was the only woman with
fifteen men on the *Equator*. Louis stands on the far left.

At a royal banquet hosted by Hawaiian king David
Kalākaua. Louis and Margaret sit near the king in
back; Lloyd and Belle are near the foreground.

Clockwise, from top left: Margaret, Belle, Lloyd,
Fanny, and Louis, with their cook, Ah Foo, in Waikiki

Louis and Lloyd in Tahiti in *pareus*, swaths of cloth wrapped and tied at the waist that are similar to Samoan *lavalavas*

Fanny and Louis lounging in the sun in the Gilbert Islands with friends Nan Tok (left) and his spouse, High Chief Nei Takauti

The Vailima household, from left: back row: Joe Strong, Margaret, Lloyd, Louis, Fanny, and the butler Simi; second row (seated): Margaret's maid Mary Carter, cook Taloja, Austin Strong, Belle, cattleman Lafaele, and assistant cook Tomasi (standing); front row: plantation worker Savea, laundress Elena, and pantryman Arrick

The Stevensons' Samoan home, Vailima, today.
It has been restored as a museum.

Louis dictating to Belle at Vailima.
Belle said the sentences flowed from him
though he rarely had any notes.

Fanny, Louis, Belle, and Margaret sat for a photo in Sydney, Australia, in March 1893. Fanny looks serene, but she was in the throes of a mental breakdown.

The London periodical *Funny Folks* christened the author "Robert Louis the First of Samoa" in the caption for this 1892 cartoon.

The birth of Belle's son, Austin, in 1881 had not made her any more conventional. She lit up a cigarette as soon as she could sit up, while nursing her baby, as her ladylike paternal grandmother, Cynthia Osbourne, looked on in horror. A hired procession of Chinese boys took Austin out daily "for an airing," including one who tied gold and silver fish ornaments from Chinatown to the end of his queue and dangled them like a mobile while he sang to the baby. A man named Sing Lee cleaned paintbrushes and did some housekeeping—a blessing for Belle, who was described as "untidy in the extreme."

The highlight of the Strongs' social life was entertaining Oscar Wilde during his 1882 American tour. Wilde had not yet written his famous works and was known in England primarily as the public face of Aestheticism, dedicated to rescuing Britain from Victorian frumpiness by injecting beauty into daily life.

Following his edict that "one should either be a work of art, or wear a work of art," twenty-seven-year-old Wilde ferried across the bay to San Francisco wearing highly polished pointed shoes, yellow gloves, a sombrero over his long locks, and a bouquet of heliotrope, daisies, and tuberoses tucked into the front of his black velvet coat. The prim pundits of the local press lost no time implying that he shared the sexual proclivities of the city's poet of "lavender verse" Charles Warren Stoddard, the Stevensons' friend and baby Austin's godfather. For the most part, however, San Francisco offered Wilde a relatively friendly welcome. Sunflowers adorned shop windows and flower stands, and the city's social leaders showed him the sights.

Decked out in his Little Lord Fauntleroy ensemble of lace and velvet knee breeches for his lectures on home decoration and dress, Wilde tore into America's lack of taste. He lambasted iron stoves as "monstrous" and hat racks as "instruments of torture." He called on American men to emulate the father of their country by wearing knee breeches and stockings. This was too much for some members of the Bohemian Club, and they whisked Wilde off to their city headquarters after the lecture to get him drunk. The plan was to poke fun at the beefy Irish dandy when he was sloshed, but Wilde matched them glass for glass before, during, and after dinner, earning their respect as a "three bottle man."

At the Bohemian Club, Joe and Tavernier had issued Wilde a formal invitation to tea at their studio. To beautify the premises, Tavernier painted clusters of roses on the skylight, so that the sun would filter down softly on guests through translucent green leaves and red petals. He and Joe dressed up a life-sized female dummy Joe used for portraits. "Miss Piffle," as she was dubbed for the occasion, peeked out from under a hat and veil, a fan in one of her gloved hands. Joe decided the occasion also called for a bowl of his ultra-boozy punch.

Wilde was at his most relaxed and happiest on the tour after captivating half the city with his lectures and the other half with his drinking prowess. A whirlwind of charm (if a bit of a poser, Belle thought), he quickly put his hosts and their friends at ease, and after downing some of Joe's punch, carried on an exceedingly witty conversation with Miss Piffle. "This is where I belong!" he reputedly burst out to the guests. "I didn't know such a place existed in the whole United States."

Belle did not record whether she mentioned her stepfather to Wilde. If she did, she would have discovered that the young writer was already a surprisingly avid fan of "that delicate artist in language," as he described Louis. Though the two men would never meet, Wilde devoured Louis's work and followed his career closely. During his grueling prison confinement in England after his 1895 conviction for "gross indecency," he asked friends to send Louis's books. At the end of his two-year term, in a kind gesture to the men he was leaving behind, Wilde again requested "any new ones by Stevenson, whose *Treasure Island*, which I presented to the prison library some six weeks ago, is, I am informed by the Schoolmaster, in great request and much appreciated."

AS AMUSING AS THE STRONGS' social life could be, it was a cause for growing concern in the Stevenson household. Fanny wrote to Dora praising Joe's good heart and excellent work but lamenting his partnership with Tavernier, knowing that he shared his colleague's credo never to let business interfere with pleasure. Her distress over Joe's health continually breaking down in other letters likely referred to his increasing problem with drugs and alcohol, another proclivity he shared with Tavernier. When the Strongs' income suffered, they heatedly demanded help from Fanny and Louis.

Though at the time Belle described her mother and stepfather to a friend as "the most entertaining folks alive," the hostile tone the Stevensons found in her letters suggests that she was still angry with them. She seemed to feel that Louis owed her, perhaps literally, for breaking up her parents' marriage. Fanny was angry that the younger couple expected to be bailed out repeatedly by her sickly husband or even his parents. And she was humiliated when Louis shared with his friends his own infuriation, outraging them on his behalf. "We have just been bled of £20 which we can ill afford . . . ," he fumed to Henley in a letter he dictated to Fanny, "begging letters three parts insult are the only communications that reach us from that happy strand."

When Belle had announced her pregnancy with Austin, both Stevensons saw it as a misfortune—or in Louis's surprisingly sour assessment, a "vulgar error." Fanny was openly harsh about it to Dora—and curiously unempathetic, given the difficulties of her own first marriage. She did send the couple a deed to an Oakland lot she owned and tried to put her "best foot foremost" about the baby to Belle. But both gestures fell woefully short in the eyes of Belle and Joe, and they cut off communication with her. Fanny blamed herself in part for this.

"You wonder at my patience with them," she wrote to Dora. "After all they belong to me whether or no, and I probably spoiled Belle by overindulgence and have to blame myself somewhat for her selfishness." Fanny knew the Strongs would resume writing when they were broke again, but "we hope to be able to harden our hearts and let them beg on the other side of the house," she sighed in another note. However, Sam Osbourne remained unencumbered by the financial concerns of his children and instead put his money in a twenty-eight-acre vineyard in Sonoma.

At the urging of Joe's concerned Bohemian Club pals, sugar tycoon

John D. Spreckels commissioned Joe to paint landscapes of Hawaii for the San Francisco office of his new venture, the Oceanic Steamship Company passenger line, to help promote travel to the islands. Fanny and Louis helped provide the funds for the couple to start a new life, but in Hawaii, they fell back into a "hectic" social life and Joe's health deteriorated further. When Fanny found out that her daughter was pregnant again, her response was bitter. "Belle I hear is going to have another baby and her dog is dead," she remarked coldly to Dora. "I'm *not* going to have another baby and my dog is not dead."

Belle named the baby after Hervey, her brother who had died. It was no doubt meant as a tribute, but she also knew it would be an agonizing reminder to Fanny of her son's hideous death at the age of five. Sadly, Hervey Strong died in infancy, even younger than his namesake, probably from a wave of dysentery that was sweeping Hawaii. For all her acrimony toward Fanny, losing a child was now an experience Belle would share with her mother for life.

ON THE OTHER SIDE of the world, Fanny turned attempts to cope with her new life in Europe into comical anecdotes in her letters and later memoirs. Her curiosity about other cultures did not keep her from criticizing or finding humor in them, but she believed all people found foreigners' ways silly and strange. She recalled the Highland proprietor of a vacation rental who cleaned plates with her handkerchief. When Fanny showed her a spoon that was still dirty, the woman licked it clean. Fanny had to convince a hired housekeeper in St. Marcel to wash the dinner knives before she brought them to the table. "She could hardly believe at first that I was serious in wanting clean knives when there was no company," she wrote to Margaret.

Fanny also made fun of her own bungling attempts to deal with the women the Stevensons hired to help with housekeeping or cooking whenever they moved. One regularly muttered to Louis in French that his wife was an "imbecile," though she treated Fanny with "kindly toleration." Some guarded their secrets when she nosed around in the kitchen. Still, through sign language, occasional spying, and bartering, Fanny managed to pick up some new techniques. In return for sharing her own recipes for salsa and curry with mango and grated-coconut milk, she expanded her repertoire to include bouillabaisse and brandade.

Things went smoother in the household when the Stevensons hired Valentine Roch, a young village woman, to do housekeeping in Hyères, and she became an indispensable member of the household for the next six years. But Fanny's ineptitude with language remained a problem when she stepped outside of the house in France.

Fanny's entertaining stories were partly an attempt to parry other people's critiques of her temper and roughness with humor. She might sign a letter to the elder Stevensons "The Vandergrifter" or "Cassandra," the nicknames Thomas had given her, or urge one of Louis's friends to visit to save him from being alone with "a cross dog and an overbearing wife." Yet Fanny also found a certain liberation in embracing her perceived character flaws. Why let them go to waste? Once accused by her friend Timothy Rearden of coming to him only when she needed something, she answered, "Having the character given me, I might as well make some use of it."

When she had time for correspondence, Fanny's letters were effusive, colorful, and thoughtful. Writing to her in-laws in large script because they requested it, she thanked them for gifts when their son forgot and tried to answer their questions because he would not. She pressed a marguerite daisy from her garden into one note to Margaret as a "sort of sentimental reminder of you."

Her letters also reveal a woman who was often addled and distracted. In their disordered household, the Stevensons misplaced manuscripts and even publishers' checks. (They were equally careless at keeping track of dates: Fanny forgot her birthday and Louis's mother had to remind him of his wedding date.) Fanny scrawled letters on scraps of paper torn from Louis's notebooks or was obliged midway through a letter to give up her pen for her husband's use. Sometimes she was called away to write business letters for

Louis. She confessed to Gosse that she felt like an inadequate medium, and the task gave her less time to do her own writing. She longed to have a studio where she could escape the chaos.

WITHIN THE RELATIVE DISARRAY of their lives, Fanny and Louis's love flourished. When Lloyd was away at a country school in Bournemouth, England, they were alone for the first and what would be the only substantial time in their married life. They avoided separations, which were especially torturous for "uxorious Billy," as Louis described himself to Colvin. When they were apart, Fanny wrote letters of encouragement and sent kisses for each pound Louis gained when his appetite rallied. He sent her silly love poems he composed, including one about their blissful reunion, when "the fat and lean / shall then convene." Otherwise, they did almost everything together, as Fanny explained to her mother-in-law: If one had an errand, the other usually went along; if one wanted to go for a walk, they both did. Louis would remember their time at Chalet La Solitude as the happiest in his life.

Hyères was the honeymoon the couple had never had. On the eve of their fourth wedding anniversary, Louis wrote of his wife to Margaret:

> *I love her better than ever and admire her more; and I cannot think what I have done to deserve so good a gift. This sudden re-mark came out of my pen; it is not like me; but in case you did not know, I may as well tell you, that my marriage has been the most successful in the world. . . . She is everything to me: wife, brother, sister, daughter and dear companion; and I would not change to get a goddess or a saint.*

Louis's words struck at the heart of the couple's deep connection. Fanny and Louis could be more fully themselves with each other than with anyone else, exposing all their considerable oddities—the exhilarating creative bursts and extravagant mood swings, the physical ailments and emotional neediness, the passion for adventure and an unconventional life. Their marriage was like a kaleidoscope, with all the vivid bits of their colorful personalities tilting together and shifting apart into ever-changing patterns.

Fanny wrote to Dora of how her admiration for her husband grew with her love:

> *You are right when you speak of his as a sweet soul. It is sound, sweet and wholesome, and his mind is always just and right in its conclusions, while his manner is so gentle that everyone loves him. I think it is a proud boast to be able to say of one's husband that you can always learn from him to be both better and wiser. That boast is mine.*

Louis's improved health was the only thing she could ask for, "to have the most perfect life that any woman could have," she would write to Margaret.

The tranquility of the French countryside was a balm for the couple's excitable temperaments. Living in France had always suited Louis. He was fluent in the language and literature, and his pelerine cape did not attract stares there as it did in Britain. During their extended stay in the country, he grew the chin hair, or "soul patch," that he would keep for the rest of his life. When Louis was well, the couple slipped into a simple routine. He wrote from the early morning until noon, while Fanny attended to household duties. After lunch—perhaps an asparagus omelet, black olives with oil and lemon, figs with cream, and mocha coffee—he read his work aloud and she offered criticism and suggestions. Then they strolled in the garden or walked up to the castle ruins with Woggs. After dinner, they talked or read aloud.

Fanny and Louis adored children, but neither seemed to feel that they needed a baby to make their life complete. It is easy to imagine Fanny's reasoning: In 1883, she was forty-three years old, her younger child was nearly grown, Louis needed care, and their finances were shaky. But when it looked like she might be pregnant that spring, her younger husband discovered that his emotions were more mixed. His initial forebodings of financial ruin and a sickly offspring turned into fantasies of fatherhood. When the alarm passed, he relayed his sadness to his friend Walter Simpson as a "joke." But the relief was bittersweet.

In their seclusion, the Stevensons showered attention on their devoted Scottish terrier. To others, there was nothing charming about Woggs—he picked fights with other dogs and bit people, including Colvin. Yet to Fanny and Louis, he was an adorable scamp. Louis loved his fighting spirit and Fanny believed he had a superior intellect. Her father-in-law was as sentimental about dogs as she was—Thomas Stevenson believed, against his religion, that they had souls. Still, when the suggestion slipped from Heriot Row that Woggs was an "idiot," Fanny rushed to her little bully's defense. "Why that dog does nothing but think; that's what's the matter with him, he thinks too much for his size," she insisted. "I don't think enough for mine, and that's what's the matter with me."

PROFESSIONALLY, THE SIXTEEN MONTHS in Hyères were a time of productivity and change for Louis. Despite his rocky health, he published several essays, completed two minor novels, and prepared much of his older work for republication. He broke off his relationship with *Cornhill* after Leslie Stephen resigned and the new editor, James Payn, rejected his story "The Treasure of Franchard" as inappropriate for a family magazine. Louis shifted his allegiance to *Longman's*, a new magazine from the publisher Longmans, Green and Company, which ran the story and serialized the second half of *The Amateur Emigrant*. A giddy review in the *Fifeshire Journal* declared the excerpt Shakespearean in parts and contended, "No one wields the English language as [Stevenson] does," prompting Louis to observe that the reviewer "seems a very excitable fellow. I cannot understand his fervour: however, it is not for me to be critical."

Louis had already cooled his relationship with the publishing house of C. Kegan Paul, a onetime clergyman whom he felt was enormously stingy with writers. (Louis once characterized the publisher in Jekyllesque terms: "Kegan is an excellent fellow, but Paul is a publisher.") Paul's meager payment of £20 for Louis's collection of essays *Virginibus Puerisque* had filled the author's mind with fantasies of grabbing him by his beard and banging his head against the wall.

Louis always maintained a healthy cynicism toward publishers. (After Cassell turned down one of his books, he made a list of fictitious titles the publishing house had also rejected that week, including "The Holy Bible: a new edition, thoroughly revised and much extended by the Holy Ghost.") But he was relatively happy with Chatto and Windus. In 1882 the company had released *Familiar Studies of Men and Books*, a compilation of his essays, and *New Arabian Nights*—a two-volume collection of his magazine fiction, including the "Suicide Club" stories. The publisher also paid Louis £100 for *The Silverado Squatters*, which he had dedicated to Dora and Virgil Williams.

In summer 1882, Louis had advised a young portrait painter, Trevor Haddon, "about any art, think last of what it pays, first of what pleases." Yet he was thinking first of what it paid the following spring when he wrote *The Black Arrow*, the story of a young man's coming-of-age during England's bloody fifteenth-century Wars of the Roses. Not that Louis considered the endeavor *art*. He had put off *Young Folks* editor James Henderson's request for a new boys' adventure serial until he was so "uncoiny" and "busted up" in health that he felt unfit to do anything else. Then he dashed off most of the manuscript of nearly eighty thousand words in two months, deriding it as "tushery" from the start.

Louis did not have his wife to cheer him on. Fanny thought the story was beneath him and could not get through a reading. Even Louis was so indifferent to his tale that he forgot the fates of some characters after he sent off the early installments and had to wait to see the proofs before he could finish it.

Though it does not compare with its swashbuckling predecessor in literary quality, *The Black Arrow* again upends the black-and-white code of boys' romantic fiction with morally murky characters and alliances, albeit within the standard formula of cliff-hanging action and narrow escapes. The hero, Dick Shelton, starts out subscribing to the idea of war as an exhilarating adventure and ends up recognizing the massive devastation that underlies the glory of victory. However, the story's continual action likely accounted for its huge success when it splashed onto the pages of *Young Folks* in June 1883, under Louis's adventure serial nom de plume Captain George North. The magazine's circulation jumped by hundreds of copies each week it ran.

Louis claimed that he disliked *The Black Arrow* so much, he never reread it. Neither he nor any British publishing house was interested in reprinting it, and it languished for five years until Charles Scribner's Sons published *The Black Arrow: A Tale of the Two Roses* in 1888. Louis wrote a playful but sharp-edged dedication to his "Critic on the Hearth," Fanny:

> No one but myself knows what I have suffered, nor what my books have gained, by your unsleeping watchfulness and admirable pertinacity. And now here is a volume that goes into the world and lacks your imprimatur: a strange thing in our joint lives; and the reason of it stranger still! I have watched with interest, with pain, and at length with amusement, your unavailing attempts to peruse The Black Arrow; and I think I should lack humor indeed, if I let the occasion slip and did not place your name on the fly-leaf of the only book of mine that you have never read—and never will read.

Louis called *The Black Arrow* serial and the old work that he was reviving and repackaging "games"—relatively easy projects he took on primarily to meet the staggering costs of moving and medical care, and schooling for "dear but costly" Lloyd. At the time, *Treasure Island* had not yet been published as a book, and he could see little ahead beyond a succession of "games" stretching in a line to his expected early death. At thirty-three, he feared that he would never be more than a hack—the "cheesy sort of shit" he had envisioned to Bob a decade before.

His American friend Will Low was suffering a similar early midlife crisis. A Francophile like Louis, Low considered himself in exile in New York, where he was living with his French wife, Berthe, in the Rembrandt, an artists' co-op on West Fifty-Seventh Street. Low fondly recalled the sunny idealism of their days in Grez and Paris with Louis's exuberant cousin Bob. "When I said farewell to him I shut the door on a good part of my life," he wrote to Louis. "I felt it then. I know it now." At the age of thirty, Low was struggling to make a living as an illustrator—a far cry from his dreams of being a fine art painter. He and Louis both saw their dedication to art for art's sake slipping away with their youth. Louis wrote to Low:

> *Nearly three years ago, that fatal Thirty struck; and yet the great work is not yet done—not yet even conceived. . . . Eight years ago, if I could have slung ink as I can now, I should have thought myself well on the road after Shakespeare; and now—I find I have only got a pair of walking shoes and not yet begun to travel.*

Prince Otto was to be the "great work"—his first serious novel for adults, set in the mythical German state of Grünewald. It features the weak and somewhat effeminate prince; his wife, who has "manlike ambitions" and has taken control of the government; and the Countess von Rosen, a "lady of a dishevelled reputation," who is sleeping with a devious prime minister who is plotting to overthrow Otto. Louis told Henley that the risqué countess was based on a coquettish older Russian woman he had met in Menton. He envisioned her fictional counterpart to be "a jolly, elderly—how shall I say?—'fuckstress.'" Yet one cannot help but be reminded of Fanny by the countess's "dishevelled reputation" and propensity to make scandals rather than prevent them.

Louis later called *Otto* his "hardest effort." He worked on it for months, writing, rewriting, and polishing some chapters up to half a dozen times. One chapter was redone nine times, with Fanny rewriting the penultimate version. But Louis's great ambition for the novel was matched by his uncertainty about its quality, and when it appeared in print in 1885, the critics recognized this. "We all expected that 'Prince Otto' was to prove the *magnum opus*," an *Academy* reviewer wrote. "Well, we were wrong." Still, Louis always retained a fondness for the story and named the countess one of his favorite female characters.

Today *Prince Otto* is notable for its amusing gender-bending and casual attitude toward extramarital sex. In the end, the "fuckstress" countess is not just a jolly character; she is a rather kinky one. Considered by the prince his "manly friend," she insists that Otto address her as "Count" when she meets him on one occasion disguised as her younger brother, and she embraces him while in drag, sending a "convulsion" through his body.

Louis and Fanny had originally planned to collaborate on the story as a play, and Fanny stayed particularly involved in the composition of the countess. Like many of Louis's readers and critics, she felt that his fictional women were somewhat thinly drawn—or, as he told Henley, she "hates and loathes and slates" them. Fanny fought for the portrayal of the countess "inch by inch," she told Margaret, and she was happy with the end result. Despite the mixed reception for the novel as a whole, the racy and unpredictable countess was and still is recognized as one of the book's successes. Two years later, when Fanny would collaborate with Louis on another unconventional female character, they would create a new kind of hero in fiction.

IN THE UNITED STATES, the good news was that a market for Louis's work was developing. The bad news was that it was not helping him make a living—largely because bootleggers were stealing his work. In the absence of an international copyright law, American publishers paid him little or nothing, releasing his work often without his consent or knowledge, and sometimes without his name. Dickens had complained about pirating on his

U.S. tour forty years earlier, but it had done little to change the practice. Louis had discovered this when he arrived in the U.S. in 1879, hungry and broke, and found a pirated American edition of *Travels with a Donkey in the Cévennes* for sale and two of his short stories running in American periodicals anonymously.

Three years later, two pirated editions of *New Arabian Nights* were released in the States a few months after its publication in Britain: a twenty-cent version from Seaside Library and a dollar edition from Henry Holt and Company. When Louis saw that Holt had misspelled his name "Stephenson" in an advertisement in *The Critic*, he "boiled," he told Low: "It is so easy to know the name of the man whose book you have stolen; for there it is, at full length on the title page of your booty."

Yet the pirated *New Arabian Nights* would actually help make Louis's name in the U.S. After dispatching a clerk at the *Century Magazine* to purchase the cheap Seaside edition, the American journalist and novelist H. C. Bunner gave the book a glowing review in the magazine in 1883. Until then, Louis had earned little recognition in the U.S. beyond being an "Englishman who is both a good traveler and a good writer," in the words of *The Publishers' Weekly*. But the review by a respected critic in a prominent periodical changed that. Bunner wrote of Louis as an exciting literary discovery.

Fanny was so ecstatic, she told Margaret that she woke at night just thinking of the review. With the *Century*'s wide U.S. circulation, she basked in the idea that everyone she knew would read it—especially those who had doubted Louis's talent and condemned her marriage to the sickly younger man.

The review also prompted the magazine's editor, Richard Watson Gilder, to take a closer look at Louis's work. Gilder and his wife, Helena (a painter and onetime romantic interest of Winslow Homer), shared a "camping-out passion" with the author of *Travels with a Donkey in the Cévennes*, he wrote to Louis. And he felt even more camaraderie with the author because of their mutual friendship with Low and others in the American artist community who had known Louis in France. "A lot of us younger men and women have had a kind of revival—love-feast and experience meeting over your books lately," he raved. "I would blush to tell you how much we think of them."

Louis wrote giddily to the elder Stevensons, "'In eighteen hundred and eighty-three, / America discovered me!' I am Columbus outside in." He boasted that he seemed to be "a kind of success nowadays," though he still needed to inquire, a few lines down, about a check he had been expecting from his ever-generous parents. Both the *Century* and *Lippincott's* offered him travel assignments, which he ended up turning down because of his precarious health. But he sent Gilder *The Silverado Squatters* and was pleasantly surprised when the editor offered him £40 to serialize it. Louis's colorful tale of squatting on an abandoned mine ran in the *Century* in the closing months of 1883.

For another American editor, Thomas Niles Jr., a partner at the Boston publisher Roberts Brothers, Louis had growing contempt. Niles had keen commercial instincts for potential juvenile classics. He had convinced Louisa May Alcott to write *Little Women*, something she agreed to only for financial reasons because, aside from her sisters, she "never liked girls or knew many." And Niles would have the foresight to snatch up *Treasure Island* for U.S. publication two months after its release in Britain. Though Roberts Brothers paid the British publisher Cassell to reprint the book, Niles offered Louis nothing for that or his previous two books that the company had pirated. Still, he seemed to believe he had an informal agreement with Louis that Roberts Brothers was his American publisher.

Louis did not see it that way. Instead, when he sent *A Child's Garden of Verses* to Low to illustrate in 1885, he gave his friend free rein to find a U.S. publisher. Low went to Charles Scribner's Sons. Whether Scribner's was more scrupulous or simply shrewder about the value of compensating a writer whose star was rising, the New York publisher offered Louis 10 percent royalties for his book of children's verse. The proposal was so generous by comparison, Louis felt compelled to write a personal note of thanks. "A man were more than human, if he did not sometimes complain of the way in which things go in the States;" he wrote, "but I have the greater pleasure in recognising conduct so handsome as yours." The publisher's comparative generosity would be rewarded when Louis also offered them the American editions of *Strange Case of Dr Jekyll and Mr Hyde* and *Kidnapped.*

The partnership still did not guarantee substantial earnings for the author, however. In the cutthroat American market for cheap books, publishers like Scribner's still had to contend with a flood of inexpensive reprints slashing into their sales. Until Congress passed the International Copyright Act in 1891, pirating of Louis's work in the U.S. increased hand in hand with its popularity. During the decade when he would write his biggest sellers, Americans would purchase mostly pirated editions of his books.

There were times, Louis wrote to his cousin Katharine, when "terror of the bailiff spoils my work." As fast as he wrote, he could not stay ahead of his family's expenses. He admitted to Henley that he bent under the constant financial strain and his perennial dependence on his parents. And there was no knowing how long he could count on their aid. Thomas's brother and business partner David was suffering from mental illness that caused difficulties at the family engineering firm. In his late sixties, Thomas had become slower and more melancholy, and his doctor was suggesting that he retire.

At other times, Louis could view the vicissitudes of his health and livelihood with laughable equanimity. "I am going to make a fortune," he wrote to Frances Sitwell, "it has not yet begun, for I am not yet clear of debt; but as soon as I am, I begin upon the fortune." His humor veered into hysterics in a letter to Charles Baxter, his friend and financial adviser. What began as a sober discussion of funds quickly dissolved into a jumble of silly verse rhyming with "finance" before sputtering to an end.

As Fanny observed to Margaret, "Illness is such an expensive and dull amusement." So the couple sometimes splurged on happier diversions when cash was in hand. Louis spent a chunk of his *Treasure Island* earnings on expensive prints by the famous Japanese artist Hokusai and on a new dress and matching watch inlaid with turquoise and rubies for Fanny in Marseille. Though Louis was not particularly handy at purchasing the practical items she asked him to pick up when he was out, she wrote to Dora: "I must say, though, that he is a fine person to take to a dressmaker. He went to a place with me that is very celebrated for its costumes, and ordered the loveliest things imaginable."

For people who were often ill or broke or both, Louis and Fanny could be remarkably resilient and upbeat. In spring 1884, they fled Hyères to escape a spread of cholera that had reached epidemic proportions in nearby Toulon. They left behind their little oasis of calm and their dreams of settling down in France. Yet when they arrived to visit Lloyd in Bournemouth, England, he recalled, "They were in the highest spirits; everything pleased them; and although they were carrying all they possessed with them, and had neither home nor plans . . . they were as happy as grigs, and seemed not to have a care in the world." They ended up settling in the resort town on the southern coast of England for the next three years.

Rich or poor, one thing remained the same: Louis's long hair and sloppy wardrobe universally antagonized the financial men in trim frock coats and bespoke trousers. Colvin later recounted one of Louis's rare victories at a bank in Clermont-Ferrand, where he stopped to collect on circular notes that had been sent from Britain. "His appearance had the usual, almost magical, effect of arousing in the business mind suspicions, amounting to conviction, of his dishonesty," Colvin wrote. Suspecting fraud, the clerks insisted they had received no documents from Britain and gave Louis five minutes to vacate the premises before they called the police.

"For once he kept his head and temper, outwardly at least," Colvin went on. Louis refused to leave, insisted that the police be summoned, and somehow rummaged through bank papers in front of the astonished clerks until he located the correspondence. Then he unleashed a "torrent of scornful eloquence" on the managers, stressing with particular glee the bank's potential ruin for such ill treatment of customers. By the time he finished, they could not fawn enough over their suddenly distinguished client as they cashed the notes and escorted him to the door. The next day, Louis had a medal engraved in Latin, which translated: "Overthrow of the Bankers. At last RLS has taken vengeance on the bankers for many injustices. To God alone be the Glory."

IN SUMMER 1884, Louis and Henley were curiously possessed with the idea that the path to gold lay through the stage. It was curious because Louis had been gripped by doubts about their joint work on *Deacon Brodie* several years before, and reviews of the play when it ran for a single night in London were not encouraging. Yet Henley's irrepressible faith in playwriting as the way out of poverty seemed to infuse their collaboration with magical thinking.

Henley had more riding on the partnership than Louis. He was living with his wife, Anna, on his meager salary as a journalist in the gritty Shepherd's Bush area of London, where he was also providing for his widowed mother and four brothers. Henley would go on to earn recognition as an influential critic and editor—championing Auguste Rodin and James McNeill Whistler, as well as J. M. Barrie, Rudyard Kipling, H. G. Wells, Joseph Conrad, and other young male writers who became known as "Henley's Regatta." And he had already worked tirelessly and without pay to promote Louis's career. But he would never have his friend's cachet as a writer, and he knew Louis's name would boost their prospects of success.

Fanny was also convinced that a fortune from the theater would provide a cushion to ease her husband's mind and liberate him from doing "games." She invited Henley to visit often and engaged in jocular sparring with him to ease the tension between them. She nicknamed him "Buffalo William" for his rowdiness and he addressed her as "you wicked woman" and promised a ruby bracelet for one of her editorial suggestions when they made their fortunes. Though it was always something of a relief when he departed—especially since he routinely flouted the rules she set to protect Louis's health—the house seemed "very dull without Henley's big jolly red face and electrified hair" when he was gone, she confessed to Margaret Stevenson.

Louis and Henley worked together and apart from summer 1884 into the following winter on three plays: *Beau Austin*, *Admiral Guinea*, and *Macaire*.

Louis set the terms, which would govern all his future collaborations. His partner would create the structure and compose the first draft, and Louis would revise and command final authority. Fanny made the fatal error, at least in Henley's eyes, of believing that she was part of the project as well. For her, it was a creative escape from the day-to-day burden of being a caregiver. She confided to Henley that some nights she lay awake repeating every line of *Admiral Guinea* and acting out her favorite parts. But Henley bristled that a novice was butting into the work of two professionals. "The match is no longer equal," he wrote to Baxter in July 1884. "Louis has grown faster than I have; and then there's the Bedlamite. I love her; but I won't collaborate with her *and* her husband, and I begin to feel that the one means both."

The collaboration was ultimately unsuccessful. The two men had no real talent for playwriting and little interest in contemporary theater. (Even Louis called *Admiral Guinea* "vomitable in many parts.") When Louis finally gave up on the plays, Henley condemned Fanny—outrageously, because her enthusiasm for the joint project had continued after Louis had begun to express doubts.

The time swallowed up in playwriting was not only failing to make the Stevensons wealthy; it was further depleting their bank account. Frantically casting about for a relatively easy project when, as Fanny later put it, "money was absolutely necessary," they turned to stories she had made up for Louis months before, when he was very ill in Hyères. At the time, Louis could not write, read, or even see because he had bandages covering his eyes. Desperate for entertainment, he asked his wife to take a walk every day and make up a tale to tell him when she returned. Stories of action and intrigue, not "important" literature, were a drug that Louis took "like opium" when he was ailing, he once wrote to a friend.

Fanny recalled her task as "a sort of Arabian Nights Entertainment where I was to take the part of Scheherazade." Some days, her caregiving duties confined her to the walkway outside their front door, but her imagination was boundless. Every day she created a new tale about a female criminal— not a poor woman who turned to crime in desperation but a young revolutionary in the campaign for Irish independence. At the time, England was reeling from the first urban bombing campaign in history, which was led by Irish exiles in the United States. Radical Irish separatists, the Fenians, had planted a series of bombs in public spaces such as railway and underground stations in British metropolitan centers—a new form of terrorism made possible by the invention of dynamite and advances in clockwork mechanisms.

Fanny's tales had been forgotten as Louis was able to resume work on other projects, but now the couple hoped to quickly turn them into a sequel to *New Arabian Nights*. In November 1884, Fanny reported to her mother-in-law that she was busy making up stories for Louis. Then he revised them and created an overarching framework, filling it out with other material. For Fanny, the project was not only a chance to help support the family, it was also her turn to step out of the shadows into the public role of coauthor.

More New Arabian Nights: The Dynamiter is a labyrinthian collection of tales within tales, a strangely humorous and fanciful satire on terrorism. It begins in a Soho cigar shop owned by Louis's *New Arabian Nights* hero Prince Florizel, now going by the name Theophilus Godall. Three broke and drifting friends lounging there—Edward Challoner, Harry Desborough, and Paul Somerset—see a newspaper notice offering a reward for information about a suspicious man who was seen wearing a sealskin coat. They decide on the spot to become detectives, "the only profession for a gentleman."

They quickly become easy prey for a team of Fenian terrorists masquerading as ordinary citizens. Somerset's life becomes entwined with that of Mr. Jones, whom he eventually discovers to be a famous dynamiter, Zero, when he spies the man's sealskin coat. Zero has grandiose visions of "the fall of England, the massacre of thousands, the yell of fear and execration," though his bombs usually fizzle. In the end, he is blown up by one of his few successful devices.

All three men cross paths with Fanny's criminal creation, named Clara Luxmore in the book, a young British woman who has run away from her comfortable home to join the revolution. Alluring, independent, and defiant of social conventions, Luxmore shines out from the pack of colorless and blathering male characters. From the moment Challoner sees her tumble out of a hissing building in a cloud of smoke, smoothing her dress and gloves, it is clear she is going to take him and his hapless chums on a wild ride. Luxmore is a shape-shifter who impersonates other women to fabricate tales that appeal to the men for protection, stirring their sense of gallantry and national honor. Instead of thwarting the dynamiters, they end up assisting them by unwittingly transporting bombs and money.

The Stevensons' antihero bears a striking physical resemblance to a younger Fanny—most likely at Louis's hand. Her face is "rich in color" and her figure "full and soft in all the womanly contours, was yet alive and active, light with excess of life." The men are taken by the "conduct of [her] sweeping skirt." Like Fanny, she also explodes conventional views of gender. She is both a "lady" and an "adventuress," a seductive woman who acts with the agency of a man. Unlike so many cunning fictional females, she does not use lies to lure men into marriage but to support a political cause. In fact, she seems to have little need for marriage—her stories enable her to rove freely through the world of men by running circles around them. She is as dangerous for the threats she poses to the social order as she is for her association with dynamite.

Luxmore's outrageous stories draw on popular fiction genres, headline news, and Fanny's personal memories. Her familiarity with Mormon women in the American West informed the first tale Fanny created, which became "Story of the Destroying Angel." In it, Luxmore masquerades as Asenath Fonblanque, a runaway from a forced marriage to a man in the Destroying Angels, an authentic violent Mormon secret society of the time. A variation of the racist slur Fanny was taunted with as a child—"N——, n——, never die, / Black face and shining eye"—becomes an odious password that Challoner must say in another story.

Most provocatively, Luxmore pretends to be Teresa Valdevia, the daughter of a Scotch Spanish father and black African mother in the "Story of the Fair Cuban," a sensationalized resurrection of the American slave narrative set in the Caribbean country where slavery was still legal. As Allison

Francis, a scholar of gender and ethnicity in literature, has pointed out, the Stevensons' decision to present a female British national impersonating a Cuban mixed-race slave is problematic, yet seen in the context of its time, they were attempting to challenge notions of gender and race in bold ways through the complex characterization of Luxmore. Francis notes that the authors also discarded the fictional slave narrative trope of the mulatta hero—a beautiful, light-skinned girl—gaining freedom only to commit suicide after being shunned by both black and white societies. In their version, the "tragic mulatta" Valdevia enjoys wealth and power.

The Stevensons' decision to craft their critique of terrorism as farce has perplexed modern scholars, but it is worth noting that the Irish campaign was relatively nonviolent. Though the Fenians staged an impressive blast at the division of Scotland Yard established to investigate the bombings, their goal was to hit iconic public spaces when they were empty, which resulted in only one civilian casualty in five years. Comic weeklies routinely ridiculed the dynamiters, relying on popular anti-Irish stereotypes to lampoon them as intellectually inept, especially the blustery leader Jeremiah O'Donovan Rossa, the likely the model for Zero. Louis despised Rossa, who advocated that everyone in Ireland carry a "bit" of explosive in their pocket. "If I cannot make dynamite horrible, I would fain make it ridiculous," Louis explained to Henley.

Fanny and Louis opposed terrorism, regardless of the cause, and found indiscriminate bombings especially cowardly. But Louis also believed that the British Empire lacked moral authority and that Liberal prime minister William Gladstone encouraged the violence by yielding to the Fenians' demands. In *The Dynamiter*, the government appears as incompetent at stopping bombs as the terrorists are at setting them off. The three young men, or "three futiles," are stand-ins for England: easily flattered and bumbling. Despite the Stevensons' absurd take on terrorism, however, they did not make light of its potential gravity, which sits in the shadows of the stories like a ticking parcel.

The book ends where it began, in Godall's cigar shop, where the three friends have reconvened, along with Luxmore. She and Desborough have married after his earnest devotion to her ultimately captured her heart and induced her to confess her deceit. His friends are shocked by his marriage to such a dangerous woman (echoing the reaction of Louis's friends to his marriage to Fanny). Godall, however, welcomes it as an indication that domesticity will tame Luxmore's political passions, and he sermonizes on traditional marriage and family as the cornerstone of Britain's national superiority. But Luxmore challenges his view. She insists that she married only for love and that she regrets her terrorist activities but not the conviction that motivated them; she was willing to give her life for what she believed. There is no suggestion that she will relinquish her political involvement as incompatible with marriage. "I may have been a criminal, in short," she says in her memorable closing words, "but I never was a fool."

In real life, Fanny and Louis were hammering out their own marriage construct, one that was both complicated and enhanced by their creative partnership. Though Louis seems to have had control of their joint project at this point, as he had with Henley, he considered Fanny a coauthor whose stories he felt free to embellish with some of his own ideas. Correcting his mother's impression that all the "Cuban stories" were Fanny's, he claimed that one of them was more his, adding the caveat: "I mean, for a book whose authorship is so mixed up."

Fanny felt very involved in the composition as well as the conceptualization of *The Dynamiter*. "I always have to fight hard for my changes, but in most Henley has borne me out . . . ," she wrote to her mother-in-law. "The field is always covered with my own dead and wounded, and often I am forced to a compromise. Still I make a very good fight." Fanny did not delude herself that she had her husband's writing talent, but she hoped to improve her craft by working with him. "Our joint book is a rather mad thing; naturally it must be if I have anything to do with it," she wrote to Dora with her self-deprecating humor. "We have had great fun over it, so if nobody else likes it, we have had our enjoyment at least."

Of the decade's popular dynamite narratives—including Oscar Wilde's play *Vera* and Henry James's novel *The Princess Casamassima*—the Stevensons' was the only one to deal with the Irish terrorist campaign that was convulsing England. By setting her stories within the campaign, Fanny had given the book an immediacy that the others lacked. A sense of chaos and confusion about reality runs through the tales, seeming to mirror the jittery public psyche. At times during the composition, fact and fiction must have seemed strangely intermingled for Fanny and Louis as the terrorist campaign escalated. Just before Louis signed a book contract with Longmans, Green and Company, in February 1885, the most alarming event occurred: Bombs planted in the House of Commons, the Tower of London, and Westminster Hall detonated nearly simultaneously. Four civilians were injured and the incident, known as Dynamite Saturday, caused an international sensation. Fanny and Louis dedicated the book to the only heroes they could discern in the conflict, two policemen who were injured when the Westminster bomb they were trying to remove exploded.

As outraged as they were by the latest incidents, the cash-starved couple could not help but be aware that they boosted the book's commercial potential. Fanny wrote to Frances Sitwell deploring Dynamite Saturday and praising the police officers, but she also noted with her usual bluntness that the incident was a "great advertisement" for the book. And on the eve of its publication in April 1885, Louis spurned his friend Andrew Lang's suggestion to go with the less exploitive, or "catch penny," title *The Man in the Sealskin Coat*. Three months after Dynamite Saturday, *More New Arabian Nights: The Dynamiter* by Robert Louis and Fanny Van de Grift Stevenson arrived in bookstores.

THE BOOK WAS AN IMMEDIATE hit with the public. While Louis's plays with Henley languished, his collaboration with his wife galloped into three editions in four months, replenishing the Stevensons' bank account. Readers enjoyed Luxmore's gripping and outrageous tales, and reviewers praised "The Fair Cuban" and "The Destroying Angel" as "highly imaginative" and "equal, if not superior, to anything Mr. Stevenson has ever done."

Despite the generally glowing reviews, Fanny felt slighted or ignored by some critics, at least early on. Most reviews acknowledged the book as a collaboration while singling out only Louis for praise. Fanny confided to her mother-in-law:

> *I thought in the beginning that I shouldn't mind being Louis's scapegoat, but it is rather hard to be treated like a comma, and a superfluous one at that;—and then in one paper, which I will send you, the only one in which I am mentioned the critic refers to me as "undoubtedly Mr. Stevenson's sister." Why, pray? Surely there can be nothing in the book that points to sister in particular.*

Fanny's fears of being Louis's "scapegoat" proved to be prophetic. In a prefatory note to the book for an edition of her husband's work eleven years after his death, she recounted *The Dynamiter*'s genesis, taking credit for originating "The Fair Cuban" and "The Destroying Angel." After that, the book's reputation plummeted, and Fanny was blamed for its flaws. To Audrey Murfin, an expert in Stevenson collaborations, this is not surprising: Modern critics commonly credit Louis for books they consider significant and credit his less talented collaborators for books they want to dismiss.

Murfin notes another factor that has shaded assessments of Louis's wife. "Of all of Fanny's perceived flaws, none has more offended the critical establishment than this: she dared to nurse literary ambitions—ambitions that may have exceeded her literary gifts." This does not seem like a particularly heinous offense; many writers' ambitions exceed their capabilities. Yet had Fanny not claimed her collaborative role in *The Dynamiter* and instead stayed a silent partner, in the tradition of many writers' wives, she undoubtedly would have fared better with Stevenson critics. Instead, the book is often held up as an example of her "literary pretensions" and "delusions of grandeur about her status as a writer," and her claims to the stories are dismissed as lies or exaggerations. Some critics have insisted her contributions were trivial, while others have accused her of wresting control of the book from her husband (just as Luxmore sometimes takes over the narrative in the book); still others have claimed both were true.

In 2015, digital humanities scholars at the University of Edinburgh sought to introduce more objective evidence into the debate by conducting a stylometric analysis of the writing styles in *The Dynamiter* and in separate works by Fanny and Louis. While the results suggest that Louis's hand predominated in their book, the researchers concluded that Fanny and Louis had individually composed the stories she credited to each, and the other tales appeared to be a blend of their writing styles.

In recent years, more critics have come to regard *The Dynamiter* as a bold and inventive book, and Fanny's contributions have earned more recognition. As Louis's most political collaborator, she connected their joint project to contemporary politics and challenged gender roles in adventure fiction. Rather than demonstrating that Fanny contaminated her husband's work, Stevenson scholar Penny Fielding observes, the book is "a tribute to the volatile, inventive and intense partnership of their lives together."

Clara Luxmore's symbolic fight for independence reflects feminist themes that run through much of Fanny's other writing. Luxmore was one of the charismatic new bad girls that emerged in fiction at the moment when the "woman question" was unsettling British society even more than the "Irish question." Her ability to slip through the knots of social convention and get away with it provided female readers with an exciting channel for their fantasies of liberation. According to Elizabeth Carolyn Miller, an expert in late Victorian British literature, irresistibly likable criminals like Luxmore were a link to the New Woman, who would soon become a feminist icon. As Miller has noted, the rise of fictional revolutionaries such as Luxmore was followed by "an outburst of *real* female political criminals": militant suffragists, one of whom called the suppression of women "an invitation to dynamite."

Fanny and Louis would not collaborate formally again, but he would continue to draw on his wife's insights to enrich his writing—especially in the creation of his next work, one of the most haunting tales in English literature.

ELEVEN

There was no cure for what ailed Robert Louis Stevenson in 1885 or 1886 or 1887. Though he would try nearly anything to stop his hemorrhages, he could not turn that insidiously reliable partner out of his bed; "Bluidy Jack," as he named them, was wasting away his body, his time, his life. During the three years the family lived in Bournemouth, Lloyd recalled, "There could be no pretense that he was not an invalid and a very sick man."

Bluidy Jack was a maddening intruder, arriving without warning and often leaving carnage in his wake. Occasionally he produced no more than a crimson blotch on Louis's handkerchief. Other times, "bowlfuls" of bright red blood spurted over his clothes and bedsheets. Coughing fits and hemorrhages could go on for hours, or even days. During one attack, in 1887, Louis would cough blood intermittently for two weeks. His worst hemorrhage had come on in Hyères when he had cajoled Fanny and their maid, Valentine Roch, to dance with him around a bonfire after a journalist he despised was found guilty of criminal libel. But Jack seemed to take any pleasure—a little travel or a visit from a friend—as an invitation to trample down the last vestiges of youth of that "lean, feverish, voluble and whiskyfied Scot, who once sparked through France and Britain, bent on art and the pleasures of the flesh."

What medical condition accounted for Louis's hemorrhages is uncertain. His symptoms are most often attributed to pulmonary tuberculosis—a disease that enjoyed a macabre romanticism in the 1800s because of its reputation as the "robber of youth." Like John Keats and Percy Shelley, Louis was among the young writers whose association with the disease lent them a certain morbid glamour, and still does. But he was never actually diagnosed with active tuberculosis, leading two prominent specialists who treated him in his thirties, Carl Rüedi and Edward Livingston Trudeau, to speculate that it was inactive by then. Louis also lived a relatively long time for an afflicted man and never infected anyone in his household.

Some modern researchers have suggested that he had bronchiectasis—a condition of damaged bronchial tubes that is characterized by repeated infections and a persistent, sometimes bloody cough. Childhood illnesses such as whooping cough, flu, croup, and bronchitis would have predisposed Louis to the disease, and its vicious cycle of lung inflammation and infection could explain why he never seemed to recover from one illness before the next one knocked him down. Tuberculosis increases the risk for bronchiectasis, so it is also possible that he suffered from both. Neither would have been improved by his chain-smoking.

Louis claimed a number of other maladies. Difficulty urinating was a recurring problem—at one point, he could not pass urine for thirty-six hours—which could have been caused by prostatitis or scarring from venereal disease. At various times, he suffered from cholera, tapeworm, painful kidneys, "pleuritic rub," a "recalcitrant liver," a "constipated gall-duct," chronic digestive disorders (that once turned his face red for three days), rheumatism, and night sweats. But Bluidy Jack was the scariest, with the dreaded aftermaths—the "long spells when he was doomed to lie motionless on his bed lest the slightest movement should restart the flow," Lloyd recalled, "when he would speak in whispers, and one sat beside him and tried to be entertaining—in that room he was only too likely to leave in his coffin."

Of course, Louis also tried to entertain those around him, especially Fanny; they shared a gallows humor that carried them through some desperate moments. During a severe hemorrhaging episode, when he was too choked with blood to talk and Fanny was too shaky to measure out his medicine, Louis did it himself and scribbled a note: "Don't be frightened; if this is death, it is an easy one." Fanny also tried to put a humorous slant on Louis's long periods of enforced idleness in her correspondence with his friends and family. She noted to William Henley that Louis was allowed to see no one—"at least he is to see no one whose conversation could be of any possible interest." And when a doctor instructed her that in order to remain calm, Louis must never be contradicted, she drolly observed to his mother that the order "will give me some training, will it not?"

Louis could not always mask his misery to those in his immediate household. Valentine, who often cared for Louis when Fanny was away, later said that if anything made him question whether he should have married, it was his poor health. "I do not ask you to love me any more," he once wrote to Fanny. "I am too much trouble. . . . You cannot put up with such a man." He was such a withered, homely version of himself in Bournemouth—"so spectral, so emaciated, so unkempt and tragic a figure," as Lloyd described him—he could hardly have felt like a seductive sexual partner for his wife. And relying on her to clean up his blood and carry him to urinate when he was weak was not the kind of marital intimacy he wished for either of them. "I don't want you when I'm ill; at least, it's only one half of me that wants you," he wrote to her. He preferred to be miserable than to subject her to that. But he could never fully suppress the sunny side that had him calling on her to come to him and produce a "tonic effect on your papa," insisting, "If you don't think I want to see you, you are a great Ass."

The difficulty for Fanny was not always knowing which side of her husband she would encounter. "Taking care of Louis is as you must know, very like angling for sly trout," she had lightly observed to her mother-in-law early on, "one must understand when to pay out the line, and exercise the greatest caution in drawing him in." But his violent mood swings did not make that easy. He was "a volcano raging inside" when he could not work, she reported back to Margaret after two years of marriage, "and you know how much harm he does himself when he gets in a wild state." He could also create hell for Fanny when he directed his anger and frustration with his invalidism at her. He vented his loathing for certain drugs on her when she tried to administer them. He turned up his nose at the special dishes she prepared to stimulate his appetite. He resented her when she tried to limit his socializing.

Fanny could not count on much emotional support from Louis's friends, for whom he put on a cheerier face. By then they were fed up with health alarms from his wife, who turned even the smallest incident into a full-blown crisis, they believed. Sidney Colvin's patience had run out when Louis, while journeying solo to Nice in 1883, had failed to get word to Fanny that he had arrived safely after hemorrhaging on the way. After several days of silence, Fanny put everyone on high alert and set out to find her husband with her son and her gun. With her flair for storytelling, she described her search in letters as a dramatic misadventure, with train station personnel at each stop rebuking her for allowing her ill husband—whom they all fondly recalled—to travel alone, and who was no doubt now lying dead or dying somewhere.

Louis, whom she finally found obliviously reading in bed in a Nice hotel, treated her arrival as the punch line to a great joke, but Colvin was not amused. He was outraged that a friend of his had witnessed Fanny's distress on a train and felt compelled to help her. Though his friend supported her version of events, Colvin raged at Fanny's "love of harrowing her own and other people's feelings" with what he regarded as her hysterical ineptitude. "I will never let myself be frightened by that maniac partner of his again, and she may cry Wolf till she is hoarse," he wrote to Charles Baxter.

The elder Stevensons also chalked up the event to Fanny being "Cassandra" and suggested that the high-strung couple overreacted to the slightest tickle in Louis's throat. This prompted him to send an angry letter of rebuke. "[Fanny] has taken it into her head, being horrid depressed, that you think that she is *bad for me!*" he chided them. "What she is to me, no language can describe, and she can never learn. . . . This talk of nervousness is the talk of sick children, and is fair neither to Fanny nor to me."

Louis's friends also doubted Fanny's credibility because he might seem perfectly well in a letter one day while the next day she dispatched one in full panic mode. However, Louis's condition could change overnight, and she was at the mercy of doctors who offered conflicting opinions and advice. On another trip to the Riviera with Baxter and Henley, the two friends had left for home when Louis had a slight cold. By the time Fanny arrived to collect him, a doctor proclaimed her husband near death and urged her to telegraph for a male family member to join her. Fanny stayed up alone for two terrified nights watching Louis's every breath and hoping someone would agree to come. Then a second doctor refuted the first, cheerfully assuring her that Louis could well live until seventy if he did not travel. At a time when much medical advice was largely guesswork, this sort of ambiguity was typical but frustrating.

Not surprisingly, Fanny later huffed to Margaret, "If [all the doctors] agree upon one point, I should think there was something in it; and if they all differ, as they likely will, I shall think the truth is in none of them." She had seen Louis pull through enough times to believe that a visit from Bob Stevenson, who did answer her call for help, could be as healing as any medicine. Still, the incident seemed to confirm that she was an "alarmist," in Henley's words. "They all think I wanted a nurse or courier and hadn't sense to hire one," she wrote, wearily defending herself to Margaret. "The doctors supposing Louis to be dying wanted someone to be here to take charge of things afterward. I wanted someone to help me keep him alive." Fanny felt she could never convince others how ill Louis truly was.

Two women who witnessed the extremes in his health did seem to understand, however. Coggie Ferrier, the sister of Louis's college friend Walter Ferrier, was with the couple during a long hemorrhaging episode and marveled at Fanny's fortitude and competence throughout. "She is really *no alarmist*," Ferrier wrote to Henley. Adelaide Boodle, a neighbor and frequent visitor in Bournemouth, later wrote of her youthful worship of the couple in her memoir, *R. L. S. and His Sine Qua Non*. Boodle understood how Louis's illness drove him to "erratic moods, in which all caution went to the winds," but she also believed they tried Fanny's nerves "almost to a breaking point," though she doubted that Fanny ever revealed that to him.

Fanny certainly was not always a ministering angel—she was often bedridden with her own illnesses, which left her grumpy and irritable. She was diagnosed with extreme anemia, gallstones, stomach problems, and "neural-gic rheumatism of the heart and kidneys," which caused painful, swollen joints. But her most relentless ailment was the nineteenth-century condition known as "brain fever," "brain inflammation," or "brain exhaustion"—a Victorian catchall diagnosis for symptoms such as violent head pain, mental confusion, erratic behavior, forgetfulness, irritability, and delirium. When Fanny suffered an "attack," the inside of her head whirled and roared, her hands shook, and sometimes she could not hear or walk.

Like tuberculosis, brain fever was a popular nineteenth-century literary device because of its dramatic onset and symptoms. In her short story "The Warlock's Shadow," Fanny even afflicted her female narrator with a "nervous exhaustion" that no Western medicine could cure. What exactly plagued Fanny remains unclear. It is possible that she suffered from a psychological condition such as bipolar disorder or post-traumatic stress disorder from losing her son. However, her "brain fever" could have also been a manifestation of one or more underlying physical illnesses that cause neurological and psychological symptoms. For example, mosquito-borne illnesses like malaria can cause inflammation of the brain, encephalitis, or meningitis. Fanny's complaint of a recurring face rash could suggest lupus, which can lead to many symptoms that were attributed to her "brain fever," including confusion, delirium, memory loss, and tremors. (Aggravated by stress, lupus, like rheumatoid arthritis, is inflammatory, which would also account for her painful and swollen joints.)

The nineteenth-century medical establishment considered women more susceptible to brain fever because of their "fragile" nervous systems. Fanny tied her condition to her tough circumstances. "I have had too worrying a life," she wrote to Dora, "neither my brain nor my heart have been able to stand it, to say nothing of my nerves." The trauma of her son Hervey's death from tuberculosis had triggered her first memory gaps and fevered imaginings, and Louis's repeated brushes with death must have forced her to relive the anguish of her son's final days.

The burdens of caregiving undoubtedly accounted for some of her symptoms as well. Today, the fatigue, tension, anger, and depression she experienced are considered common in a caregiver to a spouse with a chronic illness. They would have made every shift in her husband's health loom larger; she might have actually experienced each new downturn as catastrophic, rather than deliberately exaggerating it. Like most caregivers, Fanny neglected her own health and often fell ill when Louis was recovering. Yet retreating to her bed also provided an occasional escape from nursing her invalid husband that she would otherwise not allow herself. "The awkwardness is that I *must* be well on Louis's account, and I don't seem able to manage it," she wrote to Colvin from Bournemouth.

LIKE MANY PATIENTS in the nineteenth century, the Stevensons were prescribed treatments that seem odd today. A few were benign, such as the donkey rides prescribed for Fanny, and for Louis, the wool bandage called a "cholera belt," which was guaranteed to prevent colds when worn with a leather under-waistcoat with satin sleeves. ("All the doctors here wear them," Fanny wrote hopefully to Margaret from France.) A few, like Swedish massage for Fanny's rheumatism, were no doubt helpful. Yet some treatments were appalling. One physician proposed removing Louis's uvula to clear his throat, and even George Balfour, his physician uncle, advised blistering his feet to keep him from walking when he was ordered to rest. In Davos, Louis had reported to his parents that the "mania" of Fanny's doctor included "experimenting away upon her with red-hot needles"—or burning her skin in spots, supposedly to steady her nerves. Neither "mania" nor "experiment" is a reassuring word when applied to medical treatments, nor was Louis's offhand comment, "I don't imagine [the scourging of flesh] can do harm." Fanny found it painful to fasten clothing over those areas for the rest of her life.

With Louis's father footing the bill, in June 1884 the couple also took the waters at a spa in Royat, a French town built on the side of a volcano, where guests were carried from their rooms to the bathing pavilion in sedan chairs with curtains. However, spas and sanatoriums were only occasional options, depending on the generosity of Thomas Stevenson. Faster and less expensive relief was available on the apothecary shelf, in the many tonics, powders, and pills that contained opiates, cannabis, and cocaine. Warnings about addiction had begun to circulate by the 1880s, but most physicians were slow to heed them, in part because they had so little other relief to offer. Antibiotics were still decades away, and even aspirin did not appear until the turn of the century.

Fanny and Louis took a dizzying array of dangerous drugs over the course of their lives—enough to suggest that they were, under medical direction, more than occasional drug users. Neither may have developed an addiction, but the powerful preparations must have done their bodies and minds more harm than good—beginning, for Louis, with the poisonous antimonial wine he was given as a child, which George Balfour believed ruined his constitution.

The "blue pill" that Louis took as an adult was full of mercury, as was calomel, or mercurous chloride, which he claimed in 1885 was the only medication that could stop his hemorrhages. (Louisa May Alcott had discovered calomel's toxicity when a regimen of the drug left her with lifelong trembling, sleeplessness, and delirium, which she treated with opium and morphine.) For pleurisy and painful breathing, Louis also took aconite, a highly dangerous medication made with toxins that can damage the heart, muscles, and nerves. At the very least, it probably caused some of the nausea, weakness, sweating, and breathing problems that often plagued him.

Opiates were the cornerstone of tuberculosis treatment in the nineteenth century and stocked even at tobacco shops and stationers as the British Empire expanded its reach—and drug trafficking—around the world. In Bournemouth Louis took opium or morphine to ease his cough, though the latter induced vomiting and nightmares and made him too mentally foggy to work. "I am never really awake, but wander narcotised," he wrote to Henley in winter 1886.

Opiates were also the panacea for a host of "female problems"—from menstrual cramps to hysteria, depression, and fainting fits, known collectively as "the vapours." At the Royat spa in June 1884, Louis reported to his parents that Fanny was on opiates half the time for an internal strain. "These female games are so ticklish," he added, "and by the right men, sometimes so easily cured." Like Louis, Fanny also took laudanum, the infamous reddish-brown tincture of opium that was prescribed so often, it is known as the "aspirin of the nineteenth century." Florence Nightingale, Elizabeth Barrett Browning, and the Pre-Raphaelite model and artist Elizabeth Siddal are among those who became addicted to it. Though a laudanum comedown could cause restlessness and depression, the double bang of opium and alcohol made for a particularly euphoric high, which Charlotte Brontë captured in her novel *Villette*. The hero, Lucy Snowe, takes a moonlight stroll after being given laudanum to help her sleep and is dazzled to find an ordinary garden "sprinkled with coloured meteors" and "sparks of purple and ruby and golden fire gemming the foliage."

In Davos, Fanny wrote to Edmund Gosse's wife, Ellen, "Laudanum has become my daily beverage, while Louis regales himself upon hasheesh." Today this casual disclosure seems rather stunning. How did it play out in the couple's daily life? One imagines them sometimes floating in a fantastical world like the one Lewis Carroll had dreamed up twenty years before—Fanny tippling her magical "drink me" potion and Louis, like the hookah-smoking caterpillar, blowing smoke rings in her face. Even the dog, Woggs, sometimes wandered in a haze from the bromide prescribed for his fits.

While Louis was groggy from morphine in Bournemouth, his exhausted caregiver got a lift from the popular tonic Vin Mariani, a mix of Bordeaux wine and cocaine. By the 1880s the medical establishment and drug companies hailed cocaine as the cure for everything from flatulence and anemia to tuberculosis, depression, and morphine addiction. Consumers of the wine were encouraged to drink two to three cups a day, each of which was spiked with 43.2 milligrams of cocaine, to refresh the mind and restore health and vitality. Angelo Mariani, its creator, sent a case of it to Louis and other celebrities—including Thomas Edison, Auguste Rodin, and Arthur Conan Doyle, all of whom wrote glowing letters in response (some of which were used in the company's advertising). Queen Victoria also testified to its benefits, as did Fanny in a letter to Colvin in June 1885, describing it as "a blessing and a boon."

Louis was sometimes wary of the wonder pills and potions, but he still reached for the closest one to stop his hemorrhages, whatever the adverse effects. One of these was a psychoactive drug based on ergot, a chemical derivative of a wheat fungus that is a main component of LSD. Ergotin presumably curbed bleeding by constricting blood vessels, but just a tiny dropful constituted a dose, and overdoses must have been fairly common. Neither of the Stevensons liked it; Fanny thought it gave Louis bowel and bladder problems, and she blamed it for his bizarre behavior in September 1885, when he suffered one of the worst hemorrhages in his life.

AFTER MONTHS INSIDE THE HOUSE—"like a weevil in a biscuit," as Louis described it—he decided to pursue his personal remedy for illness: a change of scenery. So he, Fanny, and Lloyd ventured out for an inexpensive holiday in a farmhouse in the Dartmoor area of southern England. They took along Louis's cousin Katharine, a divorcée who was trying to cobble together a living writing short stories and book reviews. Fanny arranged for Katharine to leave her two children with Valentine in Bournemouth, so she would be free to work. On the way, the party stopped to visit Thomas Hardy in Dorchester. Louis admired *Far from the Madding Crowd*, which had rocketed Hardy to success and helped him and his wife, Emma, build their new home, Max Gate.

Like Louis, Hardy had married an unconventional woman. He had been attracted to Emma Gifford's wildness and eccentricity from the moment he glimpsed her riding her horse on the North Cornwall cliffs, her loose hair streaming behind her in the wind, like his hero Bathsheba Everdene. But the Hardys were not kindred spirits. Emma was hurt that her husband did not encourage her ambitions as a writer or credit her for her contributions to his work. As he withdrew into his writing, she grew more peculiar and withdrawn from him, eventually moving into the attic at Max Gate until her death. Fanny noted in a letter to Dora that Emma already "recoiled" from the new house and preferred rooms in the attic. Emma, who was openly critical of Hardy's writing, also chose the visit with Louis and his entourage to congratulate Katharine on "not being married to a literary man."

In other circumstances, Fanny might have felt empathy for Emma, but in this case she was rather relieved by her refusal to play the genial hostess. "I had the literary man quite to myself," she boasted to Dora, "and we had a most charming talk—on his side, I mean." Though Hardy was nervous and painfully shy at first, he warmed up when he told her about the construction of the house and the Roman relics unearthed in the process.

The visit turned out to be the highlight of the Stevensons' journey because the next night, Bluidy Jack found his way to their Exeter hotel. Theories later abounded on what had summoned Jack—perhaps Louis had read aloud (as Henley heard) or had suffered a chill or was agitated by the hotel noise. Whatever the trigger, he coughed blood more violently than ever—so much that Fanny feared it might strangle him—until she injected him with ergotin. Weeks later, she confided, surprisingly, to Emma Hardy, "I cannot get used to the terror of [the hemorrhage]. The feeling that my husband's life depends upon my dexterity of hand and quickness of thought keeps me in a continual terror. So far, all has gone well, but the next time?"

It was perhaps an overstatement to say that *all* had gone well, because Louis had acted a bit out of his mind. As usual, he would not use an "invalid appliance" to urinate when he was too weak to walk, preferring his tiny forty-five-year-old wife to lift and carry him to relieve himself instead. But now he insisted that she observe a bizarre ritual each time. First she was to return him to bed face down and in a kneeling position. Then she was to lift him, still kneeling, and somehow turn him over in the air before lowering him back into bed face up. Finally she was to pick him up a third time so that he could draw out his feet in the air before she lowered him again.

Fanny worried that she was going to break her back or hurt her fragile husband—"if not to kill him," she wrote to Henley, "at least to snap his little bones somewhere" (a phrase hauntingly reminiscent of Hervey's final days). She was sleepless and she had to write to Louis's friends to ease their concerns and to the elder Stevensons to request funds for their extended hotel stay, but Louis would not let anyone else wait on him. After lifting him several times in one night, she wrote to Sitwell, "He was quite off his head and could not be contradicted because he was bleeding at the lungs at the same time and got into such furies when I wasn't quick enough."

It must have been terrifying to Louis to be thrust unintentionally into a hallucinatory state. His cousin Katharine was frightened too and "a good deal appalled at Louis' mad behavior, of which you have seen something," Fanny related to Henley. However, Fanny was relatively composed. She had seen her husband's strange transformations on ergotin before, but she sighed plaintively to Henley, "I wish I had him back." She was not going to get him back, however—not until he could harness the turbulence roiling inside him and overtaking his sleep into a masterpiece.

A MAN IS RUNNING for his life, a pack of other men nipping at his heels. In a small chamber, he finds something: a vial, some chemical powders—an escape. As his pursuers press in, he tips a mixture in the vial to his lips and becomes someone else.

That is how it went in the dream, at least that is how Louis usually recalled it after the dream made him famous, when he recounted the genesis of *Strange Case of Dr Jekyll and Mr Hyde* over and over to the packs of men who nipped at his heels, notebooks in hand, around the world. Like the crowd chasing the man in his dream, they were after his life, or a little part of it— whatever they could use to feed the legend taking flight around the book.

For a week or so after the Stevensons returned from Exeter, Louis had been racking his brain for a "plot of any sort" for a short story for the Christmas market, though he was also still groggy and having terrifying nightmares. Perhaps he was still taking ergotin or had switched to morphine, which always troubled his sleep. Or perhaps pain or fever made him delirious at night. The morning after the dream, however, he set out to capture it in a burst of creative energy.

Jekyll and Hyde reads like a fever dream—a disorienting journey through dim, mazelike streets where nothing is as it seems. The story focuses on a circle of male friends in London who are privileged professionals—upholders and safekeepers of the British patriarchy. Two are doctors: Hastie Lanyon, who sees patients at his home on "that citadel of medicine," Cavendish Square, and his prominent colleague Henry Jekyll (pronounced Jee-kill). Dr. Jekyll is more of a renegade, pushing the limits of science with his chemical experiments, though he is also obsessed with his public image and "the very pink of the proprieties." Gabriel Utterson is an austere lawyer, but as legal counselor and confidant to his friends, he is privy to their sensitive affairs and trusted to keep them safe.

The men's exclusive circle is about to be penetrated by an outsider—a boorish degenerate named Edward Hyde. Utterson first learns of Hyde on a walk with his kinsman Richard Enfield, when they pass a back door in a "sinister block of building." Enfield says that late one night, he saw a man named Edward Hyde trample a young girl in the street; when witnesses demanded that Hyde reimburse the child's family, he disappeared through the door and returned with a check signed by Dr. Jekyll. Utterson, secretly aware that Jekyll recently revised his will to leave all his possessions to Hyde, commits Enfield to silence on the subject. Quietly suspecting that the mysterious stranger is Jekyll's illegitimate son or a blackmailer, Utterson decides to stalk him, thinking, "If he be Mr. Hyde, I shall be Mr. Seek."

When Utterson finally confronts the hunched, dwarfish younger man, he is repulsed. Like others, he finds Hyde loathsome without quite knowing why, deformed without any obvious deformity. He describes Hyde as "hardly human" and even "troglodytic"—words that could suggest to Victorian readers that he was the hideous offspring of Jekyll's youthful indiscretion with a lower-class woman. The lawyer is determined to see that his friend's good name is not tarnished with scandal, even if it means finding a way to blackmail Hyde.

Utterson attempts to find a rational explanation in a city where the bright facades of houses obscure their dark interiors and answers seem to slip around corners into the sooty brown fog. Jekyll's assurances to Utterson that he can be rid of Hyde anytime he chooses are unsettling—especially after Hyde, with "ape-like fury," fatally thrashes a member of Parliament, Sir Danvers Carew, who stops him on the street with a query late one night. The lawyer wonders, how is it that Hyde beat a man to death with a cane Utterson had given Jekyll as a gift? (And the reader might ask, why is an upstanding member of Parliament wandering unfamiliar streets in the dead of night?) Hyde pledges to disappear and does for a time, but when Jekyll suddenly withdraws from public life, Utterson turns to his colleague, Lanyon, for insight. He finds him in shock after an encounter with Jekyll. Lanyon dies less than a week later, leaving a testimony to be read by Utterson only after Jekyll's death.

Soon it appears that Jekyll might also be dead. His alarmed butler, Poole, entreats Utterson to come urgently to Jekyll's house—Hyde has been locked in his master's study, or "cabinet," for several days and Poole believes he might have killed the doctor. The men's winding journey through Jekyll's house, garden, and surgical theater to his study is like a descent into the darkest recesses of Jekyll's mind. They break down the door and are stunned to find a fire crackling in the hearth, the kettle whistling, and the table set for tea, "the very sugar in the cup." In the midst of this picture of cozy domesticity is Hyde, lying on the floor in the last stages of dying, his body still twitching. Utterson is horrified to discover that he himself has now replaced Hyde in Jekyll's will.

Today we are so accustomed to thinking of "Jekyll and Hyde" as an idiom for two sides of one personality, it is surprising to remember that Victorian readers believed at this point—well over halfway into the novella—that it was the story of two men. They were not yet familiar with Freud's personality theories of ego and id, and the conscious and unconscious self, or their inextricability.

Only the last two chapters reveal that the two men are one. Lanyon's testimony discloses that he knew and disapproved of Jekyll's drug experiments, but when his old school chum implored him to retrieve a vial of tincture and powders from his study for a friend, he acquiesced. Hyde arrived at Lanyon's home hysterically demanding, "Have you got it?" and then gulped down the potion, metamorphosing into Henry Jekyll. The revelation that Jekyll has such a depraved, monstrous side is so unnerving to Lanyon, it kills him.

In the final chapter, a suicide note from Jekyll, the doctor explains his discovery of humans' duality—that "man is not truly one, but truly two." Jekyll writes that he could neither give up his primitive urges nor reconcile them with his professional standing and "imperious desire to carry my head high." So he resigned himself to living a double life until he discovered a chemical potion that he believed could relieve his agonizing internal war by separating his two identities.

The first time the drug was successful, Jekyll felt liberated:

> I felt younger, lighter, happier in body; within I was conscious of a heady recklessness, a current of disordered sensual images running like a mill race in my fancy, a solution of the bonds of obligation, an unknown but not an innocent freedom of the soul. I knew myself, at the first breath of this new life, to be more wicked, tenfold more wicked, sold a slave to my original evil; and the thought, in that moment, braced and delighted me like wine.

For a time, the separation worked, even as Jekyll's "undignified" pleasures turned monstrous and criminal in the hands of Hyde. The doctor might be aghast at his split personality's transgressions, but contended, "It was Hyde, after all, and Hyde alone, that was guilty." Ultimately, however, Jekyll could not stop himself from turning into Hyde, even without the potion. Realizing that he would soon, irrevocably, become Mr. Hyde, he swallowed his last dose of the drug, knowing it was the end of Dr. Jekyll.

Part of the enduring power of *Jekyll and Hyde* is the disorientation it creates in readers. The novella is laced with doubles and reflections; revelations come in envelopes sealed inside other envelopes sealed in wax. The narrative twists and turns between genres—from mystery to shilling shocker to psychological horror story. Perhaps most skillfully, Louis made readers identify with the increasingly horrified Utterson. As *Jekyll and Hyde* expert

Richard Dury has noted, the reader absorbs information at the same time as the gravely concerned lawyer, becoming part of the story as it unfolds. If Utterson is increasingly entangled in Jekyll's story, the reader is too.

THE MANY LEGENDS that surround the composition of *Jekyll and Hyde* began with Louis's own tale of his collaboration between his conscious and his subconscious self. In the 1888 essay "A Chapter on Dreams," he wrote that the horrific nightmares he suffered as a college student had pushed him into a double life, "one of the day, one of the night," until (in a clever twist on the novella) a doctor gave him a drug to stabilize his mind. He then learned to turn his dreams into commercial tales with the help of "little people" he called "Brownies"—unseen nocturnal creatures who worked while he slept to fashion stories to which he would apply the meaning. Louis's essay seems to have left out one of his most important Brownies, however: his wife. Asked by his cousin and first biographer, Graham Balfour, to recall the genesis of *Jekyll and Hyde* after Louis's death, Fanny revealed her own role in the composition.

When Louis had begun feverishly composing the story, Fanny said she feared that it might be time wasted, as much of his recent work had been. After three days, he presented what was presumably a partial draft for her to critique in writing, which was their custom. As Fanny recounted later to Balfour, she felt that Louis's haste to capture the vividness of the dream and adhere to certain elements of it had hampered the story. "He had Jekyll bad all through, and working for the Hyde change only for a disguise," she recalled. She suggested to Louis that "he had here a great moral allegory that the dream was obscuring." She also proposed that Hyde trample the little girl to establish his wickedness early on. According to Lloyd, who corroborated Fanny's account, a very heated argument between husband and wife followed. Then, Fanny said, Louis returned to his bed, where he usually wrote, and later rang his bell for her to come. He pointed to a heap of ashes on the hearth that had been the first draft; he had burned it so that it would not influence the new draft he had already begun. At that point, Fanny was too mortified to suggest other revisions.

Fanny's account of providing critical editorial advice during the composition of *Jekyll and Hyde* has been as controversial as her claim to have written stories in the book she coauthored, *The Dynamiter.* Some, such as Stevenson biographer J. C. Furnas, have accepted her anecdote. "By carrying her hotly contested point, in fact, Fanny did as much as Henley and Colvin combined toward Louis's permanent place in world literature, as well as toward the prosperity of his last eight years," Furnas wrote, though he hastily added that it did not "wholly justify her claims to be a literary strategist."

Others contend that Fanny exaggerated or even fabricated her role. They point out that her account contains inaccuracies and that Lloyd cannot be trusted as a corroborator—he was not only her son, but given to romanticizing in his much more melodramatic retellings of the incident years later. Louis also wrote that he had long been seeking a way to dramatize "man's double being" and claimed to have done so in a previous short story, "The Traveling Companion." However, it is almost inconceivable that Fanny was not influential to the composition. She was Louis's first and sharpest critic, one who shared his fondness for Gothic stories and composed her own, so it seems likely they conferred on the story more than once. Louis also burned "The Traveling Companion," so perhaps he had not fully developed the dual theme in that story or in his hastily composed first draft of *Jekyll and Hyde.*

The tendency to belittle Fanny's contributions to her husband's work fits into the long tradition of downgrading or denying the influence of famous male writers' wives. In "A Chapter on Dreams," Louis joked that while he got all the praise for his novels, the Brownies got only a share of the pudding. Unfortunately, pudding rather than praise traditionally has been the lot of wives such as Vera Nabokov, Sofia Tolstoy, and Frieda Lawrence, whose husbands, like Louis, would have been unable to function without them. Like many other unsung literary wives, Fanny provided secretarial support such as answering fan mail and handling business correspondence; she also helped brainstorm, research, and evaluate Louis's writing while running a household and nursing her medically demanding husband. With her eccentric and creative temperament, she pushed Louis in ways that a more traditional wife probably would not. Like some other authors' wives, she also harbored ambitions of her own. "What a grim sorority they make—," literary critic Parul Sehgal has written, "thwarted artists turned protectors of the solitude of Great Men, guardians of the legacy. . . . They went mad with startling frequency."

Literary wives are very often maligned as unaccomplished, manipulative, and emasculating women who were detrimental to their famous husbands' careers. Fanny is certainly no exception. In his 1992 biography *Dreams of Exile*, Ian Bell contends that Fanny's "vigorous objections" to the first draft of *Jekyll and Hyde* may have been correct, but they were not "very sensitive" and doubled the appalling amount of work her sickly husband had to put in, as if Louis had no choice in the matter. To biographer Frank McLynn, *Jekyll and Hyde*—Louis's first "adult view of sexuality"—would have been a masterpiece had not Fanny "ruined the version he wanted to publish," her thirst for money overriding Louis's "desire for truth." As Audrey Murfin points out in *Robert Louis Stevenson and the Art of Collaboration*, Louis's burning of the first manuscript illustrates, for some, how Fanny's influence was destructive. But this view ignores the fact that destruction is often an essential part of the creative process.

In being cast so often as the villain in her husband's story, Fanny is in good company. Until the publication of Sofia Tolstoy's diaries, letters, and fiction finally revealed her as an intelligent and complex woman, she was widely seen as a jealous, hysterical, and greedy shrew who sought to limit her husband's most important work. And Olivia Langdon Clemens was long painted as a hysterical hypochondriac who "irreparably" destroyed Mark Twain's "artistic integrity," until later biographies revealed her as an intellectual partner and creative asset to her husband.

Sexist attitudes, and sometimes misogyny, have fueled the derogation of Fanny's contributions and talent. Furnas might have allotted her rare credit for *Jekyll and Hyde*, but he also observed, damning with faint praise, "A writer whose wife is better than supinely dull usually shows her all his production and she usually gets enough feel of the business to make admissible comment." Bell surmised that Fanny "seemed to have suffered more than most from the delusion common to the spouses of the famous that a sexual and emotional affinity implies artistic equality." And McLynn let his animus run away with him, imagining that Louis's "philistine" wife might have shared the "pyromania common to the wives of eminent Victorians" and burned not one, but several, versions of the manuscript herself.

Fanny's contributions to Louis's work were not always beneficial, but more often they were. She was an insightful critic and observer, and had a colorful imagination, qualities that he valued and relied on when he left his day's writing by her bedside each night for her to read and critique. Yet at best, Fanny's editorial advice is usually viewed by critics as dumb luck, as if crediting her with literary insight would somehow diminish her husband's genius. This has not only shortchanged Fanny; it has discounted how much Louis's legacy is tied to his complex creative partnership with his wife. By their very nature, informal collaborations between spouses usually lack written documentation, but a diary Fanny kept when the couple was later in the South Seas reveals how much her observations influenced her husband's work.

Rather than exaggerating her impact on Louis's writing, Fanny might actually have underestimated it. Elements from her short stories are echoed in some of his fiction, including *Jekyll and Hyde*. The "Brownies" may have *revived* the idea of a transformative potion in Louis's dream, but the potion first appeared in "Story of the Destroying Angel," a *Dynamiter* story that is widely attributed to Fanny. As Stevenson scholar Hilary Beattie has noted, the sinister doctor in the story would appear to be the "prototype for Henry Jekyll." He experiments with a potion that will make him younger in order to coerce a young woman to marry him, and he travels from Utah to London to find the purest version of the necessary drug.

LOUIS WORKED ON *JEKYLL and Hyde* through October, writing to Colvin that he was "pouring forth a penny (12-penny) dreadful" that was "dam [*sic*] dreadful." His concerns about aesthetic integrity and sensationalism had made him somewhat uneasy with the project from the start, when he began to churn out the shilling shocker for the Christmas issue of *Longman's Magazine*. No doubt he was reminded of the *Pall Mall Gazette*'s advertising campaign the previous Christmas for his short story "Markheim," a powerful tale of murder and repentance. The newspaper had titillated readers with the promise "when ghosts are walking Mr Stevenson is at his weirdest" and employed a procession of men in plaster skulls and sandwich boards shaped like black coffin lids, which was eventually suppressed by the police. Despite the gruesome fanfare, the story was pulled in proofs because it was too short and the newspaper instead ran Louis's potboiler "The Body Snatcher," based on the nefarious Edinburgh doctor Robert Knox, who procured fresh bodies for dissection from an ambitious team of grave robbers turned murderers. Louis had submitted the story with a note saying that he hoped it was "blood curdling enough" for the Christmas market.

Louis was under the gun to finish *Jekyll and Hyde* not only for the holiday issue alone. In a memorable dispatch to Fanny (which begins "Dear Pig"), he wrote, "I drive on with *Jekyll*, bankruptcy at my heels." He completed the novella in six weeks—an impressive feat for any author, much less a self-described "chronic sickest." Fanny praised the finished manuscript to Colvin, and publisher Charles Longman was so impressed, he decided to skip serialization and rush it into print as a book in another four weeks. However, the Christmas market was already saturated by the time the book was ready, so Longmans, Green and Company held its release until January.

The eve of publication again seemed to arouse Louis's discomfort with his own professional dichotomy: serious author versus hack. The reception for his "serious" novel, *Prince Otto*, in November had been disappointing. In a letter to Gosse, he derided a reading public that preferred an author's work to be "dim and knotless" and "(if possible) be a little dull into the bargain." But he also had no patience for writers who bleated about commercial realities like sacrificial lambs. "We are whores," he wrote to Gosse, "some of us pretty whores, some of us not, but all whores: whores of the mind, selling the public the amusements of our fireside as the whore sells the pleasures of her bed."

꧁꧂

STRANGE CASE OF DR JEKYLL AND MR HYDE appeared first in the United States: Charles Scribner's Sons released it on January 5, 1886, four days before it was released in Britain, where some copies were sold in a brown paper wrapper for a shilling. It seems fittingly deceptive that Louis's work of art came dressed as a shilling shocker, and some reviewers were confused. The *Academy* critic noted that it appeared to belong to a class of literature usually associated with "a certain measure of contempt," but concluded that "its impressiveness as a parable is equal to its fascination as a work of art." Other reviewers called the novella "strikingly bold and original in design" (*The Brighton Telegraph*) and "startling and wholly novel" (*The Washington Post*), and likened it to the work of Nathaniel Hawthorne in unifying art and ethics or to the "gloomy grandeur" of Edgar Allan Poe, with more depth and morality (*The Times*).

The unsigned review in *The Times* in late January reputedly caused the first big bump in sales. "Nothing Mr Stevenson has written as yet has so strongly impressed us with the versatility of his very original genius," the reviewer wrote, adding that it was either "a flash of intuitive psychological research, dashed off in a burst of inspiration; or else it is the product of the most elaborate forethought, fitting together all the parts of an intricate and inscrutable puzzle." To the *Times* critic, the novella was clearly about the "essential power of Evil, which, with its malignant patience and unwearying perseverance, gains ground with each casual yielding to temptation." The clergy seized on the story as a moral message about the struggle between virtue and sin and made it the subject of countless sermons, including one at St. Paul's Cathedral. "It is very overpowering to hear one's own son talked of from the pulpit as 'one of the greatest masters of the English language now living,'" Margaret gushed in her diary after hearing a sermon in Glasgow. (Thomas wrote less enthusiastically of "Dr. Jeykill" to Louis, "I confess I can make nothing of the said work however it seems to have made its mark.")

Within weeks the *Court and Society Review* reported that "Have you read *Dr Jekyll and Mr Hyde?*" was the first topic of conversation at dinner parties.

In April Fanny heard a vendor shouting, "DOC-ter Jekyll! DOC-ter Je-kyll!" and in May Queen Victoria was reportedly reading it. By June, the book had exploded Louis into fame and commercial success. Longmans had sold forty thousand copies—making it a major bestseller by the standards of the day—and Scribner's about twenty-five thousand. Unknown to Louis, this was only a fraction of the American pirated editions sold.

The cultural impact of *Strange Case of Dr Jekyll and Mr Hyde* was immediate and enduring. It heavily influenced Oscar Wilde's 1890 novel of double life, *The Picture of Dorian Gray*. Along with Louis's *New Arabian Nights*, it established the lamplit London of toasty fireside chats and fog-shrouded streets as a staple of mysteries, particularly the soon-to-follow Sherlock Holmes series. Writers such as Italo Calvino, Vladimir Nabokov, and Jorge Luis Borges would call it a masterpiece. Elegant stylist Donna Tartt credited it with inspiring her spine-tingling 1992 blockbuster about murderous college students, *The Secret History*. "I couldn't have written or even thought to write *The Secret History* without *Dr. Jekyll and Mr. Hyde*, which is sharp and shocking as ever on the page," Tartt told an interviewer.

The novella went on to spawn dozens of sequels, prequels, comics, graphic novels, video games, and songs. Modern retellings range from Susan Sontag's 1974 short story "Doctor Jekyll," about gender politics on campus, to Victor J. Banis's 2008 book *Drag Thing, or, The Strange Case of Jackle and Hyde*, in which the hero drinks a potion and becomes an eight-foot-tall drag queen.

Few books have had such an expansive screen presence. The sixty or so film and television adaptations include the classic John Barrymore silent version; Rouben Mamoulian's innovative and slightly racy pre–Hays Code version, which won Fredric March a best actor Oscar; Victor Fleming's lamentably racist version with Spencer Tracy; and Jean Renoir's *Le Testament du Docteur Cordelier*, set in 1950s Paris. Most screen versions have veered fairly far from the novella, simplifying and sensationalizing the story by introducing dance hall girls and sexual sadism, making Hyde more monster than man and omitting the mystery of his identity by featuring one actor in both title roles.

Parodies and spoofs began almost immediately and just kept coming. The most memorable was probably *The Nutty Professor*, in which Jerry Lewis and later Eddie Murphy played a nerdy chemistry professor who turns into a suave womanizer. But Daffy Duck, Porky Pig, and a host of animated characters have had their own spin-offs. Notable among the looser film renderings are the musical *Dr. Jekyll and Mr. Hyde*, with Kirk Douglas; the gender-bending *Madame Hyde*, with Isabelle Huppert; and the blaxploitation *Dr. Black, Mr. Hyde*, with Bernie Casey and Rosalind Cash. There have been many porn adaptations.

MORE THAN A CENTURY after its publication, *Strange Case of Dr Jekyll and Mr Hyde* continues to be interpreted and reinterpreted as each generation reshapes the message to fit its own needs. Many see it as a story of addiction: Jekyll takes a drug that initially makes him feel young and free but eventually overtakes and destroys his life. Louis may have had the soul-killing effects of alcohol in mind as he wrote. He had seen drink destroy the life and promise of his college friend Walter Ferrier, and he was still mourning Ferrier's shocking death at the age of thirty-two. In 1968 The Who's John Entwistle would evoke a similar comparison when he composed the song "Dr. Jekyll and Mr. Hyde" about drummer Keith Moon's self-destructive behavior on alcohol. ("Whenever you're with me make sure it's still me," Entwistle's poignant lyrics read. "I've got to the stage I can't tell who I'll be.")

Of course, Louis had experienced the mind-altering effects of many prescribed drugs firsthand, and he might have intended to spin a sobering tale about medical overexperimentation as well as personal drug abuse. To Victorian readers, Jekyll's reddish liquid concoction might have suggested laudanum; modern movie spin-offs have updated it to cocaine and ecstasy. British author Robert Swindells made his 1996 young adult novel *Jacqueline Hyde* about the dangers of sniffing glue. In it, eleven-year-old Jacqueline takes a whiff from a vial in her grandmother's attic that sends her life spiraling downward.

One reason *Jekyll and Hyde* is so open to interpretation is because Jekyll's vices are never actually spelled out. In fact, Louis made them vaguer with each revision. In the first surviving draft, Jekyll confesses that as a boy he was secretly "the slave of disgraceful pleasures," presumably masturbation. In revisions, the young Jekyll became slave only to "certain appetites" and finally not a slave at all but guilty of a "certain impatient gaiety of disposition, such as has made the happiness of many." In the earliest draft, Jekyll states that his adult vices were "criminal in the sight of the law and abhorrent in themselves." In the printed version, he writes, "Many a man would have even blazoned such irregularities as I was guilty of."

Based largely on the original, more explicit language, some modern scholars interpret *Jekyll and Hyde* as "a fable of fin-de-siècle homosexual panic, the discovery and resistance of the homosexual self," as Elaine Showalter writes in *Sexual Anarchy*. Showalter and others cite the timing of the novella as evidence. As anxiety about male homosexuality heated up in Britain in the 1880s, masturbation was viewed as a gateway activity, and the Labouchère Amendment of the 1885 Criminal Law Amendment Act made any sexual act between males a punishable offense. Passed about a month before Louis's influential dream, the law made it easier to blackmail gay men—and was later used to convict Oscar Wilde.

Even after Louis toned down or cut out suggestive references in the text, champions of this theory point out that the novel centers around a group of unmarried men and Hyde could be Jekyll's younger lover or blackmailer rather than his son. And Louis still retained wording that could offer coded allusions to homosexuality. For example, Utterson refers to Jekyll's secret activity as a "strange preference or bondage (call it what you please)" and Hyde enters Jekyll's home through the back way. The word "queer" also appears several times (as in Enfield's comment, "The more it looks like Queer Street, the less I ask"), although the term would not be considered gay slang for nearly another decade. According to some scholars, Louis toned down the gay-specific aspects of the story in anticipation of censorship by his publisher or his wife.

This interpretation is intriguing, though finally unconvincing. Based on his letters and professional writing, Louis was not preoccupied with homosexuality and he was too sexually tolerant to criticize gay men for living a double life when it could have been deadly for them to do otherwise. He was more concerned with upper-class Britain's obsessive public denial of heterosexual passion and desire. Victorian society had long been panicked about masturbation among middle-class boys, and Louis was probably more influenced by preaching when he was a child that tied it to epilepsy and insanity than by its recent association with homosexuality. As a young man, of course, he had lived an uncomfortable double life between polite New Town drawing rooms and Old Town brothels, slipping back from his nocturnal adventures into respectability through the rear door of his parents' home. When he sent a copy of the novella to his friend Will Low, he wrote that Jekyll was "quite willing to answer to the name of Low or Stevenson."

Louis was particularly incensed when Jekyll's sexual appetite was seen as unnatural. There was no harm in "the voluptuary" or what society labels "immorality," he wrote to American editor and poet John Paul Bocock in 1888: "The harm was in Jekyll, because he was a hypocrite—not because he was fond of women. . . . The Hypocrite let out the beast in Hyde—who is no more sexual than another, but who is the essence of cruelty and malice, and selfishness and cowardice: and these are the diabolic in man."

Hypocrisy, malice, and cruelty were certainly on public display the summer before Louis began writing, when the *Pall Mall Gazette* ran an explosive series about widespread child prostitution in London. Henley excitedly sent Louis the undercover series, in which crusading journalist W. T. Stead detailed how prominent London men—including a doctor and member of Parliament—bought young girls from impoverished families and then drugged, raped, and forced them into prostitution. The Criminal Law Amendment Act, which strengthened prostitution laws and raised the age of consent for girls from thirteen to sixteen, was enacted partly in response to the exposé. (The Labouchère Amendment was only one provision of the act.) In his novella, the scenes where Hyde tramples the young girl and kills the MP who is wandering the streets after midnight may well have been allusions to the scandal.

As Stevenson scholar Julia Reid has asserted, Louis seemed intent on illustrating the danger of denying and pathologizing sexual desires, perhaps including those between men. By intricately structuring the narrative around the views and reactions of Jekyll's friends—and how they close ranks to protect him—*Jekyll and Hyde* dramatized "the hypocrisy of a professional class whose idol is reputation, and whose business it is to deny the primitive or animal side of human nature." For some people then—and certainly now— the book's exclusive male circle could represent a patriarchal society that projected its sexual anxieties onto gay men as well as non-European nations, immigrants, and the lower classes, represented by the ashen Hyde, whose deformity was unmistakable, if undefinable.

FROM THE TIME *JEKYLL AND HYDE* APPEARED, there were concerns that simply reading the novella would unleash the inner savagery of its readers. Noting that "most of us" had verged on becoming Hyde at some point, Louis's friend John Addington Symonds admonished the author, "Your Dr Jekyll seems to me capable of loosening the last threads of self-control in one who should read it while wavering between his better and worse self."

This fear reached public frenzy when Thomas Russell Sullivan's stage adaption, *Dr. Jekyll and Mr. Hyde*, opened at the Lyceum Theatre in London in August 1888. Starring the acclaimed actor Richard Mansfield, the play was the first version of the novella to add a woman—Jekyll's fiancée, who is killed by Hyde—and Mansfield played the dual role as a sadistic sex addict who could satisfy his lust only with violence. A highlight of Mansfield's performance was his writhing onstage conversion from Hyde to Jekyll, which was said to leave audiences both terrified and mystified at how he managed it before their eyes.

Three days after the play opened, the murdered and mutilated body of a woman named Martha Tabram was discovered in the dead of night a few miles from the theater. Another murdered woman was found a few weeks later, then another, and three more within the next two months. Like Tabram, the five women—Mary Ann Nichols, Annie Chapman, Catherine Eddowes, Elizabeth Stride, and Mary Jane Kelly—were prostitutes who were murdered at night in or around the Whitechapel area. In September the press received a letter claiming credit for the crimes that was signed "Jack the Ripper."

It was an eerie coincidence that the string of murders began just as *Dr. Jekyll and Mr. Hyde* debuted in the very city where the story was set. The Lyceum Theatre was in the fashionable, affluent West End. The murders took place on the edge of the notoriously poor, crime-ridden East End, where many foreign immigrants and refugees had settled. The proximity of Whitechapel made it a prowling ground for West End men looking to slum it. The split character of Jekyll and Hyde embodied the two parts of London—and the respectable city's desire to sever itself from its seamier side.

It did not take long for someone to make a connection between the novella and the murders and perhaps not surprisingly, that person was W. T. Stead, the journalist who had exposed child prostitution in London. Stead was the first to suggest that the serial killer, who was reported to cut out the sexual organs of his victims, might not be a "horrid ruffian" but a sadistic bourgeois pervert, and he called for the police to broaden their investigation to outwardly respectable gentlemen as well. Daily newspapers quickly latched on to the "Jekyll and Hyde" theory. "Mr Hyde at large in Whitechapel" one *Pall Mall Gazette* headline blared, and a *Star* correspondent confidently asserted, "The murderer is a Mr Hyde, who seeks in the repose and comparative respectability of Dr Jekyll security from the crimes he commits in his baser shape."

Press reports that the murderer had shown particular skill at removing his victims' organs enhanced the connection by arousing speculation that he might also be a mad doctor or a surgeon. Whiffs of Louis's short story "The Body Snatcher" even permeated the air when a coroner suggested that the Ripper was selling the organs to medical schools—an idea that the medical establishment immediately tried to quash.

The "Jekyll and Hyde" theory did not just posit that the Ripper might be a dual personality like the fictional character Louis created. Its proponents also claimed that Mansfield was a role model for the serial killer, whose "diseased brain" had been provoked by watching the actor's riveting performance. Some correspondents and readers even accused Mansfield of *being* the killer because he played one so convincingly.

Not surprisingly, the police paid little heed to the speculation about Mansfield. But it would have been reasonable for them to take Stead's theory seriously, considering that some clients of Whitechapel prostitutes were West End men. Instead, as Judith R. Walkowitz points out in *City of Dreadful Delight*, they confined arrests and house searches to the usual outcasts and "ruffians" in the East End. "Long-standing patterns of deference and assumption of bourgeois respectability ultimately prevailed over speculations about bourgeois criminality circulating in the press," Walkowitz observes of the case, which was never solved.

Still, the specter of Mansfield's baffling nightly transformation from the fiendish Hyde to the smiling Jekyll preyed too heavily on public fears that autumn. *Dr. Jekyll and Mr. Hyde* was shut down in October and proceeds from the final performance were donated to night refuges for homeless women. When Mansfield announced that he would replace the dark drama with a comedy, the *Daily Telegraph* breathed a sigh of relief that the stage lights would go back up on "a pleasant side of human nature."

TWELVE

Like other Bournemouth residents in spring 1885, Adelaide Boodle was intrigued by the gossip about the new owners of the Sea View house. The once-tranquil fishing village on the Dorset coast was still somewhat bewildered by its rapid metamorphosis into a sprawling health resort, with attractions like the fir-lined "invalid's walk" to the beach that advertised both sea and pine remedies for respiratory congestion. Ashen-faced invaders, desperate to escape the choking fog and overcrowding of industrial centers like London, were pouring into the new suburban villas. But even among the "weird-looking" migrants, the man whose wife carried him up and down the stairs was said to be peculiar. "He was not, we were told, like anything human," recalled Boodle, who had moved to Bournemouth with her mother and sisters for her own lung issues, "he was just an animated bundle of shawls and wraps, with long thin hair and burning eyes."

At the time, *Jekyll and Hyde* had not yet rocketed Robert Louis Stevenson into fame, and Boodle knew little of his work. But she and her mother worked up the courage to pay a surprise social call on their new neighbor. For an unmarried twenty-six-year-old living a quiet, conventional life, the experience was like stepping through a looking glass. Louis, "curiously clad" in a bohemian velvet jacket and a dark red tie, and Fanny, in a voluminous sack that was probably a painting apron, welcomed them into a room disarrayed with packing boxes and rolled-up carpets. As if they were in a well-appointed parlor, the couple called for tea and conducted Boodle's mother across the floor, strewn with packing straw, to the room's sole chair. Then Louis perched on a box and began to enchant them with one story after another, sipping tea and punctuating the air with his teaspoon as he spoke. Boodle found herself equally entranced by Fanny, the depth of whose eyes seemed "full of yearning kindness that one's heart might draw from inexhaustibly in time of need." Boodle, who would become something of a fixture at the house during the Stevensons' residence there, would recall it in her memoir, *R. L. S. and His Sine Qua Non*, as a home "wholly unlike any other."

The Sea View was an ivy-covered yellow brick house with a blue slate roof, set above a creek valley, or chine, that cut through the cliffs to the sea, making it a onetime favored spot for tea, brandy, and tobacco smugglers. Thomas Stevenson had purchased the house as both a wedding present for Fanny and a ploy to keep her and Louis near, so that he and Margaret could visit frequently—a mixed blessing for the younger couple, for whom their presence was often oppressive and wearing. Still, Fanny would have been thrilled with her new home for practical reasons alone. Her marriage thus far had been a long stretch of resettling and refurbishing rentals; in Bournemouth alone, this was their fifth move in nine months. And she welcomed the escape from hunting down doctors and medicines on the run and facing hotel staff who cast a cold eye on guests coughing up blood. "It is very comfortable to know that we have a home really and truly, and no more will be like Noahs dove, flying about with an olive branch, and trying to pretend that we have found a bit of dry ground to perch upon," she wrote to Frances Sitwell.

A London shopping spree with Thomas gave Fanny a chance to indulge her unique and modern taste. Steering clear of the usual Victorian clutter, she set out to make the drawing room casual, with wicker chairs, an oak coffer for a window seat, and a divan she fashioned out of old, battered oak boxes and covered with yellow silk cushions. She wrote to Colvin that the room demanded to be painted blue; perhaps the Dutch in her called for it to be the cornflower shade favored by Vermeer, which she complemented with a display of blue and white china from Margaret and Japanese vases from Louis's cousin Katharine de Mattos. (In the same letter, Fanny thanked Colvin for furniture he helped her procure in London, noting, "The small dwarf chairs suit the small dwarf sideboard, and the small dwarf madwoman admirably.")

On a large oak cabinet in the "Blue Room," where she spent most afternoons, she placed a plaster cast of Auguste Rodin's entangled naked lovers, *L'Eternel printemps*, a gift from the artist after Louis defended him in *The Times* against charges of vulgarity. Rodin, who thought highly of "The Suicide Club" and *Treasure Island*, recognized a kindred independent spirit in Louis, and the two men shared a warm correspondence in French.

Upstairs, in a bedroom with a view of the sea, Louis usually worked in bed, papers scattered around him. The couple renamed the house after Alan Stevenson's spectacular lighthouse Skerryvore and paid homage to the family business throughout. In the dining room, which demanded red walls, J. M. W. Turner's engraving of Bell Rock lighthouse hung above the fireplace, a granite model of Skerryvore lit up the entrance to the house, and a ship bell graced the garden. "Skerryvore will not look much like other people's houses," Fanny wrote to Margaret Stevenson, "but it will please me so much more than if it did." She made the home a harmonious blend of the couple's personalities: Her statues of wooden angels with broken noses mingled with Louis's collection of buccaneering weapons.

As always, Fanny lavished attention on the grounds, where the woody aroma of heather and pine scented the air. Lloyd Osbourne always remembered the soothing cooing of doves fluttering on the lawn and in the dovecote, and the drama critic William Archer praised the clever network of paths and stairways Fanny devised, with "tempting seats and unexpected arbors at every turn." Fanny procured sugar pea, corn, nutmeg, and cantaloupe seeds from Will Low in the United States. Boodle recalled that the kitchen garden's sweet corn and tomatoes, and the hydrangeas in the yard, seemed very "foreign looking" at the time. Fanny's perpetual status as an outsider seemed to inspire her desire to make her native plants thrive wherever she went.

The incongruity of the Stevensons becoming bourgeois homeowners was no less striking to them than it was to everyone else. Fanny dreaded the expected suburban social whirl, she wrote to Dora, but "as [Henry] James heroines say, 'it will be an experience.'" Louis was mortified that he was now a "beastly householder," as he grumbled to Edmund Gosse, adding, "the social revolution will probably cast me back upon my dung heap." Yet he took quiet pride in the house after Fanny had made it into a home. "Our drawing room is now a place so beautiful that it's like eating to sit in it . . . ," he confided to his mother. "I blush for the figure I cut in such a bower."

Adelaide Boodle's affectionate reminiscences of the Stevensons, published years later, preserve her youthful awe at being a protégé to a couple that was creative, loving, and never dull. There are glimpses of Louis's charming quirks, such as his insistence that writers can spell words as they please. One day she found him gloating over a dictionary that deferred to his misspelling of a rare American plant; he declared that it made him both immortal and infallible. Boodle writes of his love of diversion, especially when he could not work—building houses of cards, playing military games with Bob via mail, sending hoax letters to Charles Baxter, composing music, modeling wax figures, and practicing the piano or the flageolet, though he showed little talent for musical instruments and drove the rest of the household to distraction. Of course, she also depicts him pacing in his thin slippers, a remarkable sight to nearly everyone who witnessed it. His Bournemouth physician, Thomas Bodley Scott, described him gesticulating forcefully as he held forth in French, English, and sometimes Latin while he rounded the room.

In Boodle's memory, Fanny provided more consistency and strength than alarm, and she is often seen quietly harnessing her own restless energy in needlework or another craft while Louis reads his writing to her or maniacally prowls the room. Boodle recalls Fanny's response when Louis tried to surprise his wife by pruning her raspberry bushes. Surveying the damage, Fanny mourned the sawed-off shoots and broken stems as if a "young family had been massacred," but quickly feigned gratefulness when her husband approached. "Louis must never know what he has done," she whispered to

Boodle. "He did it to surprise me and thinks it has been a splendid day's work." Boodle marvels at Fanny's "infinite patience" with her impetuous husband's countless new enthusiasms, though they usually created more work for her, and the "quiet heroism of her daily and hourly self-restraint" when Fanny, knowing it was impossible to change Louis's mind once it was set, would say her piece and let it go.

THE STEVENSONS ORIGINALLY moved to Bournemouth to be near Lloyd, but in early 1885, he moved in with Louis's parents to begin studies at the University of Edinburgh. At the age of sixteen, he needed to start considering his future, though his parents typically disagreed on what form that future should take. Sam Osbourne seemed to hope his son would chase the same get-rich schemes that had failed him. When Lloyd had shown enterprise as a boy by establishing a printing business, his father had written, "If the mines pan out, you will not need any printing office or anything of that sort." Even after Lloyd began pursuing engineering studies at the university, Sam tried to persuade him to return to California to help him run his Sonoma vineyard, another dubious enterprise.

Fanny was livid that Lloyd would even think of throwing away the substantial investment Louis and his parents had made on his education to follow his father's harebrained schemes. She huffed to Dora that she would send Lloyd "on the next steamer" to San Francisco if her son's father would assume all responsibility for his future—an unlikely prospect, since he had provided so little support in the past. After her failure to "make something" of Belle, Fanny pinned her hopes on Lloyd being educated as a gentleman, presumably in the mold of Louis and his cousin Bob.

When Lloyd returned for a visit in fall, however, the most noticeable aspect of his social grooming appeared to be snobbery. While boasting to Dora that her tall, blond, attractive son now created "a good deal of commotion in the female breast," Fanny joked that he was also something of a prig who found Louis's and her frivolity "almost painful." Sam was less amused at the idea of his son becoming a dandy. He wrote to Belle that her mother said Lloyd was "a kind of dude, fond of loafing in old ladies' drawing rooms making high-toned remarks, and posing for the calm and critical.—Funny kind of outcome, isn't it, for all the good example I have set him?"

Not surprisingly, Lloyd was maturing from a confused boy into a somewhat confused young man. In spring 1886, just as *Jekyll and Hyde* was gaining popularity, his eyesight took a turn for the worse and he was said to be threatened with blindness, which sent Fanny into an anguished frenzy. Louis ordered him to come home rather than risk failing his exams—no doubt a relief for the teen, who was struggling with his engineering studies. A strong pair of eyeglasses seemed to solve the problem, but Lloyd decided to stay home and pursue a career in writing—rejecting both his father's dreams and the Stevenson family calling, just as Louis had done. Fanny seemed to have a better sense than Louis that Lloyd's writing talent and drive were modest. But one can hardly fault a seventeen-year-old for hoping to follow in the footsteps of his brilliant and loving stepfather at the height of his career.

FOR A HOUSEHOLD hobbled by illness, Skerryvore was a remarkably social place—and Fanny was praised as a vivacious host. Though socializing invariably left her and Louis exhausted, Boodle remembered both Stevensons as the "gayest of gay entertainers."

Among the couple's Bournemouth friends were Percy Florence Shelley, the only surviving child of Mary and Percy Bysshe Shelley, and Jane, his eccentric wife. Jane Shelley's pedigree was decidedly less distinguished than her husband's: She was one of nine illegitimate children of a wealthy banker and was widowed at the age of twenty-four by her previous husband, who'd left her guardianship of his own illegitimate nine-year-old son. Not surprisingly, she had immersed herself in the glow of the Shelley family's prominence and became an eager daughter to Mary Shelley. After her mother-in-law's death, she took over her role as overseer and partial creator of the Shelleys' romantic legacy. Percy Florence Shelley was amiable and sweet, a good amateur photographer and playwright who staged dramas in the theater he built in their home, Boscombe Manor. Yet Jane Shelley was the truly theatrical one, the keeper of the family shrine—and, perhaps literally, the keeper of her father-in-law's heart.

Percy Bysshe Shelley had drowned in his sailboat during a storm off the coast near Lerici, Italy, in 1822, when his son was two years old. His decomposing body washed up onshore days later, and his friends, the poet Lord Byron and the adventurer Edward Trelawny, arranged for it to be cremated on the beach. According to Trelawny, who lavishly embellished his account over time, he plunged his hand into the fire, badly burning it, to pluck out the poet's heart, which was somehow intact even as flames devoured the rest of his remains.

Whether the retrieved organ really was Shelley's heart is a matter of debate; cremation experts consulted in the 1880s surmised that the poet's liver was more likely to have withstood the heat of the fire. But Mary Shelley chose to believe it was her husband's heart, and she kept it for nearly thirty years in her traveling desk, where her son found it after her death, wrapped in Shelley's final poem, "Adonais." Jane Shelley decided that the organ deserved a loftier resting place in a shrine in the couple's drawing room, where it was illuminated by a red light. Louis was more fascinated by another relic, the death mask of Mary Wollstonecraft, who had died of a postpartum infection eleven days after giving birth to Mary Shelley and five years after writing her trailblazing feminist work, *A Vindication of the Rights of Woman*, in 1792.

It is no surprise that the son and daughter-in-law of the woman who wrote *Frankenstein*, one of the two greatest Gothic novels, would be attracted to the man who wrote the other. Yet the couple seemed to see Louis as the embodiment of the renegade Shelley, with his brilliance, youthful idealism, bohemianism, and likelihood of dying young. To crystallize the resemblance, the poet's son took a series of romantic photos of Louis with a red shawl that Jane had given him swept across his chest, which both flattered and embarrassed the author.

Fanny relished Jane Shelley's spirit and eccentricity. She described her to Colvin as "a hopeless invalid, but with all the fire of youth . . . and ready to plunge into any wild extravagance at a moment's notice." Fanny allowed that Jane was perhaps a bit "mad," but as she had written to Dora on another occasion, "The society and the friendship of mad people are so infinitely preferable to other people's." Louis later dedicated his novel *The Master of Ballantrae* to the colorful couple, and in the red room at Skerryvore, a portrait of Percy Bysshe Shelley shared a place of honor with one of Mary Wollstonecraft.

The Stevensons' favorite new friend, though, was Henry James, who accompanied his invalid sister, Alice, to Bournemouth in early 1885. Louis and James had been indifferent to each other when they met years before at the Savile Club, though Fanny admired James's writing and had defended him when Louis mocked him in letters to friends. She had more appreciation for his insight into women, particularly American expatriates, in stories like "Daisy Miller" and his novel *The Portrait of a Lady*, which had made James a celebrity.

The friendship between the men bloomed out of their debate on the art of the novel, one of the first of its kind between two authors, in the pages of *Longman's* in fall 1884. In his essay "The Art of Fiction," James wrote that the experience writers brought to composition was "a kind of huge spider-web, of the finest silken threads, suspended in the chamber of consciousness and catching every air-borne particle in its tissue." James defended realism, contending that literature was not reality but should have the "air of reality" and "compete with life." In Louis's essay "A Humble Remonstrance," published three months later, he responded that novels were not a "transcript of life," and that the art of fiction lay in its distance from life:

> Life is monstrous, infinite, illogical, abrupt and poignant; a
> work of art, in comparison, is neat, finite, self-contained, ra-
> tional, flowing and emasculate. Life imposes by brute energy,
> like inarticulate thunder; art catches the ear, among the far
> louder noises of experience, like an air artificially made by a
> discreet musician.

Though all fiction was "artificial," the wonder was that it could touch something deep in readers who had never experienced it.

James followed up with a letter to Louis commending his writing style that "floats pearls and diamonds." Louis replied that he was a "lout and slouch of the first water" as a writer compared to James. When the forty-two-year-old James arrived in Bournemouth—where he was immediately disgruntled by the town's "almost American newness and ugliness"—Louis invited him over for a bottle of claret. James came to Skerryvore, asked if he might return the next evening, and continued to drop in after dinner most nights during his extended stay on the coast.

Fanny was awed to have the celebrated American author in her home. To Dora, she wrote that James was "slow and hesitating in his speech, sometimes falling into a stammer, but meets your meaning before you have begun to give it utterance." Yet Fanny was often barred from enjoying her compatriot's company. A couple of months later, she wrote to Colvin, "I think there is no question but that he likes Louis; naturally, I have hardly been allowed to speak to him, though fain I would. He seems very gentle and comfortable, and I worship in silence—enforced silence,—enforced by the elegant though brutal Mr. Stevenson."

James and Louis could not talk enough, however. They could discuss literary philosophy and technique on a level unmatched with their other peers, and their relationship quickly developed into one of glowing appreciation between equals. "I pant for the hours of our reunion," James gushed in one note to Louis. He visited Skerryvore so often, the Stevensons christened Louis's grandfather's armchair "Henry James's chair."

James appreciated the range of Louis's work more than his British friends. In a later essay, he called Louis's American travelogue *Across the Plains* a "little masterpiece" and applauded his experimentation in novels like *Prince Otto*. He may have been the only critic to mention Fanny separately in his discussion of *The Dynamiter,* suggesting that her hand in the composition was "a light and practiced one." Louis returned the praise for James's craftsmanship except, strangely, for *The Portrait of a Lady,* his masterpiece about an expatriate American woman's doomed attempt to take control of her fate.

Louis later wrote to James that he thought it "BELOW YOU to write and me to read" and begged him to compose "no more of the like." James was suitably bewildered by his colleague's scorn. "'Tis surely a fanciful, ingenious, elaborate work—with too many pages, but with (I think) an interesting subject & a good deal of life and style," James responded, defending his novel. "There! <u>All</u> my works may be damnable, but I don't perceive the particular damnability of this one."

Despite her limited access to James, Fanny bonded with him over their love of cats, domestic gossip, and magazines for young women, for which, he confessed to her, "having a secret weakness." She saw that James's gaze could be withering—"His small scornful, chilly smile is about the most unpleasant thing I ever met with, and explains why many people do not like him," she wrote to Dora. However, he was affectionate and sympathetic to her. He was sensitive to the difficulties of her situation and not put off by her forceful personality. He visited Fanny alone sometimes and the two corresponded for years.

In May 1885 Fanny and Louis invited James and Katharine de Mattos to dinner for their fifth wedding anniversary, the first time in their married life that Louis was well enough to celebrate it. Fanny poured her creativity into planning an elaborate American feast for the occasion. She proudly recounted each dish to her mother-in-law: American oyster soup ("the only oyster soup really fit to eat in my opinion"), curried calves' feet, lamb sweetbreads sauteed in butter with petits pois, roast chicken with stuffed tomatoes and tiny new potatoes in cream, paper cups of cheese soufflé, and an American apricot tart with vanilla whipped cream. Katharine had been too ill to attend, but Fanny triumphantly reported that the portly James lavished praise on each course and repeatedly asked for double helpings.

James found Louis's "strange California wife" romantic and "almost as interesting" as her husband, he wrote to fellow American Owen Wister, author of the quintessential western *The Virginian*, adding, "If you like the gulch and the canyon, you will like her." However, his sister's assessment of Fanny was scathing. According to her biographer, Jean Strouse, Alice James was a brilliant but tormented "career invalid" who shut herself off from the world and was known for her spiteful judgments. After meeting Alice on one of her rare public outings, Fanny praised her to her brother, likening her eyes to "Highland pools in a burn." Alice was not so generous. In her diary, she described Fanny as "an appendage to a hand organ, I believe she is possessed of great wifely virtues and I have heard some excellent letters written by her to H.," she went on, "—but such egotism and so naked!! giving one the strangest feeling of being in the presence of an unclothed being."

Perhaps Alice James was slightly jealous. Fanny's lively home was a refuge for Henry James in Bournemouth, and the Stevensons' appetite for life in the face of so much illness was in stark contrast to Alice's contempt for life. James dutifully visited his sister daily, but he could not wait to press his "sedentary part" against the "dear old fireside chair" at the home of Fanny and Louis.

WHEN JAMES RETURNED to London in July 1885, Fanny sighed to Colvin, "After ten weeks of Henry James the evenings seem very empty, though the room is always full of people." The rooms at Skerryvore were often bursting with guests, especially old Stevenson friends eager to take advantage of the couple's convenient location. This "magic circle," as Boodle called it, was referred to in correspondence by a variety of honorific titles. Some members were elevated to the status of entity: the Lloyd, *le* Henley, or, in Colvin's case, the Monument, because he resided in the British Museum, where he also worked. Louis showered wackier sobriquets on his college prankster buddy Charles Baxter: "Crapulous Bloated One," "Capacious Belly," "Capricious Banker," "Conscientious Bottle-holder," "Cheerful Blackguard," and "Corpulent Brute" in one letter alone. Louis's nicknames for his wife included Wild Woman of the West and Folly Vandegrift.

Some critics have portrayed Fanny as jealous or unwelcoming to Louis's friends at Skerryvore, but this is unfair. Her letters show that she encouraged visits when she and Louis were well (and sometimes when they were not), even though the brunt of preparing and hosting fell on her. And shortly before his death, Colvin wrote in a note for future biographers, "I can testify from my own experience that she was not moved by the kind of jealousy which a wife commonly feels towards the friends of her husband's bachelor days."

Fanny never stopped exasperating Colvin and the two would always bicker, but they also developed a genuine affection for each other. Fanny wrote to Dora, "He is a sweet creature, and one of the most elegant writers of English living and possessed of an amount of learning that is truly awful to me at least" and "There is nobody in the world to compare with him." And early on, at least, she generally welcomed the most difficult visitor— rowdy, bullying, hard-drinking but irrepressible William Henley, whose flamboyant personality alone could fill a room.

Fanny had also made some female friends through Louis. She enjoyed the chummy camaraderie of Coggie Ferrier, who told racy jokes and was very fond of Katharine, who came often with her children, Helen (nicknamed "Snoodie") and Richard, after her divorce. After one visit, Fanny wrote to Henley, "I may truly say that we loved her more at her going and that one can say of how few. The best of us sometimes grate and jar, but she never."

Still, Fanny sometimes felt very lonely. James was not the only visitor to whom her access was limited. In a letter to Anne Jenkin, the widow of Louis's mentor, Fleeming Jenkin, she wrote of expecting a visit from friends of her husband's "to whom I shall not be able to talk, nor, I fear, take any interest in." She sometimes felt like hired help—taking dictation, answering Louis's letters, keeping house, entertaining visitors, and doing much of the cooking. She missed the comfort of her sisters and the ease of Dora's gatherings, where guests might pitch in to make omelets.

Fanny's unjust reputation is due in part to the measures she was willing to take to guard her husband's health. Like other Victorian women, she was expected to provide extensive nursing with no medical education and inadequate home manuals, such as Florence Nightingale's *Notes on Nursing*, first published in 1859 and well outdated by the 1880s. So she took the unusual step of subscribing to the professional medical journal *The Lancet*. An early believer in germ theory, Fanny drew the ire of visitors when she decided to bar them from her husband if they had colds. "I am like a dragon at the door . . . ," she wrote to Henley. "I am sure I have garnered the everlasting enmity of all Louis' friends."

While reading *The Lancet* might have fed Fanny's agitation about her husband's ill health and seemed eccentric to others, her knowledge about bacteria and infection probably helped her keep him alive. Lloyd later wrote of his mother to Stevenson biographer George Hellman:

> *Whatever you may find to criticise in her remember always that it was she who kept Stevenson alive; and in keeping him alive— guarding him, watching over him, subordinating her whole life to him, she necessarily offended many people. Her life in many ways was a very sad one—a life of unending apprehension; death was always snatching at Stevenson, and there she was always interpos- ing herself.*

Fanny could also feel overwhelmed by the sheer volume of visitors to Skerryvore. One party in summer 1885 included Thomas and Margaret, "Aunt Alan" (the widow of Louis's uncle Alan Stevenson, also named Mar- garet), Coggie Ferrier, and William Henley and his brother Teddy. James was still in town; Bob and Katharine, and their families, were also staying nearby; and Lloyd was home from college. "It has been such a difficult party that I quite broke down under the strain," Fanny wrote to Colvin. With a mix of amusement and exasperation, she described to Dora Louis's friends' jealous bickering over their time with him. "Henley, for instance, won't sit in the chair at Skerryvore that is called Henry James' chair, and Henry James makes long eyes and gets sullen and goes away if the Taylor girls stay too long," she wrote.

Fanny once proudly observed that nearly everyone who came into contact with her husband adored him. Louis's grace, wit, and courage inspired de- votion from a vast array of men and women. Both straight and gay men were attracted to him. This devotion from other men has led some critics to speculate that Louis was gay or bisexual, but there is no evidence that he ever had a sexual relationship with a man or desired one, and much evidence of his strong sex drive for women.

Though it seems unlikely that Louis was ever sexually or romantically involved with men, there was a queerness about him—with his long hair, shabby chic style, and sensitivity. He was not afraid to venture beyond the rigid gender conformity of his time to embrace his feminine side. Like her husband, Fanny also refused to be boxed in by unbending concepts of masculinity and femininity. Both seemed comfortable with a kind of gender duality contained in one person. This was part of the sexual attraction between them. Louis celebrated both sides of his wife in his poem "Dark Women." As both a tiger and tiger lily, he wrote, she played a "double part":

> All woman in the body
> And all the man at heart.
> She shall be brave and tender,
> She shall be soft and high,
> *She* to lie in my bosom
> And *He* to fight and die.

ADELAIDE BOODLE'S ROSE-TINTED view of the Stevensons' marriage did not suggest that it was one of quiet harmony. As she observed, they argued often and vociferously. "There were moments when the casual looker-on might have felt it his duty to shout for the police—hastening their steps perhaps with cries of 'murder!'" she recalled. Fanny's fits of temper are well-known, but Louis could also be hotheaded. As Lloyd recalled, "when roused, he had a most violent temper," earning him the family nickname "Old Man Virulent." And he had always loved a good fight, calling battle the "spice of life." Many of those who knew the Stevensons as a couple insisted that both of them relished their intellectual sparring.

Boodle saw two strong personalities expressing their feelings without censorship as a part of a healthy marriage, not a troubled one. Another Skerryvore visitor had a different perception of their relationship. In 1885 John Singer Sargent painted a bizarre and almost photographic portrait of Louis and Fanny, set against the crimson walls of their drawing room. Some who have analyzed the painting since, including the critic Elaine Showalter, have concluded that the American painter intended to show Louis "trapped by domesticity and femininity." In fact, Fanny is depicted less as an over-weening presence than as a superfluous one, a strange part of the décor. Sargent's interpretation is often treated as a document of the Stevensons' marriage when it more accurately might be a projection of the painter's own attraction to Louis and ambivalence about his wife.

Sargent's fellow student Will Low described him as a "sad prig," but the Stevensons liked him. "We both lost our hearts to him," Louis wrote to Henley, "a person with a kind of exhibition manner and English accent who proves on examination, simple, bashful, honest, enthusiastic, and rude with a perfect (but quite inoffensive) English rudeness." Sargent was initially rattled by Louis, who insisted that *Huckleberry Finn* be read aloud while he sat for his portrait. The artist told his friend Henry James that Louis was the most intense creature he had ever met. Unhappy with his first painting, Sargent wanted to do another that captured Louis's manic energy—and his eccentric wife.

In the resulting painting, Fanny, depicted on the right margin like an apparition in the Henry James chair, is enveloped in a white shimmery garment from her head to her barefoot toes. (For the portrait, Sargent "could not resist" wrapping her in an Indian sari Margaret had given her, she told Dora.) On the left side, Louis, in his customary velvet jacket, paces away from her in long strides, twisting his mustache and looking at the viewer as if suddenly caught in midthought. Between them, a door opens onto a dark hallway, suggesting tension. One senses that Sargent would have liked Louis to continue walking off the canvas and out of the domestic scene.

It is difficult to reconcile the view of the couple in Sargent's painting with their letters to each other at the time. Shortly before he arrived, Fanny described to her mother-in-law how Louis demanded that she parade in her new dresses and then be kissed before she left the house. And in letters to Fanny when she was away, Louis waxed about his adoration for her and their home. At any rate, they were not sure what to make of the painting, which Sargent himself jokingly referred to as "the caged animal lecturing about the foreign specimen in the corner" in a letter to Louis. The author confessed to Low that it was excellent but eccentric:

> *I am at one extreme corner; my wife, in this wild dress and looking like a ghost, is at the extreme other end; between us an open door exhibits my palatial entrance hall and a part of my respected staircase. All this is touched in lovely, with that witty touch of Sargent's; but of course, it looks dam queer as a whole.*

Fanny was intrigued. She described it as "a very insane, most charming picture" to Dora and likened it to "an open box of jewels" to her mother-in-law. The Stevensons apparently did not see it as a biting critique of their marriage because they hung it in the dining room where it was painted.

Fanny was not completely blind to Sargent's unflattering view of her, however. With characteristic humor, she wrote to Colvin that she told the painter, "'I am but a cipher under the shadow,' to which he too eagerly assented." Of course, she was getting used to being demonized or dismissed. As Boodle observed, the press would often represent her as she appeared in the portrait, as a "kind of lurking shadow" in her famous husband's story. (Fanny once exasperatedly wrote to Louis of her "summary disposal" in an article in *The American: A National Journal*, where writer Olive Logan had described her as "a California lady, a widow who had some name, though I forget what that name was, in local literature.")

Fanny's bare feet in the painting also fed her image as crude and uncivilized. In Nellie Van de Grift Sanchez's biography, *The Life of Mrs. Robert Louis Stevenson*, her sister noted that the portrait generated an enduring rumor that when Fanny first came to London, "she was such a savage that she went to dinners and evening entertainments barefoot." Fanny generally ignored demeaning gossip even if, as Dora knew, it was fairly common. When the American Exhibition came to England in 1887, Dora commented drolly to her friend, "I suppose they think you an excellent specimen of the squaw American."

LOUIS ONCE CHARACTERIZED marriage as "one long conversation, chequered by disputes." It should be no surprise that this description captured the nature of his marriage to Fanny: the relationships of famous writers (primarily male) and their spouses are notoriously "stormy, short-lived, and mutually destructive," in the words of Carmela Ciuraru, whose 2023 book *Lives of the Wives* is a study of such marriages.

When a writer's spouse has her own ambitions, literary marriages can be even more tempestuous. Rather than being idyllic meeting grounds of the mind, they're often combat zones for the competing demands of the partners' work pressures and domestic expectations. Power struggles, resentment, and insecurity are inevitable and infidelity common. There have always been exceptions, and some contemporary writing couples strive for and sometimes even succeed in achieving fundamentally egalitarian arrangements for their writing time. But many such unions do not survive. The marriages of Martha Gellhorn and Ernest Hemingway, Sylvia Plath and Ted Hughes, Elizabeth Jane Howard and Kingsley Amis, and Elaine Dundy and Kenneth Tynan are among the twentieth-century casualties.

Louis described one of his marital skirmishes in a letter to Henry James. Fanny had complained about an atmosphere of excessive cheerfulness when Louis was with his mother, and he countered that Fanny was a dreary pessimist. Sniping to James that she was "a woman (as you know) not without art: the art of extracting the gloom of the eclipse from sunshine," he went on:

> She tackled me savagely for being a canary-bird; I replied (bleat-
> ingly) protesting that there was no use turning life into King Lear;

presently it was discovered that there were two dead combatants upon the field, each slain by an arrow of the truth, and we tenderly carried off each other's corpses. Here is a little comedy for Henry James to write!

Some critics contend that Louis was confiding to James that he felt suffocated in his marriage. But Louis's recounting of the incident actually revealed mutual amusement at a partner's foibles as much as frustration over them, along with mutual acceptance of some painful truths. Fanny apparently helped compose the anecdote in the letter, which Louis signed as "the kindest recollections from the canary-bird and from King Lear, from the Tragic Woman and the Flimsy Man." Fanny embellished the humor with a postscript referring to herself as the "doleful woman," signed "D.W."

Victorian literature scholar Katherine Linehan has pointed out that Louis's humorous recounting of the couple's argument to James mirrors the way he depicted marital turbulence in his work. His mature couples share a "fellowship in imperfection that allows the cherishing of the best in a loved other, while knowing the worst," she wrote. Linehan's description captures the complex nature of the Stevensons' relationship as well. Louis's cousin and first biographer, Graham Balfour, who lived with them for more than two years, later wrote, "Fanny and Louis were high-tempered, outspoken people, but their affection nobody but a fool could doubt." Many who have condemned the marriage do not acknowledge that the sparring between Fanny and Louis did not hinder their mutual affection.

Many of the couple's disagreements centered on Louis's work. Boodle recalled Louis telling her repeatedly that Fanny's "critical faculty was keener and more to be relied upon than his own," and Fanny could be a stubborn and demanding critic.

When Louis and Henley were in the midst of composing one play, Fanny wrote to Henley complaining about the artificiality of a female character who was not "to swear, to cry, nor to show a suspicion of a trouser leg underneath her petticoats." Fanny added that when she pressed the point with Louis, the scene between them was more dramatic than anything in the play. The next day, Louis famously complained to Henley, "I got my little finger into a steam press called the Vandergrifter (patent) and my whole body and soul had to go through after it." Fanny too had suffered, he wrote, but "I am what she has made me. The embers of the once gay R.L.S."

Louis might issue companionable gripes about his wife's stubbornness to his friends, but he saw conflict in creative partnership much as he did in marriage, as inevitable and stimulating. Out of the tumult, he believed, creativity blossomed. As critic Audrey Murfin wrote of the couple's later collaboration in the South Pacific, "far from resenting the intrusion of his wife's voice and ideas," Louis welcomed "conflict and struggle into his work as a central part of his artistic practice." He carefully considered Fanny's opinions but felt free to disregard them and rely on his own judgment.

Fanny may have been less open to criticism of her own writing. She once had to send a profuse apology to Frances Sitwell for her petulance after Sitwell criticized her work on *The Hanging Judge,* a play Louis had discarded and Fanny was trying to salvage. "I have really what the lady novelists call a 'pent up volcano in my heart,' and shall not be decently myself until the—at least my own—horizon is black with smoke and ashes," Fanny wrote to Sitwell. Louis also commented to Boodle that as writers, "women, as a rule, were impossible creatures" when it came to receiving criticism.

But Louis could be a particularly brutal critic. Boodle experienced his caustic editorial style firsthand when she requested writing lessons. At first, Fanny intercepted her to spare Louis's time and energy. Saying "I write too, a little," she told Boodle she would provide some guidance first, which Boodle later credited with softening the "full blast" of Louis's judgment.

Louis assigned Boodle to write about a place she loved, and she picked her garden. When she arrived at the Blue Room for his feedback, Fanny appeared to be asleep on the divan, but Louis launched headlong into his critique. Boodle's writing "could hardly be worse," he bellowed; indeed, he had never read a worse description and hoped to never read one even half as bad. It was not until Fanny, "like a couching lioness," reared her curly head and attacked her husband's manner that he apologized and softened his blows.

As Boodle choked back tears, Louis gently admonished her for using adjectives instead of descriptive verbs: "If you want me to see your garden, don't, for pity's sake, talk about 'climbing roses' or 'green, mossy lawns.' Tell me, if you like, that roses twined themselves around the apple trees and fell in showers from the branches." The phrase "green grass" seemed to raise his blood again, however. "Tell me how the lawn was flecked with shadows," he exclaimed. "I know perfectly well that grass is green. So does everybody else in England. . . . Make me see what it was that made your garden distinct from a thousand others." In the end, Louis advised his student to disregard English grammar because French and Latin were superior for building style. And he forbade her to use the word "green" in composition more than once in her life.

THIRTEEN

On July 14, 1886, an astonishing six months after the Gothic mystery *Jekyll and Hyde* appeared in print, Louis published an adventure novel that would cement his reputation as one of the brightest talents of his time. *Kidnapped; or, The Lad with the Silver Button* began serialization in fourteen weekly installments in the juvenile magazine *Young Folks* in May 1886. Two months later, the book *Kidnapped: Being Memoirs of the Adventures of David Balfour in the Year 1751 . . .* was published simultaneously in Britain, by Cassell and Company, and New York, by Charles Scribner's Sons. Louis's midthirties may have been the worst of times for his health, but they were the best of times for his reputation, when in just three years he published his triumvirate of classics: *Treasure Island*, *Dr Jekyll and Mr Hyde*, and *Kidnapped*.

In the novel's dedication to his Edinburgh pal Charles Baxter, Louis branded *Kidnapped* as nothing more than a "young gentleman's" entertainment, but Henry James knew better. He proclaimed it Louis's best book—a shining example of "what the novel can do at its best and what nothing else can do so well." The book soars far above conventional young adult fare because of its moral complexity, sophisticated view of the fraught history of Scottish nationalism, and "lustrous prose," in the words of Scottish novelist Margot Livesey.

Kidnapped is the tale of David Balfour (either sixteen or seventeen years old, in the estimation of the author), an orphaned country lad from the Lowlands who embarks on "a great Odyssey" to claim his family inheritance and become a man. David's journey takes him from the decrepit manse that turns out to be his hidden inheritance to servitude on a brig bound for the slave fields of the Carolinas. It propels him from a nightmarish shipboard brawl and sea wreck to the bloody heart of Scottish rebellion against harsh English rule to wild flight across the Highlands and heather with an outlaw hero named Alan Breck and finally back to confront his wicked uncle Ebenezer and lay rightful claim to his estate. During his trek, David encounters brigands, bamboozlers, and vain, sometimes foolish clan chiefs and warriors—a gallery of colorful characters rivaled only by those of Mark Twain. But the story is anchored in his knotty relationship with the Jacobite rebel Alan Breck, whom he finds charming but with a "dancing madness" in his eyes.

Kidnapped is set just five years after Britain's crushing defeat of the rebel Scottish army—under Charles Edward Stuart, or "Bonnie Prince Charlie"—in the 1746 Battle of Culloden. In less than an hour, about 1,300 men were killed, all but 50 of them among the greatly overpowered rebel forces. Loyal to the exiled claimant to the British throne, James Stuart, the surviving Jacobites (the name is derived from Jacobus, the Latin for James) dispersed throughout the remote Highlands, where many of their homes were burned and they were killed or forced to flee. In the novel, Alan and David—a self-professed Whig, loyal to the British king George—form an unlikely partnership when they become suspects in the Appin Murder, the assassination of the despised king's agent Colin Roy Campbell, or "the Red Fox." (Alan's seemingly innocent kinsman James Stewart later becomes a scapegoat and is put on trial.) Their harrowing flight across Scotland is essentially a trek across the neglected terrain of the nation's history after the 1745 uprising and a powerful portrait of the destruction of Scottish Indigenous culture.

Highland visits in 1880 and 1881 had first inspired Louis's interest in writing a nonfiction history of the area in the aftermath of Scotland's eighteenth-century union with England. Among the research materials he acquired were transcripts of James Stewart's trial for the murder of Colin Campbell, who had ordered several evictions on the forfeited lands of the Stewart clan. Alan Breck Stewart, the man upon whom Louis based his character, was the chief suspect in the case but escaped to France. In his absence, James Stewart was convicted and sentenced to death in a corrupt trial and his body left hanging for several years in a gruesome show of British authority.

Fanny, who was trying to write a play set in the same era, recalled that in Bournemouth, both she and Louis were engrossed in the accounts of Stewart's trial. By then Louis had reimagined the project as an opportunity to expose harsh Scottish history in the easy-to-digest form of an adventure story. He would interweave rich detail from original sources, down to the smallpox scars on Alan's face and his flamboyant dress of ostrich feathers, lace, and silver buttons. Louis also incorporated memories and knowledge from his engineering apprenticeship on Earraid and Mull. The shipwreck of the brig that is to take David to the colonies occurs a century before the construction of the lighthouse that would have prevented it, Thomas Stevenson's Dhu Heartach. For days, David believes he is marooned on an island until he discovers that he can walk to the mainland during low tide.

The episode is one of many that show how David, like his Lowland creator, was very much a "foreigner at home," in the evocative title phrase of Louis's 1882 essay about the national divisions and cultural and political differences with England that made Scots feel like strangers in their own land. David cannot decipher the regional dialect of Alan Breck and his compatriots, much less their predominate tongue, Scots Gaelic. Louis agreed to editor James Henderson's request that he minimize Scots dialogue for juvenile readers in the serial for *Young Folks*, but in the book Louis employed long passages of it as hammers against the soft ears of his English readers.

Louis's literary genius shines in his complex portrait of Alan and his relationship with David—a pair who seem to reflect the divisions within their creator. Alan thinks the idealistic adolescent an insufferable prig at times, but he admires his pluck. David looks up to the man who is twice his age while also looking down on him—but he knows that he'll never have the courage, martial skills, or passion of that "bonny fighter." He is on the verge of "twyning," or breaking, from him altogether, when he suspects Alan of taking part in the Red Fox's assassination. But again and again, the teenager decides to stick with Alan, despite the growing peril of his association with the notorious outlaw.

In doing so, he witnesses the grim campaign to destroy Highland culture after "the '45"—wretched poverty and starvation, the outlawing of tartans and bagpipe music, the shattered social attachments of the clan system, the imperial swagger of the occupying redcoats that he too comes to fear and hate, and the Highlanders' rugged resistance. He evolves from dispassionate observer steeped in the widespread stereotypes of Highlanders as primitive and lawless to sympathetic ally of their cause, if never fully developing an affinity for them. In the end, he looks forward to a comfortable future while Alan is forced into hiding.

Louis wrote most of *Kidnapped* in about five months. He later claimed that David and Alan were his only characters who ever "became detached from the flat paper, they turned their backs on me and walked off bodily" and "wrote the remainder of the story." Yet their creator sounded as exhausted as his fictional heroes must have been near the end of their remarkable journey. Feeling stuck and worked out, as he had with *Treasure Island*, Louis pressed on toward a conclusion "without interest or inspiration," rewriting the last chapter several times. He cut his drinking down to one grog a night, he told his parents, but found teetotaling overrated. To his friend Ida Taylor, he wrote, "Time blows by me like smoke, and the earth is of the consistency of cotton. A fine, bland, vasty obscurity sits on my bosom; and it is equally difficult for me to stop writing, or to write anything to the purpose."

He must have sensed that *Kidnapped* was a special tale, however, because William Henley, Sidney Colvin, and Fanny all liked it. And Louis's mood lifted considerably when Colvin suggested that he break off the story when David claims his inheritance and save the rest of his material for a sequel, a plan to which *Young Folks* agreed. To some critics now and then, the novel closes abruptly—or "stops without ending," in the words of Henry James.

But to James, this did not tarnish Louis's triumphant creation, Alan Breck—"a wonderful picture of the union of courage and swagger," whom his creator both saw through and admired.

KIDNAPPED CAN BE ENJOYED simply as an exhilarating adventure story, as some contemporary critics classed it when it appeared in print. As Scottish literature expert Ian Duncan has noted, the physically immersive writing in episodes such as David's island ordeal and the flight in the heather are the "racing heart" of the book. "It is not arrival or homecoming but the flight itself that matters—the pure rush of sensation . . . ," Duncan writes. "As though to be kidnapped, snatched out of everyday life, and then a fugitive from justice is to find oneself, mysteriously, set free." (Some critics and friends—and even its author—also welcomed the novel as a relief from the "evil odour" of his darker fare, like "Markheim" and *Jekyll and Hyde.*)

As a coming-of-age novel, *Kidnapped* is also enriched by Louis's deep insights into a teenager's roiling emotions, including the terrifying moments before David's first armed combat, which he is convinced will leave him dead before his life has fully begun. "I do not know if I was what you call afraid, but my heart beat like a bird's, both quick and little; and there was a dimness came before my eyes, which I continually rubbed away and which continually returned." Louis's evocative staccato about young life on the edge of "cold steel" would later find echoes in the battle literature of Stephen Crane and Ernest Hemingway.

Modern scholars such as Alan Sandison have labeled the tale "a novel of arrested development," arguing that David remains resolutely stuck in adolescence, repeatedly rejecting the grown-up world. It is true that nearly all the men in *Kidnapped* are villains, rogues, or weaklings. When David is being bundled off to sea, his last glimpse of the greedy uncle who has consigned him to his fate shows Ebenezer's face "full of cruelty and terror." And Captain Hoseason of the piously named ship the *Covenant* looks more dignified than "a judge upon the bench" but turns out to be as darkly du-plicitous as David's uncle.

Twentieth-century critics who reduced Louis to merely a storybook writer and *Kidnapped* to a simple boys' adventure tale sometimes argued that Louis himself never really progressed past adolescence. "It is no longer possible for a serious critic to place [Stevenson] among the great writers, because in no department of letters—except the boy's book and the short story—has he written work of first-class importance," insisted the English critic and nov-elist Frank Swinnerton in 1914. Louis was forced by his "physical delicacy" to lead a life that was "intellectually timid and spiritually cautious," accord-ing to Swinnerton, and had "to allow himself to be looked after."

This perspective not only overlooks Louis's own physical heroism and his mastery of several literary genres, it also belittles his acute mature percep-tion of the psychologically harrowing challenges of achieving adulthood with one's youthful idealism intact. Louis's complex understanding of char-acter is exhibited in the passages where David butts heads with the world of men—a world filled with father figures he longs to respect but invariably questions and disputes. This conflict would rise to the level of classic gen-erational duel in the *Kidnapped* sequel, published as *Catriona* in Britain and *David Balfour* in the U.S. Running the gauntlet to manhood might seem a trivial subject to grown men who have forgotten or repressed the agonies of their youth. But in Stevenson's hands, the boy-to-man drama achieves the status of great literature.

And it is not only men and boys who relate to the book's themes. British author Hilary Mantel dismissed the idea of *Kidnapped* as a "boy's book," noting that it was the novel she most identified with as an eight-year-old girl, and it became the model of storytelling she carried with her the rest of her life. "I think a lot of my ambitions as a writer, and many of my own per-sisting themes, originate there: friendship, courage, the need to go out into the world and make your fate," she said in an interview. "I reread it every couple of years, and get more interested in it, not less."

In burrowing into the literary territory of his towering Scottish predeces-sor, Walter Scott, Louis was engaged in his own generational duel. Scott's

historic Waverley novels created the myth of Highland people as picturesque and romantic but stranded in a "feudal" stage of development, in
keeping with contemporary anthropological and philosophical theory. Scott
saw the Anglicization of Scotland as inevitable and necessary to create a
commercial class of Lowlanders, pushing them up the evolutionary ladder.
As Julia Reid notes, *Kidnapped*, by contrast, exposed what Scott had largely
ignored: the devastation to Highland culture and fragmentation of Scotland
caused by the union with England.

Before *Kidnapped* was published, the critic Edward Purcell contrasted
Walter Scott's moral certitude with Louis's "brilliant but seemingly troubled" take on life, "where all is doubt and difficulty." Louis replied to Purcell, "Sir Walter was a good man, and a good man content with a more or
less conventional solution, whereas I am only a man who would be content
to be good if I knew what goodness was—and could lay hold of it." As with
most of his best work, Louis's restless disillusionment thrums in the background of *Kidnapped*'s melodic prose.

AS LOUIS'S REPUTATION GREW, he began to attract the adoration of
strangers as well as friends and acquaintances. His neighbor Adelaide Boodle recalled people showing up at the door of Skerryvore demanding to
know what the author was doing, what he was like, or what color his eyes
were. One woman intent on snagging a piece of his writing to auction off at
a local bazaar pushed in past the maid, Valentine Roch, and pressed Louis
even after he assured her he had no good samples of his work to provide. "It
doesn't really matter *how* stupid it is," she spluttered at him, "or *how badly
written!*"

Louis enlisted Fanny to help respond to his growing fan mail, but there
were limits to her tolerance of his female admirers. Even Thomas Stevenson
advised her to "look after" his son's letters to some of the "American ladies."
So when the U.S. poet and editor Harriet Monroe sent Louis her picture

and he responded that his spirits had been lifted by her "pretty" verse and photo—"so much prettier still"—Fanny decided it was time to step in. To Louis's flowery note, she added a succinct postscript making it clear that his wife had also enjoyed the poet's letter and photo.

Fanny was not above a little flirtation herself. Many charming men came into her orbit through Louis, though she was reluctant to elaborate on their attractions even to her close friend Dora, fearing that her letters might get lost or mislaid and wind up in print, an increasing problem. She laughed at her old friend Timothy Rearden's suggestion that she flirt with Colvin, telling Dora that she would have to first quote Greek poetry, "then trip lightly into philology (about which I should first have to be taught)" and finally "wax passionate over an undeciphered Egyptian inscription." Yet she admitted that she was drawn to the handsome Scottish poet and author Andrew Lang, with his lustrous gazelle eyes. And she confided to Dora that she *did* flirt with the writer George Meredith, who was at the height of his popularity after the success of his novel *The Egoist.* Fanny regretted that her fun had been dampened by the presence of Louis's mother, who did not care for Meredith. "Still his strong willingness to join [in the flirtation]—I won't be too modest, the overtures came from him—was the most complimentary thing that ever happened to me."

WRITING WAS MORE than a livelihood for Robert Louis Stevenson. He wrote to live; writing affirmed his very existence. He articulated its importance to Henley:

> *I sleep upon my art for a pillow; I waken in my art; I am unready for death, because I hate to leave it. I love my wife, I do not know how much, nor can, nor shall, unless I lost her; but while I can conceive my being widowed, I refuse the offering of life without my art. I am not but in my art, it is me; I am the body of it merely.*

Fanny's attention to the more material aspects of the couple's daily life made it possible for her husband to lose himself in his work. "His time was not intruded on by a multitude of petty cares and petty engagements," Lloyd recalled, "he could read and write and think—in peace; he could let himself live in his stories without any jarring interruption."

Fanny did not have the luxury of time to devote to developing her writing—her life was defined by interruptions and demands. She had to write wherever, whenever, and however she could. In the Stevensons' marital arrangement, Louis's health came first, his work second, and Fanny's needs last. Every time she turned away to do something creative, her domestic and nursing duties seemed to pull her back. In many ways, she was a woman always caught in the middle—between her husband and death, between his needs and hers, and between traditional and changing concepts of womanhood.

Fanny was generally humble about her writing skills, complaining of the "dry nippedness" and "woodenness" of her style, and was eager to improve. She never forgot that her husband was a brilliant talent as well as the breadwinner. Yet she also wished to express her own ideas in writing and was frustrated when she could not. She was simply a "buffer," she sighed to Colvin after a difficult visit from Louis's parents. "A buffer's life is a wearisome one. I can get no time for anything, to write, to think, to be conscious of my own identity." Fanny's anxiety about self-expression is echoed in her short story "The Warlock's Shadow." The female narrator has a recurring nightmare of losing her voice—she believes she is singing only to discover that her lips are moving but it is someone else's song.

Short on time and confronted with an almost exclusively male literary establishment, Victorian women writers like Fanny turned to magazines as the most accessible route to publication. While male writers relied on literary networks to get published, female writers had to be even shrewder. Some women got past the gatekeepers by adopting masculine pseudonyms, but Fanny used another savvy method, declaring her status as a married woman with an esteemed author for a husband by sometimes using the byline "Mrs. Robert Louis Stevenson."

Along with *The Dynamiter*, two book-length travel narratives, and several nonfiction essays, Fanny published eight known short stories. They are adventurous and experimental, bending and sometimes blurring Gothic, New Woman, regional, supernatural, and other genres. Though her stories have usually been dismissed or ignored by her husband's biographers—and even by her own—they are being reconsidered by a new generation of scholars. To Robyn Joanne Pritzker, whose assessment of Fanny's fiction is the most comprehensive to date, Fanny's stories may seem rudimentary and messy—ranging "often wildly, across genre"—but they were a key part of the transition to the modernist style that writers like Edith Wharton, Katherine Mansfield, and Virginia Woolf would develop in the next century.

It is difficult to see Fanny's fiction soaring to the polished heights of Wharton or Woolf based on the stories she did publish. However, had she been able to devote more time to writing, her stories might well have gained more nuance and depth over time. As they are, they sit comfortably and creditably among those of other female magazine writers of her day.

Fanny's stories include at least three additional unpublished tales that she left with Timothy Rearden before she sailed to Europe to study art. They are marked by the bold themes and striking images that characterize her published work. "Borriballoo" is a macabre fairy tale about the exploitation of young women. In the story's Roald Dahl–like opener, a girl is hanging by a hook in a giant's kitchen, being measured for a frying pan. The giant decides to spare her life, only so he can fatten her up to marry the royal "grand Borriballoo" and consolidate his political power. He takes her down from the hook, he says, to have her "served with my guests instead of to them."

Another unpublished story, "The Hunchback," is a critique of a society that treats difference as a deformity to be corrected. In this variation on the Icarus myth, a boy's parents fit him with painful straps and buckles to correct his deformity, but the harnesses cut to his "very soul" and stunt his psychological development as well. When the hump on his back develops into "two great wings of purple and gold," he falls to his death trying to fly. In a particularly memorable image, a "gleam of color" catches the eye of a bird flying over the marshes and he swoops down to discover the boy's body, his gold and purple wings lifeless in a slump of oozing green.

In early 1887, Adelaide Boodle arrived for a writing lesson to find Fanny rushing through the house with a manuscript in hand. "I am writing for my life . . . ," she blurted out to the young woman. "Money is needed for a dear friend of ours who is expecting another child soon." Fanny was hurrying to prepare a short story, "Miss Pringle's Neighbors," to be mailed to Scribner's with one of Louis's essays. The tale appeared in *Scribner's Magazine* in June 1887 under the byline "Fanny Van de Grift Stevenson." She passed on her fee of £30 to her needy friend.

Like much of the British populace, Fanny had been preoccupied that winter with sensational press accounts of the divorce trial of Colin Campbell, son of the eighth Duke of Argyll, and his wife, Gertrude Elizabeth Blood, whom he had accused of adultery with four men. Fanny had met Lady Campbell and admired her. "She seemed like a walk in the woods, and fine, supple, wild beasts, and all those things that I love, and a woman besides," she wrote to Colvin. "Any of us can be a woman, and some of us are very nice ones, but it is only given to a few to be so much more of nature." Yet newspaper articles foaming with salacious details from the divorce trial also stirred Fanny's fears that her adulterous affair with Louis (and perhaps flings with other men) might stain her husband's growing reputation. "How do you think I should stand a trial like Lady Colin's?" she wrote to Colvin rather agitatedly. "Anything, and everything, could easily be proved against me."

These thoughts were very likely on her mind when she wrote "Miss Pringle's Neighbors." In the story, the title's eponymous character is a pious older woman whose orderly life is intruded on by a new neighbor, Helen Mainwaring, a vivacious young singer who dresses in black not because she is a widow but because she thinks it is stylish. An atheist, Helen is also the unwed mother of Felix, a curly-headed and interestingly bratty prodigy, who is the product of her dalliance with another artist. She rebuffs Miss Pringle's efforts to save her soul with religion; referencing Mary Wollstonecraft and George Sand, Helen declares the "forcible binding of the marriage relation" by law "monstrous." The older woman closes her windows and curtains to shut out the joyous sounds of the "wicked heathen goddess" playing with her son in the garden below. But when Felix dies suddenly and a distraught Helen shows up at her door, Miss Pringle realizes she has been unchristian. She and Helen now find common ground and solace in each other's company. Felix comes to his mother in a vision at the cottage and Helen wills herself to die so that she may reunite with him, leaving the fading sounds of "a child's laugh of joyous surprise" trailing behind.

In "Miss Pringle's Neighbors," Fanny seems in part to have been grappling with the trauma of her son Hervey's death—and perhaps her own feelings of guilt or ambivalence about going to Paris to pursue her artistic ambitions. Yet her difficulty in working through these issues affected the quality of the writing. The storytelling is somewhat jerky, especially the abrupt handling of the deaths of mother and son. Fanny treats Felix's death in particular in a brusque, cursory manner—perhaps to avoid reliving her own son's long, tortured death. The story might have been richer had she been able to mine the depths of her own experience, which she articulated so movingly in her letters. But perhaps her own painful memories were the very reason she could not bear to do so in fiction.

It seems that Fanny did not intend "Miss Pringle's Neighbors" to be primarily about parental grief, however. She was interested in illuminating the tensions between career, motherhood, and marriage that conventional morality imposed on women. The strikingly modern hero Helen is a brazen atheist and sexually active single woman who is also a devoted mother. Though she ultimately finds freedom only in a deathly reunion with her son—perhaps Fanny's concession to Victorian morality—the forward-thinking story suggests that a woman's happiness and her decision to bear children should not hinge on marriage. Pritzker suggests that the fledgling friendship between Helen and Miss Pringle even offers the radical possibility that two women could "replace the matrimonial bond with one of sympathetic friendship."

Shortly after "Miss Pringle's Neighbors" appeared in print, Fanny asked Louis's cousin Katharine if she could rewrite a short story Katharine had read or discussed at a gathering at Henley's house. Katharine had been unable to sell the story, about a man's encounter on a train with a girl who has escaped from an asylum. She was not interested in collaborating on a new version as Fanny reimagined it—with the female character as a nixie, or mythological water sprite—but agreed to turn it over to Fanny. "The Nixie" appeared in *Scribner's Magazine* in March 1888.

The haunting tale is written from the perspective of a young British gentleman, Willoughby, who has set out on a fishing trip in the countryside when his leisure is disturbed by the "animal-like shriek" of a bedraggled girl cowering in the shadows of his first-class train compartment. With her ill-fitting dress and heavy boots, she strikes him as a runaway "workhouse brat," and he is irritated that "his privacy, for which he had paid liberally, had been violated, and his comfort destroyed." When the two step off the train near a river, however, the girl suddenly seems older and more self-assured. Willoughby becomes entranced by her wildness and graceful oneness with nature, and he begins to feel a strange and giddy "kinship with the earth." But when the two take a boat on the river, he starts to suspect she is playing tricks on him. Suddenly she disappears, and he looks like a fool talking to himself. Her face reappears to him in reflections in the water, and it seems to him that she is trying to lure him into drowning.

"The Nixie" ridicules class snobbery, but it is primarily an exploration of late Victorian anxiety about the breakdown of gender roles, a theme that also runs through "Miss Pringle's Neighbors" and *The Dynamiter.* The young gentleman in the story is surprised to find that images of his conventional "destined bride" suddenly dull in the presence of this female free spirit who seems to discard social expectations as carelessly as she sheds her stodgy dress in the river. He becomes intoxicated with her. But as she grows more willful and independent, his attraction curdles into a fear of losing control of his own identity. She begins to seem less enticing and even malevolent.

It is clear why Fanny envisioned the story's female hero as a creature of nature rather than an artist, like Helen Mainwaring, or a criminal, like Clara Luxmore in *The Dynamiter,* or a woman branded insane, as Katharine had conceived her. A female whose vital life force blossoms in nature posed a pointed challenge to the Victorian ideology that women's biologically determined sphere was the home. The nixie symbolized the "untamed spirit" and "eternal wildness" that New Woman writer George Egerton would encourage women to unleash in her short story "A Cross Line" the next decade. These were also qualities polite society found disturbing in Fanny. With the characters of the nixie and the "wicked heathen goddess" Helen Mainwaring, Fanny slyly alluded to common perceptions of her.

When Fanny's short stories were published, Dora and Margaret Stevenson sent praise and encouraged her to write more. Strangely, how Louis felt about his wife's fiction is a mystery. He usually reserved comment when he sent it on her behalf to his publishers, and the glaring lack of praise in his surviving letters and other written documents implies that he did not think highly of it. He may have felt that Fanny's stories were unpolished or uncompelling female fare. Or perhaps he thought his wife's talent was better employed contributing to his own work.

Whatever his opinion, Fanny continued to write and get published. It took nerve and self-confidence to do so. She knew she was the lesser talent in her relationship, and she faced additional barriers as a woman, yet she pressed on because she believed she had something to say. Her husband might not have always encouraged her, but neither did he try to hold her back.

BY 1887 DEATH seemed to be closing in on the house in Bournemouth. The previous spring, the Stevensons' beloved terrier, Woggs, was killed attacking a dog at a pet hospital where he was already recuperating from another skirmish. The couple buried him in Fanny's garden and Louis consoled himself that Woggs would have chosen to die as he did, in battle, "for military glory was more in his line than the domestic virtues."

In January, Fanny and Louis received word from Dora that her husband, their friend Virgil Williams, had died of a heart attack after returning from a sketching trip. Fanny was still reeling from Virgil's death when more distressing news arrived from San Francisco in April: Sam Osbourne had disappeared mysteriously. He had asked his second wife, Rebecca Paul, to have supper waiting for him after a night-court session and never returned.

The *San Francisco Chronicle* eagerly seized on rumors that the charming, popular, and roguish local fixture had fled east with a young female typist in his office. Apparently, his wife, who went by the nickname "Paulie," suspected as much because she contacted the woman's parents, who provided a "satisfactory reply regarding her whereabouts," the newspaper reported. Still, the *Chronicle* referred to Sam's disappearance as an "apparent desertion" that left Paul destitute and in debt for the Sonoma vineyard he had purchased in her name.

As bitter as Fanny was about her ex-husband, she did not believe he would abandon his wife to run off with another woman. "That he probably brought the girl to grief, I do not doubt, but it was not in him to do more," she wrote to Colvin. Other rumors drifted up and down the hilly streets that Sam had been killed by robbers or shanghaied, as his children preferred to believe, or later, that he had been seen in Africa. Like Sam's friends who knew the darkness under his sunny demeanor, Fanny suspected suicide. The discovery of a pile of clothing on the beach that was too weathered to be identified as his was convincing enough evidence to many.

Fearing that unsavory revelations about his father might tarnish his stepfather's reputation, Samuel Lloyd—who until then had gone by "Sam"—abandoned his patronymic for his middle name. ("Lloyd" has been used consistently in this book to avoid confusion.) Fanny had tried to bury Sam once, in a way, when she had declared herself a widow on her marriage record. Now she supported, or even urged, her son to do the same. "The name must be changed, as his father named him for himself, I adding the Lloyd," she wrote to Colvin, as if this were a rational reason. Sam's disappearance did seem to draw Lloyd closer to Louis, who soon declared to Henley, "Happy am I, to be even thus much of a father!"

Louis had more pressing concerns on his mind that winter. He was struggling to complete a memoir of his mentor and father figure, Fleeming Jenkin, who had died suddenly after minor surgery at the age of fifty-two. At the same time, his father's mind was steadily deteriorating. In January Thomas Stevenson's doctors ordered him to take a three-month rest that ended in his retirement from the family engineering firm. With increasing depression and likely dementia, Thomas had grown even more moody, and he was forgetful and frustrated when words eluded him.

Thomas's anguished son saw him sinking into a forlorn state from which the father he knew would never return. "[A] very beautiful, simple, honourable, high-spirited and childlike (and childish) man is now in process of deserting us piece-meal," he sighed to Colvin. Yet Louis could never quite shake his irritation and impatience with the old man. Fanny was more tolerant and sat with Thomas while he confided his fears to her, until his son approached and he tried to put on a happier face.

Looking for some kind of escape from his worries, Louis came up with a misguided plan to intervene in Irish politics. More than a year before, nationalist Moonlighters had raided a County Kerry farm seeking firearms, and the loyalist tenant farmer and one of the raiders were killed. Since then, the local community had boycotted the farm and persecuted the man's widow and children. Louis decided that he, Fanny, and Lloyd should move in with the largely female household, and, if necessary, be killed to publicize their plight. Louis thought England had no place in Ireland and had "majestically proved her incapacity to rule it." Yet he felt that persecuting the family, like dynamiting, was morally indefensible.

Fanny did not think highly of Louis's scheme. She later admitted that she snapped something like: "I don't so much mind your dying as your being a fool." Yet she agreed to accompany him if he insisted on going, she recalled in a glowing reminiscence about her husband's quixotic idealism and powers of persuasion. Apparently she also knew that the plan would never come off because she also noted, "While he was making out lists of provisions, guns and ammunition that we were to take to Ireland with us, he had to be lifted up in his bed to eat his meals from an invalid table laid across his knees."

The Irish suicide mission was tabled in spring by the news that Thomas's death was imminent. When Fanny and Louis reached his parents' Edinburgh home, Thomas no longer recognized his son. He died two days later, at age sixty-nine, on May 8, 1887. Louis organized a large funeral, with a procession of dozens of carriages to the cemetery, which he was too ill to join.

By late May, Thomas's son could write to Colvin that he was glad the "suffering changeling" had passed on and that his father would "return to us in the course of time as he was and as we loved him." Yet Louis's feeling about Thomas's death were more complex. He still felt guilt and anger, but he also felt freed from his father's domination, rigid Calvinist ideology, and obsessive fears of social impropriety. Thomas's will provided Louis and Fanny with some financial freedom as well. He left most of his estate to the church and his wife, but Louis's inheritance of £3,000 could finance a much-desired change of scenery. Whatever quarrels Thomas had with his son's chosen path, he once again funded it in death as he had in life.

Louis might have seized on the moment to put his Irish plan into effect, but instead he and Fanny began to dream of wintering in the United States. Fanny had not set foot on her native soil in seven years and she was eager to see her aging mother and her grieving friend Dora. Louis's doctors all seemed to agree that the dry climate and fresh mountain air of Colorado Springs could benefit his ailing lungs.

Louis remained ill in Edinburgh until the day he and Fanny headed to Waverley Station to return to Bournemouth. The man who had stood above that station as a boy, dreaming of train voyages that would take him away, was about to embark on an adventure from which he would never return. Fanny was finally going home, but Louis was leaving his home for the last time, though he did not know it then.

FANNY AND LOUIS agreed that they would not travel to the States without Margaret Stevenson, who was reluctant to leave Heriot Row and insisted she would be a drag on the younger couple. Fanny sought to assure Margaret that she was as eager as Louis to have her join them. "You have only Louis left now, and I could not take him away from you, even for his good,"

she wrote. "As to your being a wet blanket to us, how do you think we would feel knowing we had left you behind with your sad heart? . . . Come with us, dear, and let us try to be to you what we can."

Fanny also tried to dazzle Margaret with some of the attractions of her native country. The American millionaire Charles Fairchild—who had commissioned one of John Singer Sargent's portraits of Louis as a birthday present for his wife, Elizabeth—had offered to oversee (and perhaps bankroll) some of the couple's U.S. travel. Fairfield also suggested that they spend time at his lavish Newport, Rhode Island, summer residence. Fanny wrote to Margaret that she was excited for her to see "a swell American watering place." Margaret finally agreed and offered to help finance the trip.

While Fanny was organizing her family's departure from Skerryvore, Adelaide Boodle and the couple's friend Coggie Ferrier decided to put on a private concert as a parting gift to Louis. With Boodle accompanying on the fiddle, Ferrier sang an old Jacobite air, "The Skye Boat Song," with new lyrics that Louis had composed. (The tune and Louis's lyrics, slightly altered, were used for the theme song of the long-running television series *Outlander*.) Set in the aftermath of the Culloden battle, the original folk song celebrated the escape to Skye of Bonnie Prince Charlie and defiantly insisted that he would return to claim his crown. Louis was more interested in probing the psyche of a twenty-five-year-old who sailed away knowing he would never return, his idealism and hopes for glory crushed. His plaintive version (which was published as a poem called "Over the Sea to Skye") began "Sing me a song of a lad that is gone" and ended:

> *Billow and breeze, islands and seas,*
> *Mountains of rain and sun,*
> *All that was good, all that was fair,*
> *All that was me is gone.*

The poignant longing for lost youth was a repeated refrain in Louis's life and work, one that also evokes David Balfour's arduous journey to adulthood after his father's death in *Kidnapped*. Unlike David, Louis was still wandering at thirty-six years old, an ill and weary man who might not survive the Atlantic crossing but retained his youthful hope that something better awaited him if he did.

Fanny's eagerness to return to the United States was dampened by her heartache at leaving the little "nest" she had created for her family. Before their departure, she gathered Boodle and the gardener, John Phillips, to assign some tasks while she was gone. She asked Boodle to watch over the stray cats and pigeons, and to break the ice if the birds' water supply should freeze in winter. Then, to lighten the trio's mutual sadness, she turned to Phillips with a warning. If Boodle should ever catch him taking his pruning knife to her creepers, Fanny said, "I solemnly charge her . . . to snatch it from your hand and plunge it into your heart."

The Stevenson travel party—Margaret, Lloyd, Louis, Fanny, and their faithful maid, Valentine—arrived in London in August for two nights in a Finsbury hotel before setting sail. Those who came to say goodbye included Henley, James, and the critic William Archer, who brought a lawyer because Louis wished to draft a codicil to his will before he embarked. Aunt Alan, Katharine, and his childhood nanny, Cummy, also dropped by. Colvin stayed the last night at the hotel so he could see them off at the dock, just as he had met their ship in Liverpool when they arrived from the United States seven years before.

Among the well-wishers who filled the Stevensons' hotel suite, Edmund Gosse noticed that Louis's face was pale and his eyes a bit "dazzled." But his hair was brushed to a shine and he looked elegant and refined in his black mourning clothes and silk tie, instead of "like a Lascar out of employment, as he generally does." Louis "prowled about the room, in his usual noiseless panther fashion," Gosse wrote to a friend, "talking all the time, full of wit and feeling and sweetness, as charming as ever he was, but with a little more sadness and sense of crisis than usual."

Louis's doctors might have unanimously cheered his going to America, but his friends were apprehensive, as they had been when he had followed Fanny there a decade before. Henry James was almost alone in greeting the venture as another intriguing chapter in a colorful couple's life, and he sent along a case of champagne for the journey. "They are a romantic lot," he later wrote to Colvin, "and I delight in them."

As soon as the Stevensons' ship, the *Ludgate Hill*, crossed the Channel, the party discovered complications. Prioritizing space over luxury, Fanny had followed the advice of Colvin's brother, Bazett, to go with one of the less popular lines. At Le Havre, they discovered that they were on a cattle ship when more than a hundred horses and some apes bound for American zoos lumbered aboard. The ship was already dirty and uncomfortable, and now the scent of animal dung mingled with the fine sea air that blew in through the portholes, Margaret reported to her sister Jane. Yet Louis's fifty-seven-year-old mother proved to be a remarkably resilient and upbeat traveler. "After consultation we agree to look upon it as an adventure & make the best of it," she recorded in her diary.

The voyage was less of an adventure for Fanny, who always suffered from seasickness. But her husband was in his element rolling on the high seas with their odd floating menagerie. He roamed the deck, dispensed James's champagne to the seasick, and befriended an ape named Jacko, who sat in his arms and ruined his new clothing. He wrote ecstatically to Bob, "I had literally forgotten what happiness was." Louis could not then know of the health and fame that awaited him on the other side of the world. He only knew that he could breathe again.

FOURTEEN

On the Stevensons' seventeenth day at sea, the low Manhattan skyline emerged out of the fog that had kept the *Ludgate Hill* from landing in New York the previous day. It had been eight years since Robert Louis Stevenson had first taken in that view, on the demoralizing visit when he was rebuffed by publishers and departed with empty pockets and "the itch." Here and there an eleven- or twelve-story building now jutted above the rest, though they were dwarfed by the spire of the old Trinity Church and the masts of the sailing ships at the South Street piers. The Statue of Liberty, erected the year before, glowed in the distance like a copper penny and the Brooklyn Bridge stretched above the East River like a lacy spiderweb.

The Atlantic crossing had been rocky but entertaining—if one considers horses peeping through the saloon portholes at mealtimes entertaining, which Louis did. Now he planned to slip in and out of New York unnoticed, seeing as few people as possible. He had no idea how unlikely that would be. He got his first clue when he heard the grouchy pilot guiding the ship through the harbor referred to as "Hyde," while his more amiable partner was called "Jekyll."

The dock was lined with people awaiting Louis's arrival. *Scribner's Magazine* editor Edward Burlingame was there, as was Will Low. Louis's old artist chum could not get near the author, however, because reporters mobbed him before he could even disembark. The American millionaire Charles Fairchild had foreseen this reception, warning Fanny when he visited Skerry-vore that Americans were "Louis mad." Fairchild had a carriage waiting to whisk the travel party to the lavish Victoria Hotel, where they would stay as his guests.

The dazed author had stepped off a cattle ship into the blinding light of celebrity. An estimated 250,000 copies of *Jekyll and Hyde* had sold in North America, unknown to Louis because the vast majority were pirated. *Kidnapped* followed as an overnight American bestseller—Scribner's estimated that 10,000 copies were snapped up in the first ten days. By the time Louis arrived in the U.S., unscrupulous publishers had issued three bootleg *Kidnapped* editions and were cashing in on the new literary sensation with more than twenty pirated reissues of his old books. The stage adaptation of *Jekyll and Hyde*, starring Richard Mansfield, was opening that week at Madison Square Theatre, where it would become a huge hit. Even Louis's clunky play with William Henley, *Deacon Brodie*, was about to go on tour with Henley's actor brother Teddy in the lead.

The Victoria Hotel, which sprawled over an entire block between Broadway and Fifth Avenue at Twenty-Seventh Street, offered little respite for the weary traveler. The ornate lobby was buzzing with callers and reporters, who followed the Stevensons to their suite. Louis quickly retreated to bed, perhaps as much for refuge as rest. He conducted several interviews from there—a nice touch of color for the American press, which was eager to exploit the "courageous invalid" angle that already gripped the public imagination. The obliging author fed reporters a scoop—announcing for the first time that *Jekyll and Hyde* had come to him in a dream—and issued a plea for Americans not to buy pirated editions of his work (which earned him nothing). The next day, stories of his arrival were splashed across the front page of the New York newspapers.

Robert Louis Stevenson had "passed from one epoch of his life to another" on the voyage across the Atlantic, Lloyd Osbourne later wrote. "From that time until his death he became, indeed, one of the most conspicuous figures in contemporary literature."

Lloyd felt that fame boosted his stepfather's confidence and he exulted in it. Yet Louis greeted his first dose of American-style celebrity with a mix of wonder and disdain. "America is as I remembered a fine place to eat in, and a great place for kindness, but Lord what a silly thing is popularity," he reported to Henry James, even claiming to miss Skerryvore. To his British friend Sidney Colvin, he had a more biting commentary. "My reception here was idiotic to the last degree; if Jesus Christ came, they would make less fuss." Stevenson scholar Duncan Milne has called this Louis's "bigger than Jesus" moment, akin to John Lennon's remark to the press eighty years later that the Beatles were "more popular than Jesus." Fortunately, Louis had confided it to a friend and did not have to pay for it publicly as Lennon would.

Louis fled with a cold to the Fairchilds' estate in Newport, Rhode Island, the next day. Fanny and Margaret Stevenson briefly stayed behind to attend the New York premiere of *Dr. Jekyll and Mr. Hyde*, where they were honored with the author's box. Louis's cheerful mother was delighted by much in the big city. She found Mansfield's Jekyll-Hyde conversion astounding and thrilled to the deafening applause when the curtain fell, though she could not imagine that such a grim play could ever really be a hit. She also marveled at modern amenities like ice water and "lifts" at the hotel but was rattled to see water faucets mounted above the bathroom sink, confessing to her sister Jane her fear that she would put her eyes out while washing her face.

At the Fairchilds' summer home, where a painting of Louis by John Singer Sargent graced a wall, the author spent most of his visit in bed, puffing cigarettes and pouring forth a stream of brilliant talk that left visitors "tingling," according to one. (On the other hand, Fairchild's daughter Sally would remember him primarily for being dirty, smoking too much, and burning holes in the bedsheets.) By the time the Stevensons returned to New York, he and Fanny had decided to forgo the rigorous train trek to Colorado, opting instead for Saranac Lake, a remote village in the Adirondack Mountains near the Canadian border. Fanny and Lloyd sailed by steamer up the Hudson to make arrangements while Louis stayed in the city to handle some business.

Though perpetually teetering on the brink of bankruptcy, Louis was stunned and finally uncomfortable with the hefty New World fees that his celebrity could command. After accepting a deal with *Scribner's Magazine* to write twelve monthly pieces for about $3,500, he wrote to the British critic William Archer, "I am like to be a millionaire if this goes on, and be publicly hanged at the social revolution . . . a godsend to my biographer, if ever I have one." He was discovering that "it costs you a pound to sneeze, and 50 to blow your nose" in the U.S., a country that would "make the devil a socialist." Still, he found Joseph Pulitzer's offer of $10,000 a year to write short weekly articles for the *New York World* unconscionably extravagant and flatly turned it down.

Samuel Sidney McClure, a rising young publisher who had made the offer on Pulitzer's behalf, was a tenacious Ulster Scot who had grown up largely in poverty and would go on to pioneer muckraking journalism in *McClure's Magazine*. At thirty years old, he was determined to procure Louis's name for the publishing syndicate he had founded to sell articles to newspapers. His persistence paid off later when his revival of Louis's old story *The Black Arrow* in spring 1888 became his most successful novel serialization. Yet Louis was flummoxed when McClure then offered him a whopping $8,000 to serialize his next book, whatever it was. "He blushed and looked confused and said that his price was £800 ($4,000), and that he must consult his wife and Will Low before he made any agreement," McClure revealed in his autobiography. "He went on to say that he didn't think any novel of his was worth as much as £800."

Despite his reservations, Louis finally accepted S. S. McClure's offer, joking to his Scottish pal Charles Baxter, "I'm awfü grand, noo, and läng may it last!" He then realized he had violated his agreement with Scribner's to handle all his U.S. books, leaving him in the humiliating position of having to plead to company president Charles Scribner II that he had been an "unintentional swindler." Instead of chalking up the blunder to inexperience, he took it as a moral lesson. He had been too "greedy and hasty," he wrote to his friend Anne Jenkin: "I have done with big prices from now out. Wealth and self-respect seem, in my case, to be strangers."

Twenty-three days as a literary sensation was enough for Robert Louis Stevenson. In late September, he happily left behind the madding crowd in New York City to take refuge in the calm and isolation of the Adirondack Mountains.

A DECADE EARLIER, Edward Livingston Trudeau, a young New York physician, had made a remarkable recovery from pulmonary tuberculosis in the Adirondack wilderness. In 1885 the pioneering doctor (the great-grandfather of *Doonesbury* cartoonist Garry Trudeau) founded the first American TB research laboratory and open-air treatment center, the Adirondack Cottage Sanitarium, where he advocated the "fresh air" and "rest" cures for the disease. When the Stevensons arrived in Saranac Lake, the town was still largely a rugged outpost for logging, hunting, and fishing, and their quarters were part of a larger cottage owned by a mountain guide, Andrew Baker.

Arriving by buggy, Louis was entranced with the setting. The streams and lakes gave the area a Highland feel, and the trees were festooned with leaves of flaming shades he had seen only in his Skelt toy theater paintbox as a child. As usual, Fanny had already worked to make their new rustic quarters cozier, caulking the windows with cotton and putty and nailing up the front door to keep out the cold. She stocked the larder with venison and partridge, procured brook trout and maple sugar, and baked bread. When the travel party arrived, the five-foot dynamo was in a petticoat and jacket at the stove, busy cooking dinner.

The cottage was small, with no running water (a schoolboy was hired to haul it from a river), but there were stoves in the bedrooms and a large timber-burning fireplace in the sitting room. "Fortunately Fanny understands such things and teaches us the mysteries of 'gathering log,'" Margaret recorded in her diary. (Her son found his wife's practical competence something of a sensual turn-on and once reputedly remarked, "To see her turn the flapjacks by a simple twist of the wrist is a delight not soon to be forgotten, and my joy is to see her hanging clothes on the line in a high wind.") Margaret was baffled that even a backwoods lodging could be without an egg cup, however. When she and Lloyd tried to find one in the local store, the bewildered clerk offered her a small jug instead, prompting Lloyd to ask if he had an egg sized to match.

Fanny left soon after their arrival to visit her mother and sister Josephine in Indiana. She returned in late October by way of Montreal so that she could purchase "extraordinary garments made by Canadian Indians" before winter, she wrote to her Bournemouth protégé, Adelaide Boodle. By then, Louis had immersed himself in the romance of living in a hunter's cabin, as if he were a frontiersman in a James Fenimore Cooper novel. He refused to let his mother ruin the ambience by covering a stained table with a cloth and insisted that she warm her feet on a cut log instead of a footstool. He decorated the mantel with a whiskey bottle, flanked by two red tobacco boxes. His pioneer wife's arrival with buffalo-skin coats, astrakhan hats, snowshoes, and fur capes completed the picture. Louis had his photo taken in his new wardrobe, "hoping to pass for a mighty hunter or sly trapper," Fanny reported to Boodle.

Winter descended on the Adirondacks within days of Fanny's return. "Sleighs, snow-shoes, and frozen lakes; *voyageurs* in quaint costumes and with French to match; red-hot stoves and streaming windows . . . snow-storms, snow-drifts, Arctic cold," Lloyd later wrote, describing the scene. He, Louis, and Fanny gamely joined the consumptives in colorful hats and mittens who went sledding, and Louis skated on the nearby ice pond. But by February, when Margaret reported that the temperature had dropped to forty-eight degrees below zero, the drafty cottage was miserable. Louis's buffalo coat froze to the kitchen door and ink hardened in the well. A lunch meal of venison crunched with ice after an hour in the oven and bitterly cold air wafted down the chimney of the big fireplace. Even during the day, the cottage dwellers were often comfortable only in bed with a warm soapstone at their feet, although bed was not always a solace: Louis dreamed one night that a rat was nibbling on his ears and woke to discover it was frostbite.

"The place does not suit [Fanny]—it is my private opinion that no place does," Louis wrote to Boodle in December, a somewhat rude remark given his wife's willingness to tough it out for his health when the cold and altitude were hard on her heart and joints. The truth was that Saranac Lake suited no one in the party but him, and even he admitted that the weather was "really infinitely disagreeable." The group spent the winter trading colds. Fanny escaped as often as she could and even Margaret was relieved to descend to the comparative warmth of Boston for a time.

A few visitors braved the icy weather to see Louis, including the generous Fairchilds (whom Fanny briefly turned away because they had colds) and a young man who tramped fifty miles on snowshoes just for a glimpse of him. S. S. McClure also came to woo and skate with Louis and got to know Fanny as well. The publisher was comfortable with rough Midwestern American women because he too had spent much of his childhood in rural Indiana. McClure liked Fanny's writing and later syndicated some of her work. He also admired her energetic embrace of Louis's unsettled lifestyle. "She had a really creative imagination, which she expressed in living," he wrote. "She always lived with great intensity, had come more into contact with the real world than Stevenson had done at the time when they met, had tried more kinds of life, known more kinds of people. When he married her, he married a woman rich in knowledge of life and the world."

On one of McClure's visits, Louis told him of his wish to charter a yacht and live at sea for a time. The two irrepressible men soon brainstormed a Stevenson cruise of the South Seas, partly financed by a series of articles that Louis would send back for McClure to syndicate. Louis would take along cameras and a phonograph on which he could record "the sounds of the sea and wind, the songs and speech of the natives." He would then play them for audiences at a lecture and magic-lantern-slide tour. While the snow drove against the frozen windows and their buffalo coats steamed in a corner, Lloyd and Louis dreamed out the details of the trip, which Fanny, of course, would make happen.

Edward Trudeau treated Louis for five months in Saranac Lake, though his lab tests showed that the patient did not have active disease. The two men never became close, however. Louis was revolted by some of Trudeau's experiments and the doctor—who later founded the American Lung Association—disapproved of his patient's chain-smoking, which even Andrew Baker's wife claimed was the most excessive she had ever seen. Despite his steady tobacco consumption, Louis benefited from his time there—he would go for fifteen months without a serious hemorrhage.

"THE DREADFUL DEPRESSION and collapse of last summer has quite passed away," Louis wrote to his old friend Walter Simpson, "it was a thorough change I wanted." Happy and relatively well, he knocked off his twelve pieces for *Scribner's* in just six months. Edward Burlingame asked that Louis withdraw only one essay, out of sensitivity to Irish American support for the uprising in Ireland: In "Confessions of a Unionist," Louis had condemned the British presence in the nation yet opposed terrorism and immediate home rule.

Away from Britain and free of his father's censorship, Louis's work began to move in a more provocative and complex direction. In his essay "Pulvis et Umbra," he contemplated the limits of human idealism in a universe devoid of meaning. He also began writing *The Master of Ballantrae*, a novel about a family shattered by the 1745 Jacobite rebellion that was much darker than *Kidnapped*. In contrast to his post–*Jekyll and Hyde* assertion that art should be a "piece of pleasure set afloat," he planned for the story about a brothers' quarrel to lead to "a perfectly cold-blooded murder of which I wish (and mean) the reader to approve," he wrote to James.

To aid his poor eyesight, Lloyd was now writing on a typewriter, the bell of the carriage return tinkling agreeably in another room. The nineteen-year-old was pounding away on his first novel, a light comedy involving fraud, false identities, and a traveling corpse that turns up, among other places, hidden in a piano. According to Lloyd, Louis told him the first draft was "not at all bad"—even "devilishly funny" in parts—but that he had thrown away much of the best material because he did not know how to use it. Louis thought he could make it more marketable. Ultimately he extensively revised the story while sticking closely to Lloyd's initial structure and characters.

Was Louis's new collaboration a welcome diversion from more serious work or just a favor to his stepson? In letters to friends, he was effusive about the book. "Lloyd's story was so damned funny and absurd that I lost my heart to it, and am now about half through my version . . . ," he waxed to Henley in March. "I have laughed consumedly as I wrote." His observation that Fanny's son had "a genuine talent of a kind" no doubt rankled his abandoned collaborator. Louis continued to chuckle through the revisions until the end, telling Baxter, "If it is not funny, I'm sure I don't know what is."

The Wrong Box was published with a double byline in June 1889. Not many have shared Louis's enthusiasm for it. Sam McClure believed the novel was impressive for a budding writer like Lloyd but cautioned Louis against putting his name on it. Scribner's, on the other hand, considered Louis's name its main selling point and agreed to his terms only if it went first on the title page and preface. The novel was considered a comic tour de force by authors such as G. K. Chesterton, Rudyard Kipling, and V. S. Pritchett, to whom the praise "a farce that slips down the throat with the nicety of an oyster" has often been attributed by publishers. But many critics and readers view it as a flimsy effort not worthy of Louis's talents.

For better or worse, the partnership between Louis and Lloyd would yield three more novels and many intriguing but unrealized projects, including a murder mystery set in San Francisco's Chinatown and a political drama about a company's fight against a copper-mining monopoly. For the time being, the collaboration seemed to suit both men's work ethics—Louis could sit back and let Lloyd hammer out the first draft, and Lloyd could sit back and let Louis make it sing.

Meanwhile, Fanny was also putting the finishing touches on the short story "The Nixie." With slightly less reserve than usual about his wife's work, Louis wrote to Edward Burlingame, "If it smiles on you, I believe she means a series of Demigods in Exile; and I think the idea rather plummy."

In spring 1888, when "The Nixie" appeared in *Scribner's Magazine*, it would ignite a literary scandal. Not surprisingly, Louis's complicated friendship with Henley was at the heart of it.

THE STEVENSONS HAD BEEN HOPING that some of Louis's good fortune in the U.S. would spill over to their perpetually strapped friend overseas. Fanny sent Henley a notice when *Deacon Brodie* was a success in Chicago (though it failed elsewhere), and both she and Louis promoted him to editors and publishers. In January 1888, Louis reported to Henley that Fanny was in New York "blowing your praises in [McClure's] ear" and that his friend might very well become the publisher's permanent London agent "if you play your part." Louis advised him to be his most charming when McClure met with him in London, where he was traveling to establish literary connections overseas.

When McClure met with Henley and some of Louis's other friends, he was shocked to find them jealous and irritated by Louis's success in the U.S. Some of them claimed that Louis's talent was overrated and his cousin Bob Stevenson was the real family genius. "Henley was particularly emphatic," McClure recalled. "He believed that his own influence on Stevenson's work was not sufficiently recognized." Henry James was the only exception; McClure would not forget how he lit up with warmth and admiration when he talked about his fellow author.

Bob's sister, Katharine de Mattos, was part of that literary circle—reputedly a rather special part to Henley. Louis was close to his cousin, though in a poem he described her in her teens as "pale and sharp . . . a strong and bitter virgin." But Henley nursed an unreciprocated crush on her. Alan Stevenson's deterioration from illness had cast a long shadow over Katharine's childhood, and she had made an unfortunate marriage to a rampant womanizer. Before and after her divorce, Louis helped her financially, as he did Bob and Henley, but he was less supportive of her writing.

Henley's patronage helped her establish a prolific career as a reviewer for various prestigious publications, though her fiction (later often written under the pseudonym Theodor Hertz-Garten) would never meet with success.

It appears that Henley had failed to sell Katharine's story about a chance train meeting between a man and a female escapee from a mental asylum, and he was not present when she reluctantly agreed to let Fanny rewrite it with the main character as a nixie. After Henley read "The Nixie" in *Scribner's*, where it was the lead story, he decided that Fanny had plagiarized it by using aspects of Katharine's narrative, setting, and imagery. In an otherwise chatty letter to Louis, he conveyed astonishment: "It's Katharine's; surely it's Katharine's? . . . It is all better focussed, no doubt; but I think it has lost as much (at least) as it has gained, and why there wasn't a double signature is what I've not been able to understand."

Henley should have known that a casual attack on his wife's honor would ignite Louis's quick temper. "I write with indescribable difficulty; and if not with perfect temper, you are to remember how very rarely a husband is expected to receive such accusations against his wife," Louis replied. He appealed to Henley to verify the facts from Katharine: that she had turned down Fanny's offer to collaborate but agreed that she could rework the story, asking only that Fanny send her a copy if it was published. Both Louis and Fanny waited for Katharine to confirm this and settle the matter. Fanny, who was then on her way to California to secure a yacht for the South Seas cruise, reminded Louis that they "must not judge" Katharine without hearing from her.

But Katharine was evasive, refusing to confirm or deny her consent. To her mind, it was clear in her polite social circle that her demurring permission was a refusal, but Fanny did not belong to that circle and instead took her quiet passivity for agreement. Louis later recalled that he had advised Fanny not to proceed with the rewrite, but she had charged on, all heady with her ideas.

While Fanny might have misread or simply ignored Katharine's clues, however, Katharine did not act forthrightly. Possibly miffed that Fanny had published a story that she could not, she sniffed to Louis that Henley and anyone else who read it "had a perfect right to be astonished" but insisted that she was "far from wishing . . . to criticize [Fanny] in any way." And after the story was published, she claimed to have praised it to their mutual friends and even wrote to Fanny to tell her it was "well managed." (Katharine later claimed she had done so only to please Louis.)

Katharine's original draft has been lost, so how closely "The Nixie" resembled it is unknown, though Fanny's story is livelier and better told than some of Katharine's surviving fiction. (One modern critic remarked that Katharine "would have drained the life" from the story.) To what extent Fanny can be said to have plagiarized an unpublished story she had permission to rework is debatable. While the story should have carried a double byline, as Henley and some critics have contended, collaborations must be consensual. Fanny might have been happy to share the byline, but Katharine was unequivocal about only one thing—that she did not want to collaborate with Fanny. Nonetheless, Fanny could have given Katharine part of her payment—and there is no record that she did.

On the surface, the tempest swirled around two women with strong literary ambitions, but the controversy—remembered as the "Henley-Stevenson quarrel"—was more about the two men's deteriorating friendship than it was about intellectual property theft. Louis viewed Henley's stand as the culmination of years of backbiting, jealousy, and bitterness over the failure of their plays, and even resentment of his financial support. (It did not help that concurrently, a tour of *Deacon Brodie* starring Henley's brother Teddy was shut down after the star got into a liquor-fueled brawl in Philadelphia, and the "drunken, whoreson bugger," in Louis's words, then asked Fanny for money.) Henley, in turn, thought "Lewis" was spoiled and blind to his wife's meddling and deviousness, in contrast to his own loyal honesty. He recruited an ally in Bob Stevenson, who quietly took his sister's side. "We believe that F. stole the story," Henley boldly asserted to Baxter, who was trying to act as a mediator. In another letter, he added, "[Louis] can't have slept with Fanny all these years, and not have caught her in the act of lying."

Unfortunately, just as Henley demonized Fanny, Louis convinced himself that Katharine was the "petticoat" behind his friend's charges. Eventually

Henley apologized for offending Louis, but not for the accusations against his wife. Katharine, now deeply hurt that her cousin considered her the instigator of the whole furor, apologized to him too. "If I have failed to understand anything said to me at Bournemouth or put a wrong construction on things I am more grieved than ever but I cannot say it has been intentional," she wrote Louis. Yet she did not mention Fanny or acknowledge the possibility that Fanny too might have unintentionally put "a wrong construction on things" said in Bournemouth.

Fanny was understandably hurt by all the acrimony. Since Henley's charge, none of Louis's friends, who she liked to think were now her friends too, had written to her. "I gave up my own country and my own friends for Louis, and God knows, and I almost think you will believe me, I was sincere," she wrote to Baxter. "I loved them all." But she also reacted with bitter reproaches. In San Francisco, where she learned she would need surgery to remove a throat tumor, she dramatically added that her accusers had nearly "murdered" Louis and driven her to suicide. "While they eat their bread from my hand—and oh, they will do that—I shall smile and wish it were poison that might wither their bodies as they have my heart," she wrote. With her usual remorse after an outburst, she later sent him a profuse apology.

Louis was temperamentally incapable of his wife's bitterness, but he was equally capable of hysteria. In the middle of the squabble, he wrote to friends that he had to resort to taking opiates for sleep and lamented in several letters that he had not died in Hyères, the happiest time in his life because he "had still enough health for pleasure, and my wife and I were alone." Even when he was about to embark on his lifelong dream of voyaging in the South Seas, he moaned that it might be better if the ship went down with him (presumably also drowning his mother, wife, stepson, and their maid, Valentine Roch).

Louis's old circle would never recover. If Henley had hoped to drive a wedge between Louis and Fanny that he might slip into, it backfired. The couple grew closer than ever. Louis grudgingly continued but reduced his financial support to his friend and cousins. He never forgave Katharine, but he patched together a semblance of a relationship with Henley and Bob for a time. Fanny was saddened too. She had been fond of Bob as well as Katharine—Adelaide Boodle recalled how welcome he had been at Skerryvore. And she even had a soft spot for the maddening but undeniably likable Henley. Years later, Fanny reminisced to his widow, Anna, about a happy trip the couples had made to Paris and warmly recalled Henley's infectious laugh—"one of the most beautiful things I ever heard."

RESTLESS AND MISSING his wife in California, Louis left Saranac Lake and slipped quietly into the St. Stephen Hotel in Greenwich Village in April, for the most part managing to dodge reporters. Edward Bok, a young man who delivered proofs to him and was later the editor of *Ladies' Home Journal*, remembered him as "an author whom it was better to read than to see": his skin sallow, his hair disheveled, his fingernails long and stained by tobacco. Perhaps Louis made a more favorable impression on another visitor, Harriet Monroe, the American poet whose photo had rankled Fanny. "Monroe of the photograph, the entrancing Harriet," as Louis had described her to Henley, took a train from Chicago to meet him.

In New York, Louis met with another fan, Mark Twain. The two were mutual admirers—Twain already owned several of Louis's books and Louis assured him that he had read *Huckleberry Finn* four times and was ready to do so again. They spent an afternoon chatting on a bench in Washington Square "among the nursemaids like a couple of characters out of a story by Henry James," as Louis later recapped it to Twain. The conversation between the two world-famous authors, whose boys' novels confounded standard notions of Victorian masculinity, would have been an extraordinary earful for any eavesdropping nanny. They likely traded notes on fame, writing, their colorful youths, and perhaps the strong, modern American women who had married them and greatly influenced their work.

Like most observers, Twain was mesmerized by Louis's eyes. "He was most scantily furnished with flesh, his clothes seemed to fall into hollows as if there might be nothing inside but the frame for a sculptor's statue," Twain recalled in his autobiography. But Louis's eyes burned "with a smoldering rich fire under the pent-house of his brows and they made him beautiful." Two decades later, on his deathbed, Twain's last words were about dual personality and *Jekyll and Hyde*.

The two authors share another distinction, though they could not have known it then. *Kidnapped* and *The Adventures of Huckleberry Finn* would establish the epic buddy road trip—the literary and later film genre in which two often-mismatched people, historically men, embark on an odyssey filled with mishaps and adventure. They were the template for novels like *On the Road* and countless films, from *Butch Cassidy and the Sundance Kid* to the *Lethal Weapon* movies to the British comedy series *The Trip*.

Will Low introduced Louis to another fan, the celebrated American sculptor Augustus Saint-Gaudens. The artist visited Louis often at the St. Stephen while he designed a medallion of him working in bed, smoking a cigarette. At the time, Saint-Gaudens was also working on a bust of the famous American Civil War legend William Tecumseh Sherman, whom Louis hero-worshipped. Louis had gobbled up Sherman's memoir, but the general seemed to be one of the few people in New York who had never heard of him. "Stevenson?" he replied when Saint-Gaudens suggested a meeting. "Who is he, one of 'my boys'?" Louis did not really care who Sherman thought he was as long as he could meet and talk military strategy with the heroic (if ruthless) man of action, who had lived life as he never could. Together they went over maps and new material in a second edition of Sherman's book, which he suggested that Louis buy. "All this just as simply as you or I—," the starstruck author marveled to Low, "and to think that he has led armies!"

Louis and Fanny were apart for their eighth wedding anniversary in May, but Louis sent "my dearest fellow" a belated and poignant reminiscence of their courtship and marriage day:

> Not that I think so much of that day; if I had some other dates I
> would think more of them: that of the day when I looked through
> the window [at Grez], or the day when I came to see you in Paris

after the first absence, for example. But the marriage day we
know, and it was a mighty good day too, for me: for you, I wish I
was sure. It would have been better, if my health had been so, that
I do believe. The longer I go on, the more I think the worst of me is
my health.

Even with his regained strength in the Adirondacks, illness never left him. At low moments, he questioned whether Fanny should have saved his life but felt that his gratitude to her (and to some degree, his friends) obligated him to fight on. The South Seas voyage was not only an adventure but a desperate bid for the warm climate and sea air to "set him up," as Fanny knew. As much as he tried to protect her emotionally, in reality she was the only person who bore witness to his anguish, misery, and fears about illness and death. He intuitively understood that his friends and mother recoiled from seeing that side of the "General Exhilarator," whom they relied on to lift them up.

Low got a rare glimpse of that side of his friend in Manasquan, a New Jersey beach town where he hustled Louis when New York had tired him out. Fanny had just wired that a gorgeous yacht could be ready to sail from San Francisco in ten days, and Louis took a break from his departure preparations to walk with his friend on the beach. Louis told Low that when he felt free to leave Britain after his father's death, he had decided to make a new effort to live—not as he had been living in recent years, because he did not consider that life.

"No one knows, no one can know, the tedium of it," he reflected wearily. Of course, he did not hope to ever be the wild bohemian Low had known in Fontainebleau. At thirty-seven years old, he simply wished to be "an invalid gentleman" who could swim a little and ride a horse and know his body's enemy but get the better of him. "That's not a very wild ambition, is it?" he sighed. Louis did not discuss his health with Low again, but when it was time to part, he suggested they drink a bottle of Beaujolais to his bon voyage instead of saying goodbye at the train station. Both men knew this could be the last time they saw each other, and it was.

—⚜—

IF THE ESCAPE TO SARANAC LAKE had been good for Louis, the return to California worked wonders for Fanny. She did not have to contend with the seasickness, cold, or high altitude that she'd endured for her husband's sake; she had only herself to take care of, could go where she wanted, and slept well (unlike Louis, who always slept worse without her). The growth on her throat, though frightening, was successfully removed. Above all, she was back in the warm embrace of friends and family. She had not felt that well in years.

With her sister and brother-in-law, Nellie and Adulfo Sanchez, and their son, Louis, she barbecued over bonfires on the beach in Monterey. And she visited Jules Simoneau, a bedraggled restaurateur who had offered Louis friendship and free meals when he was a sickly stranger in the town. Simoneau and his wife scavenged in the woods for roots and herbs traditionally used in Native American remedies for lung ailments. Fanny eagerly accepted them for the upcoming voyage and sent some on to Louis to brew into a tea.

In San Francisco, she was happily reunited with Dora Williams and visited with her old friends and possible lovers Timothy Rearden and John Lloyd. She also received a surprise visit from Sam Osbourne's widow, Paulie, whom she invited to stay for lunch. The contrast of the two women's fates was never more pronounced: While the local press breathlessly awaited the arrival of Fanny's prominent husband, it had made Paulie's life miserable with speculation about her husband fleeing with another woman to escape her or his debts. Paulie grimly joked to Fanny that their rendezvous would be an irresistible scoop if reporters had known about it. "Imagine how humble I felt in my good fortune when I sat side by side with that poor woman whose case might have been mine—but for you," Fanny wrote passionately to Louis after their lunch. "Everything seems small and slight that might happen besides that."

After years of strained relations with her daughter, Fanny reconciled with Belle and met her seven-year-old grandson, Austin. Belle's marriage to Joe Strong was in turmoil, and she had fled to San Francisco for what was likely a tryst with Frank Unger, a dashing journalist who had been part of their bohemian set but was now married with a child in New York. None of this was a surprise to Fanny, and her daughter's tumultuous reentry into her life must have been bittersweet. But Fanny's usual frustration with Belle softened into pity and sympathy upon seeing her. And she happily welcomed her grandson into her life: She and Austin adored each other immediately and for the rest of their lives.

When Fanny greeted the rest of the Stevenson party at the train station in Sacramento, she looked so well and pretty in a new hat, Margaret noted it in her diary. But Fanny's days of relative relaxation were now over. The yacht she had located was not quite ready to sail, as she had promised. The owner, Samuel Merritt, was reluctant to entrust his elegant vessel, with its velvet sofas and gleaming brass work, to a man who he had gathered from articles was "kind of a crank."

"You may think your husband loves *you*," Merritt told Fanny, "but I can assure you I love my yacht a great deal better." Meeting Louis convinced him that the author was sensible. He agreed to let Louis charter his ninety-five-foot, two-masted schooner, the *Casco*, for seven months at an exorbitant $3,500, plus all cruise expenses.

Inundated by reporters and suffering again from a bad cold, Louis fled the Occidental Hotel in San Francisco to wait out their departure on the *Casco*, where it was anchored at Oakland Creek. While Belle and Frank showed Margaret around the city, Fanny scrambled to get provisions for eleven people for seven months at sea. She stocked up on healthy foods, as well as medical reference books and remedies, and saw that everyone was vaccinated for smallpox except Louis, who was too ill. For him, she procured a vial of "lymph" to inject in an emergency. She began to carry two items that were emblematic of her longing to settle down and her perpetual need to move on. She kept seeds for planting—sugar peas, sweet corn, nutmeg, flowers—in a pocket of her dress and a vial of medicine sewed into the hem, to rip out and inject immediately if her husband should start bleeding from the lungs. Many times the seeds would not have time to take root before Louis's hemorrhages sent them on the road again.

At Belle's suggestion, Fanny also went to a Chinatown dressmaker to order holokus—long-sleeved, yoked dresses that fell loose from the shoulders and were an airy alternative to fitted gowns that required corsets and stays. Holokus were originally introduced in Hawaii by missionaries, but Belle knew they had become standard and stylish dress there, sometimes embellished with lace and ruffles and accessorized with parasols and ostrich-plumed hats. In the U.S. and Britain, their shapeless counterpart, known as the "Mother Hubbard," still carried a subversive whiff of the emancipated woman, however. Once their ship set sail, Fanny and Valentine would gladly slip into theirs, but Margaret fretted that she would be a "queer-looking customer" in one and vowed to hold off as long as possible, though she did take off her stockings.

In the wee hours of June 2, 1888, Belle's troubles were still on her mother's mind. From the *Casco*, Fanny dispatched a heartfelt note to her daughter, gently urging her to realize that her affair with Frank Unger must end. Belle was so touched, she wrote back that she would keep the letter for the rest of her life. Belle knew then she would return to Hawaii and Unger would return to New York. At dawn, she and Dora waved goodbye as the *Casco* was towed through the Golden Gate and let loose, with Louis and Fanny, on the open sea.

FIFTEEN

I can see her now—a small woman in a blue dress, sitting barefoot on the roof of the aftercabin of a trading schooner in the South Seas," Fanny's grandson, Austin Strong, would write many years later:

> Her Panama hat, set at a rakish angle, shades a face of breath-taking beauty. She is holding a large silvered revolver in each hand, shooting sharks with deadly accuracy. . . . Infinitely feminine, self-effacing and gentle, nevertheless she gave the impression of holding a secret power not to be trifled with.

The South Seas opened Fanny and Louis to a whole new way of being. The ocean breeze tasted of freedom, from which there was no turning back. When they set sail from San Francisco for French Polynesia in June 1888, they intended to return to Europe within a year. Instead, the voyage was the first of three cruises that continued for two years, and they would never return.

The islands the Stevensons visited on the first cruise—such as Nuku Hiva, Fakarava, and Tahiti—had been written about by explorers and others, including Herman Melville and their friend Charles Warren Stoddard. By the time the *Casco* made its final stop in Hawaii after seven months at sea, Louis was eager to go beyond the areas under French domain to explore the less traveled independent kingdoms of the Pacific. Fanny's perennial seasickness had prompted her to vow that she would never leave land once she set foot in Hawaii, but six months later, in June 1889, she and Louis were on a ship bound for Micronesia, not Europe.

Though the Western imagination was gripped by the fantasy of the Pacific Islands as an exotic utopia, it was uncommon for white men, let alone white couples, to travel that far. It was especially unusual for a Victorian woman to venture to the more mysterious islands and face the discomforts of the Stevensons' next two cruises. Fanny's diary of her experience, later published, would be one of the rare accounts of nineteenth-century South Seas travel by a white woman.

Instead of chartering a luxury yacht on their second tour, the Stevensons were passengers on the small, sixty-two-ton trading schooner *Equator*, which stopped to exchange items like sewing machines, cloth, and tinned foods for dried coconut meat, or copra, used to produce coconut oil and butter for soap, cosmetics, and medicine. And they would be touring the Gilbert Islands (now part of the Republic of Kiribati). Even traders seldom visited these equatorial islands, which were considered wilder and less hospitable by white Western travelers, so Margaret Stevenson returned to Britain, where Fanny and Louis intended to join her at the end of the cruise. This time Fanny was the only woman with fifteen men on a cramped ship that looked like "a tiny cockle shell" among the cargo ships and men-of-war in port, Belle thought as she saw her mother off. "If the boat had been an ocean liner with every luxury, she could not have looked more pleased and serene."

Touring the Pacific turned out to be better for Louis than he and Fanny had dared to hope. "I did not dream there were such places or such races. . . . I am browner than the berry; only my trunk and the aristocratic spot on which I sit, retains the vile whiteness of the north," Louis wrote to Sidney Colvin. Though he had a few bouts of illness, he gained strength. To others he might still appear fragile, Lloyd wrote, but to his family, the change was astonishing—his hair was shiny, his complexion ruddy, his eyes without the "strange fire of disease." By the end of their second tour, Fanny and Louis were so enamored with the Pacific Islands—and so convinced that it was the only place where he could enjoy good health—they decided to settle permanently in Samoa. They purchased about 315 hilly acres on the island of Upolu at ten dollars an acre and arranged to have the land cleared and temporary living quarters erected while they headed for Australia. This time they intended to return by steamer to England only to sell Skerryvore and visit friends.

Louis was aware that two sea journeys had asked much of his queasy wife. "Fanny has stood the hardships of this rough cruise wonderfully," he reported to Margaret as the *Equator* tour neared an end after six months, "but I do not think I could expose her to 'another of the same.'" In Sydney, however, he fell so ill, the only remedy either of them could think of was to get him back to sea, but not back to Britain. Within weeks, they set sail again, this time on the *Janet Nicoll*, a six-hundred-ton, iron-screw trading steamer rigged with topsails.

On the *Janet Nicoll* the party had no say over the itinerary and no idea where they would stop. The four-month cruise took them to about thirty-five isles—as far east as Penrhyn in the Cook Islands, then back through the Ellice Islands (now Tuvalu) and north to the Gilberts and Marshalls before finishing in Nouméa, New Caledonia. As usual, the heat and fresh air eased Louis's physical ailments, but "being at sea" was clearly a mental remedy as well—a cure for melancholy, boredom, societal pressures, and his inner turmoil. "So soon as I cease from cruising, the nerves are strained, the decline commences, and I steer slowly but surely back to bedward," he reported to Colvin.

As much as Louis thrived at sea, all the voyages were physically challenging—food supplies ran low, dry rot in the ship masts kept them stranded on land for weeks, and sleep was difficult. (Fanny sometimes slept inside under drying shark fins or outside, with an open umbrella to hold above her if it rained and between her feet if the wind blew.) And it was rough sailing through areas such as Tuamotu Archipelago, known as the "Dangerous Archipelago" because of its treacherous coral reefs and narrow passages. Sometimes their ships were tossed about in squalls and hurricanes, then landed in dead calms when they seemed to be sitting still for days. Between Tahiti and Hawaii, the *Casco* encountered a raging hurricane, and the captain, A. H. Otis, decided to run with it instead of riding it out. As the yacht was swept "like a toy across the sea," the Stevensons were confined to their cabins and the crew tied to their posts so they would not be swept overboard.

The Pacific excursions were working voyages for Fanny, Lloyd, and Louis. Lloyd took hundreds of photos and they all kept diaries to provide source material for Louis's South Seas letters, which were helping finance the tours. But writing in cabins overheated by steam engines or bouncing on the waves was not easy. "You never saw such a bitch to roll," Louis wrote to *Scribner's* editor Edward Burlingame after being nearly thrown out of his bunk while trying to write on the "Jumping Janet," as the *Janet Nicoll* was nicknamed. Other times sweat poured from his brow onto his papers as he clutched them in place with one hand and tried to spear the ink bottle "like a flying fish" with the other. Fanny recalled that she composed the entries to her *Janet Nicoll* diary "on the damp, upturned bottom of a canoe or whaleboat, sometimes when lying face down on the burning sands of the tropic beach, often in copra sheds in the midst of a pandemonium of noise and confusion . . . but never in comfortable surroundings." It was all worth it for the tapestry of life that unfurled before them on land.

"THE FIRST EXPERIENCE can never be repeated," Louis wrote of the *Casco*'s arrival in Anaho Bay in Nuku Hiva, the largest of the Marquesas Islands, twenty-two days into their first cruise. "The first love, the first sunrise, the first South Sea island, are memories apart and touched a virginity of sense." The Stevensons would also visit low-lying coral isles and atolls, but Nuku Hiva was a stunning introduction to the high volcanic islands, with its monumental waterfalls and towering precipices. "The land heaved up in peaks and rising vales; it fell in cliffs and buttresses; its colour ran through 50 modulations in a scale of pearl and rose and olive; and it was crowned above by opalescent clouds," he wrote.

The first landfall was also something of a shock, as the local men, rumored to be cannibals, paddled out to the ship and trampled aboard without offering any cordial greetings. Being surrounded by men "in every stage of undress" was a particularly eye-popping exercise for Margaret. "Two most respectable-looking old gentlemen wore nothing but small red and yellow loin-cloths and *very* cutty sarks on top," she gasped in a letter to her sister Jane. "There were even some who wore less!" But Margaret was rarely ruffled for long, and she noted that the men's bare legs were decorated with such intricate and beautiful tattoos, they looked as if they were wearing "open-work silk tights." An obstreperous group of men and women paraded through the yacht's cabins later, gawking at the travelers, fingering their belongings, and admiring themselves in the beveled mirrors. One woman hoisted up her dress and slid her bare bottom across the velvet cushions, luxuriating in the silky rub.

The encounter revealed how little Fanny and Louis knew about what lay ahead of them. Trade was usually the main interaction between Pacific Islanders and travelers, and the Marquesans who brought out their wares were disgruntled that the Stevensons showed little interest in them. Fanny also realized that the little trinkets she had purchased in San Francisco were woefully inadequate for gifts or trade (especially when she later received highly valued presents such as an old man's beard and a necklace of human teeth). Louis felt intimidated and frustrated by his inability to communicate with the local people. He despaired that the Marquesans were "beyond the reach of articulate communication, like furred animals, or folk born deaf, or the dwellers of some alien planet."

His uncharacteristically derogatory view was forgotten as the party spent the following weeks getting to know people in Anaho and Tai-o-hae, on the other side of the island. Soon Margaret was taking a moonlight stroll on the beach with a gentleman attired only in a handkerchief, Fanny delightedly reported to Henry James. Louis picked up bits of the Polynesian language, and his fluent French was an asset as well. From the looks of the

Casco, the local men determined him a rich man—christening him with the prestigious if inaccurate honorific "ona," or owner—and like men everywhere, soon began to vie for proximity to him.

On the whole, however, Ona and his brood must have struck the islanders as a bit like dwellers from another planet: Margaret, in a white starched widow's cap with organdy streamers that trailed down her straight back, in the manner of Queen Victoria, whose photo she eagerly shared; Louis's dark, boyish wife darting about in bare feet, big-hooped earrings, and short hair; and Lloyd—whose spectacles earned him the title Mata-Gahali, or "glass eyes"—also sporting two gold hoops after having his ears pierced in San Francisco.

The Stevensons were not the type of travelers to stand back and observe local life at a distance; they planned to immerse themselves in it wherever they could. Over time, as Fanny learned more about the women on different islands, she sought out items they desired for trade and gifts: bolts of fabric in pretty prints, red India combs, perfume, framed mirrors, needles and thread. When the Stevensons reached Hawaii, she and Belle would string beads and make wreaths of artificial flowers for her to take to the atolls, where they were coveted in the absence of fresh flowers. Fanny joined island women in crafts like plaiting hats out of bamboo shavings and sugarcane, a diversion she equated to watercolor painting for European ladies.

As always, Fanny's interest in cooking was also a way into local life. In the Marquesas, Margaret described her marching ashore with a bowl and a beater, going from house to house to learn how to make a dish of breadfruit roasted over an open fire, then mashed and drenched in coconut cream. The Stevensons still clung to their coffee, wine, and salt, but they gobbled up native dishes such as taro popoi and raw fish with miti sauce, which Fanny also learned to prepare.

"It is wonderful how quickly one takes up the ways of a people when you live with them as intimately as we do," Fanny wrote to Colvin, no doubt confirming the prevailing view that Louis's wife, with her dark skin (even darker now) and American birth, was already nearly "savage." But Margaret admired the aplomb with which her daughter-in-law embraced new customs. By the time the party reached Tahiti, she would write that Fanny was "quite *une femme Tahitienne* in her *holaku* [*sic*] and bare feet. She lies on a pillow in the chief's smoking room . . . and can even take a whiff of a native cigarette and pass it on to the other members of the company in the approved way."

Louis immersed himself in recording native folklore and traditions, usually passed on orally, that were being lost or outlawed as Western powers and Christian missionaries sought to force change on the islanders' way of life. In the Marquesas, a sweeping ban of cannibalism had included anything vaguely associated with it, such as traditional songs, dances, tattooing, and other native arts and pleasures. Louis interpreted local life through the lens of his Scottish heritage. "When I desired any detail of savage custom, or of superstitious belief, I cast back in the story of my fathers, and fished for what I wanted with some trait of equal barbarism," he wrote in his South Seas letters. In his view, "the native was no longer ashamed, his sense of kinship grew warmer, and his lips were opened." Louis's Scottish ancestry also shaded his sense of the costs of political upheaval in the Pacific. The Marquesas were in "the same convulsive and transitory state" as the Scottish Highlands and islands a century before, he wrote: "In both cases an alien authority enforced, the clans disarmed, the chiefs deposed, new customs introduced, and chiefly that fashion of regarding money as the means and object of existence."

Louis viewed the Pacific cultures he visited through the eyes of a white man, and his accounts (and Fanny's) sometimes include racist stereotypes. (Other times they use stereotypical words like "savages" ironically.) But Louis was less interested in labeling people or judging their rituals and superstitions than in understanding how they fit into the fabric of local life, and in the social consequences when they were denied. This was something of a challenge in the case of cannibalism, which both horrified and titillated the Western world. With her usual abandon, Fanny deemed the practice merely a "freak of fashion." For readers of his South Seas letters, Louis more thoughtfully sought to equate conventional Western attitudes toward man-eaters with Buddhist and vegetarian views of meat-eaters, who "consume the carcases of creatures of like appetites, passions, and organs with ourselves." And he disputed the idea that anthropophagites like the Marquesans were by nature cruel. Eating an enemy after killing him was considered the final triumph in local wartime ritual. "Rightly speaking," Louis asserted, "to eat a man's flesh after he is dead is far less hateful than to oppress him whilst he lives."

Still, Louis's tolerance was tested when he met Moipu, a former high-ranking chief of Atuona and reputedly one of the last cannibals on the island of Hiva Oa. The French had replaced Moipu with their own appointee, Paaaeua, but the ousted chief was clearly still the people's favorite. With his impeccable manners and dapper Western dress—a muslin shirt and black trousers—he would hardly seem threatening. But in the 1880s, many Marquesans had taken to flaunting their reputation for eating flesh, or "long pig," to ridicule European stereotypes and build a protective barrier around themselves—and Moipu had made his predilection for human flesh well-known. Louis despised him from the start, and he was somewhat beside himself when Moipu squeezed Fanny's hand, the body part for which he was known to have a special appetite. Intriguingly, the women in the Stevenson party were much more relaxed about the charismatic former chief—a "magnificent figure," in Fanny's words, at well over six feet. In a rare show of irritation, Margaret even scoffed at her daughter-in-law's claim that Moipu had eaten hundreds of people "when you know he only ate 11 men."

Louis and Fanny became fascinated by the weird and often disturbing manifestations of the collision between Old and New World cultures in the Pacific. Both of them recorded how Marquesans got around the taboo on eating a slain enemy in the usual public festival: They quietly divided the man's cooked remains in Swedish matchboxes for each warrior to take home and observe the rite in secret. "The barbarous substance of the drama and the European properties employed offer a seizing contrast to the imagination," Louis wrote.

At a time when travel literature generally boosted the imperialist agenda, the Stevensons wrote about the destructive ways it played out in the Pacific. As Julia Reid has noted, even Louis's celebration of island folklore was radical for its time: It blurred the distinction between "civilization" and "savagery" upon which imperial ideology, and the anthropological theory that justified it, was based. But everywhere Louis and Fanny looked, those lines were blurred. And they saw that it was not only Western powers that were changing the face of the Pacific; the cross-pollination of missionaries, beachcombers, traders, and Indigenous people was creating a new hybrid culture. Louis would weave the vast range of characters they met, and the tangled relations between them, throughout his later fiction.

WHEN THE STEVENSONS sailed into Honolulu harbor at the end of their first cruise, a couple of weeks late and nearly starving on food rations that had shriveled to salt beef and biscuits, two thoughts were uppermost in Louis's mind: to eat and to find out if he had any money. The first was easily remedied. The travel party—along with Belle, Joe, and Austin—indulged in a fancy roast beef dinner at the grand Royal Hawaiian Hotel. The second issue was more complicated. There were no checks among the seven months of mail waiting for Louis, and the steep bills for Captain Otis and the *Casco* cruise were due.

Honolulu was the prosperous capital of the independent Kingdom of Hawaii, a bustling city with a music hall, a racecourse, and one of the most advanced telephone systems in the world. After the travelers' harrowing passage from Tahiti, one might think they would welcome amenities like running water for a change, but they did not relish their return to "civilization." They had already experienced a distaste for Papeete, the shabby French colonial capital in Tahiti, which even Margaret had described as "a sort of halfway house between savage life and civilisation, with the drawbacks of both and the advantages of neither."

Hawaii's gleaming capital was even worse, its smooth paved streets choked with traffic and overrun by Americans and other haoles. "What is a *haole*?" Louis wrote to Charles Baxter. "You are one; and so, I am sorry to say, am I." Fanny was equally dismayed. "I cannot bear colonial people," she wrote to Dora, "give me my gentle Anaho savages; I have seen none yet to equal them in beauty or manners."

Fanny's daughter, on the other hand, had taken to Honolulu perhaps too enthusiastically in the seven years since she and Joe Strong had moved to the Hawaiian Kingdom. When they had arrived, their socially savvy friend Charles Warren Stoddard had presented them with a choice: Would they run with the straitlaced missionaries or with King David Kalākaua's royal set? This was no dilemma for Belle, since the royals liked dancing and late-night supper parties in the king's bathhouse (which were *not* "orgies," she took pains to point out in her memoir). And the missionaries disapproved of her girlfriends in the royal set, who smoked and galloped around the island riding their horses astride rather than sidesaddle. Island equestrians had devised a clever way to do this: They hoisted up their fancy dresses and pulled on culotte skirts made of yards of fabric that flowed elegantly past their stirrups.

Apparently Belle did not consider whether so much sociability was likely to help her husband conquer the drinking problem that had driven them to the islands in the first place. Joe did some commissions for Kalākaua and helped establish the Volcano school, a regional artistic movement that took painters into craters to capture the heat and fiery plumes of lava on canvas. But after his nervous breakdown, Joe descended further into alcohol, opium, and debt. Belle pieced together work teaching dance and drawing and doing designs for Kalākaua, and eventually she developed a colorful line of fortune-telling cards. But the couple's piecemeal income was not enough to support Joe's lavish lifestyle, and by the time the Stevensons arrived, he had been barred from leaving the island until his debts were paid.

Bracing for an extended stay on land, Louis sent the *Casco* back to San Francisco and moved everyone but Belle and Austin into a bungalow on Waikiki, where he could keep an eye on Joe and "make a little money to take us home," in Margaret's sunny version of events. He and Lloyd finished the last chapters of their comic novel *The Wrong Box* and Louis aggressively negotiated a $5,000 fee for it from Scribner's—possibly the only time he insisted that one of his books was worth more than it actually was. He struggled through the conclusion of *The Master of Ballantrae* and sent it off to *Scribner's Magazine*, where the novel began serialization in fall. He also wrote "The Song of Rahero" and "The Feast of Famine," two ballads based on Polynesian legends.

Fanny spruced up the lanai in their bungalow, one of a handful of houses scattered among the coconut groves and rice fields at Waikiki. She decorated it with easy chairs and a grand piano, hung island weapons and woven mats on the walls, and lined the sea-facing windows with shells. Every weekend, Belle and Austin hopped off one of Honolulu's new mule-driven streetcars at the gate, which was flanked by two big barrels of goldfish, and walked in through a garden blooming with oleander and hibiscus flowers. To Belle, "this was always an exciting moment, like the rising of a curtain in the theatre," as the sounds of lively conversation and laughter, and guitar and piano music, spilled outside. Still, she noted, her mother managed to break up social gatherings at the first sign of fatigue from Louis in such a clever way that no one, especially the guests, realized why they were leaving.

By then Valentine Roch had left the travel party, ostensibly because of a sexual indiscretion with a crew member of the *Casco*. Louis bought her a ticket back to Europe, but she stopped off in San Francisco and settled down with a Sonoma farmer. Surprisingly, Louis described the parting with their faithful employee as one of "mutual glee." Valentine might well have welcomed an escape from the demands of Fanny, who in turn suspected that the maid swiped some small trinkets of theirs on her way out. But Fanny had a ready replacement. In the Marquesas the *Casco* had picked up a cook named Ah Fu—a tall, muscular man who sported a shaved head and queue in the Chinese fashion though he had lived in Polynesia since he was marooned there as a boy. No doubt his skills were more suited than Valentine's to the Stevensons' new way of life: He could catch a fish with his hands, climb a coconut tree, and use a jagged piece of rock for a knife. Ah Fu swore like the American sailors from whom he had learned English, to Fanny's chagrin when he served their guests, but he adored her and would sharpen his cooking skills under her tutelage on the next cruise. Fanny told Belle he was much more to her taste than a lady's maid.

Each morning at dawn, Ah Fu brought tea and toast to a dilapidated shack where Louis chose to work among centipedes, lizards, and a mouse he trained to nibble toast next to his morning tray. When Louis was not working, he swam, rode horses, and bathed in lagoons—activities that would have been unimaginable the year before. "And if you could only see him!" Fanny rhapsodized to Colvin and Sitwell about her husband, who now often went about in a pareu, or sarong, with a flower tucked behind his ear. "It is a delight to me beyond words, as it would be to you to see him bare-footed and half clothed, flying about with his usual impetuosity, accompanied by no fear of danger." To his friend Alice Taylor, Louis wrote, "Words cannot depict how much fun we have."

Louis also traveled to other islands to gather material, escape haoles, and work in peace. The highlight of these was his pilgrimage to the Kalawao leper colony on Molokai, where native Hawaiians with Hansen's disease had been quarantined since the 1860s (and would be for another hundred years). After twelve days there, Louis wrote, "I have seen sights that cannot be told, and heard stories that cannot be repeated: yet I never admired my poor race so much, nor (strange as it may seem) loved life more, than in the settlement."

Back in Waikiki, the thorny issue of what to do with Joe, Belle, and Austin awaited him. Louis laid down rules that his son-in-law continually broke, but he found Joe such a "lovable fellow"—much more lovable than Belle, in Louis's eyes—that it was difficult to turn him away. After a particularly severe falling-out, Joe pleaded for forgiveness and agreed to put all his affairs in Louis's hands. His remorse and shame were so moving, even Fanny softened. Joe could be selfish and devious but also kind and affectionate—the sort of person "you always love, worse luck," she confided to Colvin—and she agreed he deserved one more chance.

Financial responsibility for three more family members was a burden Louis did not need, though he did not ease the burden by sending them out to find work on their own. Instead, he paid off Joe's debts and put him to work on their next cruise painting island scenes on magic lantern slides. Lloyd would earn his keep by taking photos and collecting material for a book and lecture tour.

To Belle's shock, Louis ordered her to sail with Austin on the next steamer to Sydney and stay out of trouble until the rest of the family joined her there at the end of the *Equator* cruise. Belle screamed and cried, then washed her face and cheerfully began to pack. She was never one to dwell on unpleasantness, and she really had no choice. She consoled herself with the thought that at least she did not have to worry about Joe. He was Louis and Fanny's problem now.

THE STEVENSONS HAD UNINTENTIONALLY landed in the Pacific during one of the ugliest times in its history. Europe and the United States were carving up the region to expand their empires, aided by rival Catholic and Protestant missionaries who saw it as their duty to prepare the "savage" islands for Western control. On their travels, Fanny and Louis met two very different monarchs who were fighting to retain national sovereignty in the face of overwhelming odds.

David Kalākaua was an intellectual and an arts patron, a cosmopolitan ruler who had brought prosperity to Hawaii by brokering a free-trade agreement with the U.S. banning tariffs on Hawaiian sugar. He was the first Hawaiian monarch to travel to the United States, Asia, and Europe, and he modeled his lavish new Iolani Palace after European courts. After meeting with Thomas Edison, he installed electric lighting in the palace five years before it appeared in the White House. When Louis was presented to the king, his letters of introduction were unnecessary; Kalākaua, who was fluent in English, had already read *Treasure Island* and *Jekyll and Hyde*.

Kalākaua was trying to ensure his state's survival by incorporating some modern Western practices while reviving island traditions that had been prohibited. He created a renaissance in Hawaiian culture, bringing back surfing, native medical remedies, and the hula, which a previous monarch had banned because of its chants evoking Hawaiian legends and myths. Kalākaua worked with scholars to produce a book of native verse and traditions, and he and Louis pored for hours over the notebooks where he had recorded ancient lore.

Known as "the Merrie Monarch," Kalākaua was too merry for some. "O, Charles! what a crop for the drink!" Louis reported to Baxter after the king polished off five bottles of champagne in less than four hours one afternoon but rose from the occasion "perceptibly more dignified." By then Kalākaua had not much left but his dignity. An alliance of missionaries and wealthy plantation owners had been steadily discrediting him, accelerating their efforts to quash his administration after he attempted to create a league of independent Pacific islands. A year and a half before the Stevensons arrived, he had been forced by a largely white, armed militia to sign the "Bayonet Constitution," which ceded much of his power to a legislature more friendly to American business interests. For the rest of his reign, he was largely a figurehead.

In June 1889, the Stevensons left Hawaii for the Gilbert Islands, a group of sixteen small coral isles and atolls—ring-shaped coral reefs that enclose lagoons. In the Gilberts, Fanny and Louis met Tem Binoka, king of the islands of Abemama, Aranuka, and Kuria. Unlike Kalākaua and the rulers of other nearby Gilbert Islands, Tem Binoka had held the line against the Western assault largely by keeping white people out of his kingdom.

Tem Binoka was a much-feared tyrant, "the last erect visage of a dead society," Louis wrote. He was suspicious of all foreigners and white traders, whom he divided into three categories: those who cheated a little, those who cheated "plenty," and those who cheated "too much." He told Louis that he had to look into his eyes long and hard before concluding that he was not a liar. He agreed to let the Stevensons live on Abemama temporarily on the condition that they not give or sell liquor or tobacco to his people.

Tem Binoka was one of the most extraordinary characters in Louis's South Seas letters. A huge man with a beaked nose and thick mane of long black hair, he was a musician and historian but had only recently broken with the royal tradition of being carried and begun to walk. He tightly controlled his kingdom's copra business, boarding visiting ships himself because he delighted in traders' offerings, if not their company. The palace buildings were filled like closets with clocks, music boxes, umbrellas, blue spectacles (a special passion), tools, rifles, stoves, and sewing machines. Tem Binoka fashioned the fabrics and clothing he collected to his own unique taste. Here was another glimpse of that strange intermingling of cultures in the Pacific: Sometimes the king wore a naval uniform, sometimes a woman's dress (which he might couple with a pith helmet and blue spectacles), sometimes a green velvet or cardinal-red silk suit of his own design. The last outfit "becomes him admirably," Louis wrote. "In the woman's frock he looks ominous and weird beyond belief."

The Stevensons stayed in thatched huts on Abemama for six weeks, managing largely on onions and radishes Fanny planted and the occasional turtle, washed down with the last of their California claret. While Ah Fu chased chickens and prepared meals, Joe sketched and Louis worked on his South Seas letters and a new novel, *The Wrecker*, with Lloyd. Fanny designed a flag for Tem Binoka's kingdom that featured a black shark jumping across a bed of green, red, and yellow stripes, to honor the legend that had descended from the union of a shark god and a female chief. When the Stevensons left, she took the design to Sydney to have it sewn into a flag. The king had grown quite fond of these white people by then. Outfitted in his naval uniform, he cried as he saw them off.

Roslyn Jolly, a scholar of the Stevensons in the Pacific, has pointed out that Louis and especially Fanny were less critical of the brutality of Tem Binoka's reign than they should have been. But their connection to the king gave them unprecedented insight into a world usually barred to whites—"an insight that became even more valuable when that world suddenly vanished," Jolly wrote. The Stevensons visited Tem Binoka once more, on their third cruise, but they never saw David Kalākaua again. When both monarchs died in 1891, their struggles for independent nationhood died with them. Within two years, Britain had annexed the Gilbert Islands and the

Hawaiian monarchy was overthrown, paving the way for the United States to annex Hawaii in 1898.

THE LONGER FANNY AND LOUIS were away from "civilization," the harder it was to come back. When they arrived in Sydney in February 1890, Belle was not quite prepared for the scene that greeted her at the posh Union Hotel, where they were checking in. The couple's odd luggage—palm leaf baskets and cedar chests tied together with rope, canvas-covered buckets made of scooped-out tree trunks, coconut shells and calabashes tied in fish netting—was scattered on the polished lobby floor. Belle, who had resumed wearing Western clothes in the cosmopolitan Australian capital, realized that her mother and stepfather were "as odd-looking as their belongings." Louis, in a floppy straw hat and suit rumpled from six months in the hold of a ship, was berating the hotel clerk for disrespecting his wishes, while Fanny, in a baggy gray holoku and straw hat, looked on nervously. Belle quickly defused the scene by suggesting that the travelers move to the less fancy but still comfortable Oxford Hotel.

The reception for Louis in Australia rivaled that in the United States. The next day Sydney newspapers heralded his arrival with front-page articles and, to the horror of the Union Hotel manager, photos of the unkempt eccentric his staff had snubbed. Mortified, the manager marched over to the Oxford with the offending clerk to apologize and offer Louis a whole floor of rooms at a reduced rate. But the man being hailed as "the greatest author living" was quite pleased with his current accommodations, he told them.

As invitations poured in for speeches and dinners, Louis predictably fell ill and moved to the Union Club, where he could work peacefully in bed. He finished several chapters of *The Wrecker* there, but he also coughed up blood and seemed headed for pleurisy. He and Fanny agreed that he needed to get back to sea, but that seemed impossible—Australian seamen and dockworkers were about to walk out on the job in what would become the biggest maritime strike in Australian history.

Undaunted, Fanny marched through crowds of disgruntled seamen milling around the wharves and shipping offices, insisting that getting her husband to sea was a matter of life and death, until she found a vessel that would take her family as passengers. Two months after Louis had walked onto the dock in Sydney, he was carried onto the *Janet Nicoll* "rolled like a mummy in a blanket," according to Belle, and the ship slipped out of the harbor with the Stevensons and a nonunion crew of mostly Solomon Islanders.

On their virgin Pacific cruise, Fanny had been one of three women among eleven men on a luxury yacht. On the *Janet Nicoll*, she was the only woman with forty-five men on a trading steamer for more than three months. She earned the respect of the captain and crew by proving herself exceptionally tough and resourceful. She mended the men's clothes, doctored them, repaired camera bellows when cockroaches ate through them, and was, according to the captain, bitterly disappointed when a threatened shipwreck did not occur. She developed an easy camaraderie with the ship company and wrote admiringly of the Melanesian crew. The Stevensons celebrated their tenth anniversary with champagne set to cool on wet towels and performances that culminated in a sermon delivered by Louis, based on an advertisement for the pain remedy St. John's Oil.

The *Janet Nicoll* cruise gave the fullest rein to the many qualities Louis loved in Fanny—her unconventionality, unfussiness, resourcefulness, independence, and openness to new experiences. An edited version of Fanny's diary of the expedition was published in 1914 (with the ship's name misspelled) as *The Cruise of the "Janet Nichol" Among the South Sea Islands*. Like her, the published diary is passionate, unpolished, insightful, and entertaining. Like most diaries, it flows randomly through events both ordinary and significant. One day Fanny is shaking hands with a person with leprosy whose fingers are "dropping off." Another day she is jotting down a recipe for a pudding of taro pounded with pandan syrup and coconut milk, then baked in taro leaves underground.

One night Fanny writes a lovely entry about sea-bathing in the evening rain. When the raindrops strike the ocean, "each producing a spark like a star," she finds her bath "blazing like liquid fireworks," she writes, as if the heavens had fallen into the sea. Another night she opens her eyes to find an immense white rat with red eyes scurrying over her in bed. The ship is full of them, and when Captain Ernest Henry announces that he is going to tame one for a pet—"the loveliest rat in the world," in his estimation—she runs to help him catch it in his cabin. Suddenly, the rat jumps out from under the bed, hitting Henry and rebounding off Fanny's breast "like a fluff of white cotton wool." The "loveliest rat in the world" escapes to freedom, leaving Fanny and the captain screaming and laughing hysterically.

Fanny quickly recognized the harsh realities in the Pacific and did not hesitate to record them. She wrote passionately about "blackbirding," a practice of relocating islanders, usually by trickery or kidnapping, for work in white-owned mines and plantations. French, German, British, American, and Australian labor-traders engaged in the practice, euphemistically called "recruiting" and more accurately known as "slaving," which was at its height in the Pacific when she was there. On the Ellice island of Fanafuti, Fanny recorded a trader's story of two American vessels sailing under the Peruvian flag that "recruited" two-thirds of the islanders with gifts and promises of education. "It is needless to add that the vessels were slavers, and the entrapped islanders were never seen again," she reported. On the *Janet Nicoll*, she wrote about laborers she met who were returning to their families, including one boy who had been enslaved for five years and had waited three more for passage home.

Fanny blamed the islanders' fear and distrust for an incident at Niutau, when the ship captain half dragged a young local woman down to the saloon to observe the female visitor. Fanny believed the woman feared that he intended to kidnap her for enslavement, and she broke away and flung herself at Fanny. "I could feel her heart beating against my breast and she was trembling from head to foot," Fanny wrote. When Fanny tried to soothe her, the woman smiled. "Plainer than words her smile said: 'You are a woman, too; I can trust you; you will protect me, will you not?'" Jolly notes that it was imperial arrogance for Fanny to fancy that she could read the thoughts of a woman from a different culture. Yet Fanny strongly believed that women could bond together across cultures to overcome male control.

Among the handful of Victorian female travelers who wrote about the Pacific, Fanny's casual mixing with island women and curiosity about their lives was unusual. She borrowed local women's clothing, a familiarity frowned upon by whites, and lined her fingers with gold rings "that I might take them from my own hand to offer as presents." More than once, local women "took possession" of her: whisking her off for a viewing at one of their homes, where she was admired, petted, poked, and gawked at. On one occasion, before a crowd of men and children, the women tried to take off her dress, which made her cry, and then settled for peeking at her knees and sniffing her arms. "Their taste differed from mine, for, while I was thinking what a cold, ugly colour a white arm looked beside their warm, brown ones, they were crying out in admiration," she observed. One local woman wanted Fanny to stay on the island with her. "I really think she had some hope that she might keep me as a sort of pet monkey."

Fanny's praise for the skin color of Pacific Island women has been viewed as an example of white Western travelers' exotic gaze. But it was more complicated coming from a woman whom the blueblood American historian Henry Adams would soon describe as a "half-breed Mexican" and "Apache squaw" when he met her in Samoa. Fanny never rested easily in her "whiteness," from the time fair-skinned children taunted her for her olive coloring. No one in polite society ever openly speculated that Louis's wife was of mixed race, but they certainly implied it.

In the Pacific, Fanny wrote a story called "The Half-White," about a part-Hawaiian young woman named Lulani who was largely raised by a white priest since her mother was sent to the Molokai leper colony when the girl was a child. The lead story in the March 1891 issue of *Scribner's Magazine*, it was a searing condemnation of the Christian mission in the Pacific. The priest claims Lulani has leprosy, purportedly to protect her against sexual exploitation, but in reality so that he can control her physically and sexually. In the tale's melodramatic climax, he confesses that it is his body, not hers, that is riddled with leprosy. Much like Teresa Valdevia, the fictional woman in the Stevensons' book *The Dynamiter*, Lulani escapes a disease that eats away at a predatory white man—as if her mixed racial heritage blessed her with a special resilience or life force.

LOUIS NEVER CEASED to be mystified and intrigued by his unpredictable and free-spirited wife. In the Pacific, as elsewhere, Fanny's brave and sometimes reckless insistence on going her own way shaped his travel writing, opening them up to experiences they would not otherwise have had. In Tahiti, Louis spit blood and fell into a feverish stupor in Papeete, and Fanny determined to get him across the island to a healthier climate in Tautira. With the help of Lloyd and Valentine, she transported her husband sixteen miles in a horse-drawn wagon through dense forests and across numerous streams, sustaining him with small doses of "coca." Their arrival attracted the attention of the subchief Ori-a-Ori and his wife, Princess Moë, who sheltered the Stevensons when they had no way to repay them. The princess helped nurse Louis back to health and the couples cemented their friendship in bonding ceremonies. When Louis was well enough to leave, Ori asked Fanny to prepare the farewell feast of roast pigs and pudding.

Even Fanny's rebellious ventures into trouble provided lively material for Louis's writing. When their travel party landed on the Gilbert atoll Butaritari, it was in the midst of an island-wide, nine-day bender after the king had temporarily lifted the tapu, or taboo, on foreigners selling alcohol to the islanders. Some of the people were hungover and ornery, and violence erupted. Fanny ignored her husband's instructions to stay safe on their premises and headed off to collect shells instead. As she wandered, a haggard-looking couple started to walk next to her, then argued about her, and finally seized her by the arms and pushed her down a crooked path into a heavy woodland of coconut trees. Fanny was starting to feel alarmed when the woman drew a clay pipe out of an enormous hole in her ear, lit it and puffed on it, and then shoved it into Fanny's mouth. After Fanny nervously took a few puffs, the couple resumed pushing her through the palm grove and eventually all the way back to her lodging.

The incident was the beginning of a warm friendship between Fanny and Louis and the couple, Nei Takauti and Nan Tok. As the islanders later recounted, they had been concerned when they saw Fanny wandering through the woods alone and decided to escort her back to safety. Nei Takauti had given Fanny the pipe to calm "a supposed fiery gleam in my eyes that disconcerted them," Fanny humorously recalled. Louis's account of the marriage between the aging woman and her much younger husband became a colorful passage in his South Seas letters. Nei Takauti was a high chief, a small but imperious woman with an eye of "sombre fire," while her high-spirited husband "changed to view like a kaleidoscope." Whenever Fanny gave Nei Takauti a string of beads or a pretty ribbon as a gift, it appeared on Nan Tok the next day. "It was plain he was a clothes-horse," Louis wrote, "that he wore livery; that, in a word, he was his wife's wife." The couple's relationship turned other conventional Western marital roles on their head. Nan Tok was a tender nurturer while his wife appeared to practice tough love. When Nei Takauti was ill, her husband was solicitous; when he had a toothache, she jeered at him. When he dared to snicker about her to his buddies within her earshot, she lobbed a coconut at his head.

The couples became close during the Stevensons' stay on Butaritari. A photo of them relaxing together on a sunny hillside shows an easy familiarity that is more reminiscent of the 1960s than the 1880s. The women are holding hands, sitting on the ground in flowing dresses and chunky beaded necklaces, flanked by their barefoot husbands. Louis, in a loose shirt and pants, lies next to Nei Takauti while Nan Tok, who is shirtless, lounges beside Fanny. Louis and Fanny have garlands of blossoms in their hair, and Fanny holds a cigarette in one hand like a joint. Except for the banana trees and vines in the background, they could easily be "flower children" on a sunny day in a meadow in Golden Gate Park.

BY THE TIME the Stevensons' travels came to an end, Louis had determined that he would not simply compile the South Seas letters he was writing for syndication into a travel book. Instead, he saw them as material for a magnum opus—a sixty-chapter, authoritative political, cultural, historical, and anthropological study, along with personal impressions of the Pacific region, or "*the* big book on the South Seas," as he described it to French writer Marcel Schwob. What he might have lacked in expertise for the complex enterprise, he made up for in ambition: The theme would be the "extinction" of Pacific Islanders by Western civilization. He felt that it was a less commercial project than his previous travel books but also a more important one.

Fanny was against the book, but not simply because she had her eye on the bottom line. She had supported her husband's experimental work in the past. But in this case, she felt that Louis would be wasting both his best talents and incredibly enchanting material. She complained to Colvin:

> *He has taken into his Scotch Stevenson head, that a stern duty lies before him, and that his book must be a sort of scientific and historical impersonal thing, comparing the different languages (of which he knows nothing, really) and the different peoples, the object being to settle the question as to whether they be of common Malay origin or not.*

Fanny even claimed that she could write a better book and kept copious notes on their adventures for him to use if he ever came to his senses. In her eyes, the world was not waiting for an authoritative reference book from Robert Louis Stevenson; it was waiting for another work of art. "What a thing it is to have a 'man of genius' to deal with," she griped to Colvin. "It is like managing an overbred horse."

The South Seas letters were a kind of testing ground for the public appetite, and their reception was not encouraging. S. S. McClure had brokered a deal with the *New York Sun* for the American rights for fifty letters at $200 each, but when the *Sun* received the first fifteen letters in late 1890, it reneged on the deal, ostensibly because they were not in the form of letters. Other newspapers followed suit. In the end, McClure had to syndicate them in Britain, the United States, and Australia at a much lower rate, earning Louis about a third of what he had expected. Like Fanny, McClure felt that editors and readers had expected something different from the author of *An Inland Voyage* and *Travels with a Donkey in the Cévennes*. "Contrary to our expectation, it was the moralist and not the romancer which his observations in the South Seas awoke in him, and the public found the moralist less interesting than the romancer," he later wrote.

McClure was perhaps not the best judge of the new critical direction the author was attempting to take, but even Louis's stalwart defender Henry James was perplexed. He found the letters dry and wrote to Louis that he missed "the *visible* in them—I mean as regards people, things, objects, faces, bodies, costumes, features, gestures, manners, the introductory, the *personal* painter-touch."

Louis promised the "painter-touch" would be incorporated into his epic book, and he worked on it for two years before abandoning it in 1891, grumbling as he did that he preferred Fanny's "peace of mind" to his own ideas. Clearly, he was wearied by the sustained campaign she and Colvin waged against it, but he also seemed to have some of his own doubts about the unwieldy tome by then.

It is difficult to imagine that Louis would have finished the projected massive book when he often struggled to sustain his interest long enough to see even his much less formidable projects through to the end. Jolly notes that he never found the right form for the disparate material, and he complained several times that he was uninspired. It may have been easier to blame Fanny for his decision to quit than to admit that his ambitious multidimensional approach did not come together as he had imagined it would.

When Charles Scribner's Sons posthumously published *In the South Seas*, a compilation of the letters (though not as Louis envisioned them in the book), it met with mixed reviews. Despite Fanny's claim that Louis's theories on civilization and depopulation would be of little interest, the *New York Times* praised the book and commended Louis for the sympathetic and rational view that "enabled him to distinguish among 'the barbarians' so often lumped under that vague title." American readers were more taken by the book than those in Britain, but overall its reception was lackluster.

Eighteen years later, Scribner's published *The Cruise of the "Janet Nichol" Among the South Sea Islands*, which Fanny prepared for publication just before her death. "However dull it may seem to others," she wrote humbly in the preface, "it can boast of at least one reader, for I have gone over this record of perhaps the happiest period of my life with thrilling interest."

The book attracted little public attention. Stevenson scholars have regarded it primarily as a supplement to Louis's writing, but more recently it has received recognition as an engaging nineteenth-century travel memoir by an intrepid woman. To Heather Waldroup, an expert on the intersection of Western and Oceanic cultures, Fanny's presentation of the complexities of imperialism is unusual for Victorian travel literature. "[Fanny] certainly takes pleasure in describing, in the telling of a story," Waldroup writes, "yet her writings suggest both enchantment with island life and an understanding of the sometimes harsh realities of that life."

Fanny notes in the book that she included some material that her husband had entered into her diary. At some points, she expressly cites Louis when she quotes longer passages from him. But Audrey Murfin, who has studied the couple's Pacific diaries, has pointed out that Fanny did not credit Louis for other lines that she copied "word for word" from his unpublished notes. The uncredited material Murfin discusses appears to constitute a couple of pages out of nearly two hundred, and the book's most memorable entries are Fanny's. Still, her failure to completely acknowledge her husband's contributions may be seen to echo her role in publishing the short story "The Nixie."

The nature of Fanny and Louis's creative partnership was always somewhat murky, however—perhaps more so in the Pacific, where, Murfin notes, his writing was very much a "family venture." Fanny, Louis, and Lloyd read one another's diaries, and the couple composed some recollections together. Louis sometimes incorporated Fanny's perspective and sharp observations into his own accounts of people, places, and ceremonies. And he used some of her colorful *Janet Nicoll* sketches of the island people and travelers they met to create his fictional characters.

IN SEPTEMBER 1890, the Stevensons headed for the island of Upolu, their new home. They had picked Samoa because it was an independent nation but was relatively near New South Wales, so it also boasted relatively fast mail service—one month to London and three weeks to New York.

As Fanny prepared to go, she must have wondered if this might finally be the reward for a journey that had taken them from Silverado to Switzerland to Saranac Lake, and now Samoa, in search of better health for Louis. It was a last chance in a ten-year marriage that had been built on chances, beginning when Fanny left her first husband for a man who might not live ten weeks. Creating a life in the South Seas would be the biggest challenge yet. But already, to her, Samoa felt like home. "Breaths of the land breeze began to come out to us, intoxicating with the odours of the earth, of growing trees, sweet flowers and fruits," she wrote in her diary as the *Janet Nicoll* approached Upolu, "and dominating all, the clean wholesome smell of breadfruit baking in hot stones."

SIXTEEN

A massive volcano rose from the Pacific to create the island of Upolu. It settled into mountains that rippled across the island like soft folds in a blanket. Its lava rivers cooled into coastal cliffs. On the flatter land, Indigenous people constructed fales—round, open-air huts with egg-shaped roofs of woven coconut leaves and reeds. They clustered together in aigas, extended family groups under the care and leadership of a matai, who was often a native chief. On these communal sites, they welcomed babies into the world and buried their dead.

According to one of their legends, Mt. Vaea, on the north-central coast, formed not from a volcanic eruption but when a warrior married a Fijian princess who took their baby back home to show her family. The warrior watched for his wife's return for so long, he turned into stone that became the mountain. When the princess returned and saw him, her tears formed the waterfalls and streams that spilled down its sides.

Thick forests covered the slopes of Mt. Vaea. Pacific tree boas heaved up the twisted trunks of the trees and "flying foxes"—large bats with fox-like heads—clambered through the upper branches foraging for fruit and nectar. Blue-eyed mao honeyeaters nested there too, laying their speckled eggs in sticky nests. The air was filled with the sounds of giant flapping wings, screeching and caterwauling, and shrill cries like cats mewing to be fed.

This is where the Stevensons chose to build their home. Fanny transformed a mountainside tangled with trees and creepers into a lofty family aerie and lush garden high above the sweltering, muggy town of Apia, a settlement of traders' dens, stores, bars, and churches huddled at the foot of a pier. The name of the Stevensons' new home, "Vailima," translated to "water in the hand." Though most of their three-hundred-acre property would remain bush, the cool breezes, streams, and bathing pool made Vailima an attractive site for building a new life.

At the age of fifty, Fanny was no longer the energetic young mother who had gamely wrestled with the hardships of life in a silver mining camp. But she still relished a challenge. Building their wooden home on a remote mountainside would demand even more of her. Supplies had to be brought up by pack saddle three miles from Apia and there was no connecting road. The property had no electricity or running water. Fanny sold Skerryvore, her gift from Thomas Stevenson, to finance the construction of the house (which Louis said he would bequeath to her in his will), but their living quarters were just the beginning of the couple's grand ambitions. They planned to start a small farm of livestock, fruit, and vegetables, which would quickly expand to a cacao or coffee plantation to support them.

The American historian Henry Adams and the painter John La Farge visited them early on, when Fanny and Louis were clearing brush and sometimes scrounging for food, and they were stunned by the couple's dirty, primitive living conditions. Adams could see that their travels had left Fanny almost paralyzed with rheumatism, while her husband gloated over their discomforts. Despite his grimy first impressions, Adams found the couple charming and friendly. He wrote to a friend that Fanny was "more human" than her husband, whom he memorably described as "an insane stork." Adams noted that Louis greeted their guests wearing trousers; filthy, mismatched, heelless socks; and a flannel shirt with the sleeves rolled up above his shoulders, "displaying a pair of the thinnest white arms I ever beheld, which he brandished in the air habitually as though he wanted to throw them away."

The Stevensons' architect drew up a plan for a house with a hefty price tag of $20,000, which they streamlined into a two-bedroom home for about

$7,500. Yet almost as soon as it was completed in 1891, their quarters seemed cramped. Belle, Joe, and Austin were joining them—at Louis's request, according to Belle, because he told her he wanted his family with him in Samoa, though he also must have reasoned that putting Joe to work at Vailima would be less costly than supporting him and Belle in Sydney. And Lloyd gave up his professed dream of enrolling at Cambridge or Oxford to stay and help the family, but no doubt the laid-back island lifestyle was more to the twenty-three-year-old's taste than rigorous collegiate study.

Margaret Stevenson also arrived with a lady's maid and carts of belongings from Heriot Row. She was initially thrilled with her room (which Fanny had taken great pains to prepare) but decided she needed a sitting room as well and pushed hard for an extension to the house, which she helped finance. As construction on a new wing went ahead, Louis complained constantly of the skyrocketing costs, yet even he had insisted that the house include some extravagant features—a fireplace, which was virtually unheard of in Samoa, and a great hall for entertaining. Imported California redwood, bricks, sand, and cement were hauled up the mountain on a track, as were the twelve carts of Margaret's possessions. Eleven native men carried up a piano hung from poles.

While the building progressed, Fanny hurled herself into projects to develop the grounds that were breathtaking. From a modest early planting of melons, lima beans, and tomatoes, she experimented with all kinds of seeds, establishing a garden that soon provided Vailima's fruits and vegetables. She took farming seriously, consulting with experts from Kew Gardens and keeping detailed records of her efforts. She burned the soil that imported plants were packed in to avoid introducing new diseases to the island. Out of her efforts grew modern Samoa's premier botanical gardens.

Among Fanny's engineering projects (including supervising the building of a bridge), she designed an irrigation system from a mountain spring to ensure that Vailima had water during the dry season. As with planting, she did some of the hands-on work of building the reservoir—her grandson, Austin, recalled her asking him to rub her fingers to unlock them when they were stiff from cementing the retaining wall.

In their early days on the island, Fanny and Louis sometimes dined on bread and onions or a single avocado. By summer 1893, the farm had hens, cocks, pigs, sows, a boar, and a cow. Louis boasted to Colvin, "We have salad, beans, cabbages, tomatoes, asparagus, kohl-rabi, oranges, limes, barbadines, pineapples, cape gooseberries—galore; pints of milk and cream, fresh meat five days a week." The Stevensons were also among the planters who pioneered the cultivation of cacao, used in chocolate and cocoa butter, as a cash crop on the island. Fanny served warm cups of cocoa to the workers each morning to inspire them. In May 1892 Margaret marveled in a letter to her sister Jane that her daughter-in-law had supervised the planting of nearly eight thousand cacao trees.

FANNY ACCOMPLISHED ALL of this in the face of enormous difficulties. She had to fight off the wrath of Colvin and others who blamed her for the couple's decision to settle in the Pacific, despite Louis's own insistence that he needed to be there for his health. There were early mistakes—wildlife ate the hens, the pigs escaped over a fence, and a carpenter's horse trampled on a nest of eggs, making an "omelette of our hopes," Louis quipped to Colvin. The Samoan workers the Stevensons hired were conscientious but not particularly interested in farming or the regimented Western work schedule, and Fanny, who had no facility for new languages, had trouble communicating precise instructions to them.

The traditional belief in "aitus," spirits who could inhabit people and terrorize or even kill them, was a particular cultural challenge. Some of the staff refused to work in areas of Vailima that were haunted by aitus, especially a banana patch that was said to be infested with them. Ironically, the rise of German-owned plantations on the island had breathed new life into this ancient belief. The fields were primarily worked by people who were "recruited" with deception—or often kidnapped—from Melanesian islands. Those laborers who fled beatings and starvation were shunned even by native Samoans (often under the influence of missionary racial attitudes) for their darker skin. To survive, they lived and foraged in the jungle and stole food in the village.

The "black boys" almost seemed to take on the mythical status of aitus; like the evil spirits, they haunted the bush and were rumored to kill and eat their victims. Even Western settlers were infected with the idea of aitus. Belle and Lloyd would not go near the banana patch, Louis reported "bright eyes" watching him in the woods, and Fanny heard strange sounds coming from under the garden. In the light of day, the couple suspected there were runaways living in caves on their land, but in the pitch-dark woods at night—where decaying trees cast an eeric phosphorescent glow "like a grating over a pale hell"—their minds could play tricks on them.

In addition to her house and plantation work, Fanny had the responsibility of providing medical and psychological care in Vailima's relatively isolated location. She created a dedicated "medicine room" stocked with medications, natural therapies, and copies of *The Lancet* for reference. She and Belle nursed more than twenty Samoans there during a flu epidemic that swept the island. Fanny's medical prowess earned her a reputation for possessing slightly mystical powers, which she exploited to deal with less conventional ailments as well.

When the servant Lafaele had a sore toe, a native doctor told him that an aitu had entered his foot and was traveling up his leg in order to take possession of his body. Fanny rubbed the possessed toe with ointment while reminding Lafaele that "no Samoan devil can do harm to a man that belongs to me." That was probably true, the native doctor retorted, but he estimated that the aitu had entered the servant's toe before he had ever met Fanny. Her deeply loyal servant assured her that he trusted her to protect him, but she noted that afterward Lafaele sang very loudly when he was alone.

Louis necessarily spent most of his time writing, but he was very involved in planning the estate and he helped out on the grounds. Clearing the brush even became one of his fleeting manias—more gratifying than writing books, he insisted. "The life of the plants comes through my fingertips, their struggles go to my heart like supplications," he wrote in one letter.

"*Nothing* is so interesting as weeding," he gushed in another. While Louis dabbled in garden work, however, it was Fanny who shouldered the burden of the supervising, clearing, and planting. The family worried that she was working too hard, yet she probably felt pressured to move quickly. The couple planned for the plantation to support them within five or six years. Once the cacao trees were in the ground, it would be another five years before they produced pods and generated the profit that would allow Louis to ease up on his work schedule.

So when Louis took a potshot at Fanny for the exhausting work that she felt she was doing to benefit the family, she was deeply hurt. "Louis says that I have the soul of a peasant . . . ," she wrote in her diary in October 1890. "Had I the soul of an artist, the stupidity of possessions would have no power over me." (This and other passages on his comment were marked out of her diary by an unknown hand but recovered by Charles Neider for *Our Samoan Adventure*, his 1955 compilation of the couple's writing.) Fanny went on to justify (to herself) her passion for nature and belief that working the earth with her own hands *was* an act of creativity. "When I plant a seed or a root, I plant a bit of my heart with it . . . ," she wrote. "My heart melts over a bed of young peas, and a blossom on my rose tree is like a poem written by my son."

Louis's cutting remark did not merit mention in any of his letters, but it stayed fresh in Fanny's mind. "My vanity, like a newly felled tree, lies prone and bleeding," she recorded two weeks later. Apparently Louis had intended his remark as a commentary not just on Fanny's agrarian interests but on her opposition to his planned anthrohistorical tome *In the South Seas*. In January she elaborated to Colvin:

> *I plunged into the work of the plantation with so much interest that [Louis] says I have the true peasant nature, and lack the artistic temperament, therefore my advice on artistic matters, such as a book on the South Seas, must be received with extreme caution. He says I do not take the broad view of an artist, but hold the cheap opinion of the general public that a book must be interesting.*

Louis and Fanny had disagreed about his work before, but this cut deeper into her soul because he was attacking her intellect, and he must have known it would leave a scar.

One day at about this time, Fanny took a colorful inventory of her bedroom for her diary. Horse bridles and ropes hung among her dresses. Pincers and chisels lay beside her comb and toothbrush on the wood trunk that served as her dressing table. There were a pistol and cartridges, cameras and hats, strings of teeth ("fish, human and beast"). "My little cot bed seems to have got into its place by mistake," she sighed. Today the image seems emblematic of the yearning ambitions, and often conflicting responsibilities, that this vibrant Victorian woman crowded into her life. But in her day, as she noted, it would not be considered the room of a lady. And except for an easel that was shoved into one corner, it was hardly the room of an artist.

THE STEVENSONS WERE able to achieve their grand ambitions for Vailima only through the labor of many servants and other workers. Literary scholar Carla Manfredi has pointed out that as an employer, Louis exhibited an "idealistic flexibility" that somewhat contradicted his public stands. Initially at least, he relied on Harry Jay Moors, a successful American trader and planter, to hire dozens of men—some indentured workers—to clear the land and build their house. Moors had been a "recruiter" in the labor trade and a onetime manager on a German plantation, where he was known as a "driving and callous overseer" who made considerable use of corporal punishment. When a female field worker fled with her son, who subsequently died in the bush, Moors flogged her savagely in public after having her brought back lashed to a pole like a hunted animal.

Louis knew some, if not the full extent, of the wily American's misdeeds, yet he became friends with Moors, borrowed money from him, and consulted with him on his writing. Moors was a wonderful talker, and Louis spent evenings at his home discussing British and American literature over a bottle of whiskey. Louis admitted that Moors was not of the best character, but he rationalized that bad character and deceit were so endemic in whites living in the Pacific that "any exclusiveness becomes impossible; they are all in the same boat."

Though Louis and Fanny repeatedly rejected the characterization, they imposed some aspects of the colonialist mentality on the island people who worked for them. Louis grafted the Scottish clan system on his domain, likening it to traditional Samoan aigas. Louis was the undisputed head—or "chief and father," as he described himself—of the Vailima clan. He Anglicized the customary Samoan wraparound skirt, the lavalava, by having some made from Royal Stewart tartan cloth, like kilts, to be worn by his male servants on special occasions. In an interview with a New Zealand journalist, the "chief and father" boasted that he paid the lowest wages and got the best service from Samoans because he treated his employees fairly. In fact, he and Fanny liked to say their servants were "family," a paternalistic sentiment that some of the staff may not have shared. There is little doubt that working in the Stevenson household was an emblem of prestige, and that Fanny and Louis were benevolent employers and relatively enlightened Westerners, but they were still part of the colonial system of exploitation in the Pacific.

Victorian male travelers and settlers greeted the Pacific Islands as a phantasmagoria of eroticism—a place where everything, including the women, was ripe for the picking. While the Stevensons lived in Samoa, the artist Paul Gauguin was in Tahiti fathering children with young girls and producing paintings that promoted the islands as a sexual paradise for Western men. Louis admitted to being distracted at work sometimes by the sensual beauty of the half-naked Samoan women on his staff as they went about their chores. To Colvin, he described the servant Java stooping to pump the bellows at his hearth fire: "The inside of Java's knees, when she kilts her *lava-lava* high, is a thing I never saw equaled in a statue." He had a particular attraction to Lafaele's beautiful and rather young wife, Faauma, whose arms and "little hips" were "masterpieces." He later described her washing the windows in his study "in a black *lava-lava* . . . with a red handkerchief hanging from round her neck between her breasts; not another stitch." (Colvin prudishly deleted both passages from Louis's letters for publication after his death.)

Louis admitted to Colvin that he was sometimes glad to be too "elderly and sick and overworked" to feel temptation. Yet unlike many Western men, he was also too morally principled to sexually exploit island women and girls or be unfaithful to his wife. And he was still attracted to Fanny, whose "touch" alone made the difficulties, defeats, and victories of life worthwhile, he wrote in his poem "Dark Women." In the verse, a protest against the tyranny of the Victorian ideal of light-skinned, blond female beauty, he singled her out:

> Dark as a wayside gypsy,
>   Lithe as a hedgerow hare,
> She moves, a glowing shadow,
>   Through the sunshine of the fair.
> Golden hue and orange,
>   Bosom and hand and head,
> She blooms, a tiger lily,
>   In the snowdrift of the bed.

THE STEVENSONS' PEACOCK-BLUE house, wrapped with wide verandas and topped with a red iron roof, became legendary. There were tennis courts (though Louis's play there was curtailed by a hemorrhage) and a broad lawn in front of the house for croquet and cricket. Fanny hung Samoan tapa cloth on the walls and Indian gauze lined with soft orange silk on the windows, and spread plush Samoan mats and rugs on the floors. It was "beautiful beyond dreams," Louis wrote to Gosse, and he insisted on having the windows blazing with candles and lamps when he rode up on his horse from Apia at night.

When he was not swelling with pride for Vailima, Louis was anxiously churning out stories to support it. He began work at five or six in the morning and broke at eleven to give Austin a history lesson before lunch. In the early afternoon, the family played musical instruments and helped themselves to the mildly hallucinogenic drink kava that was set out like punch in a large, traditional legged wooden bowl. (Made from a pepper plant root that has been pounded or chewed, kava was a symbol of hospitality and an integral part of Samoan social and religious rituals.) Then Louis worked for a couple more hours before taking a dip in a bathing pool under a waterfall. Sometimes he dined with friends like Moors or hung out at beachcomber bars and danced with "islandresses." According to Belle, when business or socializing took him to Apia in the afternoon, he was likely to return for dinner with a native chief or a naval officer, or to invite an entire ship crew for lunch the next day.

Vailima became one of the liveliest social centers on Upolu. The Stevensons hosted native feasts, dinner parties, picnics, afternoon teas, and balls that stretched well into the night. Any holiday was an excuse for celebration—including the birthdays of George Washington and Queen Victoria, as well as Bastille Day. The couple delighted in entertaining traders, Samoan chiefs, colonial officials, British ship officers, and missionaries. "Everybody felt thoroughly at home at Vailima," Moors recalled.

Celebrations in the sixty-foot-long redwood great hall were grand affairs, with Margaret's heirloom silver and crystal glassware glittering under lamps and colored paper lanterns (sixty-five at one event alone). One feast included sixteen pigs roasted underground, four hundred pounds each of salt beef and pork, two hundred heads of taro, and eight hundred pineapples from their patch, as well as bananas, oranges, sugarcane, and ship biscuits. After dinner, guests commonly retired to the veranda and sipped coffee with sugar soaked in burnt brandy.

⁕

"A WRITER WHO amounts to anything is constantly dying and being reborn," Louis once told his stepson. As a writer, Robert Louis Stevenson died and was reborn several times during his stay in the Pacific. Feeling less boxed in by the narrow expectations of his literary guardians back in Britain, he wrote fiction, journalism, history, and mythological stories, which ranged from the light and fanciful to the grimly realistic.

Among the small gems is "The Enchantress," a feminist tale that was not published until 1989, when it was discovered buried among some of Louis's papers. It is the story of a young British gentleman, Edward Hatfield, who has gambled away his fortune and decides to use his charms to fleece a young heiress, Emmeline Croft. But Hatfield falls in love with his target, and when Croft proposes, he agrees to marry her under whatever terms she chooses, which she insists will benefit him. "You are the man in this story, I the woman," he notes. Croft ditches Hatfield on a street corner minutes after they are married, with a pledge of £300 a year and the explanation that she could access her inheritance only through marriage—and could gain her independence only through subsequent divorce. Victorian literature scholar Lena Wånggren notes that Louis wrote the story, which dramatizes "the lengths to which women must go to gain independence," at the height of the heated late Victorian debate about marriage inequality and women's freedom, establishing him as a New Woman writer.

In another little jewel, "The Persons of the Tale," two of Louis's fictional creations from *Treasure Island*—the upstanding Captain Smollett and the charming rogue Long John Silver—take a break between chapters to speculate on the author's intentions for them and argue over who is his favorite. In this clever bit of metafiction, Smollett points out that the author respects him, but Silver scoffs, "He does me fathoms better'n he does you—fathoms, he does. And he likes doing me. He keeps me on deck mostly all the time, crutch and all; and he leaves you measling in the hold, where nobody can't see you, nor wants to, and you may lay to that!"

The story was published posthumously in *Fables*, but two other equally inventive and humorous tales that were to be included in the collection were never quite finished. In "The Clockmaker," microbes in a glass of water engage in a philosophical debate about science, religion, and the origins of their world until a thirsty worker who comes into the room to adjust a clock grabs the glass and gulps down the water, wiping out them and their theories. In "The Scientific Ape," a community of West Indian apes being subject to extinction by a vivisecting colonizer kidnap the man's baby and contemplate whether experimenting on his child will put them on the fast track to becoming men, who are only "promoted apes," as one notes. Exclaiming, "Can apes descend to such barbarity?" their outraged chief convinces them that answering one brutal act with another is beneath them. They return the baby to the colonizer, who begins three new experiments the same day.

For the most part, Louis was intent on shedding a starker light on the dark imperial machinations in the Pacific. Like other islands he and Fanny had visited on their cruises, Samoa was in political and social turmoil. By the 1880s, a few German firms had taken over much of the land for plantations. While Samoan aigas were at war with one another, Germany attempted to seize control of the government, and Britain and the United States intervened. The Western powers played native Samoan factions against one another as they vied to protect their own financial, political, and strategic interests. Based on eyewitness testimony and documents, Louis recounted the destruction and near war brought on by their bickering, brinkmanship, and folly in a slim book, *A Footnote to History: Eight Years of Trouble in Samoa.*

Samoa's wealth was fought over "like a bone between two dogs, each growling, each clutching his own end," Louis wrote. The showdown between the powers escalated in March 1889, when all three crowded their warships into Apia harbor in a show of might just as a hurricane was about to strike. In intense and harrowing detail, Louis re-created the near biblical disaster, which left the land untouched but blew six ships to pieces and killed many men. He also recounted the Samoans' effort to rescue the foreign sailors, despite the suspicions of some they sought to help.

When Louis and Fanny sailed into Apia eighteen months after the hurricane, the ruins of the vessels were still rotting in the bay, like harbingers of the decaying situation on land. By then the three powers had signed a treaty in Berlin agreeing to a tripartite government. They installed a puppet Samoan king, Malietoa Laupepa, but that did little to assuage Samoan resistance and unrest in places like Apia, where, Louis wrote, "the handful of whites have everything; the natives walk in a foreign town." Even before they arrived (or met him), Fanny and Louis pledged allegiance to Laupepa's rival, Mata'afa Iosefo, whom many Samoans believed was a stronger leader because his army had defeated German forces in battle. Louis thought Samoa should temporarily become a British colony while the two chiefs were reconciled, and eventually they should govern jointly, in keeping with Samoa's traditional decentralized leadership.

In *A Footnote to History* and several letters to *The Times*, Louis called on his legal training to attack the deeply flawed Berlin treaty, which ignored the needs and rights of Samoans, and the incompetence of the European officials who were charged with administering it. Fanny encouraged Louis to write the book, though they both knew it was unlikely to be as lucrative as the history of Scotland for boys that he set aside in order to do it. Louis even insisted that he would finance its printing himself if the book was turned down by publishers, but it was not. In August 1892, Charles Scribner's Sons and Cassell and Company simultaneously published *A Footnote to History: Eight Years of Trouble in Samoa* in the United States and Britain.

"It is impossible to live here and not feel very sorely the consequences of the horrid white mismanagement," Louis wrote in one of his few letters to his cousin Bob Stevenson from Samoa. "I tried standing by and looking on, and it became too much for me." Not surprisingly, the author's intrusion into politics raised the ire of local treaty officials, as well as the three powers' consuls and some in the missionary society whom he had also criticized. Louis was threatened with a libel suit and rumors about his possible deportation circulated, which both concerned and pleased him.

In Britain, the book did raise some concern about the country's international conduct among the statesmen Louis had hoped to reach. And several reviewers praised it, including a critic for the *Daily Chronicle*, who overheatedly gushed, "When his novels are forgotten, his pamphlet on Samoa will be remembered." But most critics found the plight of brown islanders in a far-off corner of the world of only vague interest.

Astonishingly, *The Times* published Louis's angry letters about Samoa even as it questioned their veracity, prefacing one with the disclaimer that the "very fury" of his views might have "warped his judgment." It seems that Louis's imagination in fiction was a liability when he wrote about factual issues. Stevenson expert Roslyn Jolly has pointed out that after British and German government reports vindicated Louis's accounts, *The Times* sheepishly apologized in an editorial, attributing its own skepticism to "the extraordinary condition of affairs described by Mr. Stevenson, and to his acknowledged power of telling a story."

Others simply felt that Louis was wasting his talents by getting involved in parochial politics. "I see that romantic surroundings are the worst surroundings possible for a romantic writer," Oscar Wilde later sniped. "In Gower Street Stevenson could have written a new *Trois Mousquetaires*. In Samoa he wrote letters to *The Times* about Germans." In Louis's personal letters, he also dwelt at length on the Samoan situation and the lives and concerns of people on his staff, to the fatigue of friends like Henry James. Had he so gone native that he had lost all interest in "the main currents of human affairs," Colvin demanded in exasperation:

> For three letters or more you have not uttered a single word about anything but your beloved blacks—or chocolates—confound them . . . so much less interesting than any dog, cat, mouse, house or jenny-wren of our known and hereditary associations, loves and latitudes. . . . Please let us have a letter or two with something besides native politics, prisons, kava *feasts*, and such things as our Cockney stomachs can ill assimilate.

Louis replied to his friend's racist outburst with restrained anger:

> Please remember that my life passes among my "blacks or chocolates." . . . You must try to exercise a trifle of imagination, and

*put yourself, perhaps with an effort, into some sort of sympathy
with these people, or how am I to write to you?*

Colvin later apologized to Louis for being a "beast," but his sentiments
were not unusual. "Our friends at home take such bitter exception to our
'blacks' or 'darkies' as they call them, that I fear to say a word about our life
here, which is so entirely mixed up with the native element that I cannot
disentangle it," Fanny wrote to Edmund Gosse. "We foreigners here do not
use the words 'black,' 'darkie,' or 'n——' when speaking of the Samoans,
who are really very little darker than I am."

Among Louis's colleagues, some of his most recent work also revived old
fears about his talent diminishing in direct proportion to his distance from
London. A poetry collection, *Ballads*, was panned on its release in 1890. A
second Stevenson-Osbourne collaboration, *The Wrecker*, received mixed reviews when it was published in 1892. Louis had conceptualized the novel as
a way to finance one of his brief obsessions, to purchase a schooner and become a part-time trader, before he decided that the profession was morally
dubious at best. The novel centers on the global zigzagging and misadven-
tures of a fortune hunter and a Michigan art student who sink their money
into a shipwrecked schooner they believe is packed with opium that will
make them wealthy. Louis was shocked when the book sold poorly, especially in the United States. Charles Scribner and Edward Burlingame
thought the collaboration with Lloyd was hurting sales and that Louis was
beginning to glut the market with inferior work.

Ironically, while Louis's sales were sagging, his celebrity was skyrocketing because of his exile. The public was fascinated that the author of a classic high seas adventure tale was now living among "savages" on a tropical
island. A cartoon in a British periodical depicted him as a kind of bohemian
South Seas monarch in his velvet jacket, cigarette in hand, casually rising
above a crowd of smiling, dancing natives draped in robes rather than Samoan lavalavas.

"Since Byron was in Greece, nothing has appealed to the ordinary literary
man as so picturesque as that you should be in the South Seas," Gosse had

beamed to Louis when he was cruising the Pacific. Prominent authors such as John Galsworthy, Arthur Conan Doyle, and J. M. Barrie became correspondents. (Conan Doyle thanked Louis "for all the pleasure you have given me during my lifetime—more than any other living man" and hoped that Louis would remember him for his historical adventure *The White Company* rather than his phenomenally successful Sherlock Holmes series.) Still, the literary men in London shook their heads over his work. "The fact seems to be that it is very nice to *live* in Samoa, but not healthy to *write* there," Gosse sniffed to a friend. "Within a three-mile radius of Charing Cross is the literary atmosphere, I suspect."

LOUIS'S TALENT HAD HARDLY diminished; once again, his colleagues did not appreciate that his interests were evolving and he was stretching beyond his literary comfort zone, as he had when he wrote *The Amateur Emigrant*. To Louis, living on a Pacific island on the front lines of the global imperial struggle offered much more compelling material for high drama than writing in bed in Bournemouth. "You don't know what news is, nor what politics, nor what the life of man, till you see it on so small a scale and with your own liberty on the board for stake," he exclaimed to James. "I would not have missed it for much. And anxious friends beg me to stay home and study human nature in Brompton drawing-rooms!" For the first time in his life, Louis was healthy enough to be an active participant in local life and politics. This inspired him to write fiction that expressed his growing anti-imperialist views.

The stark, modern opening line of *The Ebb-Tide*, cowritten with Lloyd Osbourne, emphatically dispels any notions that it is a cozy Stevenson romance: "Throughout the island world of the Pacific, scattered men of many European races and from almost every grade of society carry activity and disseminate disease." The novel notes that some of these men prosper, some marry native women who support them "in sheer idleness," and some become degenerate and destitute. *The Ebb-Tide* centers on three members of the last group.

The "troop of swine," as Louis described them to James, is made up of Davis, a disgraced alcoholic American sea captain; Huish, an immoral Cockney clerk; and Herrick, a failed Oxford graduate. When Davis is given command of the *Farallone*, a smallpox-infected schooner transporting California champagne to Sydney, the greedy, inept trio hatch a plan to hijack the ship and its brown-skinned crew to Peru, where they can pocket the profits themselves. At sea they discover they have been duped and are sitting on mostly worthless bottled water. As their provisions run short, the men stumble on an uncharted island at the fraying edge of empire, where a maverick British trader, Attwater, has created a personal kingdom that is a nightmare of the imperialist dream. Much of the novel focuses on the trio's dealings with Attwater—a refined, Cambridge-educated religious zealot and violent outlaw slaver who kills one of them.

Lloyd claimed that he began the first draft of *The Ebb-Tide* while the family was staying in Hawaii but abandoned it when Louis's praise for his writing soured after the first few chapters. In February 1893, Louis decided to finish the novel, writing the entire second half himself. He used notes from Fanny's *Janet Nicoll* diary to provide color and depict a penal colony and ghost settlement. He modeled the amiable brown-skinned sailors who manned the *Farallone* after the Pacific Island crew that Fanny had praised in her diary, shedding light on people who were more often relegated to the shadows of South Seas literature of the time.

Louis was pleased with the final result, but Colvin fretted that publishing the grim story in book form could hurt the Stevenson brand. When it was released in 1894 by William Heinemann in Britain and Stone and Kimball in the United States, a *Speaker* reviewer conveyed the favorable, if somewhat perplexed, view typical of the critics' response: "This is not the Stevenson we love, but it is something to be read and remembered, nevertheless." Most notable among those who read and remembered it was a young Polish merchant seaman and budding author. Joseph Conrad was clearly thinking of

The Ebb-Tide when, a decade later, he created the evil genius Kurtz, who rules over his own hellish colonial enterprise in *Heart of Darkness*.

The idea for what became Louis's most powerful piece of Pacific fiction shot through him "like a bullet" while he was weeding. *The Beach of Falesá* is a masterful interracial love story, a gripping adventure, and a critique of colonialism and economic exploitation. Again, Louis used anecdotes from Fanny's *Janet Nicoll* diary to develop characters and create a powerful narrative about traders who would stop at nothing, including murder, to destroy their rivals.

On the fictional island of Falesá, John Wiltshire, a newcomer who works for a copra trading company, encounters a rival trader, Case, who convinces him he must have a wife. Wiltshire is attracted to Uma, the beautiful woman Case offers him, and he agrees to marry her under the terms of an obscene marriage contract Case draws up. Not translated to the bride, it specifies that she "is illegally married to *Mr John Wiltshire* for one night, and Mr John Wiltshire is at liberty to send her to hell next morning." Wiltshire feels a twinge of shame that Uma believes the contract will legally bind them in marriage. "That was a nice paper to put in a girl's hand and see her hide away like gold," he reflects. "A man might easily feel cheap for less."

Louis entwines Uma's sexual exploitation with the commercial exploitation widespread in the South Seas. Like Louis's friend Moors, his fictional character Wiltshire is the ambiguous kind of man he heard about and encountered throughout the Pacific. Despite Wiltshire's momentary discomfort with the marriage contract, he represents Western insouciance, entitlement, and profiteering. Outraged when the islanders shun his store, Wiltshire tells Case to inform the local chiefs, "I'm a white man, and a British Subject, and no end of a big chief at home; and I've come here to do them good and bring them civilization. . . . And tell them plain, that I demand the reason of this treatment as a White Man and a British subject." He adds that the only real laws on island nations are "what you've got to knock into their heads."

Louis's novella is not entirely free of exotic literature tropes, but he broke through some stereotypes in his depiction of Wiltshire's native wife. Uma is not a clichéd innocent victim but a dignified, smart, and assertive woman whom the trader grows to respect and love. Explaining to Wiltshire that he has been shunned because of a taboo set on her, she offers to leave him. But he realizes that the taboo is just one of the maneuvers (including murder) that Case uses to drive his competitors out of business so he can monopolize the island's copra trade. With a network of shady local accomplices, including a corrupt missionary, Case also overcharges the native people and terrorizes them by using mirrors and other devices in the bush to exploit their fear of aitus. With Uma's help, Wiltshire decides to challenge his authority and expose him as a fraud. During an ensuing fight, he fatally stabs Case.

Louis might have made Wiltshire into an unequivocal hero at the end: He frees the island from the stranglehold of the malevolent Case, enlists a respectable missionary to marry Uma and him "right," and promises the cleric that he will "deal fairly with the natives" in business. Instead, Louis keeps him ambiguous to the end, his enlightenment situational. When Wiltshire's firm moves him to another station, he admits he is pleased that he can freely exploit the native islanders there. And despite his marriage to an island woman, he maintains that "kanakas" are not good enough to marry his own mixed-race daughters. Pondering the future of his girls, he reflects, "Nobody thinks less of half castes than I do; but they're mine, and about all I've got . . . and I'd like to know where I'm to find them whites?"

Editors and publishers were somewhat startled by the story, with its morally dubious hero and interracial sexual relationship that ended in a happy marriage rather than tragedy. They worried that the pidgin English, Beach-la-mar (a language developed through the contact of different cultures in the Pacific), and rough sailor jargon would offend Victorian readers' sensibilities. When it was edited for serial publication, wording was softened or deleted, rendering sentences and whole passages confusing. Some of this can be attributed to the one-month mail time that made negotiating changes cumbersome. Louis also authorized Colvin, probably the least fervent admirer of his Pacific fiction, to make some decisions on his behalf.

Other changes were made without Louis's knowledge or consent, rendering the novella the "most mutilated" of his texts, according to Stevenson scholar Barry Menikoff. The real problem, Menikoff writes, was not the story's rough language but Louis's critique of the existing order: It "took for its subjects miscegenation, colonialism, the exploitation of brown people, and, indeed, the very idea of the white man's presence in the Pacific."

Especially troublesome to editors and publishers was the wording of the marriage contract used to bait Uma into sex, which Louis duplicated from ones he had seen in the Gilbert Islands and elsewhere. Clement Shorter, editor at the *Illustrated London News*, where the story was to be serialized, preferred that Uma and Wiltshire be married properly before "that night." Louis disagreed, and without further consultation, Shorter simply dropped the marriage certificate altogether. He later admitted that the story hung on the fake contract but said he felt duty bound to omit it for a family newspaper. "No editor who knows his business would worry himself about the feelings of an author, however great, when he had such a point for decision," he audaciously concluded.

Book publishers did not labor under the same constraints as periodical editors, but even they were unnerved by the contract. A team of "bearded gentlemen" engaged by Cassell and Company to come up with a solution for the British publication proposed that the story be edited so that Uma was illegally married to Wiltshire for one week rather one night. Charles Scribner's Sons simply omitted the "one night" and softened the stipulation that Wiltshire could "send his wife to hell next morning" with the more innocuous "send her packing when he pleases." The original, unbowdlerized story did not appear in print for another ninety-one years, when Menikoff restored Louis's original wording for publication in 1984.

Against Louis's wishes, *The Beach of Falesá* was published in the 1893 book *Island Nights Entertainments* with "The Isle of Voices," a Polynesian fable, and "The Bottle Imp," a traditional German folk story that he reset in Hawaii. ("The Bottle Imp" was the first piece of fiction printed in Samoan, enhancing Louis's local reputation as the "teller of tales," or Tusitala.)

Even in its more hobbled form, critics were impressed with the novella's gritty realism. A reviewer at the British periodical *Black and White* contended that it lifted readers "clean out of the atmosphere of books and bookish things" and plunged them into "life itself." A *New York Times* critic marveled at Louis's realistic dialogue (though the credit for this might more accurately belong to Lloyd). "Where or how did he ever catch the roughness of the beach comber, words of the past and present that are the slang of Seven Dials or Five Points, such as are vollied from the mouths of the toughest of the tough?" the critic asked. In *The Nation*, English literature scholar George Lyman Kittredge pronounced it "almost as good a story as ever was written."

Louis certainly considered *The Beach of Falesá* one of the best stories *he* had ever written. In a letter to Colvin in September 1891, he called it "the first realistic South Sea Story" and contended, "You will know more about the South Seas after you have read my little tale, than if you had read a library," though he questioned whether it would find favor with "that great, hulking, bullering whale, the public."

Like other Stevenson stories, *The Beach of Falesá* had an intriguing afterlife. Years after its publication, Dylan Thomas based a screenplay on the novella, and after his death in 1953, his fellow Welshman Richard Burton bought the rights to the script and enlisted the novelist Christopher Isherwood to work on it. Burton never got the story to the screen, where he reputedly intended to play Wiltshire and cast his wife at the time, Elizabeth Taylor, as the native woman Uma.

WHILE READERS EMBRACED Louis's sojourn in Samoa as a romantic adventure, they preferred him to cast his imagination closer to home. When he rewarded them with a sequel to *Kidnapped* in 1893, they were gratified to be back on familiar ground, in the company of the plucky young Scot David Balfour and his swashbuckling sidekick, Alan Breck Stewart.

Published simultaneously as *Catriona* by Cassell and Company in Britain and as *David Balfour* by Charles Scribner's Sons in the United States, the sequel picks up the young man's odyssey where the book *Kidnapped* left off seven years earlier. The first half of the novel centers on David's attempts to find justice for James Stewart, the defendant in the Appin Murder trial of 1752. In the second half, David focuses his affections on Catriona Drummond, a high-spirited Highland lass who is alternately bemused, incensed, and swept off her feet by his youthful gallantry. Their romantic union is disrupted by many complications and misunderstandings, but they finally wed in the end.

Like David, Louis had evolved in the seven years since *Kidnapped* was published. Away from his native land, he reimagined Scotland's past through the filter of Samoa's present. *Catriona* was about clan rivalries, lost freedoms, and men in power imposing corrupt laws for personal gain— dynamics Louis witnessed in Samoa and applied to his depiction of British rule after the Battle of Culloden. As a result, the story was deeper, darker, and more overtly political than *Kidnapped*.

Yet *Catriona* also lost the propulsive, breathtaking storytelling of *Kidnapped*. The sequel is marred by long and sometimes dull expositional passages about Scottish nationalism and English cruelty. The pace is gripping only near the end, with the romantic complications between David and Catriona providing most of the drama.

The novel was a commercial success, though it never gained the popularity of *Kidnapped* because critics and readers felt that it was simply not as good a yarn. As reviewer Arthur Quiller-Couch wrote at the time, *Catriona*'s "wordy, politic intrigue" appealed less than *Kidnapped*'s "rough-and-tumble intrigue." Readers responded more to the novel's love story and were pleasantly surprised with Louis's complex portrait of a female character. As Andrew Lang noted, Louis had "drawn a good petticoat at last."

Unbeknown to Lang or any of his friends, Louis had developed the character Catriona—a woman who is excluded from the life of male adventure she longs for—when his wife appeared to be losing her mind.

SEVENTEEN

The first clue that the threads that held together Fanny's mind were unraveling might have come as early as January 1891. She had boiled a variety of ferns she'd gathered in the woods and slathered them with lime juice and butter to serve to her husband. Louis refused to eat them without assurance that none were poisonous, but Fanny defiantly ate them all just to find out. She woke in the night with stomach cramps and a "deathly" feeling.

Or perhaps the first sign that her mind was slipping was in a letter to Frances Sitwell, when she confided her alarm at finding her head "going wrong in the middle of the night." Fanny had suffered attacks of "brain fever" before, but this time Louis was in Sydney, and the beating in her head seemed as if it would never stop. Over the next months, her attacks seemed to get longer and harder to manage. Even laudanum, the powerhouse tincture of opium, sometimes failed to dull the pain. From Scotland, Louis's uncle George Balfour diagnosed a brain aneurysm and put her on the knockout drug chlorodyne—laudanum pumped up with cannabis tincture and chloroform. "The remedy is as bad as illness, too, as weakening as disease," she wrote to Sitwell.

Louis first felt something was amiss when Fanny became more argumentative and histrionic than usual. She had always bickered with Belle, but now she was squabbling incessantly with her mother-in-law—about everything from the best way to keep a horse to whether quarreling with the government officials in Samoa would lower their social status, as Margaret feared. Living roughly and communally in the bush, Fanny was irked that Margaret's servant, Mary Carter, refused any menial jobs that fell outside the duties of a proper lady's maid. And Fanny grew impatient with her mother-in-law's prim life of making social calls and awarding prizes to missionary school students for mastering skills such as ironing. Margaret, in turn, could not understand why Fanny refused to ease up on her manic plantation work, which everyone could see was making her ill and irritable. She was becoming obsessive about it—digging "like a demented beast," as Louis wrote in a poem. Fanny showed up late to meals, her frizzy hair matted, her eyes bleary, her signature blue holoku or trousers spotted with mold or mud.

Margaret eventually returned to Scotland to sell the Heriot Row house, neatly escaping her daughter-in-law's wrath. But then Fanny directed most of her venom at Louis—so much that finally he isolated himself in his own room to shut her "anxious shrillness about nothing" out of his ears. For nearly a year and a half—through various fits and diagnoses and treatments—she careened between pettiness and hysteria, grumbly kindness and belligerence, wistful hallucinations and terrifying delusions.

Fanny's symptoms reached a fever pitch when she and Louis were confronted with serious family problems. A decade earlier she had confided to Dora Williams her fear that Belle's feckless family would descend on her and Louis and never leave. At best, Belle barely pulled her weight at Vailima. Joe had gone back on his agreement to stop drinking and was likely still using opium. But then one night Louis caught him stealing from their cellar, using a duplicate key he had made. And Louis and Fanny learned that Joe secretly had a Samoan "wife" in Apia and was likely involved with their servant Faauma.

This time Joe's pleas for forgiveness fell on deaf ears. Fanny had an attack of angina, and Louis told Belle her husband had to go. Then the couple pushed Fanny's passive daughter through divorce proceedings. (In a letter to Charles Warren Stoddard, in which Belle claimed that Joe had once tried to kill her in a drug-induced mania, she admitted that she would never have filed for divorce, but it was probably for the best.) Hoping to remove Austin from his father's influence, Louis offered his debauched son-in-law funds to get to Sydney or Japan and set up a new life. But Joe stayed on the island instead, spreading slurs about his mother-in-law and her children in town. Further antagonizing Fanny, Louis's friend Moors disliked her and sided with Joe. The Michigan trader, who had a Samoan wife but was called "the greatest whoremaster on the beach," hired Joe to paint murals for his Apia "hotel," rumored to be a brothel. So Louis sent Austin to a prep school in California, to live with Fanny's sister Nellie Sanchez, whose husband, Adulfo, had died of tuberculosis. Just as Louis had footed the bill for raising Sam Osbourne's son, he now took on the responsibility of supporting his grandson.

Lloyd was also involved with an Indigenous woman, Sosifina, the daughter of an island chief. Fanny and Louis became unsettled when Sosifina appeared to be moving into their house, without clear-cut recognition of her position in Lloyd's life. They gave Lloyd an ultimatum: If he intended to marry her, he should do it, and if he did not, he would have to tell her to leave. Lloyd refused to marry or quarrel with Sosifina, and somehow the situation was resolved with the construction of a new house for the young woman in her village. The public shame that Lloyd and Joe brought on the household—and even worse, on Fanny's prominent husband—seemed to push her over the edge.

"Well, there's no disguise possible: Fanny is not well, and we are miserably anxious," Louis confessed to Colvin in April 1893, his first mention of the breakdown that had consumed him for well over a year by then. "You know about F. there's nothing you can say is *wrong*, only it ain't *right;* it ain't *she*." Louis painfully recounted "a hell of a scene which lasted all night—I will never tell anyone what about, it could not be believed, and was so unlike herself or any of us—in which Belle and I held her for about two hours; she wanted to run away."

Earlier, Louis had taken Fanny on a "month's lark" in Sydney to try to pull her out of her frenzied state. All went well at first: Fanny wrote that she had never seen Louis happier and she sat with Margaret, him, and Belle for photos, looking youthful, beautiful, and surprisingly placid in a black velvet dress. Yet after a few weeks, the shrillness crept back into her voice and she claimed to see Louis's Edinburgh buddy Charles Baxter on the street. Fairfax Ross, a Sydney doctor who examined her, was not reassuring about her physical or mental condition.

Ross also told Louis he needed to rest and relax, but Fanny's husband had no time for either. In a touching role reversal, Louis became the hands-on caregiver to his wife. Just as Fanny had spent sleepless nights watching his chest rise and fall, mopping up blood, and lifting and carrying his wrecked body, now he sat anxiously by her bed, afraid to leave her alone, refusing to give in to the unthinkable possibility that he was losing her to madness. He was alarmed by the sedatives a local doctor prescribed, which kept her nearly catatonic, but he was too afraid to stop them.

Above the bed where his wife lay in a stupor was a single footprint on the redwood ceiling of her bedroom. It was made by a worker who had stepped on the plank before it was nailed up, but the Vailima servants knew it was really the "ghostly track" of an aitu whom Fanny had scared off with her special powers. Now, it seemed, the aitu possessed Louis's wife.

Louis told Colvin he was as "tired as a man could be" and "broken on the wheel." Margaret was gone, but he did not have to weather his wife's mental breakdown alone. Fanny's children helped with her care and became a surprising source of comfort and strength to him. It was an important turning point in Louis's relationship with Belle, the first compensation for his declared wish to have family around him. "Belle has her faults and plenty of them," he wrote to Colvin, "but she has been a blessed friend to me."

Then Fanny's special powers returned—or at least the "extraordinary recuperative power" that Louis had witnessed over and over and had clung to when her doctors had given him little hope. By fall he could report that she was herself again, "only with some old illusions not yet—probably never to be—eradicated." It was as if the veil that had concealed his wife had lifted, the way the morning mists on Mt. Vaea receded to reveal the trees.

What had "possessed" Fanny—pushed her beyond the occasional "brain fever" attacks to a full-blown breakdown? Later in Hawaii, she was diagnosed with "Bright's disease," an inflammatory kidney disease now known as nephritis, which can be a complication of lupus. Yet this would not explain her volatile mood swings and hallucinations. Biographers have speculated that her breakdown was triggered by menopause, jealousy of Louis's success, or feeling less needed by him as caregiver or literary critic. Any or all of these might well have played a role, but the rigors of nursing her husband and the exhausting demands of life at sea and in Samoa probably played a greater one.

The episodic nature of Fanny's symptoms might suggest bipolar disorder, which worsens over time. This could also explain her sudden irritability, restlessness, and manic energy in the garden, although the length of the flare-up would be unusual and there is no record of recurring episodes. The side effects of the potent medications she was given can also cause many of the symptoms she experienced, such as agitation and hallucinations. Whatever underlying mental condition might have afflicted Fanny, the drugs used to treat it very likely made it worse.

Some biographers contend that Fanny's breakdown, along with her dark and combative moods, finally ground down Louis and made him deeply disheartened with his marriage. Toward the end of his life, Louis seemed more exhausted by Fanny and their clashes about his work. It would not be surprising if Fanny too longed for an escape from the unending demands of putting her husband's needs before her own. Yet even in their worst times, the couple seemed to prefer being unhappy together to being happy apart because they were bonded by deep love and need. In the depths of his wife's nervous collapse, Louis wrote to Anne Jenkin of his marriage, "As I look back, I think it was the best move I ever made in my life. Not only would I do it again; I cannot conceive the idea of not doing it."

On Fanny's fifty-fourth birthday, Louis wrote a poem about his "stormy petrel" that was her favorite gift. The opening words were perhaps his best evocation of what she was to him: "ever precious and perilous, like an ember from the fire or gem from a volcano." Loving Fanny had always been perilous, from the moment Louis had set eyes on Sam Osbourne's runaway wife in Grez. But the peril of almost losing her had made him realize how precious she was to him.

-⚜-

FANNY'S BREAKDOWN AWAKENED in her a healthy longing for some lib-eration from her husband's enormous shadow. "I wish I were able to write a little tale that I might save some money of my own," she wrote in her diary shortly after her recovery.

This is curious because just the month before, *McClure's Magazine* had run her little tale "Under Sentence of the Law," about a charming and free-spirited dog named Rick. Tried and sentenced to die for murdering a sheep, Rick refuses to let the system break him: He curls up for a nap at his solici-tor's feet during his trial and when he wins a reprieve on condition that he wear a muzzle, he cheerfully trots around town with it "not often on his nose" but dangling from his chin. Fanny had been allotted only part of her $150 story payment from the family coffers, and she had sent her share to an ailing brother-in-law. Men control the purse, she wrote in her diary, doling out money to their wives for clothing and other necessary expenses as if they were a gift. "I wonder what would become of a man, and to what he would degenerate, if his life was that of a woman's . . . to be always under bonds of the deepest gratitude for any further sums," she complained. "I would work very hard to earn a couple of pounds a month, and I could easily earn much more, but there is my position as Louis's wife, therefore I cannot."

Stevenson biographer Frank McLynn dismisses Fanny's private lament as a pompous delusion that she had writing talent—a fantasy he contends is common to intimates of writers. "'Easily earn much more' at what?" McLynn demands to know. "She had not been notably successful as an earner before she teamed up with Louis." But Fanny had been building a project of her own, a series of personal essays that earned her quite a bit more than a few pounds in the following months. And she convinced her relatively enlight-ened husband to arrange for her earnings to go directly to her.

Fanny's essays came out of a cookery book she had begun to write on the *Casco* cruise. The book was not intended to be a conventional compilation of instructions but a series of lively vignettes about her experiences around the world, with relevant recipes dropped into the text. Combining her humorous storytelling, cultural curiosity, and love of cooking, the mash-up was the perfect showcase for her particular writing talent and experiences—as innovative and eccentric as she was. A century before Nora Ephron's *Heartburn* and Laura Esquivel's *Like Water for Chocolate*, Fanny was spicing up personal stories with personal cooking advice. Fifteen chapters, stretching from Indiana to Samoa, would form "Ramblings of a Housewife"—or, as she liked to refer to it, "The Diary of a Mad Housewife."

In 1893 and 1894, Fanny published seven essays that appear to have been chapter prototypes in the *Philadelphia Inquirer* and the *Scranton Republican* in the U.S. and in *The Queen* and *The Woman at Home* (sometimes called *Annie S. Swan's Magazine*) in Britain. Others might have been published elsewhere. An 1894 profile of Fanny in *Ladies' Home Journal* commended her writing and referred to a series of her articles about Pacific Island life in a British journal at around the same time, though these might not have been intended as part of the cookbook.

Louis must have felt that Fanny had found a good form for her writing. Perhaps he also realized how much his "peasant" remark had hurt her, and he wanted to make amends. Far from discouraging his wife's project, he enthusiastically took a supporting role in it. Louis wrote to Baxter in 1894 that he and Fanny planned to gather her articles into a cookery book, and he began to solicit "sham anecdotes" from his colleagues for what he described as a companion volume.

Fanny drew on handwritten recipes from her colorful home cookbooks, two of which survive. The recipes in the published essays range from desperation entries like faux honey from the Nevada silver mining camp to sophisticated thyme-and-saffron-scented bouillabaisse from Marseille. They include quirky advice, such as Fanny's tip on handling garlic tenderly: "Treat the savory bulb coarsely and it will be coarse to you in turn, but handle it with tact, with consideration, as if you love it, and you will be repaid a thousandfold." Some of the recipes evolve as they accompany Fanny around the globe: A frozen cream from Indiana is infused with a tip from French chefs, and "confectioners gingerbread" becomes a popular dish served at native Samoan feasts.

In her vignette "A Backwoods Childhood," based on her memories of primitive homemaking customs in Indiana, Fanny suggests gathering bacon rind or scraps of fat left on dinner plates to make soap, and she dives head-first into her father's method for making scrapple with a lesson on how to dissect a pig. She admits that to some readers, regional traditions such as these might seem "sordid" (and indeed, the scrapple recipe was excised for British audiences), but to her, they evoked a disappearing way of life. Her South Seas chapters likely would have included other instructions from her home cookbook—for dishes such as "Ah Foo's pig's head," ginger beer Akamama, and Butaritari pudding, as well as guidance on how to build a Samoan oven.

The wildest published piece is "At the Undertaker's," in which Fanny recalls cavorting at the home of a childhood friend whose father was a funeral director—until she was banned from the premises for using some of his coffins to stage plays. And the recipe? As she notes, her friend's home was the only one in the neighborhood that had ice in the summer, and the undertaker's wife, "Mrs. W," made the best of this ghoulish perk by using it to churn homemade ice cream. Mrs. W's recipe is there, along with Fanny's memory of licking the sweet cream off a big wooden spoon when Mrs. W opened the freezer to stir it.

DRUMBEATS PIERCED THE QUIET evenings on Upolu in spring 1893. Pumped-up young men blackened their faces for battle and brandished knives and axes and Winchester rifles. Women cut their hair and wove it into war headdresses for the chiefs.

Louis's efforts to broker peace between the nominal Indigenous ruler, Malietoa Laupepa, and the ousted chief, Mata'afa Iosefo, had ultimately been unsuccessful. As Iosefo and his supporters geared up for a revolt and rumors of a crackdown by the foreign powers circulated, Louis soberly warned of impending war in his *Times* letters.

Though Louis took his diplomatic efforts seriously, they also aroused in him a kind of boyish excitement that Fanny found silly and sometimes reckless. She had bristled over one incident during her breakdown, when Margaret Child-Villiers—wife of the seventh Earl of Jersey, who was also the New South Wales governor—had come to Samoa to visit. Louis did not hide his delight in Lady Jersey's English manners and vivacity, which was in stark contrast to his ailing wife's frowning sourness. He turned a diplomatic mission to Iosefo into a rollicking adventure that involved hiding in a thicket and Child-Villiers masquerading as his fictional cousin "Amelia Balfour." The countess later admitted that the burlesque was probably not politically advisable but wrote that Louis "was not only a writer of romance, but a hero of romance."

As unrest on the island heated up, the eve of war seemed to excite the armchair soldier in Louis. When he rode out to observe the warriors' preparations with his cousin Graham Balfour, who was part of the Vailima household for several months, he excitedly turned to him and said, "After all there are only two things worth while—to have women and to kill men." Fanny groaned when the two returned "quite wild with excitement, burning to join the fray" and noted in her diary that it was going to be "a difficult task to keep Louis from losing his head altogether."

Fanny also rolled her eyes at her husband's fantasies about protecting her. He seemed to expect her to retreat into the role of quivering female while he was busy stockpiling arms to defend Vailima. "I suppose if our house should be attacked, Belle and I must retire to a back apartment with some crochet work and not ask what is going on," she bristled in her diary. "A strange thing that would be for a person of my spirit." She did not add that she and Balfour were the most experienced shooters in the household, should it become necessary to use the stockpiled arms.

When war erupted in July, it lasted only nine days. Laupepa attacked Iosefo's forces, quickly driving them back. Then the three powers, which had stood by as the country hurtled toward bloodshed, sent warships to help crush the revolt. In keeping with Samoan tradition, Laupepa's warriors paraded the heads of several slain fighters as war trophies, a practice that horrified Fanny and Louis. For the first time, the Samoan warriors also violated their own code of honor by displaying the heads of three girls. Yet this and other atrocities went unpunished. As Stevenson expert Roslyn Jolly notes, instead of bringing the rule of law to "lawless, savage people," Western intervention in Samoa had actually invited "a descent *into* lawless savagery."

Louis continued to advocate diplomacy, insisting that it was necessary to work through the proper channels and stay friendly with the colonial officials to bring peace. But Fanny was too enraged to remain calm. She believed the white men in power had provoked the war and was fed up with Western political and economic exploitation. In her diary, she railed against the white traders who "called the Samoans 'n——' and made them walk behind like dogs" and asserted that if she were Samoan, she would agitate for a "massacre of the whites." If Fanny had worried that Louis might "lose his head," Louis thought Fanny already had. He called her an "idiotic Enthusiast." She returned the insult.

The couple did remain united in their support of Iosefo, who was deported with several of his leading chiefs to the German-controlled Marshall Islands for five years. Louis protested his exile and sent him gifts and necessities. He and Fanny also provided food and support to other chiefs who had fought with Iosefo and were imprisoned on Upolu after the war. They celebrated Louis's forty-third birthday with the jailed Samoan rebels, and the prisoners' families later hosted a lavish feast in the jail to pay tribute to the Stevensons. Fanny was honored at the kava ceremony, while Louis received gifts and was named the "only friend" of the captive chiefs. "No such feast was ever made for a single family, and no such present ever given to a single white man," Louis wrote proudly to Colvin.

When the imprisoned Samoans were released, they were so grateful for the Stevensons' support and Louis's untiring diplomatic efforts, they built a road connecting Vailima to the main highway. At a feast Fanny and Louis threw to celebrate the completion of the "Road of the Loving Heart," Louis gave a speech reiterating his firm belief that Samoans needed to work the land and stop warring among themselves if they were to hold on to their country. "There is only one way to defend Samoa," he said. "Hear it before it is too late. It is to make roads, and gardens, and care for your trees, and sell their produce wisely, and, in one word, to occupy and use your country. If you do not, others will."

Louis continued to develop a plan to unite the Samoan royal factions, but his views grew more radical over time. In an interview in Honolulu after the short-lived war, he advocated going beyond compromise "to follow the demand of the Samoan people that the Berlin act be rescinded, *while the three Powers withdraw absolutely*, and the natives be let alone, and allowed to govern the islands as they choose."

Independence would not come to Samoa for another seven decades—and then, not fully. Six years after the war, the three powers carved up the islands against the wishes of the Samoan people. The United States was given the eastern islands and still administers them as American Samoa. Germany annexed the western islands, including Upolu, in return for concessions to Britain elsewhere in the world. Later, New Zealand ousted Germany and governed Western Samoa under a League of Nations mandate for several decades. During this time, the nonviolent Mau movement continued to agitate for independence. Finally, in 1962, Western Samoa gained its independence from New Zealand, following a path to freedom similar to the one Louis had outlined. Eventually, Western Samoa was renamed the Independent State of Samoa.

LOUIS'S LAST YEARS in Samoa were shaded by a sense that time was running out—on his peacemaking work, on his popularity as a writer, on his earning capacity, and on his life.

Stevenson biographer J. C. Furnas estimated that Louis wrote a phenomenal seven hundred thousand words in four years on Upolu. He desperately longed to get off the work treadmill, but his constant money worries kept him bound to his pen. Louis once described juggling three projects at once, dividing them according to "most pressing," "most remunerative," and "most tempting." London literary circles gossiped that the quality of his work was suffering.

For years critics had attacked him for being too idle, Louis complained to fellow author George Meredith, and now they seemed to feel he was playing himself out. They had no concept of what it took for a sickly writer to support a family:

> *For 14 years I have not had a day's real health; I have wakened sick and gone to bed weary; and I have done my work unflinchingly. I have written in bed, and written out of it, written in hemorrhages, written in sickness, written torn by coughing, written when my head swam for weakness; and for so long, it seems to me I have won my wager and recovered my glove.*

Louis's most extraordinary feat of determination in Samoa might have been completing *The Ebb-Tide* during the four months that Fanny's ravings and hallucinations were at their worst. He seems to have wrenched out every word, sometimes completing only a page or so a day. "I break down at every paragraph, I may observe," he wrote to Colvin, "and lie here, and sweat, and curse over the blame thing, till I can get one sentence wrung out over another." He might have found *The Ebb-Tide* especially challenging because he was moving in a new realist direction, but given the stresses of his life at the time, it is remarkable that he managed to write at all.

Louis was alternately defiant and depressed about his waning popularity, excited about experimenting and concerned that he had lost his way. Sometimes the Stevenson legacy of black moods seemed to be overtaking the Balfour sunniness he had inherited from his mother—"so much so that I have a painful difficulty in believing I can ever finish another book or that the public will ever read it," he wrote to his cousin Bob, who also suffered from the family depressive streak. Louis half joked to an old school chum that it would be a relief to die sooner rather than later so he could avoid seeing himself "impotent and forgotten."

Estrangement from his tight Edinburgh circle also continued to haunt him. Louis's love/hate relationship with Henley limped on in occasional awkward correspondence. He had severed ties with his old chum in a fit of pique when Henley did not call on Margaret Stevenson in Edinburgh after he moved nearby. But afterward Louis alternated between relief and regret when he recalled the man's "big presence and his welcome, wooden footstep," and he wrote to Henley when the poet's beloved only child died at five years old. Henley continued to publish some of Louis's poems and articles while also denigrating him to his young literary protégés.

Louis's feelings about his cousins Bob and Katharine did not soften. Though he had one friendly exchange of letters with Bob before he died, Louis complained to Baxter that his cousins were generally unfriendly and did not write. After Fanny's breakdown, he was moved by the support of Belle and Lloyd to shift his family allegiance to his stepchildren. Louis decided that he would honor his father's wish to leave something to Alan Stevenson's children, but he altered his will to favor Belle, Lloyd, and Austin.

Even though the Pacific climate clearly benefited Louis's lungs, he continued to suffer from other physical and mental ailments. He resorted to laudanum for his "collywobbles," or nervous stomach. He complained of "brain fag" from overwork and he still needed to use a tube for urinating, presumably for an enlarged prostate or scarring from venereal disease. He also developed a new problem, migraine headaches, and tried once again to give up alcohol, except for brandy in his coffee. Suffering his worst headache after a day of complete temperance, he scrapped abstinence.

Doctors and others pressed Louis to ease up on his relentless chain-smoking, which he described to Barrie as "cigarettes without intermission except when coughing or kissing." As always, he made light of his half-hearted attempts to quit. He sent a note of thanks to Lillie Hitchcock Coit for prompting one "gratifying relapse." Coit, the eccentric San Francisco firefighter enthusiast, had arranged for a live pig wearing a jockey cap and carrying a box of cigarettes to be delivered to Vailima after she visited. "I shall continue to *stop smoking*, until the dark-winged angel 'puts my pipe out' finally," he wrote to her, "it amuses me and does nobody any harm; and I shall continue to relapse, which amuses me a great deal more and does good at last to the tobacconists."

LOUIS'S SPIRITS LIFTED in fall 1894. His worries about Fanny had eased and he managed to take a break from writing for a few months. His mother returned to Vailima to live and Austin transferred to a school in New Zealand, so he could visit the family on holidays. The whole clan was there for the grand party Fanny threw for her husband's forty-fourth birthday in November. A hundred guests streamed in from morning until afternoon with gifts of kava bowls, finely woven mats, wreaths, and flowers. At the feast, everyone ate with their fingers, according to Samoan custom, in a gazebo constructed for the occasion with a roof of thatched coconut and banana leaves. The festivities ended with traditional Samoan dancing.

For Louis, the biggest highlight of the season was the publication of the first volumes of the *Edinburgh Edition of the Works of Robert Louis Stevenson*. Baxter had proposed a collection of Louis's works and negotiated the contract for a twenty-volume set, which Colvin would edit. Louis planned the contents with excitement, not least because advance subscriptions promised that it would solve his family's financial woes. As an added bonus, Baxter was personally delivering the first books. Louis had been worried about his old college drinking buddy, who slipped into full-blown alcoholism after the death of his wife, Grace. Louis and Fanny urged Baxter to visit and in late 1894, he set sail from Scotland with the volumes in his bag.

Louis was also invigorated to be devoting himself exclusively to a Scottish story he had worked on only intermittently for four years. He had ideas for several other Scottish tales as well. He knew that he was unlikely to ever see "Auld Reekie" again or feel the heather crunch under his boots, but his imagination was drawn back to his native country by what he called "identities of sensation" that evoked extraordinary emotions in him. He described one such experience to Colvin, when, standing on his veranda in Samoa, a storm blowing in from the west filled his head with images of "Highland huts, and peat smoke, and the brown swirling rivers, and wet clothes, and whisky, and the romance of the past, and that indescribable bite of the whole thing at a man's heart, which is—or rather lies at the bottom of—a story."

Louis did not intend for the book he was working on, *Weir of Hermiston*, to be a sweet whiff of Scottish nostalgia. The grim novel (originally called *The Justice-Clerk*) centers on the struggle between a young lawyer, Archie Weir, and his father, Lord Hermiston, known as "the hanging judge" for the harsh sentences he hands down. An inspiration for the justice-clerk was the real eighteenth-century "hanging judge" Lord Braxfield, who was known for pronouncements such as "Hang a thief when he's young, and he'll no steal when he's auld."

Louis's coarse, emotionally repressed judge pours his passion into his work rather than his wife and son. After Archie denounces capital punishment at the hanging of a man his father sentenced to die, Lord Hermiston banishes him to the family estate in the moorland parish of Hermiston, where Archie falls in love with Kirstie Elliot, a passionate and headstrong local girl. The two rendezvous in secret, but when Archie tries to end their meetings to protect her honor, Kirstie believes he is ashamed of her because she is lower class.

Louis did not live to complete the story. According to Belle, who was acting as his amanuensis, he planned that Archie's duplicitous friend, Frank Innes, would get Kirstie pregnant and Archie would kill him. Archie is then tried and sentenced to death by his father, but he breaks out of prison and escapes with Kirstie to America, hastening Lord Hermiston's death. Irish poet and author Sidney Lysaght, who visited Louis in Samoa, had come away from a discussion about the book with a different impression. According to Lysaght, Louis envisioned the story climaxing in Kirstie's tense visit to Archie in prison, when she confesses that she is pregnant by the man he murdered. Lysaght believed this ending was "much more in harmony with the genius and conception of the story and characters" than the alternative ending sketched by Belle.

Louis had begun dictating to Belle because he suffered from writer's cramp, and working with her on the book energized them both. In a diary entry in September, she marveled at the way the words simply flowed out of Louis as he composed the story. "He had hardly more than a line or two of notes to keep him on track," she wrote, "but he never falters for a word, giving me the sentences, with capital letters and all the stops, as clearly and steadily as though he were reading from an unseen book." She later wrote that Louis told her, "I see it unfold before me without a break to the end."

Not surprisingly, Belle—whose Samoan name was Teulia, or "one who adorns things"—also acted as fashion consultant for the book. She suggested that Kirstie liven up her gray dress with a pink handkerchief when she first catches Archie's eye in church. Louis matched this with bold pink stockings, which he had seen Belle wear. Belle later claimed that Louis based young Kirstie on her, though this likely applied mostly to the character's wardrobe. *Weir of Hermiston* editor Gillian Hughes suggests that Kirstie's fiery personality and fierce pride, dark coloring, and small, thin figure were reminiscent of Fanny when Louis met her. Hughes notes that in a draft manuscript, Louis used his wife's signature flower to describe Kirstie as she appeared to Archie in church: "like a bed of tiger lilies in a city garden."

Weir of Hermiston is widely considered Louis's unfinished masterpiece because of its vivid evocation of the rolling Scottish Borders landscape and Edinburgh history, its powerful tragic story, and its compelling characterizations of women as well as men. The novel's portraits of the strong-minded Kirstie and her aunt, also named Kirstie—the Hermiston housekeeper who has a mother's love for Archie—are deep and insightful. Louis delved into the female characters' complicated feelings and told part of the story from the elder Kirstie's point of view.

The book leaves off during a quarrel between young Kirstie and Archie, as he tries in vain to understand what he said that provoked a torrent of violent emotion in her. Some of the last words Louis wrote are especially haunting—not only because they are an incisive depiction of a young man's awe and stupefaction at women's unleashed fury, but because they seem borne of the painful wisdom he had gained from caring for his wife. As Archie takes Kirstie in his arms to try to comfort her, Louis wrote:

He felt her whole body commoved by the throes of distress, and had pity upon her beyond speech. Pity, and at the same time a bewildered fear of this explosive engine in his arms, whose works he did not understand, and yet had been tampering with. There rose from before him the curtains of boyhood and he saw for the first time the ambiguous face of woman as she is.

AS EARLY AS SPRING 1889, before the Stevensons moved to Upolu, Louis wrote to Charles Baxter that overwork had brought on a distressing "attack of blood to the head," during which he could hardly see or understand words said to him. This could have been a small stroke, but Louis thought it had passed without harm. Five years later, in fall 1894, Fanny noticed that his face was often unusually flushed, a possible sign of spikes in his blood pressure. Though this might have been triggered by overwork and financial anxiety, Louis's relentless smoking, which narrows the veins, and chronic lung disease, which thickens the blood, made him dangerously vulnerable to hypertension and stroke.

It seems that Louis sensed the end might be near. Fanny recalled that he wanted to discuss death more than usual with her, and in a letter to Edmund Gosse two days before he died, Louis made the chilling remark, "I have in fact lost the path that makes it easy and natural for you to descend the hill. I am going at it straight. And where I have to go down it is a precipice."

After Belle finished work with Louis on December 3, 1894, she went to her room to write a letter while he gave Austin a French lesson on the veranda. She noticed the lesson was rather noisy, but tutoring sessions with Louis were often rambunctious, sometimes involving translations of sentences about a local editor he disliked, such as "blank is a silly ass" and "blank hasn't an idea in his fat head."

Afterward, Louis went to cheer up Fanny, whose gloomy forebodings had dimmed her mood for a few days. He retrieved a special bottle of wine from the cellar and helped her make mayonnaise for a salad he liked. Louis was dripping oil into egg yolks as Fanny whisked them when suddenly he put down the bottle and grabbed his head. According to Belle, he exclaimed, "What's that? Do I look strange?" Then he collapsed to the floor.

Sosimo, one of Louis's favorite servants, helped get him into a big leather chair and Lloyd galloped down to Apia for a doctor. Louis was unconscious and breathing heavily. Fanny, Margaret, and Belle stumbled through their shock as they rubbed his skin with brandy and put his feet in hot water. After all Fanny's efforts to suppress Louis's hemorrhages before they killed him, the women could not believe that he might die suddenly now, when he did not even seem ill. They told one another that his pulse was getting stronger or his breathing better. But when the local doctor arrived, he confirmed that Louis was dying. Then he asked that the windows be opened to let in the cool night air. It smelled of gardenias, Belle would remember, and Louis's hair curled lightly on his forehead as if he were asleep. He died about two hours after he had collapsed, of a cerebral hemorrhage, according to the doctor.

WHEN SIR WALTER Scott died in 1832, he was buried with the pomp and decorum that his family and nation felt befitted the man who had written his vision of Scotland into the hearts of his compatriots. Robert Louis Stevenson died sixty-two years later as one of the most prominent contemporary authors in the world, but he was buried simply where his wandering led him, among people he had adopted as his own.

Scott's servants and family carried him to his grave "so that no foreign hand should be allowed to touch the remains of a master so honoured and so beloved," as the *Edinburgh Courant* reported. Samoans prepared Louis for his funeral. Vailima servants helped Fanny dress her husband in his evening clothes—a white linen shirt, black trousers, and a dark blue silk sash. They took down the Union Jack that usually flew over the household and spread it over his body, along with traditional fine Samoan mats. Local chiefs and their families arrived throughout the evening and held vigil with the family all night, sitting in a semicircle on the floor. Belle recalled that some kissed Louis and bid the Teller of Tales goodbye in their native tongue, "Tofa Tusitala."

A procession of sixty-two carriages, phaetons, and gigs wound from Scott's castle-like manor, Abbotsford, through shuttered villages to a serene burial spot at the ruins of Dryburgh Abbey, on the River Tweed. The day after Louis died, forty of the Stevensons' Samoan friends, including some chiefs, hacked a path through the jungle on Mt. Vaea up to the summit, where Louis had wished to be buried. Funeral mourners climbed on foot up the mountain, a journey that was too arduous for Fanny and Margaret, to the burial site overlooking the sea. They threw flowers on the coffin and then planted a twig decorated with a tinsel cross at the head of his grave.

Fanny later had a tomb built from large blocks of cement, in the Samoan fashion. On one brass panel is a thistle and the words "The Tomb of Tusitala" in Samoan, with an excerpt from the Book of Ruth: "Thy people will be my people . . . where thou diest, will I die, and there will I be buried." The other panel is inscribed with "Requiem," the poem Louis had been composing when he lay delirious in the woods near Monterey after he had traveled across the world to get to Fanny, hardly dreaming that he would live to marry her and become one of the most famous writers of his time:

> Under the wide and starry sky,
> Dig the grave and let me lie.
> Glad did I live and gladly die,
> And I laid me down with a will.
>
> This be the verse you grave for me:
> *Here he lies where he longed to be;*
> *Home is the sailor, home from the sea,*
> *And the hunter home from the hill.*

⁕

SIDNEY COLVIN STEPPED onto the street after lunch on a stormy London day when a newspaper poster flapping in the wind caught his eye. It proclaimed in large black letters "Death of R.L. Stevenson." For ten days, Henry James refused to believe the reports—which some newspapers also questioned—until Fanny sent him a cable confirming that Louis was dead. As tributes began to emerge from all corners of the globe and condolences poured in from friends and strangers, James sent Fanny a stirring letter. "You are nearest the pain, because you were nearest the joy and the pride . . . ," he wrote. "He lighted up one whole side of the globe, and was in himself a whole province of one's imagination."

Charles Baxter learned of Louis's death in Port Said, as his ship approached the Suez Canal. He arrived in Samoa at the end of January 1895 with the first volumes of the Edinburgh Edition and left two months later with the manuscript of *Weir of Hermiston*. In London, Colvin sent the unfinished work to his influential literary friends for comments. Their consensus was that it should be published as soon as possible. One can imagine their collective sigh of relief. It was as if Louis had finally come home.

Threats of censorship followed Louis to his grave. Colvin, who edited *Weir of Hermiston* for publication, was not one to push the limits of sexual honesty in print. Fortunately, he did not have to deal with Kirstie's seduction at age thirteen because Louis died before writing the passage, which he expected would bar the story from serialization. Yet Colvin still reduced references to the girl's vanity and ardor and even jettisoned Archie's peek at her pink stockings in church. He also felt compelled to make her older, in keeping with the Criminal Law Amendment, which had raised the age of consent from thirteen to sixteen.

Literary chatter about the book was audible even before it was serialized in the new international magazine *Cosmopolis* in spring 1896. Soon after, *Weir of Hermiston: An Unfinished Romance* was released simultaneously in Britain by Chatto & Windus and in the United States by Charles Scribner's Sons. It was less popular in Britain than the U.S., where the reviews were nearly all positive. *The New York Times* praised the character of the elder Kirstie as "divined with genius and presented with perfect art," and *Literary World* called the story "one of the strongest pieces of work Stevenson has ever done." Perhaps not surprisingly for an unfinished work, sales were modest.

For more than a century, Louis's tragic death while composing a likely masterpiece has led to inevitable "What if?" questions: What literary heights and new directions might the forty-four-year-old writer have reached had he lived a full life? The novelist Graham Greene—whose grandmother was Louis's first cousin—contended that Louis did his best work in his final years. In his essay "From Feathers to Iron," Greene wrote that it was only then that Louis's "fine dandified talent began to shed its disguising graces, the granite to show through." Fanny too thought Louis had died before reaching the pinnacle of his talent. She wrote to Colvin, "He was very near the true beginning of his work."

It is not difficult to imagine that Louis's writing would strengthen with age and wisdom. His talent was certainly not played out at the time of his death. He had been experimenting with new forms, and *The Beach of Falesá* and the completed part of *Weir of Hermiston* show that he was still capable of mastering different genres. But Louis's most famous books—*Treasure Island*, *Kidnapped*, and *Strange Case of Dr Jekyll and Mr Hyde*—are the works of a master storyteller and stylist. No matter what he might have gone on to write—and how well it was received—those three books would have endured, enthralling generation after generation of new readers.

FANNY TRIED TO CONSOLE herself after her husband's death with the thought that he could not have stood to grow old. But she would live on for another twenty years. "My life, young man, resembles a wild ride on the crest of a wave that rolls on and never breaks," she told an admirer.

Fanny tried to keep Vailima running with her children's help after Louis died, but by 1897 the plantation had not paid off, perhaps because of her inexperience or the negligent oversight of Lloyd and, before him, Joe. Belle and Lloyd were eager to return to the States. Fanny sold the house and her garden of dreams to a German merchant, who in turn sold it to the German government in 1911, when it became the governor's residence. It is now restored and open to the public as a Stevenson museum.

Fanny built a home on San Francisco's Russian Hill, then known as the city's poets and writers corner. The renowned local architect Willis Polk designed the Mediterranean-style mansion overlooking the Golden Gate, which included a stained-glass window depicting the *Hispaniola*, the fictional fabled ship of *Treasure Island*. But Fanny could not seem to settle in one place and continued to roam. With her growing wealth from Louis's literary estate—which included some collections of his work that were rushed into print after his death—she bought a house in Santa Barbara, then a ranch in the Santa Cruz Mountains and then another in Ensenada.

Anyone who imagined that Fanny would settle into the role of Great Man's dignified widow, discreetly living out her final years to preserve her husband's legacy, was mistaken. Her conflicts with Louis's colleagues over his work grew sharper when her husband was no longer there to moderate them. She quarreled with Baxter when he authorized the publication of *Fables*, a story collection she told Margaret she "wouldn't let Louis publish" when he was alive, though it is well regarded now. She threw herself into seeing that Louis's official biography was published before she died and battled with Colvin because she thought he was writing it too slowly.

Lloyd, who was no diplomat, badgered Colvin into withdrawing from the biographical project, and Fanny handed it over to Louis's cousin Graham Balfour, who had interviewed Louis about his work and other experiences while he was staying with the family in Samoa. *The Life of Robert Louis Stevenson*, published in 1901, was a decent job as authorized Victorian biographies go. It touched on Louis's conflicts with his father and colorful youth without delving into the salacious details. For Fanny, it fulfilled the directive Louis had given to her years before that his biography not "inflict pain upon a snail" or "cause a pang to any one whom I have known, far less whom I have loved."

For Henley, however, the whitewashed biography provided the perfect opportunity to savage his onetime friend's character and reputation, and to take revenge on Fanny as well. In a *Pall Mall Magazine* review, he unfairly dismissed the Louis who emerged from the book as "this Seraph in Chocolate, this barley-sugar effigy of a real man." Where was the real "Lewis," Henley demanded—the riotous comrade and occasional buffoon who left for America and never returned? Settling old scores, Henley went on to criticize Louis's ego, talent, and even his invalidism.

Fanny had no quarrels with Henry James, who described her to Colvin on one visit as "gentleness and kindness and touchingness itself." To James, Fanny's sojourn in the Pacific had made her even more of a romantic figure, invoking images of an "old grizzled lioness—or resigned captive South Sea Chieftainess." But the tiny woman with the massive gray curls who wandered through San Francisco in exotic jewelry and ballet slippers continued to turn the heads of younger men. Fanny had two male protégés who were writers, both shadows of her late husband, whose work they could only hope to emulate.

Critic, humorist, and poet Gelett Burgess, whose signature uniform was a long cape with a carnation, was a popular figure in the 1890s literary scene in the Bay Area. When Fanny met him, Burgess had been dismissed from his teaching job at the University of California at Berkeley for a prank and was happily editing a popular irreverent magazine known as *The Lark*. Burgess designed the tablets for Louis's tomb in Samoa, but he fell out with Fanny when he wrote a barely veiled story about her entourage.

Fanny had a more serious relationship with Edward Salisbury Field, a feature writer and artist for the Hearst newspapers. Ned was an aspiring playwright and raconteur, known for his quick wit and humor. He was also thirty-seven years younger than Fanny and the son of one of her Indianapolis school friends. He became a member of Fanny's household—her secretary, travel companion, and likely lover—until her death. Whatever the nature of his affection, he reputedly said that she was "the only woman in the world worth dying for."

In 1907 Fanny and Ned went on a motor tour of Europe, chauffeured by

Lloyd, who was an early automobile enthusiast. Perhaps she was embarrassed by her relationship with the much younger man or wanted to keep it from leaking to the press, because she refused to give out her address and avoided some old friends. Reacting to her rather bizarre behavior, Henry James characterized her on the trip as a "poor barbarous and merely instinctive lady," though he regretted that he would not see her.

By then, Fanny's relationship with some of Louis's other friends had mellowed; Colvin and even Katharine de Mattos came to stay in the house she rented in the English countryside. The arrival of Fanny's twenty-six-year-old grandson, Austin, and his wife, Mary, must have been a triumph for her as she entertained Louis's clique. Austin was on his way to becoming a well-regarded playwright. He was in England for the London opening of *The Toymaker of Nuremburg*, one of his six plays that were turned into films. The renowned silent film version of his biggest Broadway hit, the romantic comedy *Seventh Heaven*, went on to earn three Oscars at the first Academy Awards in 1929. Colvin and Sitwell could never warm up to Louis's stepchildren, but they welcomed Austin and his wife with open arms. Rather touchingly, they liked to think of themselves as Austin and Mary's "English parents."

Fanny continued to feel connected to the island that was her husband's final resting place. While still in Samoa, she had heard about a missing half-native girl, the heir to her American father's fortune, who had disappeared when she was sent to San Francisco to attend school. Fanny found and rescued the girl from an orphanage in the city and took her into her home. Then she met with lawmakers in Washington, D.C., where she successfully proved the girl's claim and secured her property.

Fanny generously paid for the care of Louis's aging nanny, Alison Cunningham, during her final illness and proudly took Jules Simoneau, the shabby restaurateur who had befriended Louis in Monterey, as her guest to fancy RLS Society galas there. She provided a home and much financial support to her son's first wife, Katherine Durham, after Katherine's marriage to Lloyd fell apart and he seemed to slip out of the picture. Fanny did this despite the fact that Katherine, whom she had heartily approved of, came to despise Fanny, to blame her for the couple's breakup and to speak publicly and volubly about her grievances. Later, Fanny took in her grandsons, Alan and Lloyd, when their bitter and mentally unbalanced mother declared that she no longer wanted the responsibility of rearing them. But Fanny's generosity toward Lloyd's ex-wife finally wore out, and she coldly left Katherine five dollars in her will, to the dismay of Louis's friends when it became international news.

Fanny's physical ailments and age did not prevent her from camping in the woods, hanging out with copper miners in Mexico, and buying Angora goats with the idea of going into the wool business. She attended séances with Dora Williams, entertained Samoan sailors in port in San Francisco, and developed a warm friendship with muckraking journalist and novelist Frank Norris and his wife, Jeannette. She wrote several prefaces for collections of Louis's work. On her seventieth birthday, Fanny told her sister Nellie, "[I] would rather go to the well and be broken than be preserved on a dusty shelf."

Nellie Van de Grift Sanchez wrote that her sister's belief in an afterlife and ultimate reunion with Louis sustained her through her final years. This conviction was the underlying theme of Fanny's final piece of fiction, "Anne," published in *Scribner's Magazine* in 1899, about a woman's gradual realization that she is dead. Separation from her husband leaves Anne unsettled, and she is able to find peace only when he too dies and they are reunited in the afterlife. "We are one;" Anne says to her husband, "we cannot be parted."

Fanny died—like her husband, of a cerebral hemorrhage—on February 18, 1914, at the age of seventy-four, a few days after editing proofs of her Pacific diary, *The Cruise of the "Janet Nichol" Among the South Seas Islands.* Belle and Ned Field took her ashes to Samoa, where dozens of chiefs and other friends commemorated her return with a feast and procession to the summit of Mt. Vaea to place her remains in Louis's grave. A tiger lily decorates a plaque added to the tomb, along with Fanny's ethereal native name, Aolele, or "flying cloud," and a quatrain from Louis's poem "My Wife":

Teacher, tender, comrade, wife,
A fellow-farer true through life,
Heart whole and soul free,
The august father gave to Me.

LLOYD OSBOURNE WENT on to write fiction on his own after Louis's death, though he remained something of a "dude," as his father once described him. The instability of his life, his father's wavering interest and support, his stepfather's immense talent, and his mother's domineering personality seemed to cripple his ability to establish his own identity; in many ways, he remained a confused boy his entire life. Lloyd wrote light tales about "motormaniacs," some of them with anti-Semitic overtones that were unfortunately fairly common in American literature of the time. He wrote a few good stories set in the Pacific, including one from the point of view of a native woman.

While literary fame eluded him, Lloyd seemed comfortable settling back into his stepfather's shadow. He wrote affectionate reminiscences about Louis and edited a collection of his works. He aggressively took advantage of opportunities from the Stevenson estate and was said "never to have let a quote from RLS pass without extracting a fee." He was frequently seen at the New York branch of the Lambs, a theatrical London social club. Lloyd died in 1947 at the age of seventy-nine, after an undistinguished literary career and two unsuccessful marriages.

Belle also found ways to cash in on the fame of her illustrious stepfather, but she seemed to live a more charmed life than her brother. She gave lectures on Louis and wrote touching memoirs that were somewhat sloppy with facts but true to the spirit of her eventful life. An avid theatergoer, she basked in her son's popular success with hits like *Seventh Heaven* and *Three Wise Fools*.

Six months after Fanny's death, Belle married her mother's protégé. Ned Field was three years older than Belle's son and not as talented a writer, though his plays and scripts included the screwball comedy *Twin Beds*, which was made into a movie four times. Ned proved more successful in real estate, however, and he and Belle became millionaires when oil was discovered on one of his properties. He died in 1936 at the age of fifty-eight. Belle's first husband, Joe, had passed away almost four decades earlier, shortly after remarrying at the age of forty-five. Belle was ninety-four when she died in 1953, having survived both her husbands, her brother, and even her son, Austin, by one year.

Belle's marriage to Ned Field is another strange twist in the Stevenson saga that leaves some tantalizing questions. Was Field only pretending to love Fanny while secretly lusting after her daughter? Or in his grief after Fanny's death, did he reach for Belle, who most closely evoked "the only woman in the world worth dying for"?

HENLEY'S BLISTERING REVIEW of *The Life of Robert Louis Stevenson* helped set off a backlash against Louis's work. Up-and-coming writers like Stephen Crane denounced him, and the modernist Joseph Conrad tried to distance himself from "airy R L Stevenson" even as he mined Louis's ideas for his own work. H. G. Wells derided Louis's romance writing as a "pitiful instance of the way in which wrong-headed flattery, a feminine book market, and a man's own talent may triumph over his genius."

Ironically, attempts by Fanny and Colvin to manage Louis's legacy helped secure his reputation as a "non-controversial writer of children's fiction," in the words of English literature scholar Linda Dryden. Louis became sentimentalized as a lovable eccentric and optimistic invalid, quoted on calendars and inspirational greeting cards. It was not until the 1950s that scholars began to recognize that the vast reach and majesty of his writing exceeded his boyhood tales.

Some might say that Louis's hometown has still not given its restless, wayward son the recognition he deserves. A Gothic-spired memorial to another native son, Walter Scott, has soared above Princes Street Gardens since it was erected twelve years after his death. The city honored the poet Robert Burns, who was not born in Edinburgh, with a memorial styled as a Neo-Greek temple in 1831. But it was not until 2013 that a four-foot statue depicting Robert Louis Stevenson as a boy sitting on a tree stump reading a book was unveiled in the suburb of Colinton Village. (A bronze cast of Augustus Saint-Gaudens's memorial was placed in St. Giles' Cathedral in 1911 and a statue of the author's *Kidnapped* heroes was erected in 2004.) Popular mystery writer Ian Rankin lobbied for the monument for years, crediting *Dr Jekyll and Mr Hyde* with inspiring him to write modern mystery novels.

Louis had written to J. M. Barrie that Fanny was "a violent friend, a brimstone enemy . . . always either loathed or slavishly adored; indifference impossible." In death, she continued to be a lightning rod, inspiring contradictory portraits by critics and biographers. Fanny's detractors have savaged her as a greedy woman who ruined Louis's friendships, destroyed and suppressed his work, and forced him into respectability. They have found traces of her in every one of Louis's unpleasant fictional female characters, and even in the duplicitous Edward Hyde. In a more thoughtful consideration of Fanny, author Joseph Farrell attributes such interpretations to "selective sympathy . . . whereby faults in the artist-hero are analysed and explained, but deficiencies in his partner are subject to absolute censure."

The common savaging of Fanny sells Louis short as well, reinforcing views of him as a lifelong adolescent who was cowed by his wife. In reality, Louis treated the woman he married neither as an angelic mother figure, like Frances Sitwell, nor as a Victorian doll, as Thomas regarded Margaret. Theirs was a creative partnership in all senses of the word. Some of the harsh views of Fanny as selfish or "difficult" fail to acknowledge the boldness of the relatively egalitarian project she and Louis were trying to make out of their love and marriage—one that anticipated the struggles and joys of later generations of bohemians, counterculturists, and feminists.

Colvin came around to write that Fanny's character was as strong and interesting as her husband's, and to praise her for being "an inseparable sharer of all his thoughts . . . the most open-hearted of friends to all who loved him, the most shrewd and stimulating critic of his work." In another time, Fanny might have hired a caregiver for her husband and devoted herself to pursuing her own career. But the version of marriage that the Stevensons conceived in the late nineteenth century allowed them to transcend some of the limitations imposed on Fanny as a Victorian woman and on Louis as a sickly man. Their partnership enabled each to lead a more adventurous and creative life than either could have without the other or in a more traditional marriage.

Without Fanny, there would be no Robert Louis Stevenson as we know him. Toward the end of his life, Louis publicly recognized his essential literary collaboration with his wife. In his dedication of the unfinished *Weir of Hermiston* to Fanny, he praised her not as a tender comrade or wife but as a creative partner whose steadfast support and sometimes harsh critiques yielded their shared triumph, the book he believed would be his masterpiece:

> Take thou the writing: thine it is. For who
> Burnished the sword, blew on the drowsy coal,
> Held still the target higher, chary of praise
> And prodigal of counsel—who but thou?
> So now, in the end, if this the least be good,
> If any deed be done, if any fire
> Burn in the imperfect page, the praise be thine.

The stories of Fanny and Robert Louis Stevenson are impossible to separate. The couple is forever frozen together in time like the entangled lovers in the Rodin statue that they carried with them around the world. Fanny once said that her husband taught her how to live. She made his life and art possible. In their manifold imperfections, Fanny and Louis were perfect for each other.

ACKNOWLEDGMENTS

Thanks, first and always, to my brilliant sister-in-law Margaret Talbot, who made this book possible in more ways than I can count. Margaret introduced me to Fanny, the remarkable woman who inspired this book, and was by my side to the end, as a sensitive reader, astute editorial adviser, and tireless cheerleader. I can't imagine having written the book without her.

I am grateful for the wonderful team at Viking Penguin who shepherded this book into print. My special thanks to Amber Qureshi, who saw that the Stevensons' story could resonate with a generation of readers more than a century later; Paul Slovak, for his sensitive and rigorous editing; Allie Merola, whose discerning judgment and lively enthusiasm kept the book happily afloat to the end; and Jason Ramirez, for designing a beautiful book cover that could not fail to invite readers inside. No one could hope for a more loyal agent than Kristine Dahl, at Creative Artists Agency, who was with me in the trenches with unwavering support.

One of the happiest rewards of my research was recovering some of Fanny's long-forgotten published writing from the dust heaps where it had been buried for 150 years. Fortunately, Lena Wånngren at the University of Edinburgh was on the same mission. Many thanks to Lena for sharing her discoveries and thoughts about Fanny with me.

Roger Swearingen provided the heartiest welcome into the Robert Louis Stevenson community that a newcomer could hope for and remained an ever enthusiastic and erudite guide. Richard Dury's generosity and prodigious scholarship was most helpful. Special thanks also to Stevenson scholars Linda Dryden, Hillary J. Beattie, Alison Frances, Gillian Hughes, and Duncan Milne for their time and rich insights; and to the Robert Louis Stevenson Club of Edinburgh, which staged for me a lively luncheon debate over Fanny Stevenson's suitability as a mate for RLS.

I am grateful to the late Professor Francis Parker of Ball State University for sharing his vast knowledge of Indiana transportation and railroad history, which helped me visualize Fanny's "escape" to Indianapolis with her children. Maritime historian Richard Brouwer provided me with details that recalled the look and feel of New York harbor when Fanny and Louis arrived there in 1887.

It was pure serendipity to discover that Nancy Everett, the great niece of Fanny's close friend Dora Williams, had not only written an article about her ancestor, but lived just a few blocks from my home in San Francisco. We chatted in Everett's kitchen over coffee one afternoon, much as Fanny and Dora must have done in this city a century and a half ago.

In following the Stevensons' trail from Scotland to Samoa, Nat Talbot and Ruth Henrich were the best of travel companions. In Edinburgh, John and Felicitas MacFie were most accommodating hosts at the Stevenson House. John MacFie was an excellent guide to RLS's life, and the opportunity to stay in the author's childhood home helped me imagine him as a boy playing in the nursery and as a young man sneaking in through the back door at night.

In Grez-sur-Loing, many thanks to Christina Backman and Bernadette Plissard of the Hasselblad Foundation for procuring permission for me to stay at Hôtel Chevillon, the lodging where Fanny and Louis met and which is now a residency program for artists from around the world. In the U.S., I am grateful to Andy and Susan Howard, whose generosity allowed me many quiet writing hours in their little "garret" in Nevada City.

I am indebted to the enthusiastic efforts of many librarians and archivists. Thanks to Marissa Schleicher and Barret Dahl for making the Robert Louis Stevenson Museum in St. Helena, California, an essential resource and a cool oasis of calm for researchers. In Indiana, Reann Poray at the Plainfield-Guilford Township Public Library, Dagny Villegas at the Indianapolis Public Library, and Andrea Glenn at the Indiana Division of the Indiana State Library supplied me with handwritten letters, photos, and other documents related to Fanny's early life there. History curator Denise Brace warmed up a blustery afternoon of research in the turret of the wonderful Writers' Museum in Edinburgh with her high spirits and cups of hot tea. The staff of the Robert Louis Stevenson Museum, in the couple's former home in Apia, Samoa, was particularly helpful in expanding my knowledge of the nation's culture and history.

Thanks as well to the Beinecke Rare Book and Manuscript Library at Yale University, which is a Stevenson scholar's dream, as well as the National Library of Scotland, the Bancroft Library at the University of California at Berkeley, the Berg Collection at New York Public Library, and the San Francisco History Center at San Francisco Public Library.

I am indebted to Dr. Cynthia Talbot, psychotherapist Samuel Chase, and medical historian Helen Bynum for their expertise and understanding of physical and psychological conditions and treatments in the age before aspirin, antibiotics, and Freud. Author and therapist Beverly Burch provided additional insights.

Thanks to Dylan Weir for chasing down suicide clubs and to Emily and Sue Peri for tech assistance and patiently transcribing the Stevensons' nearly illegible handwriting.

Warmest thanks to the friends and fellow writers who made this book better just by being there. To Connie Matthiessen, my barometer for good storytelling; to Gary Kamiya, for his knowledge and boundless enthusiasm; and to Ruth Henrich, for letting me talk incessantly about Fanny and Louis as if they were our friends. I'm also grateful for the patience, suggestions, and support of Carla Sorey-Reed, Quincy McCoy, Louise Rubacky, Cheryl Nardi, Linda Khatami, Jim Khatami, Richard Ravin, Carol Baum, Margaret Weir, Karen Croft, Paula Spencer Scott, Mark Schapiro, Zoe Fitzgerald Carter, Marc Bruno, Judith Pollock, and Olivia Gatwood.

As with many books, writing this one was more of a marathon than a sprint. I am eternally grateful to Hope Rugo for getting me across the finish line.

I could not have asked for a better family to cheer me on. Cynthia Talbot's warmth and wisdom kept me together during some challenging times. The generosity of Don Peri, Sue Peri, Arthur Allen, and Margaret Talbot gave me a way forward. Thanks also to Teri Peri, Bob Peri, Stephen Talbot, Pippa Gordon, and Dave Davis for their good humor and support, and to my many nieces and nephews, whose interest in Fanny and Louis showed me that their story is inspirational to young people and anyone seeking a creative life.

Finally, I am grateful to my immediate family—my husband, David, and my sons, Nat and Joe, who were always there to listen, give advice, rub a sore shoulder, and provide the right word at just the right time. Joe's great heart, matched only by his dreams, always buoyed me. Nat's warmth and help, as a research assistant and photographer, kept our travels fresh and fun, and his moral strength kept me going when the hill got steep.

I'm forever grateful to David for his wise counsel, sharp editorial judgment, irrepressible good humor, encouragement, and occasional gentle prodding when, like RLS's donkey Modestine, I sometimes stalled in my tracks.

NOTES

ONE

8 "as if all the water-spouts": "Flood Notes," *Danville Union*, August 5, 1875, 3.

8 "The aggressive female": Fanny Vandegrift Stevenson (hereafter FVS) to Dora Williams, August 25, 1875, Edwin J. Beinecke Collection of Robert Louis Stevenson, Beinecke Rare Book and Manuscript Library, Yale University, New Haven, Connecticut. Fanny's ride is based on her account in letters as well as contemporary and historical accounts of the flood.

9 "the lady who drove": FVS to Williams, August 25, 1875, Beinecke Collection.

11 "Oh but that was romantic": Fanny Vandegrift Stevenson, "A Backwoods Childhood," quoted in Nellie Van de Grift Sanchez, *The Life of Mrs. Robert Louis Stevenson* (Fairfield, CA: James Stevenson, 2001), 13.

11 "Laid up in the trunks": Fanny Vandegrift Stevenson, "A Backwoods Childhood: Early Recollections of a Noted Woman," *Scranton Republican*, August 26, 1893, 3. See also Mrs. Robert Louis Stevenson, "A Backwoods Childhood," *The Woman at Home*, vol. 1, 1894.

11 "Fanny was what": Sanchez, *Life of Mrs. Robert Louis Stevenson*, 14–15.

12 "made money easily": Sanchez, *Life of Mrs. Robert Louis Stevenson*, 7.

12 "He had a hasty": Sanchez, *Life of Mrs. Robert Louis Stevenson*, 8.

12 "ready, like Dickens's": Vandegrift Stevenson, "A Backwoods Childhood," quoted in Sanchez, *Life of Mrs. Robert Louis Stevenson*, 21.

13 "often totally unsuited": Sanchez, *Life of Mrs. Robert Louis Stevenson*, 326.

13 "But when I looked": Vandegrift Stevenson, "A Backwoods Childhood," *Scranton Republican*, 3.

13 "stuffed with the": Vandegrift Stevenson, "A Backwoods Childhood," *Scranton Republican*, 3.

13 "With the skull-cap": Vandegrift Stevenson, "A Backwoods Childhood," *Scranton Republican*, 3.

14 "told every incident": Sanchez, *Life of Mrs. Robert Louis Stevenson*, 19–20.

14 "Fanny was always": Sanchez, *Life of Mrs. Robert Louis Stevenson*, 21.

14 "That heaven was": Fanny Van de Grift Stevenson, "At the Undertaker's: Early Recollections of a Noted Woman," *Philadelphia Inquirer*, September 3,1893, 23.

14 "N——, n——, never": FVS to Margaret Stevenson, October 21, 1882, Robert Louis Stevenson Museum Collection, St. Helena, California.

14 "She is that color": Sanchez, *Life of Mrs. Robert Louis Stevenson*, 14.

14 "piquant prettiness": Sanchez, *Life of Mrs. Robert Louis Stevenson*, 22.

15 "They looked like": Sanchez, *Life of Mrs. Robert Louis Stevenson*, 24.

15 "a honeymoon child": Isobel Field, *This Life I've Loved* (Lafayette, CA: Great West Books, 2005), 36.

16 "Perhaps, Jo, we": FVS to Josephine Marshall, April 1864, quoted in Alexandra Lapierre, *Fanny Stevenson: Muse, Adventuress and Romantic Enigma*, trans. Carol Cosman (London: Fourth Estate, 1995), 20. Fanny addressed Josephine as "Joe," but "Jo" is used in this book to avoid confusion with Fanny's son-in-law, Joe Strong.

17 "Believe me": FVS to Marshall, April 1864, quoted in Lapierre, *Fanny Stevenson*, 20.

17 "the riff-raff": FVS to Marshall, April 1864, quoted in Lapierre, *Fanny Stevenson*, 20.

18 "plenty of time": Sam Osbourne to Josephine Marshall, Stevenson Museum Collection.

19 "Beef and bread": Mrs. R. L. Stevenson, "Life Abroad—The Far West," *Queen*, March 31, 1894, 59.

20 "They would divide": Field, *This Life I've Loved*, 6.

22 "Often we felt": Mark Twain, *Roughing It* (New York: Signet Classics, 1962), 229.

22 "literally alive with": Mary McNair Mathews, *Ten Years in Nevada* (Buffalo: Baker, Jones and Co., 1880), 196. (Library of Congress facsimile.)

22 "doing splendidly": Sam Osbourne to Jacob Vandegrift, undated, quoted in Lapierre, *Fanny Stevenson*, 57.

23 "I am sure I wouldn't": FVS and Sam Osbourne to Josephine Marshall, 1865, Stevenson Family File, Plainfield-Guilford Township Public Library, Plainfield, Indiana.

23 "live after the Salt Lake": Mathews, *Ten Years in Nevada*, 193.

23 "You spoke of": FVS to Josephine Marshall, 1868, Stevenson Family File, Plainfield-Guilford Library.

Two

26 "There were bright": Isobel Field, *This Life I've Loved* (Lafayette, CA: Great West Books, 2005), 21.

27 "with a bare chest": Field, *This Life I've Loved*, 17.

27 "My mother (at the cost": Field, *This Life I've Loved*, 19.

27 "My mother, in her black": Field, *This Life I've Loved*, 20.

27 "crazily in love": Timothy Rearden to his mother and sister, June 18, 1880, Baeck Family Papers, The Bancroft Library, University of California, Berkeley, California.

29 "Your letter, containing": Sam Osbourne to Jacob Vandegrift, February 28, 1867, Stevenson Family File, Plainfield-Guilford Library.

29 "I am sure you will none": FVS to Jake Vandegrift, 1867, Stevenson Family File, Plainfield-Guilford Library.

29 "I remember when": FVS to Josephine Marshall, October 1867, Stevenson Family File, Plainfield-Guilford Library.

29 "Someone is always": FVS to Josephine Marshall, June 21, 1867, Stevenson Family File, Plainfield-Guilford Library.

30 "It is very showy": FVS, letter fragment, 1868, Stevenson Family File, Plainfield-Guilford Library.

30 "I am sure my father": Field, *This Life I've Loved*, 32–33.

30 "glorious walks": Field, *This Life I've Loved*, 34.

30 "That I should": FVS to Josephine Marshall, 1867, Stevenson Family File, Plainfield-Guilford Library.

30 "You don't know": Sam Osbourne to Jacob Vandegrift, February 28, 1867, Stevenson Family File, Plainfield-Guilford Library.

30 "If he had gone": Sam Osbourne to Jake Vandegrift, 1867, Stevenson Family File, Plainfield-Guilford Library.

31 "Wasn't that thoughtful": FVS to Josephine Marshall, October 1867, Stevenson Family File, Plainfield-Guilford Library.

31 "I think it flatters me": FVS to Josephine Marshall, June 21, 1867, Stevenson Family File, Plainfield-Guilford Library.

31 "that fit exactly": FVS to Jake Vandegrift, 1867, Stevenson Family File, Plainfield-Guilford Library.

31 "Your little child": FVS to Marshall, October 1867, Stevenson Family File, Plainfield-Guilford Library.

33 "young and slender": Nellie Van de Grift Sanchez, *The Life of Mrs. Robert Louis Stevenson* (Fairfield, CA: James Stevenson, 2001), 36.

33 "Of all the lovely gardens": Field, *This Life I've Loved*, 49.

33 "My mother influenced": Sanchez, *Life of Mrs. Robert Louis Stevenson*, 39.

33 "made me look still darker": Sanchez, *Life of Mrs. Robert Louis Stevenson*, 38.

34 "home was a pleasant": Field, *This Life I've Loved*, 36.

35 "a little tiger lily!": Sanchez, *Life of Mrs. Robert Louis Stevenson*, 14.

35 "Fanny's temper drove": Margaret Mackay, *The Violent Friend* (London: J. M. Dent & Sons, 1968), 12.

35 "the grand manner": Field, *This Life I've Loved*, 31.

35 "I never saw": Roy Morris Jr., *Declaring His Genius: Oscar Wilde in North America* (Cambridge, MA: Harvard University Press, 2013), 140.

36 "I never understood": Field, *This Life I've Loved*, 63.

36 "My father of course": Field, *This Life I've Loved*, 66.

37 "rather pleasant and lucrative": Nancy Everett, "Dora Norton Williams: A New England Yankee in San Francisco Bohemia," *Argonaut* 21, no. 1 (Spring 2010): 78.

37 "a frankness that": Field, *This Life I've Loved*, 69.

38 "features cut like": Field, *This Life I've Loved*, 69–70.

39 "I know he is peculiar": FVS to Dora Williams, November 1881, Beinecke Collection.

39 "Come and see me": FVS to Timothy Rearden, September 18, 1874, Stevenson Museum Collection.

39 "**When you marry**": FVS to Timothy Rearden, November 1874, Stevenson Museum Collection.

39 "**beautiful cultured blonde**": Anna Rearden Baeck's account of the life of her father, Timothy Rearden, Baeck Family Papers, Bancroft Library. In the Stevenson biography *Myself and the Other Fellow*, author Claire Harman suggests that Rearden was homosexual.

40 "**I came to make a friendly call**": Field, *This Life I've Loved*, 37.

THREE

43 "**After many moving**": FVS to Dora Williams, August 25, 1875, Beinecke Collection.

43 "**I watched for**": FVS to Williams, August 25, 1875, Beinecke Collection.

44 "**When in any difficulty**": Isobel Field, *This Life I've Loved* (Lafayette, CA: Great West Books, 2005), 71.

44 "**We hardly seem**": FVS to Williams, August 25, 1875, Beinecke Collection.

44 "**a city that**": FVS to Timothy Rearden, December 1875, Stevenson Museum Collection.

45 "**One of them**": FVS to Dora Williams, October 1875, Beinecke Collection.

45 "**I must say**": FVS to Dora Williams, December 1875, Beinecke Collection.

46 "**flaring gas jets**": Émile Zola, *Nana* (Oxford: Oxford University Press, 2009), 179.

46 "**crowded to suffocation**": FVS to Timothy Rearden, December 14, 1875, Stevenson Museum Collection.

46 "**He is excessively**": FVS to Rearden, December 14, 1875, Stevenson Museum Collection.

46 "**innocent, natural, and truthful**": FVS to Williams, December 1875, Beinecke Collection.

46 "**a tall willowy creature**": Field, *This Life I've Loved*, 83.

47 "**rose up and looked**": FVS to Rearden, December 14, 1875, Stevenson Museum Collection.

47 "**I have never**": Henry James, *Parisian Sketches: Letters to the New York Tribune 1875–1876*, Leon Edel and Ilsa Dusoir Lind, eds. (New York: New York University Press, 1957), 39.

47 "**threatened with scrofulous**": FVS to Rearden, December 14, 1875, Stevenson Museum Collection.

48 "**I am sure you will**": FVS to Rearden, December 14, 1875, Stevenson Museum Collection.

48 "**I have given**": FVS to Timothy Rearden, February 1876, Stevenson Museum Collection.

48 "**We are very poor**": FVS to Dora Williams, February 1876, Beinecke Collection.

48 "**The ladies at**": FVS to Rearden, February 1876, Stevenson Museum Collection.

48 "**It does not seem**": FVS to Rearden, February 1876, Stevenson Museum Collection.

49 "**We were miserably**": Lloyd Osbourne, "How I First Saw Stevenson," in Sidney Colvin et al., *Robert Louis Stevenson: His Work and His Personality* (London: Hodder and Stoughton, 1924), 33.

49 "Our poor little boy": Sam Osbourne to Timothy Rearden, April 5, 1876, Baeck Family Papers, Bancroft Library.

49 "I did not dare": FVS to Timothy Rearden, April 18, 1876, Stevenson Museum Collection.

51 "Even after all": Lloyd Osbourne, "How I First Saw Stevenson," 33.

52 "She grew paler": Field, *This Life I've Loved*, 87.

52 "I felt so light": FVS to Timothy Rearden, September 18, 1875, Stevenson Museum Collection.

52 "must be tired lying": FVS to Rearden, April 18, 1876, Stevenson Museum Collection.

FOUR

53 "From the morning": Robert Louis Stevenson (hereafter, RLS) to Bob Stevenson, March 29, 1870, *The Letters of Robert Louis Stevenson*, Bradford A. Booth and Ernest Mehew, eds., 8 vols. (New Haven and London: Yale University Press, 1994–95), 1: 193. Hereafter, *Letters*.

55 "Only a few inches": Robert Louis Stevenson, *Edinburgh: Picturesque Notes* (London: Palace Athene, 2001), 54–55.

55 "Her hair came down": Robert Louis Stevenson, "Old Mortality," *The Works of Robert Louis Stevenson*, South Seas Edition (New York: Charles Scribner's Sons, 1925), 13: 24.

55 "lean, ugly, idle": Robert Louis Stevenson, "Some College Memories," South Seas 13: 18.

55 "severe, monotonous, and lying": Stevenson, "Old Mortality," 25–26.

56 "Many winters, I": Robert Louis Stevenson, "Notes of Childhood," Beinecke Collection.

58 "the children of lovers": RLS to Frances Sitwell, January 11, 1875, *Letters*, 2: 103.

59 "I was sentimental": Robert Louis Stevenson, "Memoirs of Himself," South Seas 13: 281–82.

60 "waking from a dream": Stevenson, "Memoirs of Himself," 278.

60 "going about the town": Stevenson, "Notes of Childhood."

61 "ships in fleets": Robert Louis Stevenson, "The Land of Counterpane," *A Child's Garden of Verses* (San Francisco: Chronicle Books, 1989), 29.

61 "An opera is far more": RLS to Margaret Stevenson, August 5, 1872, *Letters*, 1: 243.

61 "The world was plain": Robert Louis Stevenson, "A Penny Plain, Twopence Coloured," South Seas 13: 120.

62 "We lived together": Stevenson, "Memoirs of Himself," 280.

62 "It is good": RLS to Margaret Stevenson, January 30, 1874, *Letters*, 1: 468.

63 "vanishing into the tunnel": Stevenson, *Edinburgh*, 119.

63 "You must understand": RLS to Margaret Stevenson, October 16, 1874, *Letters*, 2: 60.

63 "he heard the noise": John Henry Nash, *Stevenson's Baby Book* (San Francisco: John Howell, 1922), 51. (Printed on demand from Leopold Classic Library.)

64 "if he was bright": Graham Balfour, *The Life of Robert Louis Stevenson* (London: Methuen and Co., 1906), 55. (Kessinger Rare Reprints.)

64 "butt of the school": Rosaline Masson, ed., *I Can Remember Robert Louis Stevenson* (Edinburgh: W. & R. Chambers, 1922), 3.

64 "In body, Stevenson": Henry Bellyse Baildon, *Robert Louis Stevenson: A Life Study in Criticism* (London: Chatto & Windus, 1901), 20.

65 "In a pleasant": Robert Louis Stevenson, "Beggars," South Seas 13: 188.

65 "He touched on nothing": Robert Louis Stevenson, "Pastoral," South Seas 13: 54.

66 "Novels begin to touch": Stevenson, "Pastoral," 57.

66 "He had made a story": Balfour, *The Life of Robert Louis Stevenson*, 67–68.

67 "part of a mangle": RLS to Aeneas Mackay, June 1881, *Letters*, 3: 200.

67 "an extensive and highly rational": Stevenson, "Some College Memories," 21.

67 "It's quite useless": Claire Harman, *Myself and the Other Fellow* (New York: HarperCollins, 2005), 66–67.

67 "so narrow that": Stevenson, *Edinburgh*, 22.

68 "family after family": Stevenson, *Edinburgh*, 29.

68 "wilderness of square-cut stone": *The Complete Works of John Ruskin* (London: George Allen, 1904), 12: 62.

69 "continually changed by the action": Balfour, *The Life of Robert Louis Stevenson*, 84.

69 "great-haunched, blue-eyed": Robert Louis Stevenson, autobiographical fragment, National Library of Scotland.

69 "beset by fleshly frailties": Sidney Colvin, *Memories and Notes of Persons and Places* (New York: Charles Scribner's Sons, 1921), 101.

69 "was a loose fish": Papers of Sir Graham Balfour, National Library of Scotland.

70 "I give her posterity": RLS to Maud Babington, November 26, 1870, *Letters*, 1: 208.

70 "precocious, interesting, affected": Rosaline Masson, *Life of Robert Louis Stevenson* (New York: Frederick A. Stokes, 1923), 46–47.

70 "how I feared": RLS to Charles Baxter, September 6, 1888, *Letters*, 6: 207.

70 "Thus I lived with words": Robert Louis Stevenson, "A College Magazine," South Seas 13: 34.

70 "I have thus played": Stevenson, "A College Magazine," South Seas 13: 35.

71 "but *I cannot trust myself*": RLS to Bob Stevenson, October 22, 1868, *Letters*, 1: 166.

71 "My daily life": RLS to Bob Stevenson, November 17, 1868, *Letters*, 1: 169.

FIVE

73 "had in him a reserve": Robert Louis Stevenson, *Records of a Family of Engineers* (n.p.: Perfect Library, 2015), 32.

74 "I am utterly sick": RLS to Margaret Stevenson, July 28, 1868, *Letters*, 1: 136.

74 "Some twenty rounds"; "like an intoxicated sparrow": Robert Louis Stevenson, "The Education of an Engineer," *The Works of Robert Louis Stevenson*, South Seas Edition (New York: Charles Scribner's Sons, 1925), 13: 222–24.

75 "framed in the round bull's-eye": Robert Louis Stevenson, "Memoirs of an Islet," South Seas 13: 67.

75 "thought divers, that have been": Andrew Delbanco, *Melville* (New York: Vintage Books, 2005), 14.

76 "I owned I cared for": RLS to George Iles, October 29, 1887, *Letters*, 6: 47.

76 "Tom wonderfully resigned": Margaret Stevenson diary entry, April 8, 1871, quoted in *Letters*, 1: 209.

76 "I was at last able": Graham Balfour, *The Life of Robert Louis Stevenson* (London: Methuen and Co., 1906), 90. (Kessinger Rare Reprints.)

77 "radiant and soaring intelligence": Sir Walter Alexander Raleigh, *Milton* (London: Edward Arnold, 1915), Dedication, ii.

77 "a mask which he wore": William H. O'Donnell and Douglas N. Archibald, eds., *The Collected Works of W. B. Yeats* (New York: Scribner, 1999), 3: 126.

77 "changed like the patterns": Balfour, *The Life of Robert Louis Stevenson*, 87.

77 "absurd acts for the sake": Balfour, *The Life of Robert Louis Stevenson*, 93.

78 "Suddenly the man's eye": Balfour, *The Life of Robert Louis Stevenson*, 94.

78 "We did not look for Louis": Charles Guthrie, *Robert Louis Stevenson: Some Personal Recollections* (Edinburgh: W. Green & Son, 1924), 31.

78 "a slim and graceful spaniel": Rosaline Masson, ed., *I Can Remember Robert Louis Stevenson* (Edinburgh: W. & R. Chambers, 1922), 101.

79 "almost uncomfortably brilliant": Masson, *I Can Remember Robert Louis Stevenson*, 127.

79 "There kept growing": *Letters*, 1: 36.

79 "red-hot socialist": Robert Louis Stevenson, "Crabbed Age and Youth," in Jeremy Treglown, ed., *The Lantern-Bearers and Other Essays* (New York: Farrar, Straus & Giroux, 1988), 61.

80 "tumbled the world": Robert Louis Stevenson, "Books Which Have Influenced Me," in William Lyon Phelps, ed., *Essays of Robert Louis Stevenson* (New York: Charles Scribner's Sons, 1906), 139. (Pinnacle Press reprint.)

80 "ignore everything that": Claire Harman, *Myself and the Other Fellow* (New York: HarperCollins, 2005), 79.

81 "as I have done": RLS to Charles Baxter, February 2, 1873, *Letters*, 1: 273.

81 "my heart stirred": Robert Louis Stevenson, "Edifying Letters of the Rutherford Family," in Roger G. Swearingen, ed., *A Newly Discovered Long Story, an Old Song, and a Previously Unpublished Short Story, Edifying Letters of the Rutherford Family* (Hamden, CT: Archon Books, 1982), 86.

81 "a man of unfortunate temperament": E. V. Lucas, *The Colvins and Their Friends* (New York: Charles Scribner's Sons, 1928), 64.

82 "unmistakable young genius": Masson, *I Can Remember Robert Louis Stevenson*, 88.

82 "But this new Scottish youth": *Notices of the Proceedings at the Meetings of the Members of the Royal Institution of Great Britain with Abstracts of the Discourses Delivered at the Evening Meetings, Volume 20*; Meeting of February 10, 1911.

82 "fast friend": Masson, *I Can Remember Robert Louis Stevenson*, 88.

83 "He said tonight": RLS to Frances Sitwell, September 22, 1873, *Letters*, 1: 312.

83 "[Bob] said if I were": RLS to Frances Sitwell, October 2, 1873, *Letters*, 1: 328–29.

83 "already heavily over-strained": Sidney Colvin, *Memories and Notes of Persons and Places, 1852–1912* (New York: Charles Scribner's Sons, 1921), 105.

84 "like an enthusiast": Robert Louis Stevenson, "Ordered South," in Robert-Louis Abrahamson, ed., *Essays I: Virginibus Puerisque and Other Papers, The Works of*

Robert Louis Stevenson, New Edinburgh Edition (Edinburgh: Edinburgh University Press, 2018), 55.

84 "The first violet": RLS to Frances Sitwell, December 7, 1873, *Letters*, 1: 401.

84 "I had a day": RLS to Sitwell, December 7, 1873, *Letters*, 1, 402.

85 "struggle to keep from liquor": RLS to Bob Stevenson, December 1, 1874, *Letters*, 2: 86.

86 "*poseur*": Henry James to T. S. Perry, September 14, 1879, in Leon Edel, ed., *The Letters of Henry James* (Cambridge, MA: Belknap Press, 1975), 2: 255.

86 "a mere club fizzle": RLS to William Henley, February/March 1881, *Letters*, 3: 159.

86 "more like a lass": Andrew Lang, *Adventures Among Books* (New York and Bombay: Longmans, Green and Co., 1905), 51.

86 "la-de-dady Oxford": R. C. Terry, ed., *Robert Louis Stevenson: Interviews and Recollections* (Iowa City: University of Iowa Press, 1996), 57.

86 "possessed more than any man": Lang, *Adventures Among Books*, 51.

86 "at first sight": Colvin, *Memories and Notes*, 101.

87 "He was simply bubbling": Edmund Gosse, *Critical Kit-Kats* (London: William Heinemann, 1900), 279.

87 "with his legs thrown sideways": Gosse, *Critical Kit-Kats*, 281.

87 "he alone kept dancing": Gosse, *Critical Kit-Kats*, 301.

87 "in all my humours": RLS to Sitwell, September 19, 1873, *Letters*, 1: 304.

88 "I would not give up": RLS to Frances Sitwell, May 1, 1874, *Letters*, 2: 3.

88 "masculine combustions": Lucas, *Colvins and Their Friends*, 341.

88 "I can think of nothing": RLS to Sitwell, May 1, 1874, *Letters*, 2: 3.

89 "some one from whom": RLS to Fanny Stevenson, January 11, 1875, *Letters*, 2: 103.

89 "Louis breaks down": RLS to Frances Sitwell, March 7, 1875, *Letters*, 2: 123, fn 1.

89 "'going in' for literature": Will H. Low, *Chronicle of Friendships* (New York: Charles Scribner's Sons, 1908), 52.

90 "They had come from London": Robert Louis Stevenson and Lloyd Osbourne, *The Wrecker, The Novels and Tales of Robert Louis Stevenson* (New York: Charles Scribner's Sons, 1918), 10: 67.

91 "aghast": RLS to Frances Sitwell, September 12, 1873, *Letters*, 1: 299.

91 "Stick in": RLS to Bob Stevenson, September 1874, *Letters*, 2: 55.

91 "physical and moral endurance": Robert Louis Stevenson, "My First Book," in Treglown, *Lantern-Bearers and Other Essays*, 278.

92 "All eloquence & balls": William Ernest Henley, "Ballade, R.L.S.," in Edward H. Cohen, *The Henley-Stevenson Quarrel* (Gainesville: University of Florida, 1974), 18.

92 "Out of the night": William Ernest Henley, "Invictus," in John Connell, *W. E. Henley* (London: Constable and Company, 1949), 4.

93 "like a man gone": Masson, *I Can Remember Robert Louis Stevenson*, 65.

93 "Accept my hearty congratulations": Balfour, *The Life of Robert Louis Stevenson*, 119.

94 "I don't know but that": RLS to Frances Sitwell, January 7, 1876, *Letters*, 2: 170.

94 "If you were to ask": RLS to Frances Sitwell, July 9, 1876, *Letters*, 2: 176.

94 "a leaf on a river": "A Retrospect," *The Works of Robert Louis Stevenson*, Vailima Edition (New York: Peter Fenelon Collier, 1912), 9: 295.

SIX

95 "played out": Margaret B. Wright, "Bohemian Days," *Scribner's Monthly*, May 1878, 125.

95 "afoot and light-hearted": Walt Whitman, "Song of the Open Road," Poetry Foundation. Accessed online: poetryfoundation.org/poems/48859/song-of-the -open-road.

96 "pleasing voice, moderate": Robert Louis Stevenson, "Virginibus Puerisque," in Robert-Louis Abrahamson, *Essays I: Virginibus Puerisque and Other Papers, The Works of Robert Louis Stevenson*, New Edinburgh Edition (Edinburgh: Edinburgh University Press, 2018), 7–9 and 13.

96 "of the right sort": Will H. Low, *Chronicle of Friendships* (New York: Charles Scribner's Sons, 1908), 185.

97 "I was helping": FVS to Timothy Rearden, June 1876, Stevenson Museum Collection.

97 "Though she shed": Isobel Field, *This Life I've Loved* (Lafayette, CA: Great West Books, 2005), 91.

97 "that escapes geographical definition": Low, *Chronicles of Friendships*, 176.

98 "He smiled pleasantly": Lloyd Osbourne, Introduction, *The Works of Robert Louis Stevenson*, Vailima Edition (New York: Peter Fenelon Collier, 1912), 1: xii.

98 "melted the heart": Field, *This Life I've Loved*, 94.

98 "Talk about women": FVS to Timothy Rearden, July 25, 1876, Stevenson Museum Collection.

98 "where the greatest latitude": Low, *Chronicle of Friendships*, 146.

98 "They don't think so here": FVS to Timothy Rearden, July 7, 1876, Stevenson Museum Collection.

98 "the leader of a great": Birge Harrison, "With Stevenson at Grez," *Century Magazine*, December 1916, 93: 312.

99 "a sort of surprised admiration": Field, *This Life I've Loved*, 94.

100 "eyes of gold": Robert Louis Stevenson, "My Wife," in Roger C. Lewis, ed., *The Collected Poems of Robert Louis Stevenson* (Edinburgh: Edinburgh University Press, 2003), 184.

100 "Her face startled him": Robert Louis Stevenson, "The Story of a Lie," in Barry Menikoff, ed., *The Complete Stories of Robert Louis Stevenson* (New York: Modern Library, 2002), 671.

100 "It had never": Robert Louis Stevenson, *The Beach of Falesá*, in Barry Menikoff, ed., *Robert Louis Stevenson and "The Beach of Falesá": A Study in Victorian Publishing*, Original Text (Stanford: Stanford University Press, 1984), 125.

100 "the day when I looked": RLS to FVS, May 15, 1888, *Letters*, 6: 186.

100 "Her eyes took hold": Robert Louis Stevenson, "Olalla," in Menikoff, *Complete Stories*, 440.

100 "We have been living": FVS to Rearden, July 25, 1876, Stevenson Museum Collection.

101 "Art and life": Low, *Chronicle of Friendships*, 151.

101 "the respectable and well-to-do": Lloyd Osbourne, *An Intimate Portrait of R. L. S.* (New York: Charles Scribner's Sons, 1924), 3–4.

102 "There is a young Scotchman": Nellie Van de Grift Sanchez, *The Life of Mrs. Robert Louis Stevenson* (Fairfield, CA: James Stevenson, 2001), 48.

102 "These parts don't seem": Sanchez, *Life of Mrs. Robert Louis Stevenson*, 48.

102 "R L S always paid children": Osbourne, *Intimate Portrait*, 2.

102 "I can manage a canoe": FVS to Rearden, July 25, 1876, Stevenson Museum Collection.

103 "the sighting of a pistol": Margaret Mackay, *The Violent Friend* (London: J. M. Dent & Sons, 1968), photo insert caption.

103 "[Louis] has turned out": Isobel Field to unnamed friend, September 1876, excerpt, *Letters*, 2: 185.

104 "ever so much better": Sanchez, *Life of Mrs. Robert Louis Stevenson*, 48.

104 "the wittiest man": FVS to Timothy Rearden, April 11, 1877, and December 13, 1877, Stevenson Museum Collection.

104 "As long as [Louis] was": Sidney Colvin, *Memories and Notes of Persons and Places 1852–1912* (New York: Charles Scribner's Sons, 1921), 105.

104 "The air penetrates": Robert Louis Stevenson, "Forest Notes," *The Works of Robert Louis Stevenson*, Swanston Edition, 23: 106. (FQ Books facsimile.)

105 "The love I hold": Robert Louis Stevenson, "Know you the river near to Grez" in Lewis, *Collected Poems*, 268.

105 "On the stream": Robert Louis Stevenson, "Mine eyes were swift to know thee," in Stuart Campbell, *RLS in Love: The Love Poetry of Robert Louis Stevenson* (Dingwall, UK: Sandstone Press, 2009), 91.

105 "damnably in love": RLS to Charles Baxter, November 1876, *Letters*, 2: 197.

106 "illogical adventure": Robert Louis Stevenson, "On Falling in Love," in Robert-Louis Abrahamson, ed., *Essays I: Virginibus Puerisque and Other Papers*, *The Works of Robert Louis Stevenson*, New Edinburgh Edition (Edinburgh: Edinburgh University Press, 2018), 21.

106 "You must have nothing": FVS to Timothy Rearden, December 13, 1877, Stevenson Museum Collection.

106 "The ideal story": Stevenson, "On Falling in Love," 45.

107 "wholly . . . unalterably": Stevenson, "Mine eyes were swift to know thee," 91.

107 "The day when I came": RLS to FVS, May 15, 1888, *Letters*, 6: 186.

107 "Bob and I both recognized": Low, *Chronicle of Friendships*, 194.

108 "Louis has confessed": William Henley to Charles Baxter, quoted in *Letters*, 4: 269.

108 "be-ribboned battlements": Robert Louis Stevenson, "Now bare to the beholder's eye," in Lewis, *Collected Poems*, 329–30.

108 "for we are fonder": Robert Louis Stevenson, "In the Latin Quarter: A Studio of Ladies," in Jeremy Treglown, ed., *The Lantern-Bearers and Other Essays* (New York: Farrar, Straus & Giroux, 1988), 55–57.

109 "passionate love": Stevenson, "On Falling in Love," 21.

110 "I don't expect": FVS to Timothy Rearden, October 28, 1876, Stevenson Museum Collection.

110 "gay, rollicking, dissipated": FVS to Rearden, April 11, 1877, Stevenson Museum Collection.

112 "Your account of the life": RLS to Lloyd Osbourne, no date, Stevenson Museum Collection.

112 "guiding her pen": FVS to Timothy Rearden, September 1876, Stevenson Museum Collection.

112 "One day I find her": RLS to Frances Sitwell, February 1878, *Letters*, 2: 244.

112 "When he begins to laugh": FVS to Timothy Rearden, February 1877, Stevenson Museum Collection.

113 "he would bend": FVS to Rearden, February 1877, Stevenson Museum Collection.

113 "I wonder if she remembers": Sanchez, *Life of Mrs. Robert Louis Stevenson*, 27. I believe Sanchez mistakenly ties Fanny's comment to another headline about Louise Mackay in Paris.

115 "so out of place": FVS to Timothy Rearden, November 27, 1877, Stevenson Museum Collection.

115 "Now I call that": FVS to Rearden, November 27, 1877, Stevenson Museum Collection.

115 "a very enthusiastic friend": RLS to Frances Sitwell, November 7, 1877, *Letters*, 2: 226.

115 "a miserable widower": RLS to William Henley, December 1877, *Letters*, 2: 227.

116 "The snow fell over Paris": Robert Louis Stevenson, "A Lodging for the Night," in Menikoff, *Complete Stories*, 186.

116 "He cannot escape!": Field, *This Life I've Loved*, Appendix, 325.

117 "Here's your story!": Field, *This Life I've Loved*, 324–25.

117 "I want coin": RLS to Sidney Colvin, January 1, 1878, *Letters*, 2: 233.

117 "one of the most perfect": Philip Gilbert Hamerton, review of "An Inland Voyage," *Academy*, June 1878, in Paul Maixner, ed., *Robert Louis Stevenson: The Critical Heritage* (London: Routledge & Kegan Paul, 1981), 56.

117 "You may paddle": Robert Louis Stevenson, *An Inland Voyage*, ed. Tom Thomas (San Francisco: Black Oyster, 2012), 110.

118 "Queen of Bohemia": Wright, "Bohemian Days," 126–27.

118 "the tenderest, dreamiest": Wright, "Bohemian Days," 127.

118 "ugly and coarse": Margaret Bertha Wright, "Housekeeping in Normandy," *Lippincott's*, July 1883, 32: 471.

119 "spared no trouble": Field, *This Life I've Loved*, 88.

119 "Can a man": RLS to Charles Baxter, June 26, 1878, *Letters*, 2: 257.

120 "was not free": Graham Balfour, *The Life of Robert Louis Stevenson* (London: Methuen and Co., 1906), 157. (Kessinger Rare Reprints.)

120 "This is the last": RLS to Charles Baxter, June 1878, *Letters*, 2: 256.

121 "'Hurry, my lad'": Fanny Van de Grift Stevenson, Preface to *New Arabian Nights*, *The Works of Robert Louis Stevenson*, Biographical Edition (New York: Charles Scribner's Sons, 1906), 16: viii.

121 "He said that in a tight": Osbourne, *Intimate Portrait*, 9.

121 "My eyes followed him": Osbourne, *Intimate Portrait*, 13.

SEVEN

122 **"not so much"**: Mrs. Robert Louis Stevenson, "Miss Pringle's Neighbors," *Scribner's Magazine*, June 1887, 700.

123 **"read to rags"**: Nellie Van de Grift Sanchez, "Guide Posts on My Way to Happiness," unpublished, Stevenson Museum Collection.

123 **"universal popularity"**: Lloyd Osbourne, *An Intimate Portrait of R. L. S.* (New York: Charles Scribner's Sons, 1924), 20.

123 **"a noted story-teller"**: Dora Williams, "How Stevenson Courted," *Indianapolis Journal*, January 6, 1889, 2.

124 **"away from the enemy"**: E. V. Lucas, *The Colvins and Their Friends* (New York: Charles Scribner's Sons, 1928), 113. In "The Tree and the Vine," an unpublished biography of Fanny, Elinor McIntire raised the possibility that Sam had removed the children from her custody. McIntire's manuscript is at the Stevenson Museum in St. Helena.

124 **"weak brain"**: Fanny Osbourne, "Easy Reading for an Old Bachelor: The Story of the Ravening Sheep," unpublished, Stevenson Museum Collection.

125 **"the first money I can get"**: FVS to Timothy Rearden, 1879, Stevenson Museum Collection.

125 **"didn't seem at *all glad*"**: James Pope Hennessy, *Robert Louis Stevenson* (New York: Simon & Schuster, 1974), 137.

126 **"a taste for ways"**: Robert Louis Stevenson, "The Suicide Club," in Barry Menikoff, ed., *The Complete Stories of Robert Louis Stevenson* (New York: Modern Library, 2002), 3.

126 **"latest convenience"**: Sarah Ames, "'The Suicide Club': Afterlives," *Journal of Stevenson Studies* 8 (2011): 151.

127 **"fairy London"**: Daniel Balderston, "Interviews with Borges. Buenos Aires, August–September 1978." Accessed online from Borges Center, University of Pittsburgh, borges.pitt.edu/sites/default/files/0818.pdf.

127 **"I think I shall die"**: RLS to William Henley, early September 1878, *Letters*, 2: 265.

128 **"the color of"**: Robert Louis Stevenson, *Travels with a Donkey in the Cévennes* (Evanston, IL: Northwest University Press, 1996), 148.

128 **"shaken together like a diamond"**: Stevenson, *Travels with a Donkey*, 129.

128 **"Lots of it"**: RLS to Bob Stevenson, April 1879, *Letters*, 2: 313.

128 **"determined under-jaw"**: Stevenson, *Travels with a Donkey*, 21.

128 **"breathing deeply and freely"**: Stevenson, *Travels with a Donkey*, 94.

128 **"between content and longing"**: Stevenson, *Travels with a Donkey*, 96. In *Footsteps: Adventures of a Romantic Biographer* (New York: Vintage Books, 1985). Richard Holmes pointed out that Louis wore the silver band on his wedding ring finger and suggested that the passage in his book was in essence a marriage proposal to Fanny.

130 **"at breakneck speed"**: Osbourne, *Intimate Portrait*, 14.

130 **"A smile was"**: Alexandra Lapierre, *Fanny Stevenson: Muse, Adventuress and Romantic Enigma*, trans. Carol Cosman (London: Fourth Estate, 1995), 251.

130 **"There were no class distinctions"**: Isobel Field, *This Life I've Loved* (Lafayette, CA: Great West Books, 2005), 108.

131 "fraternizing with male friends": Scott A. Shields, *Artists at Continent's End: The Monterey Peninsula Art Colony, 1875–1907* (Berkeley and Los Angeles: University of California Press, 2006), 266.

131 "amazing likenesses": Field, *This Life I've Loved*, 109.

132 "You'll never believe it": FVS to Timothy Rearden, 1879, Stevenson Museum Collection.

132 "The Chinese who are": F. M. Osbourne, "A Funeral in a Chinese Fishing-Camp," *Lippincott's Magazine*, May 1880, 620.

133 "The young woman's patient sorrow": Osbourne, "A Funeral in a Chinese Fishing-Camp," 622.

134 "no indelicacy or impropriety": Paul A. Kramer, "The Case of the 22 Lewd Chinese Women," *Slate*, April 23, 2012. Accessed online: slate.com/news-and -politics/2012/04/arizonas-immigration-law-at-the-supreme-court-lessons -for-s-b-1070-via-the-case-of-the-22-lewd-chinese-women.html.

135 "The ladies will": F. M. Osbourne, "Sargent's Rodeo," *Lippincott's Magazine*, January 1880, 9.

135 "The hitherto undivulged": Osbourne, "Sargent's Rodeo," 11–12.

135 "cool violet odors": Osbourne, "Sargent's Rodeo," 12, 18, and 20.

136 "'good form' now-a-days": Unsigned review of *Edinburgh: Picturesque Notes*, in *The Scotsman*, December 1878, in Paul Maixner, ed., *Robert Louis Stevenson: The Critical Heritage* (London: Routledge & Kegan Paul, 1981), 60.

137 "weakness, languor": RLS to Sidney Colvin, April 1879, *Letters*, 2: 315.

138 "I envy you": RLS to Edmund Gosse, July 28, 1879, *Letters*, 2: 330.

138 "maddest of enterprises": Edmund Gosse, *Critical Kit-Kats* (London: William Heinemann, 1900), 284.

139 "couldn't say no": William Henley to Charles Baxter, August 16, 1879, *Letters*, 3: 4–5.

139 "I don't yet know": RLS to Sidney Colvin, August 17, 1879, *Letters*, 3: 6.

139 "No man is of any": RLS to Sidney Colvin, August 20, 1879, *Letters*, 3: 9.

140 "I seem to have died": RLS to Sidney Colvin, August 6, 1879, *Letters*, 3: 2–3.

140 "worst of emigrant life": Robert Louis Stevenson, *The Amateur Emigrant*, Julia Reid, ed., *The Works of Robert Louis Stevenson*, New Edinburgh Edition (Edinburgh: Edinburgh University Press, 2018), 7.

141 "a family of cousins": Stevenson, *Amateur Emigrant*, 76.

141 "family men broken": Stevenson, *Amateur Emigrant*, 14.

141 "greedier for small delicacies": Stevenson, *Amateur Emigrant*, 62.

142 "picking their way": Stevenson, *Amateur Emigrant*, 27.

142 "grand gentlemen": Stevenson, *Amateur Emigrant*, 66.

142 "These land stowaways": Stevenson, *Amateur Emigrant*, 118.

142 "each respiration tasted": Stevenson, *Amateur Emigrant*, 46.

142 "One sees it is a new": RLS to Colvin, August 17, 1879, *Letters*, 3: 6.

143 "I could not sh-hush!": RLS to William Henley, August 18, 1879, *Letters*, 3: 6.

144 "Children fell, and were picked": Stevenson, *Amateur Emigrant*, 86.

144 "pleasant villages, carts": Stevenson, *Amateur Emigrant*, 88, 90.

145 "He was indeed strikingly": Stevenson, *Amateur Emigrant*, 89.

145 "Equality, though conceived": Stevenson, *Amateur Emigrant*, 99–100.

146 "Were they all": Stevenson, *Amateur Emigrant*, 111–12.

146 "I do my best": Stevenson, *Amateur Emigrant*, 109.
146 "They seemed never": Stevenson, *Amateur Emigrant*, 113.
146 "over whose own hereditary continent": Stevenson, *Amateur Emigrant*, 115.
147 "It was like meeting": Stevenson, *Amateur Emigrant*, 119.
148 "He looked ill": Osbourne, *Intimate Portrait*, 16.
148 "gay and full of banter": Elsie Noble Caldwell, *Last Witness for Robert Louis Stevenson* (Norman: University of Oklahoma Press, 1960), 10.
148 "This is not a letter": RLS to Charles Baxter, September 9, 1979, *Letters*, 3: 11–12.
149 "Bury me low": In Roger C. Lewis, ed., *The Collected Poems of Robert Louis Stevenson* (Edinburgh: Edinburgh University Press, 2003), 415. This was the earliest version of "Requiem," which is on Louis's tomb in Samoa.
149 "I am lying": RLS to Charles Baxter, September 24, 1879, *Letters*, 3: 13–14.
149 "in exelent health": Joe Strong to Sidney Colvin, October 11, 1879, *Letters*, 3: 17.
150 "strangely disturbing quality": Osbourne, *Intimate Portrait*, 20–21.
150 "so colorless and yet": Osbourne, *Intimate Portrait*, 21.
150 "I want to tell you": Osbourne, *Intimate Portrait*, 21–22.
151 "The only question": RLS to Charles Baxter, October 15, 1879, *Letters*, 3: 18.
151 "So you see": FVS to Rearden, 1879, Stevenson Museum Collection.

EIGHT

152 "could look right through you": Arthur L. Price, "Why One Woman Remembers Robert Louis Stevenson," *San Francisco Call*, June 21, 1908, 12.
152 "He had such": Anne Roller Issler, *Happier for His Presence* (Stanford: Stanford University Press, 1949), 11.
153 "I sling ink": Claire Harman, *Myself and the Other Fellow* (New York: HarperCollins, 2005), 189.
154 "by God, I'll starve here": RLS to Sidney Colvin, December 26, 1879, *Letters*, 3: 39.
154 "R.L.S. used to find": RLS to Sidney Colvin, January 18, 1880, *Letters*, 3: 45–46.
155 "Go on, Mrs. Carson": Price, "Why One Woman Remembers Robert Louis Stevenson," 12.
155 "an enchanting young lady": RLS to William Henley, late January 1880, *Letters*, 3: 55.
156 "this penniless foreigner": Elsie Noble Caldwell, *Last Witness for Robert Louis Stevenson* (Norman: University of Oklahoma Press, 1960), 10.
156 "To see a person": Bob Stevenson to RLS, January 11, 1879, Beinecke Collection,
156 "a burning fiery furnace": Bob Stevenson to RLS, undated, Beinecke Collection.
157 "burdened himself with": Sidney Colvin to Charles Baxter, December 22, 1879, *Letters*, 3: 38.
157 "It is absolutely necessary": William Henley to Sidney Colvin, January 2, 1880, *Letters*, 3: 40.
157 "Of course there is always": Colvin to Baxter, December 22, 1879, *Letters*, 3: 38.
157 "the high-water mark": J. A. Hammerton, *Stevensonia* (London: Grant Richards, 1903), 241.

157 "took possession of his mind": Robert Louis Stevenson, "The Story of a Lie," in Barry Menikoff, ed., *The Complete Stories of Robert Louis Stevenson* (New York: Modern Library, 2002), 671 and 673.

158 "I lay all this": Thomas Stevenson to Sidney Colvin, January 8, 1880, *Letters*, 3: 43.

158 "the death of me": Stevenson, "The Story of a Lie," 704.

158 "Is it fair": Thomas Stevenson to Sidney Colvin, November 10, 1879, *Letters*, 3: 23.

158 "I won't desert": RLS to William Henley, November 17, 1879, *Letters*, 3: 27.

159 "Drink is more": RLS to Sidney Colvin, late February 1880, *Letters*, 3: 66.

159 "His point of view": Dora Norton Williams, "Recollections of Robert Louis Stevenson" (paper read before the Century Club of San Francisco, August 5, 1895), Robert Louis Stevenson House, Monterey, California.

159 "of the sketchiest": Isobel Field, *This Life I've Loved* (Lafayette, CA: Great West Books, 2005), 112.

159 "airs of Marseilles": Robert Louis Stevenson, "A Modern Cosmopolis" reprinted in *San Francisco: A Modern Cosmopolis* (San Francisco: Book Club of California, 1963), 26.

160 "shaken to the heart": Stevenson, "A Modern Cosmopolis," 23.

160 "One brief impression": Stevenson, "A Modern Cosmopolis," 34–35.

160 "millionaire vulgarians of": Robert Louis Stevenson, "The Old Pacific Capital," *The Works of Robert Louis Stevenson*, Tusitala Edition (London: William Heinemann: 1924), 18: 142.

160 "the heart of San Francisco": Stevenson, "A Modern Cosmopolis," 38–40.

161 "a long Smith-and-Wesson": Stevenson, "A Modern Cosmopolis," 31.

161 "From what I had once": Robert Louis Stevenson and Lloyd Osbourne, *The Wrecker, The Novels and Tales of Robert Louis Stevenson* (New York: Charles Scribner's Sons, 1918), 141–43.

161 "girls are well": Roger Austen, *Genteel Pagan* (Amherst: University of Massachusetts Press, 1991), 82.

162 "balm for the weary": RLS to Frances Sitwell, June 21, 1875, *Letters*, 2: 145.

163 "I am going for 30": RLS to Edmund Gosse, December 8, 1879, *Letters*, 3: 32.

163 "I am only beginning": RLS to Henley, late January 1880, *Letters*, 3: 56.

163 "Fortunately dulness is": RLS to Sidney Colvin, late January 1880, *Letters*, 3: 58–59.

163 "full of force": RLS to Sidney Colvin, late February 1880, *Letters*, 3: 65, fn 2.

163 "Louis Stevenson is": RLS to James Ferrier, April 8, 1880, *Letters*, 3: 74, fn 4.

164 "You rolled such a lot": RLS to Colvin, late January 1880, *Letters*, 3: 59.

164 "profound faith in": Nellie Van de Grift Sanchez, *The Life of Mrs. Robert Louis Stevenson* (Fairfield, CA: James Stevenson, 2001), 65.

164 "He has a line": FVS to Timothy Rearden, July–August 1879, Stevenson Museum Collection.

164 "I do not think many": RLS to Edmund Gosse, January 23, 1880, *Letters*, 3: 53.

165 "The second part": RLS to Sidney Colvin, mid-April 1880, *Letters*, 3: 75.

165 "lying seriously ill": Thomas Stevenson to Sidney Colvin, January 8, 1880, *Letters*, 3: 42 and 42 fn.

167 "infatuation for a young": Issler, *Happier for His Presence*, 127.

167 "was sure that Mr. Stevenson": Nellie Van de Grift Sanchez to Elizabeth Vandegrift Patterson, April 19, 1880, Stevenson Museum Collection.

168 "the ugliest woman": Issler, *Happier for His Presence*, 120.

168 "What an idiot": Thomas Stevenson to RLS, March 11, 1880, Beinecke Collection.

168 "Count on £250": RLS to Colvin, mid-April 1880, *Letters*, 3: 75.

169 "mechanical cleverness of": Sanchez, *Life of Mrs. Robert Louis Stevenson*, 66.

169 "It was not my bliss": RLS to P. G. Hamerton, early July 1881, *Letters*, 3: 203.

170 "grand blow out": RLS to Dora Williams, January or February 1880, *Letters*, 3: 153.

171 "a clique of neighbourly": Robert Louis Stevenson, *The Silverado Squatters*, *The Travels and Essays of Robert Louis Stevenson: The Amateur Emigrant, Across the Plains, The Silverado Squatters* (New York: Charles Scribner's Sons, 1903), 355.

171 "the beds made": Stevenson, *Silverado Squatters*, 415.

172 "The difference between Louis' severity": FVS to Dora Williams, May or June 1880, Beinecke Collection.

172 "like spinning wheels": Stevenson, *Silverado Squatters*, 422.

173 "and yet you": Stevenson, *Silverado Squatters*, 379.

173 "chink of money": Stevenson, *Silverado Squatters*, 358–59. Wendy R. Katz wrote about Jewish stereotypes in Stevenson's work in "Stevenson's Silverado Squatters: The Figure of 'the Jew' and the Rhetoric of Race," *Journal of Stevenson Studies* 4 (2007): 73.

174 "I hope you both understand": Margaret Stevenson to RLS, June 29, 1880, Beinecke Collection.

174 "I do so earnestly": FVS and RLS to Margaret Stevenson, July 16, 1880, *Letters*, 3: 89.

175 "If I can keep well": RLS to Jacob Vandegrift, late July 1880, *Letters*, 3: 91.

175 "a citizen of the world": Sanchez, *Life of Mrs. Robert Louis Stevenson*, 70.

175 "I call that your fate": RLS to A. Trevor Haddon, June 1882, *Letters*, 3: 335.

176 "If she doesn't make": RLS to William Henley, late January 1880, *Letters*, 3: 55 fn.

176 "port of entry": Stevenson and Osbourne, *The Wrecker*, 144.

NINE

177 "with their skins off": Lloyd Osbourne to Isobel Field, August 18, 1880, Stevenson Museum Collection.

177 "If you can love": RLS to His Parents, June 23, 1880, *Letters*, 3: 87.

178 "whether you and I": Sidney Colvin to William Henley, August 17, 1880, *Letters*, 3: 93.

178 "darker than one": William Archer, "Robert Louis Stevenson at 'Skerryvore'," *Critic*, November 5, 1887, excerpted in J. A. Hammerton, *Stevensonia* (London: Grant Richards, 1903), 77.

178 "spoke English very well": Margaret Mackay, *The Violent Friend* (London: J. M. Dent & Sons, 1968), 88.

179 "I married a *besom*": Mackay, *Violent Friend*, 90.

179 "The father is a most": FVS to Dora Williams, September 1880, Beinecke Collection.

180 "quite amusing how": "Notes from His Mother's Diary," *The Works of Robert Louis Stevenson*, Vailima Edition (New York: Peter Fenelon Collier, 1912), 26: 335.

180 "She is adored": FVS to Williams, September 1880, Beinecke Collection.

180 "what my mother": RLS to James Cunningham, August 22, 1880, *Letters*, 3: 94.

180 "plays dolls with me": FVS and RLS to Dora Williams, early October 1880, *Letters*, 3: 105.

180 "I have to dress properly": James Pope Hennessy, *Robert Louis Stevenson* (New York: Simon & Schuster, 1974), 168.

180 "They are the best": FVS to Isobel Field, fragment, Beinecke Collection.

181 "Religion seems a thing": FVS to Margaret Stevenson, December 15, 1880, Stevenson Museum Collection.

181 "filled with every manner": FVS and RLS to Williams, early October 1880, *Letters*, 3: 105

181 "This was the creature": FVS and RLS to Williams, early October 1880, 105–6.

181 "brushed every morning": Pope Hennessy, *Robert Louis Stevenson*, 168.

181 "He was a citizen": Rosaline Masson, ed., *I Can Remember Robert Louis Stevenson* (Edinburgh: W. & R. Chambers, 1922), 195.

182 "New Tarterly": RLS to Sidney Colvin, October 21, 1879, *Letters*, 3: 19, and RLS to Edmund Gosse, October 8, 1879, *Letters*, 3: 16.

182 "the breaching of bodily": Julia Reid, "'Newspaper Like in Style, and Not Worthy of R.L.S.'; Robert Louis Stevenson's 'The Amateur Emigrant,'" *The Bottle Imp*, issue 12, n.d.

183 "*Intolerably* nasty": Robert Louis Stevenson, *The Amateur Emigrant*, Julia Reid, ed., *The Works of Robert Louis Stevenson*, New Edinburgh Edition (Edinburgh: Edinburgh University Press, 2018), 136.

184 "from early morning": FVS to Margaret Stevenson, October 13, 1880, Stevenson Museum Collection.

184 "reintroduced with safety": Robert Louis Stevenson, "Talk and Talkers," in William Lyon Phelps, ed., *Essays of Robert Louis Stevenson* (New York: Charles Scribner's Sons, 1906), 81 and 84.

184 "racy flesh-pots": RLS to James Walter Ferrier, September 24, 1873, *Letters*, 1: 326.

184 "create for you": Stevenson, "Talk and Talkers," 71.

184 "a physical no less": Oscar Wilde to William Rothenstein, August 14, 1897, in Merlin Holland and Rupert Hart-Davis, eds., *The Complete Letters of Oscar Wilde* (New York: Henry Holt and Company, 2000), 925.

184 "so polished that": Stevenson, "Talk and Talkers," 74–75.

185 "excited a passionate admiration": Andrew Lang, *Adventures Among Books* (New York and Bombay: Longmans, Green and Co., 1905), 51.

185 "hypocritical Cheshire Cat": FVS to Margaret Stevenson, October 13, 1880, Stevenson Museum Collection.

186 "their life's blood": FVS to Margaret Stevenson, October 13, 1880, Stevenson Museum Collection.

187 "He stayed in bed": Mackay, *Violent Friend*, 99.

187 "People you had not seen": Lloyd Osbourne, *An Intimate Portrait of R. L. S.* (New York: Charles Scribner's Sons, 1924), 24.

188 "It seems the fashion": FVS to Margaret Stevenson, October 11, 1882, Stevenson Museum Collection.

188 "Her legs caved in": RLS to Nellie Sanchez and Belle Strong, early October 1880, *Letters*, 3: 104 and 117.

188 "little kindnesses going on": Nellie Van de Grift Sanchez, *The Life of Mrs. Robert Louis Stevenson* (Fairfield, CA: James Stevenson, 2001), 89.

189 "eager, gifted wife": Mackay, *Violent Friend*, 99.

190 "a man buried alive": Ann Thwaite, *Edmund Gosse: A Literary Landscape* (Oxford: Oxford University Press, 1985), 320.

190 "I feel pretty sure": W. G. Lockett, *Robert Louis Stevenson at Davos* (London: Hurst & Blackett, 1934), 245.

190 "wolverine on my own shoulders": RLS to Sidney Colvin, March 12, 1881, *Letters*, 3: 162.

191 "like a violin hung up": RLS to Colvin, March 12, 1881, 161.

191 "There is no denying it": FVS to Margaret Stevenson, April 25, 1881, Stevenson Museum Collection.

191 "schoolgirl of 40": William Henley to Charles Baxter, May 18, 1881, *Letters*, 3: 182.

192 "She was American": Penny Fielding, "A Dangerous Collaboration: Fanny van de Grift Stevenson and Robert Louis Stevenson," Dangerous Women Project, January 6, 2017, dangerouswomenproject.org/2017/01/06/a-dangerous-collaboration.

192 "anything in her": Henley to Baxter, May 18, 1881, *Letters*, 3: 183.

192 "I don't see why": Henry James, *An International Episode* (Doylestown, PA: Wildside Press, 2004), 61.

192 "so much fuller": FVS to Margaret and Thomas Stevenson, December 26, 1880, Stevenson Museum Collection.

193 "It's only Louis": Pope Hennessy, *Robert Louis Stevenson*, 176.

193 "a masterpiece in 13 pages": Henry James, "Robert Louis Stevenson," *Century Magazine*, April 1888, reprinted in Paul Maixner, ed., *Robert Louis Stevenson: The Critical Heritage* (London: Routledge & Kegan Paul, 1981), 300.

194 "That evening is": Fanny Van de Grift Stevenson, Prefatory Note, *The Merry Men and Other Tales and Fables*, *The Works of Robert Louis Stevenson*, Tusitala Edition (London: William Heinemann: 1924), 8: vii.

194 "denuded of so much": F. V. de G. Stevenson, "The Warlock's Shadow," *Belgravia*, March 1886, reprinted in *Belgravia: An Illustrated London Magazine* (London: Chatto & Windus, 1886), 59: 30.

194 "great lift": RLS and FVS to William Henley, July 1881, *Letters*, 3: 212.

195 "the heroine would be": RLS to William Blackwood, January 16, 1886, *Letters*, 5: 176, fn 1. Lena Wånggren wrote of the "The Warlock's Shadow" and the challenges for Fanny and other women writers in nineteenth-century publishing in "Gender and Genre in Fanny Van de Grift Stevenson's Periodical Writing," *Review of English Studies* 72, no. 305 (June 2021): 520–39. Accessed online: doi.org/10.1093/res/hgaa104.

195 "The only thing I fear": RLS and FVS to Henley, July 1881, *Letters*, 3: 212.

195 "These could be coincidences": Hilary J. Beattie, "Fanny Osbourne Stevenson's Fiction: 'The Nixie' in Context," *Journal of Stevenson Studies* 11 (2014): 133.

195 "My heart beat": FVS to RLS, June–July 1881, Stevenson Museum Collection.

196 "Oh Fanny, how could you?": Mackay, *Violent Friend*, 89.

196 "I am not allowed": FVS to Dora Williams, June–August 1882, Beinecke Collection.

196 "We have such": Margaret Stevenson to Alison Cunningham, August 3, 1883, Beinecke Collection.

196 **"I am a woman"**: FVS to Dora Williams, December 1880, Beinecke Collection.

197 **"This is a most entertaining"**: Thwaite, *Edmund Gosse*, 217.

197 **"I can recall the little"**: Lloyd Osbourne, Prefatory Note to *Treasure Island*, *The Works of Robert Louis Stevenson*, Tusitala Edition (London: William Heinemann: 1924), 2: xviii.

198 **"No trouble. No strain"**: RLS to William Henley, August 24, 1881, *Letters*, 3: 224–25.

198 **"big, hulking, chicken-hearted"**: Robert Louis Stevenson, *Treasure Island* (New York: Penguin Books, 1999), 21.

199 **"the lives of all the honest"**: Stevenson, *Treasure Island*, 56.

199 **"obvious though unsuspected shortcuts"**: Robert Louis Stevenson, "My First Book," in Jeremy Treglown, ed., *The Lantern-Bearers and Other Essays* (New York: Farrar, Straus & Giroux, 1988), 284.

199 **"Fifteen men on the dead"**: Stevenson, *Treasure Island*, 124.

199 **"a face as big"**: Stevenson, *Treasure Island*, 42 and 77.

199 **"a great, glowing"**: Osbourne, *Intimate Portrait*, 53.

200 **"his noble head"**: Fanny Van de Grift Stevenson, Prefatory Note to *Treasure Island*, *The Works of Robert Louis Stevenson*, Tusitala Edition (London: William Heinemann: 1924), 2: xx.

200 **"Louis is just now"**: FVS to Dora Williams, September 1881, Beinecke Collection.

201 **"Anybody can write"**: Stevenson, "My First Book," 278.

201 **"It has a snout"**: FVS to Williams, September 1881, Beinecke Collection.

202 **"lying, ghastly, in bed"**: Herbert M. Schueller and Robert L. Peters, eds., *The Letters of John Addington Symonds* (Detroit: Wayne State University, 1968), 2: 703.

202 **"I have never asked you"**: RLS to James Henderson, November 11, 1881, *Letters*, 3: 249.

202 **"My mother, usually the sole"**: Osbourne, *Intimate Portrait*, 36.

203 **"It is snowing"**: FVS to Margaret Stevenson, 1881, Beinecke Collection.

203 **"the pert and hypercritical"**: RLS to William Henley, February 16, 1882, *Letters*, 3: 285.

203 **"Let them write"**: RLS to William Henley, March 1882, *Letters*, 3: 294.

204 **"There's a book for you!"**: Roger Swearingen, *The Prose Writings of Robert Louis Stevenson* (London: Macmillan, 1980), 67.

204 **"a Bloody Sight"**: RLS to William Henley, May 7, 1883, *Letters*, 4: 120.

204 **"A hundred jingling"**: RLS to His Parents, May 5, 1883, *Letters*, 4: 119–20.

204 **"Boys who have lived"**: R. H. Hutton, unsigned review, *Spectator*, July 24, 1886, in Maixner, *Critical Heritage*, 235.

204 **"real hero"**: W. E. Henley, unsigned review, *Saturday Review*, December 8, 1883, in Maixner, *Critical Heritage*, 136.

205 **"He rose once"**: Stevenson, *Treasure Island*, 143. Emma-Lee Davidson's "'The Game Is Up': The Evolution of *Treasure Island* as Imperial Critique" is a particularly enlightening examination of how Louis's book subverted the glorification of imperialism in boys' adventure fiction.

205 **"twice the man"**: Stevenson, *Treasure Island*, 166.

206 **"What blood and sorrow"**: Stevenson, *Treasure Island*, 185.

206 **"negroes, and Mexican-Indians"**: Stevenson, *Treasure Island*, 189.

206 **"this fairy-tale training"**: Osbourne, *Intimate Portrait*, 39–40.

207 "[opening] my whole being": Pete Hamill, "The Death and Life of John Lennon," *New York Magazine*, March 18, 2008. Accessed online: nymag.com/news/features/45252.

207 "unfading boyishness of hope": Stevenson, "Virginibus Puerisque," Robert-Louis Abrahamson, ed., *Essays I: Virginibus Puerisque and Other Papers*, *The Works of Robert Louis Stevenson*, New Edinburgh Edition (Edinburgh: Edinburgh University Press, 2018), 14.

207 "teacher, tender, comrade, wife": Stevenson, "My Wife," in Roger C. Lewis, ed., *The Collected Poems of Robert Louis Stevenson* (Edinburgh: Edinburgh University Press, 2003), 184–85.

TEN

208 "I don't suppose our address": FVS to Dora Williams, October 1882, Beinecke Collection.

208 "full of stories": FVS to John Addington Symonds, late October 1882, *Letters*, 4: 20.

209 "in continual danger": Fanny Van de Grift Stevenson, Prefatory Note to *More New Arabian Nights: The Dynamiter*, *The Works of Robert Louis Stevenson*, Tusitala Edition (London: William Heinemann: 1924), 3: viii.

209 "a garden like": RLS to Frances Sitwell, April 18, 1883, *Letters*, 4: 102.

210 "These are rather nice rhymes": "Notes from His Mother's Diary," *The Works of Robert Louis Stevenson*, Vailima Edition (New York: Peter Fenelon Collier, 1912), 26: 338.

210 "children of the sickroom": RLS to William Dean Howells, early June 1880, *Letters*, 3: 85.

210 "When at home": Robert Louis Stevenson, "The Little Land," *A Child's Garden of Verses* (San Francisco: Chronicle Books, 1989), 86.

211 "There were brilliant": Fanny Van de Grift Stevenson, Preface, Robert Louis Stevenson, *The Works of Robert Louis Stevenson*, Biographical Edition (New York: Charles Scribner's Sons, 1908), 25: viii.

211 "High bare walls": Stevenson, "The Little Land," 88.

212 "Children, you are very little": Robert Louis Stevenson, "Good and Bad Children," in *A Child's Garden of Verses*, 49.

212 "fed on proper meat": Robert Louis Stevenson, "Foreign Children," in *A Child's Garden of Verses*, 50.

212 "showing each other marvels": RLS to William Henley, early May 1883, *Letters*, 4: 114–15.

212 "the only person": RLS to Alison Cunningham, February 16, 1883, *Letters*, 4: 76.

213 "lovely": FVS to Dora Williams, late spring 1884, Beinecke Collection.

213 "as timid as hens": J. A. Hammerton, *Stevensonia* (London: Grant Richards, 1903), 155.

213 "commonplace": RLS to Sidney Colvin, early November 1883, *Letters*, 4: 199, fn 5.

213 "State Mr Stevenson's faults": RLS to Edmund Gosse, March 12, 1885, *Letters*, 5: 85.

214 "little frosty Eskimo": Stevenson, "Foreign Children," 50.

214 "His poems were my companions": Charlotte Higgins, "Patti Smith to Pay Tribute to Poems of Robert Louis Stevenson on Stage," *The Guardian*, August 13, 2013. Accessed online: theguardian.com/music/2013/aug/13/patti-smith-robert-louis-stevenson-poetry.

215 "for an airing": Isobel Field, *This Life I've Loved* (Lafayette, CA: Great West Books, 2005), 126.

215 "untidy in the extreme": Dora Williams to FVS, March 15, 1886, Beinecke Collection.

215 "one should either be": Talia Schaffer, "Fashioning Aestheticism by Aestheticizing Fashion: Wilde, Beerbohm, and the Male Aesthetes' Sartorial Codes," *Victorian Literature and Culture* 28, no. 1 (2000): 42.

216 "This is where I belong!": Field, *This Life I've Loved*, 139.

216 "that delicate artist": Merlin Holland and Rupert Hart-Davis, eds., *The Complete Letters of Oscar Wilde* (New York: Henry Holt and Company, 2000), 524–25.

216 "any new ones by Stevenson": Holland and Hart-Davis, *Complete Letters of Oscar Wilde*, 802.

217 "the most entertaining": Margaret Mackay, *The Violent Friend* (London: J. M. Dent & Sons, 1968), 111.

217 "We have just been bled": RLS to William Henley, July 29, 1881, *Letters*, 3: 216.

217 "vulgar error": RLS to Dora Williams, January or February 1881, *Letters*, 3: 153.

217 "best foot foremost": FVS to Dora Williams, December 1880, Beinecke Collection.

217 "You wonder at my patience": FVS to Dora Williams, November or December 1881, Beinecke Collection.

217 "we hope to be able": FVS to Dora Williams, October 1882, Beinecke Collection.

218 "Belle I hear": FVS to Dora Williams, late spring 1884, Beinecke Collection.

218 "She could hardly believe": FVS to Margaret Stevenson, November 7, 1882, Stevenson Museum Collection.

219 "imbecile": Fanny Van de Grift Stevenson, "Housewife's Ramblings: Campagne Defli," *Philadelphia Inquirer*, October 1, 1893, 15.

219 "a cross dog": FVS to Charles Baxter, December 15, 1883, *Letters*, 4: 216 fn.

219 "Having the character": FVS to Timothy Rearden, n.d., Stevenson Museum Collection.

219 "sort of sentimental reminder": FVS to Margaret Stevenson, November or December 1884, Beinecke Collection.

220 "uxorious Billy": RLS to Sidney Colvin, late January/early February 1883, *Letters*, 4: 63.

220 "the fat and lean": RLS to FVS, August 3, 1882, *Letters*, 3: 343.

220 "I love her better": RLS to Margaret Stevenson, April 19, 1884, *Letters*, 4: 272.

221 "You are right": FVS letter fragment, recipient missing but most likely Dora Williams, Beinecke Collection.

221 "to have the most perfect life": FVS to Margaret Stevenson, January 20, 1885, Stevenson Museum Collection.

222 "joke": RLS to Walter Simpson, December 11, 1883, *Letters*, 4: 228.

222 "Why that dog": FVS to Margaret Stevenson, May 14, 1881, Stevenson Museum Collection.

222 "No one wields": RLS to Thomas Stevenson, August 25, 1883, *Letters*, 4: 149 and fn.

223 "Kegan is an excellent fellow": Hammerton, *Stevensonia*, 81.

223 "The Holy Bible": RLS to William Henley, March 31, 1882, *Letters*, 3: 309.

223 "about any art": RLS to Trevor Haddon, June 1882, *Letters*, 3: 333.

223 "tushery": RLS to William Henley, late May 1883, *Letters*, 4: 128.

224 "Critic on the Hearth": Robert Louis Stevenson, *The Black Arrow: A Tale of the Two Roses*, Dedication (New York: Charles Scribner's Sons, 1916).

224 "dear but costly": RLS to Katharine de Mattos, October 22, 1883, *Letters*, 4: 188.

225 "When I said farewell": Will Low to RLS, April–June 1883, Beinecke Collection.

225 "Nearly three years": RLS to Will Low, March 1883, *Letters*, 4: 87.

225 "manlike ambitions": Robert Louis Stevenson, *Prince Otto*, *The Works of Robert Louis Stevenson*, New Edinburgh Edition (Edinburgh: Edinburgh University Press, 2018), 60 and 49.

225 "a jolly, elderly": RLS to William Henley, early May 1883, *Letters*, 4: 115.

225 "hardest effort": RLS to George Iles, October 29, 1887, *Letters*, 6: 48.

226 "We all expected": E. Purcell, review, *Academy*, February 27, 1886, in Paul Maixner, ed., *Robert Louis Stevenson: The Critical Heritage* (London: Routledge & Kegan Paul, 1981), 197.

226 "manly friend": Stevenson, *Prince Otto*, 150 and 91.

226 "hates and loathes": RLS to William Henley, May 7, 1883, *Letters*, 4: 120.

226 "inch by inch": FVS to Margaret Stevenson, fragment, Beinecke Collection.

227 "It is so easy": RLS to Low, March 1883, *Letters*, 4: 87.

227 "Englishman who is": *The Publishers' Weekly*, June 7, 1879, 15: 615. Accessed online: hdl.handle.net/2027/hvd.32044092999051.

227 "camping-out passion": Richard Watson Gilder to RLS, February 17, 1883, in Rosamond Gilder, ed., *Letters of Richard Watson Gilder* (Boston and New York: Riverside Press, Houghton Mifflin, 1916), 121.

228 "'In eighteen hundred'": RLS to His Parents, February 1, 1883, *Letters*, 4: 64.

228 "never liked girls": John Matteson, "Little Woman," *Humanities* 30, no. 6 (November/December 2009).

228 "A man were": RLS to Mssrs Charles Scribner's Sons, March 12, 1885, *Letters*, 5: 86.

229 "terror of the bailiff": RLS to Katharine de Mattos, October 22, 1883, *Letters*, 4: 189.

229 "I am going to make": RLS to Frances Sitwell, April 1883, *Letters*, 4: 102.

229 "Illness is such": FVS to Margaret Stevenson, November 1884, Stevenson Museum Collection.

229 "I must say, though": FVS to Dora Williams, September or October 1883, Beinecke Collection.

230 "They were in": Lloyd Osbourne, *An Intimate Portrait of R. L. S.* (New York: Charles Scribner's Sons, 1924), 51–52.

230 "His appearance had": Sidney Colvin, *Memories of Notes of Persons and Places* (New York: Charles Scribner's Sons, 1921), 110–11.

230 "Overthrow of the Bankers": RLS to Charles Baxter, October 3, 1883, *Letters*, 4: 174, fn 4.

231 "you wicked woman": William Henley to FVS, February 2, 1884, Beinecke Collection.

231 "very dull without": FVS to Margaret Stevenson, early 1884, Stevenson Museum Collection.

232 "The match is": William Henley to Charles Baxter, July 11, 1884, *Letters*, 5: 4 fn.

232 "vomitable in many parts": RLS to William Henley, April 8, 1885, *Letters*, 5: 101.

232 "money was absolutely": Van de Grift Stevenson, Prefatory Note to *More New Arabian Nights: The Dynamiter*, *The Works of Robert Louis Stevenson*, Tusitala Edition (London: William Heinemann: 1924), 3: xii.

232 "like opium": RLS to John Meiklejohn, February 1, 1880, *Letters*, 3: 61.

232 "a sort of Arabian": Van de Grift Stevenson, Prefatory Note, *The Dynamiter*, xi.

233 "the only profession": Robert Louis Stevenson and Fanny Van de Grift Stevenson, *More New Arabian Nights: The Dynamiter* (London: Longmans, Green and Co., 1885), 6.

233 "the fall of England": Stevenson and Van de Grift Stevenson, *The Dynamiter*, 117.

234 "rich in color": Stevenson and Van de Grift Stevenson, *The Dynamiter*, 139.

234 "conduct of [her] sweeping skirt": Stevenson and Van de Grift Stevenson, *The Dynamiter*, 133.

234 "N——, n——, never": Stevenson and Van de Grift Stevenson, *The Dynamiter*, 58.

235 "tragic mulatta": Allison Francis, "'Unstable Mixtures': The Destabilization of Race and Gender in Stevenson's *The Dynamiter*," presented at the RLS Conference: Napier University, Edinburgh, Scotland. Also, email correspondence and telephone interview with author.

235 "If I cannot": RLS to William Henley, April 7, 1884, *Letters*, 4: 266.

235 "three futiles": Stevenson and Van de Grift Stevenson, *The Dynamiter*, 4.

236 "I may have been": Stevenson and Van de Grift Stevenson, *The Dynamiter*, 205.

236 "I mean, for a book": RLS to Margaret Stevenson, October 8, 1885, *Letters*, 5: 130.

236 "I always have to fight": FVS to Margaret Stevenson, January 20, 1885, *Letters*, 5: 71–72.

236 "Our joint book": FVS to Dora Williams, March 1885, Beinecke Collection.

237 "great advertisement": FVS to Frances Sitwell, February 1885, Beinecke Collection.

237 "highly imaginative": Audrey Murfin, *Robert Louis Stevenson and the Art of Collaboration* (Edinburgh: Edinburgh University Press, 2019), 6.

238 "I thought in the beginning": FVS to Margaret Stevenson, May 20, 1885, Beinecke Collection.

238 "Of all of Fanny's": Murfin, *Robert Louis Stevenson and the Art of Collaboration*, 53.

238 "literary pretensions": James Pope Hennessy, *Robert Louis Stevenson* (New York: Simon & Schuster, 1974), 187, and Frank McLynn, *Robert Louis Stevenson* (New York: Random House, 1993), 235. For information on the stylometric analysis of *The Dynamiter*, see *Deciphering The Dynamiter: A Study in Authorship Attribution*, thedynamiter.llc.ed.ac.uk/?page_id=223.

239 "a tribute to the volatile": Penny Fielding, "A Dangerous Collaboration: Fanny van de Grift Stevenson and Robert Louis Stevenson," Dangerous Women Project, January 6, 2017, dangerouswomenproject.org/2017/01/06/a-dangerous-collaboration.

239 "an outburst of *real* female": Elizabeth Carolyn Miller, *Framed: The New Woman Criminal in British Culture at the Fin de Siècle* (Ann Arbor: University of Michigan Press, 2008), 221.

Eleven

240 "There could be no pretense": Lloyd Osbourne, *An Intimate Portrait of R. L. S.* (New York: Charles Scribner's Sons, 1924), 61.

240 "lean, feverish, voluble": RLS to Bob and Louisa Stevenson, March 12, 1884, *Letters*, 4: 249.

241 "pleuritic rub": RLS to Henry James, January 24, 1887, *Letters*, 5: 348.

241 "long spells when": Osbourne, *Intimate Portrait*, 62.

242 "Don't be frightened": Graham Balfour, *The Life of Robert Louis Stevenson* (London: Methuen and Co., 1906), 213. (Kessinger Rare Reprints.)

242 "at least he is": FVS to William Henley, 1887, Beinecke Collection.

242 "will give me some training": FVS to Margaret Stevenson, May 18, 1884, *Letters*, 4: 294.

242 "I do not ask you": RLS to FVS, October 2, 1882, *Letters*, 4: 5.

242 "so spectral, so emaciated": Osbourne, *Intimate Portrait*, 60.

242 "I don't want you": RLS to FVS, October 3, 1882, *Letters*, 4: 7–8.

242 "Taking care of Louis": FVS and RLS to Margaret Stevenson, July 16, 1880, *Letters*, 3: 88.

242 "a volcano raging inside": FVS to Margaret Stevenson, November 7, 1882, Stevenson Museum Collection.

243 "love of harrowing": Sidney Colvin to Charles Baxter, January 15, 1883, *Letters*, 4: 53 fn.

243 "[Fanny] has taken it": RLS to Margaret and Thomas Stevenson, January 24, 1883, *Letters*, 4: 59.

244 "If [all the doctors] agree": FVS to Margaret Stevenson, July or August 1884, Beinecke Collection.

244 "They all think I wanted": FVS to Margaret Stevenson, January 1884, Beinecke Collection.

244 "She is really *no alarmist*": *Letters*, 4: 293.

244 "erratic moods": Adelaide A. Boodle, *R. L. S. and His Sine Qua Non* (New York: Charles Scribner's Sons, 1926), 76.

245 "I have had too worrying": FVS to Dora Williams, September 1882, Beinecke Collection.

246 "The awkwardness is": FVS to Sidney Colvin, spring 1886, Beinecke Collection.

246 "All the doctors": FVS to Margaret Stevenson, early 1884, Stevenson Museum Collection.

246 "mania": RLS to Margaret Stevenson, February/March 1883, *Letters*, 4: 86.

247 "I am never": RLS to William Henley, February 1886, *Letters*, 5: 214.

248 "female games are": RLS to Margaret and Thomas Stevenson, June 22, 1884, *Letters*, 4: 310.

248 "sprinkled with coloured meteors": Charlotte Brontë, *Villette* (New York: Vintage Books, 2009), 601.

248 "Laudanum has become": FVS to Ellen Gosse, March 16, 1882, Beinecke Collection.

248 "a blessing and a boon": FVS to Sidney Colvin, June 1885, Beinecke Collection.

249 "like a weevil": RLS to Sidney Colvin, May 1, 1892, *Letters*, 7: 280.

250 **"not being married"**: FVS to Dora Williams, October/November 1885, Beinecke Collection.

250 **"I cannot get used to"**: FVS to Emma Hardy, September 1885, Beinecke Collection.

250 **"if not to kill him"**: FVS to William Henley, August 1885, Beinecke Collection.

251 **"He was quite off"**: FVS to Frances Sitwell, 1885, E. V. Lucas, *The Colvins and Their Friends* (New York: Charles Scribner's Sons, 1928), 161.

251 **"a good deal appalled"**: FVS to Henley, August 1885, Beinecke Collection.

251 **"plot of any sort"**: Robert Louis Stevenson, "A Chapter on Dreams," *Scribner's Magazine*, January 3, 1888, in Jeremy Treglown, ed., *The Lantern-Bearers and Other Essays* (New York: Farrar, Straus & Giroux, 1988), 224.

252 **"that citadel of medicine"**: Robert Louis Stevenson, *Strange Case of Dr Jekyll and Mr Hyde*, Richard Dury, ed., *The Collected Works of Robert Louis Stevenson*, Centenary Edition (Edinburgh: Edinburgh University Press, 2004), 14.

252 **"the very pink"**: Stevenson, *Dr Jekyll and Mr Hyde*, 11.

252 **"sinister block of building"**: Stevenson, *Dr Jekyll and Mr Hyde*, 8.

252 **"If he be Mr. Hyde"**: Stevenson, *Dr Jekyll and Mr Hyde*, 16.

252 **"hardly human"**: Stevenson, *Dr Jekyll and Mr Hyde*, 18.

253 **"ape-like fury"**: Stevenson, *Dr Jekyll and Mr Hyde*, 25.

253 **"the very sugar"**: Stevenson, *Dr Jekyll and Mr Hyde*, 49.

253 **"Have you got it?"**: Stevenson, *Dr Jekyll and Mr Hyde*, 55.

254 **"man is not"**: Stevenson, *Dr Jekyll and Mr Hyde*, 59.

254 **"imperious desire to carry"**: Stevenson, *Dr Jekyll and Mr Hyde*, 58.

254 **"I felt younger"**: Stevenson, *Dr Jekyll and Mr Hyde*, 60–61.

254 **"It was Hyde, after all"**: Stevenson, *Dr Jekyll and Mr Hyde*, 63.

255 **"one of the day"**: Stevenson, "A Chapter on Dreams," 218.

255 **"little people"**: Stevenson, "A Chapter on Dreams," 223. Amusingly, like the "little people," or Brownies, in Louis's subconscious, his wife had a flair for storytelling, was often sleepless while he slumbered, shared his financial worries, and had "an eye to the bank-book." In "Demonic Disturbances of Sexual Identity: The Strange Case of Dr. Jekyll and Mr/s Hyde" (in *NOVEL: A Forum on Fiction*, Autumn 1989), Janice Doane and Devon Hodges suggest that "it is easy to read Fanny—the 'tiny' woman with the 'little, determined brown face'—as reduced to the 'Brownies,' here internalized and praised, then expelled and chastised as responsible for the weakness of peripheral elements of the story."

255 **"He had Jekyll"**: Stevenson, *Dr Jekyll and Mr Hyde*, Dury, notes, 179.

256 **"By carrying her hotly contested point"**: J. C. Furnas, *Voyage to Windward* (New York: William Sloane Associates, 1951), 246.

256 **"man's double being"**: Stevenson, "A Chapter on Dreams," 224.

257 **"What a grim sorority they make"**: Parul Sehgal, "A Rebellious Victorian Woman Rescued from History's Shadows," *New York Times*, June 24, 2020. Accessed online: nytimes.com/2020/06/24/books/review-true-history-first-mrs-meredith-diane-johnson.html.

257 **"vigorous objections"**: Ian Bell, *Dreams of Exile* (New York: Henry Holt and Company, 1992), 174–75.

257 **"adult view of sexuality"**: Frank McLynn, *Robert Louis Stevenson* (New York: Random House, 1993), 253–54.

257 "irreparably": Laura E. Skandera-Trombley, "'I Am Woman's Rights': Olivia Langdon Clemens and Her Feminist Circle," *Mark Twain Journal* 34, no. 2 (1996): 17. Accessed online: jstor.org/stable/41641429.

257 **"A writer whose wife":** Furnas, *Voyage to Windward*, 195.

258 **"seemed to have suffered":** Bell, *Dreams of Exile*, 162.

258 **"pyromania common to the wives":** McLynn, *Robert Louis Stevenson*, 255.

258 **"prototype for Henry":** Hilary J. Beattie, "Fanny Osbourne Stevenson's Fiction: 'The Nixie' in Context," *Journal of Stevenson Studies* 11 (2014): 134.

258 **"pouring forth a penny":** RLS to Sidney Colvin, late September/early October 1885, *Letters*, 5: 128.

259 **"when ghosts are walking":** RLS to Edmund Gosse, November 15, 1884, *Letters*, 5: 33, fn 2.

259 **"blood curdling enough":** RLS to Charles Morley, December 5, 1884, *Letters*, 5: 41. "Markheim" did not appear until 1886, in *Unwin's Christmas Annual*.

259 **"I drive on with *Jekyll*":** RLS to FVS, *Letters*, 5: 135.

259 **"chronic sickest":** RLS to Will Low, December 26, 1885, *Letters*, 5: 162.

259 **"dim and knotless":** RLS to Edmund Gosse, January 2, 1886, *Letters*, 5: 171.

260 **"a certain measure of contempt":** James Ashcroft Noble, review, *Academy*, January 23, 1886, in Paul Maixner, ed., *Robert Louis Stevenson: The Critical Heritage* (London: Routledge & Kegan Paul, 1981), 203 and 205.

260 **"strikingly bold":** Stevenson, *Dr Jekyll and Mr Hyde*, Dury, Introduction, xxiii–xxiv.

260 **"gloomy grandeur":** Unsigned review, *Times* (UK), January 25, 1886, in Maixner, *Critical Heritage*, 206.

260 **"Nothing Mr Stevenson has written":** Unsigned review, *Times* (UK), in Maixner, *Critical Heritage*, 205–7.

260 **"It is very overpowering":** RLS to Margaret Stevenson, September 21, 1886, *Letters*, 5: 322, fn 1.

260 **"I confess I can":** Thomas Stevenson to RLS, January 1886, Bancroft Collection.

260 **"Have you read":** Stevenson, *Dr Jekyll and Mr Hyde*, Dury, Introduction, xxv.

261 **"DOC-ter Jekyll!":** FVS to Margaret Stevenson, April 24, 1886, Beinecke Collection.

261 **"I couldn't have written":** Emily Temple, "Donna Tartt On the Books That Were Important to Her While Writing *The Secret History*," Literary Hub, December 20, 2022, https://lithub.com/donna-tartt-on-the-books-that-were-important-to-her-while-writing-the-secret-history/.

263 **"the slave of disgraceful pleasures":** William Veeder and Gordon Hirsch, eds., *Dr Jekyll and Mr Hyde After One Hundred Years* (Chicago and London: University of Chicago Press, 1988), 34–35. Stevenson, *Dr Jekyll and Mr Hyde*, 58.

263 **"a fable of fin-de-siècle":** Elaine Showalter, *Sexual Anarchy: Gender and Culture at the Fin de Siècle* (New York and London: Penguin Books, 1991), 107.

263 **"strange preference or bondage":** Stevenson, *Dr Jekyll and Mr Hyde*, 16.

263 **"The more it looks":** Stevenson, *Dr Jekyll and Mr Hyde*, 11.

264 **"quite willing to answer":** RLS to Low, December 26, 1885, *Letters*, 5: 163.

264 **"the voluptuary":** RLS to John Paul Bocock, mid-November 1887, *Letters*, 6: 56.

265 **"the hypocrisy of a professional":** Julia Reid, *Robert Louis Stevenson, Science, and the Fin de Siècle* (London: Palgrave Macmillan, 2009), 98.

265 **"most of us"**: John Addington Symonds to RLS, March 3, 1886, in Maixner, *Critical Heritage*, 211.

266 **"horrid ruffian"**: Judith R. Walkowitz, *City of Dreadful Delight* (Chicago: University of Chicago Press, 1992), 207.

266 **"Mr Hyde at large"**: Lucy Worsley, *The Art of the English Murder* (New York: Pegasus Books, 2014), 193.

267 **"diseased brain"**: Worsley, *Art of the English Murder*, 193.

267 **"Long-standing patterns"**: Walkowitz, *City of Dreadful Delight*, 212.

267 **"a pleasant side"**: Reid, *Robert Louis Stevenson, Science, and the Fin de Siècle*, 103.

TWELVE

268 **"weird-looking"**: Adelaide A. Boodle, *R. L. S. and His Sine Qua Non* (New York: Charles Scribner's Sons, 1926), 3.

269 **"full of yearning kindness"**: Boodle, *R. L. S. and His Sine Qua Non*, 9.

269 **"wholly unlike any other"**: Boodle, *R. L. S. and His Sine Qua Non*, 1.

269 **"It is very comfortable"**: FVS to Frances Sitwell, February 1885, Beinecke Collection.

270 **"The small dwarf chairs"**: FVS to Sidney Colvin, summer 1885, Beinecke Collection.

270 **"Skerryvore will not look"**: FVS to Margaret Stevenson, July 29, 1885, Stevenson Museum Collection.

270 **"tempting seats and unexpected arbors"**: William Archer, "Robert Louis Stevenson at 'Skerryvore,'" *Stevensoniana*, 76.

270 **"foreign looking"**: Boodle, *R. L. S. and His Sine Qua Non*, 1.

271 **"as [Henry] James"**: FVS to Dora Williams, spring 1884, Beinecke Collection.

271 **"beastly householder"**: RLS to Edmund Gosse, March 12, 1885, *Letters*, 5: 85.

271 **"Our drawing room"**: RLS to Margaret Stevenson, October 8, 1885, *Letters*, 5: 130.

271 **"young family had been massacred"**: Boodle, *R. L. S. and His Sine Qua Non*, 116–17.

272 **"infinite patience"**: Boodle, *R. L. S. and His Sine Qua Non*, 75–76.

272 **"If the mines pan out"**: Sam Osbourne to Lloyd Osbourne, July 20, 1881, Bancroft Collection.

272 **"on the next steamer"**: FVS to Dora Williams, April/May 1885, Beinecke Collection.

272 **"a good deal of commotion"**: FVS to Dora Williams, October/November 1885, Beinecke Collection.

273 **"a kind of dude"**: Sam Osbourne to Belle Strong, June 12, 1885, Bancroft Collection.

273 **"gayest of gay"**: Boodle, *R. L. S. and His Sine Qua Non*, 98.

275 **"a hopeless invalid"**: FVS to Sidney Colvin, July 1885, *Letters*, 5: 120.

275 **"The society and the friendship"**: FVS to Dora Williams, April or May 1885, Beinecke Collection.

275 **"a kind of huge spider-web"**: Janet Adam Smith, ed., *Henry James and Robert Louis Stevenson* (Westport, CT: Hyperion Press, 1948), 55 and 65–67.

275 **"transcript of life"**: Smith, *Henry James and Robert Louis Stevenson*, 92 and 100.

276 **"floats pearls and diamonds"**: Smith, *Henry James and Robert Louis Stevenson*, 101.

276 "lout and slouch": RLS to Henry James, December 8, 1884, *Letters*, 5: 42.

276 "almost American newness": Leon Edel, *Henry James* (New York: Harper & Row, 1985), 309.

276 "slow and hesitating": FVS to Williams, April/May 1885, Beinecke Collection.

276 "I think there is no": FVS to Colvin, summer 1885, Beinecke Collection.

276 "I pant for": Henry James to RLS, n.d., Beinecke Collection.

276 "little masterpiece": Paul Maixner, ed., *Robert Louis Stevenson: The Critical Heritage* (London: Routledge & Kegan Paul, 1981), 304.

277 "BELOW YOU to write": RLS to Henry James, November 20, 1887, *Letters*, 6: 61–62.

277 "'Tis surely a fanciful": Henry James to RLS, December 5, 1887, Beinecke Collection.

277 "having a secret weakness": Henry James to FVS, September 18, 1885, Beinecke Collection.

277 "His small scornful": FVS to Williams, October/November 1885, Beinecke Collection.

277 "the only oyster soup": FVS to Margaret Stevenson, May 20, 1885, Beinecke Collection.

277 "strange California wife": *Letters*, 1: 66.

278 "Highland pools in a burn": FVS to Henry James, June 19, 1887, *Letters*, 5: 427.

278 "an appendage to": Leon Edel, ed., *The Diary of Alice James* (Middlesex: Penguin Books, 1982), 93.

278 "sedentary part": Henry James to RLS, November 6, 1885, Beinecke Collection.

278 "After ten weeks": FVS to Colvin, summer 1885, Beinecke Collection.

278 "Crapulous Bloated One": RLS to William Henley, October 8, 1884, *Letters*, 5: 14.

279 "I can testify": E. V. Lucas, *The Colvins and Their Friends* (New York: Charles Scribner's Sons, 1928), 107.

279 "He is a sweet creature": FVS to Dora Williams, September/October 1883 and spring 1884, Beinecke Collection.

279 "I may truly": FVS to William Henley, 1887, Beinecke Collection.

279 "to whom I": FVS and RLS to Anne Jenkin, May 1886, *Letters*, 5: 250.

280 "I am like a dragon": FVS to William Henley, 1885 or 1887, Beinecke Collection.

280 "Whatever you may find": *Letters*, 1: 67.

280 "It has been such": FVS to Sidney Colvin, July 1885, *Letters*, 5: 120.

280 "Henley, for instance": FVS to Dora Williams, May 1886, Beinecke Collection.

281 "tiger and tiger lily": Robert Louis Stevenson, "Dark Women," in Roger C. Lewis, ed., *The Collected Poems of Robert Louis Stevenson* (Edinburgh: Edinburgh University Press, 2003), 175. These stanzas were not included in some published versions of the poem, possibly because they were considered too personal.

281 "There were moments": Boodle, *R. L. S. and His Sine Qua Non*, 11.

281 "when roused, he had": Lloyd Osbourne, Introduction, *The Works of Robert Louis Stevenson*, Vailima Edition (New York: Peter Fenelon Collier, 1912), 1.

281 "spice of life": Stevenson, "Talk and Talkers," in William Lyon Phelps, ed., *Essays of Robert Louis Stevenson* (New York: Charles Scribner's Sons, 1906), 65.

282 "trapped by domesticity": Elaine Showalter, *Sexual Anarchy: Gender and Culture at the Fin de Siècle* (New York and London: Penguin Books, 1991), 107.

282 "sad prig": Will Low to RLS, January 14, 1885, Beinecke Collection.

282 "We both lost": RLS to William Henley, December 17, 1884, *Letters*, 5: 51.

282 "could not resist": FVS to Dora Williams, October 1885, Beinecke Collection.

283 "the caged animal": John Singer Sargent to RLS, January 1886, Beinecke Collection.

283 "I am at one extreme": RLS to Will Low, October 22, 1885, *Letters*, 5: 137.

283 "a very insane": FVS to Williams, October 1885, and FVS to Margaret Stevenson, August 13, 1885, both Beinecke Collection.

283 "'I am but a cipher'": FVS to Sidney Colvin, summer 1885, Beinecke Collection.

283 "kind of lurking": Boodle, *R. L. S. and His Sine Qua Non*, 10.

283 "a California lady": Olive Logan, "Authors and Publishers," *The American*, August 21, 1886, 284. Accessed online: google.com/books/edition/The_American/biAgAQAAMAAJ?q=olive+logan+ro&gbpv=1. Fanny's comment is in *Letters*, 5: 302 and fn.

283 "she was such a savage": Nellie Van de Grift Sanchez, *The Life of Mrs. Robert Louis Stevenson* (Fairfield, CA: James Stevenson, 2001), 120.

284 "I suppose they": Dora Williams to FVS, June 12, 1887, Beinecke Collection.

284 "one long conversation": Stevenson, "Talk and Talkers," 84.

284 "stormy, short-lived": Carmela Ciuraru, *Lives of the Wives* (New York: Harper-Collins, 2023), 3.

284 "a woman (as you know)": RLS to Henry James, December 23, 1886, *Letters*, 5: 340.

285 "the kindest recollections": RLS to James, December 23, 1886, *Letters*, 5: 340.

285 "fellowship in imperfection": Katherine Linehan, "Revaluing Women and Marriage in Robert Louis Stevenson's Short Fiction," *English Literature in Transition, 1880–1920* 40, no. 1 (1997): 51.

285 "Fanny and Louis were": *Letters*, 1: 69.

285 "critical faculty was keener": Boodle, *R. L. S. and His Sine Qua Non*, 11.

285 "to swear, to cry": FVS and RLS to William Henley, February 5, 1886, *Letters*, 5: 196.

286 "I got my little finger": RLS to William Henley, February 6, 1886, *Letters*, 5: 196–97.

286 "far from resenting": Audrey Murfin, *Robert Louis Stevenson and the Art of Collaboration* (Edinburgh: Edinburgh University Press, 2019), 88.

286 "I have really": FVS to Sidney Colvin, April 22, 1887, *Letters*, 5: 399–400.

286 "women, as a rule": Boodle, *R. L. S. and His Sine Qua Non*, 51.

286 "I write too, a little": Boodle, *R. L. S. and His Sine Qua Non*, 32 and 35.

286 "could hardly be worse": Boodle, *R. L. S. and His Sine Qua Non*, 57 and 58.

287 "If you want me to see": Boodle, *R. L. S. and His Sine Qua Non*, 60.

THIRTEEN

288 "young gentleman's" entertainment: Robert Louis Stevenson, *Kidnapped; or, The Lad with the Silver Button: The Original Text*, ed. Barry Menikoff (San Marino: Huntington Library, 1999), vii.

288 "what the novel can do": Henry James, "Robert Louis Stevenson," in Paul Maixner, ed., *Robert Louis Stevenson: The Critical Heritage* (London: Routledge & Kegan Paul, 1981), 311.

288 "lustrous prose": Stevenson, *Kidnapped: Original Text*, Margot Livesey, Introduction, xxii.

289 "a great Odyssey": Stevenson, *Kidnapped: Original Text*, 253.

289 "dancing madness": Stevenson, *Kidnapped: Original Text*, 73.

291 "bonny fighter": Stevenson, *Kidnapped: Original Text*, 90.

291 "became detached from": Graham Balfour, *The Life of Robert Louis Stevenson* (London: Methuen and Co., 1906), 232. (Kessinger Rare Reprints.)

291 "without interest or inspiration": RLS to George Iles, October 29, 1887, *Letters*, 6: 48.

291 "Time blows by me": RLS to Ida Taylor, May 1886, *Letters*, 5: 251.

291 "stops without ending": James, "Robert Louis Stevenson," in Maixner, *Critical Heritage*, 309 and 296.

292 "racing heart": Robert Louis Stevenson, *Kidnapped*, ed. Ian Duncan, Introduction (Oxford: Oxford University Press, 2014), ix and xxii.

292 "evil odour": R. H. Hutton, unsigned review, *Spectator*, July 24, 1886, in Maixner, *Critical Heritage*, 236.

292 "I do not know if I was": Stevenson, *Kidnapped: Original Text*, 85.

292 "a novel of arrested development": Alan Sandison, *Robert Louis Stevenson and the Appearance of Modernism* (New York: St. Martin's Press, 1996), 193.

292 "full of cruelty": Stevenson, *Kidnapped: Original Text*, 56.

293 "a judge upon the bench": Stevenson, *Kidnapped: Original Text*, 50.

293 "It is no longer possible": Stevenson, *Kidnapped*, Duncan, Introduction, xi.

293 "I think a lot": EW staff, "Hilary Mantel: Books of My Life," *Entertainment Weekly*, updated October 3, 2014. Accessed online: ew.com/article/2014/10/03 /hilary-mantel-books-my-life. James Campbell, "Escape from the Margins," *The Guardian*, November 18, 2005. Accessed online: theguardian.com/books/2005 /nov/19/featuresreviews.guardianreview12.

294 "where all is doubt": E. Purcell, review, *Academy*, February 27, 1886, in Maixner, *Critical Heritage*, 195.

294 "Sir Walter was": RLS to Edward Purcell, February 27, 1886, *Letters*, 5: 213.

294 "It doesn't really matter": Adelaide A. Boodle, *R. L. S. and His Sine Qua Non* (New York: Charles Scribner's Sons, 1926), 89.

294 "look after": Thomas Stevenson to FVS, May 30, 1886, Beinecke Collection.

295 "so much prettier still": RLS to Harriet Monroe, June 30, 1886, *Letters*, 5: 272.

295 "then trip lightly": FVS to Dora Williams, March 1885, Beinecke Collection.

295 "I sleep upon my art": RLS to William Henley, March 13, 1884, *Letters*, 3: 252.

296 "His time was": Lloyd Osbourne, Introduction, *The Works of Robert Louis Stevenson*, Vailima Edition (New York: Peter Fenelon Collier, 1912), 1: xvi.

296 "dry nippedness": Nellie Van de Grift Sanchez, *The Life of Mrs. Robert Louis Stevenson* (Fairfield, CA: James Stevenson, 2001), 201 and 306.

296 "A buffer's life": FVS to Sidney Colvin, November 1886, Beinecke Collection. In "Demonic Disturbances of Sexual Identity: The Strange Case of Dr. Jekyll and Mr/s Hyde" (in *NOVEL: A Forum on Fiction*, Autumn 1989), Janice Doane and Devon Hodge suggest that some of Fanny's physical and mental ailments were related to her professional frustrations. They note that New Woman writers like Fanny, who were torn between idealized femininity and masculine possibilities for achievement, wrote "haltingly," and according to Elaine Showalter, developed

"numerous and persisting ailments." I would suggest that Fanny's use of different bylines might also be a reflection of her inner conflict about her roles and identity.

297 **"often wildly, across genre"**: Robyn Joanne Pritzker, "Fanny Van de Grift Stevenson's Short Fiction: Gender and Genre in the Late Nineteenth Century Literary Imagination," PhD thesis (University of Edinburgh, 2019), 126. Accessed online: https://era.ed.ac.uk/handle/1842/36537. Pritzker points out that literary scholarship has traditionally marginalized magazine writing in general and women's magazine writing in particular. However, some modern critics contend that Fanny and other women who found a voice in late-nineteenth-century magazines were part of an important literary transition. Their experimental stories may seem at times "uncertain, unstable, and embryonic," Pritzker writes, but they helped usher in the modernist style that the next generation would develop and polish. "What might be labeled the 'minor' writing of women like Stevenson flowed organically—and should be understood as a key part of the *fin-de-siecle* transition—into the works of 'major' women such as [Edith] Wharton, Katherine Mansfield, Willa Cather, and Virginia Woolf." (180)

297 **"served with my guests"**: Fanny Osbourne (unsigned), "Borriballoo," manuscript, Stevenson Museum Collection.

297 **"very soul"**: Fanny Osbourne (unsigned), "The Hunchback," manuscript, Stevenson Museum Collection.

298 **"I am writing for my life"**: Boodle, *R. L. S. and His Sine Qua Non*, 41.

298 **"She seemed like a walk"**: FVS to Sidney Colvin, E. V. Lucas, *The Colvins and Their Friends* (New York: Charles Scribner's Sons, 1928), 210.

298 **"How do you think"**: FVS to Sidney Colvin, spring 1886, Beinecke Collection.

298 **"forcible binding of"**: Mrs. Robert Louis Stevenson, "Miss Pringle's Neighbors," *Scribner's Magazine*, June 1887: 697, 694, and 700.

299 **"replace the matrimonial bond"**: Pritzker, "Fanny Van de Grift Stevenson's Short Fiction," 42.

300 **"animal-like shriek"**: Fanny Van de Grift Stevenson, "The Nixie," *Scribner's Magazine*, March 1888, 278 and 283.

300 **"destined bride"**: Van de Grift Stevenson, "The Nixie," 280.

301 **"untamed spirit"**: George Egerton, "A Cross Line," in Carolyn Christensen Nelson, ed., *A New Woman Reader* (Peterborough: Broadview Press, 2001), 15–16.

301 **"for military glory"**: RLS to Alison Cunningham, April 16, 1887, *Letters*, 5: 392.

302 **"satisfactory reply regarding"**: "Sam Osbourne," *San Francisco Chronicle*, April 7, 1887, 8.

302 **"That he probably"**: FVS to Sidney Colvin, May 1, 1887, Beinecke Collection.

302 **"The name must be changed"**: FVS to Colvin, May 1, 1887, Beinecke Collection.

302 **"Happy am I"**: RLS to William Henley, late April/early May 1887, *Letters*, 5: 404.

303 **"[A] very beautiful"**: RLS to Sidney Colvin, March 17, 1886, *Letters*, 5: 236.

303 **"majestically proved her"**: Robert Louis Stevenson, "Confessions of a Unionist," in Jeremy Treglown, ed., *The Lantern-Bearers and Other Essays* (New York: Farrar, Straus & Giroux, 1988), 238.

303 **"I don't so much mind"**: Fanny Stevenson, handwritten notes for use in lectures or publishing, Beinecke Collection.

304 **"suffering changeling"**: RLS to Sidney Colvin, late May 1887, *Letters*, 5: 411.

304 "You have only Louis": FVS to Margaret Stevenson, May 28, 1887, Beinecke Collection.

305 "a swell American watering place": FVS to Margaret Stevenson, June 23, 1887, Beinecke Collection.

305 "Sing me a song": Robert Louis Stevenson, "Over the Sea to Skye," in Roger C. Lewis, ed., *The Collected Poems of Robert Louis Stevenson* (Edinburgh: Edinburgh University Press, 2003), 200.

306 "I solemnly charge": Boodle, *R. L. S. and His Sine Qua Non*, 46.

306 "dazzled": Jenni Calder, *RLS: A Life Study* (New York: Oxford University Press, 1980), 228.

307 "They are a romantic lot": Henry James to Sidney Colvin, September 21, 1887, Beinecke Collection.

307 "After consultation we agree": Margaret Stevenson's diary, 1883, Beinecke Collection.

307 "I had literally forgotten": RLS to Bob Stevenson, early October, 1887, *Letters*, 6: 17.

FOURTEEN

309 "Louis mad": Claire Harman, *Myself and the Other Fellow* (New York: HarperCollins, 2005), 324.

309 "passed from one epoch": Lloyd Osbourne, *An Intimate Portrait of R. L. S.* (New York: Charles Scribner's Sons, 1924), 77.

310 "America is as I remembered": RLS to Henry James, September 18, 1887, *Letters*, 6: 7.

310 "My reception here was idiotic": RLS to Sidney Colvin, September 18, 1887, *Letters*, 6: 5.

310 "bigger than Jesus": Duncan Milne, Twitter post, September 24, 2015.

310 "tingling": RLS to Sidney Colvin, September 18, 1887, *Letters*, 6: 5, fn 1.

311 "I am like to be": RLS to William Archer, mid-October 1887, *Letters*, 6: 32.

311 "it costs you a pound": RLS to William Henley, October 8, 1887, and January 2, 1888, *Letters*, 6: 27 and 97.

311 "He blushed and looked confused": S. S. McClure, *My Autobiography* (New York: Frederick A. Stokes, 1914), 188. (Forgotten Books facsimile.)

311 "I'm awfū grand": RLS to Charles Baxter, November 18, 1887, *Letters*, 6: 58.

311 "unintentional swindler": RLS to William Henley, December 5, 1887, *Letters*, 6: 71.

311 "greedy and hasty": RLS to Anne Jenkin, December 6, 1887, *Letters*, 6: 72.

312 "Fortunately Fanny understands": "Notes from His Mother's Diary," *The Works of Robert Louis Stevenson*, Vailima Edition (New York: Peter Fenelon Collier, 1912), 26: 352.

312 "To see her turn": Elbert Hubbard, *Little Journeys to the Homes of Great Lovers: Robert Louis Stevenson and Fanny Osbourne* (East Aurora, NY: The Roycrofters, 1906), 185.

313 "extraordinary garments made": Nellie Van de Grift Sanchez, *The Life of Mrs. Robert Louis Stevenson* (Fairfield, CA: James Stevenson, 2001), 128.

313 "hoping to pass": Sanchez, *The Life of Mrs. Robert Louis Stevenson*, 128.

313 "Sleighs, snow-shoes, and frozen lakes": Osbourne, *Intimate Portrait*, 74.

314 "The place does not suit": RLS to Adelaide Boodle, December 10, 1887, *Letters*, 6: 77.

314 "really infinitely disagreeable": RLS to Charles Scribner, December 17, 1887, *Letters*, 6: 83.

314 "She had a really creative": McClure, *My Autobiography*, 198.

314 "the sounds of the sea": McClure, *My Autobiography*, 191–92.

315 "The dreadful depression": RLS to Walter Simpson, early October 1887, *Letters*, 6: 18.

315 "piece of pleasure": RLS to William Archer, October 28,1885, *Letters*, 5: 142; RLS to Henry James, late January 1888, *Letters*, 6: 105.

315 "not at all bad": Osbourne, *Intimate Portrait*, 79–80.

316 "Lloyd's story was": RLS to William Henley, early March 1888, *Letters*, 6: 125.

316 "If it is not funny": RLS to Charles Baxter, March 1889, *Letters*, 6: 263.

316 "If it smiles": RLS to Edward Burlingame, late November 1887, *Letters*, 6: 67.

317 "blowing your praises": RLS to William Henley, January 2, 1888, *Letters*, 6: 98.

317 "Henley was particularly": McClure, *My Autobiography*, 193.

317 "pale and sharp": Robert Louis Stevenson, "To K. de M.," in Roger C. Lewis, ed., *The Collected Poems of Robert Louis Stevenson* (Edinburgh: Edinburgh University Press, 2003), 78.

318 "It's Katharine's; surely": William Henley to RLS, March 9, 1888, *Letters*, 6: 130.

318 "I write with indescribable difficulty": RLS to William Henley, March 22, 1888, *Letters*, 6: 131.

318 "must not judge": Katharine de Mattos to RLS, RLS's annotation, early May 1888, *Letters*, 6: 189.

319 "had a perfect right": Katharine de Mattos to RLS, early April 1888, *Letters*, 6: 169.

319 "well managed": Hilary J. Beattie, "The Enigma of Katharine de Mattos: Reflections on Her Life and Writing," *Journal of Stevenson Studies* 4 (2007): 55–56.

319 "would have drained": Harry McGrath, "New Robert Louis Stevenson Book Examines Neglected Feud with Cousin," *The National*. Accessed online: thenational .scot/news/15713100.new-robert-louis-stevenson-book-examines-neglected -feud-with-cousin.

319 "drunken, whoreson bugger": RLS to Charles Baxter, December 30, 1887, *Letters*, 6: 93.

319 "We believe that F. stole": William Henley to Charles Baxter, April 25, 1888, *Letters*, 6: 177.

319 "[Louis] can't have slept": William Henley to Charles Baxter, July 4, 1888, *Letters*, 6: 168.

320 "If I have failed": Katharine de Mattos to RLS, June 1888, *Letters*, 6: 204.

320 "I gave up": FVS to Charles Baxter, May 10, 1888, *Letters*, 6: 181–82.

320 "had still enough health": RLS to Louisa Burgess, April 12, 1888, *Letters*, 6: 159.

321 "one of the most beautiful": FVS to Anna Boyle Henley, 1912, Beinecke Collection.

321 "an author whom": J. C. Furnas, *Voyage to Windward* (New York: William Sloane Associates, 1951), 303.

321 "Monroe of the photograph": RLS to William Henley, February 6 or 7, 1888, *Letters*, 6: 111.

321 "among the nursemaids": RLS to Mark Twain, April 16, 1893, *Letters*, 8: 57.

321 **"He was most scantily furnished"**: Mark Twain, *The Autobiography of Mark Twain* (Berkeley: University of California Press, 2010), 1: 228–29.

322 **"Stevenson?"**: Will H. Low, *Chronicle of Friendships* (New York: Charles Scribner's Sons, 1908), 52, 401, and 403.

322 **"my dearest fellow"**: RLS to FVS, May 15, 1888, *Letters*, 6: 186.

323 **"No one knows"**: Low, *Chronicle of Friendships*, 427.

324 **"Imagine how humble"**: FVS to RLS, April 1888, Beinecke Collection.

325 **"kind of a crank"**: Graham Balfour, *The Life of Robert Louis Stevenson* (London: Methuen and Co., 1906), 254. (Kessinger Rare Reprints.)

325 **"You may think your husband"**: Margaret Isabella Balfour Stevenson, *From Saranac to the Marquesas and Beyond*, ed. Marie Clothilde Balfour (New York: Charles Scribner's Sons, 1903), 55. (ULAN Press facsimile, 2023.)

326 **"queer-looking customer"**: Margaret Mackay, *The Violent Friend* (London: J. M. Dent & Sons, 1968), 180.

FIFTEEN

327 **"I can see her now"**: Austin Strong, "The Most Unforgettable Character I've Met," *Reader's Digest*, March 1946.

328 **"a tiny cockle shell"**: Isobel Field, *This Life I've Loved* (Lafayette, CA: Great West Books, 2005), 225.

328 **"I did not dream"**: RLS to Sidney Colvin, September 21, 1888, *Letters*, 6: 209.

328 **"strange fire of disease"**: Lloyd Osbourne, *An Intimate Portrait of R. L. S.* (New York: Charles Scribner's Sons, 1924), 89.

329 **"Fanny has stood"**: RLS to Margaret Stevenson, December 1, 1889, *Letters*, 6: 334.

329 **"So soon as I cease"**: RLS to Sidney Colvin, April 30, 1890, *Letters*, 6: 388.

330 **"like a toy"**: Arthur Johnstone, *Recollections of Robert Louis Stevenson in the Pacific* (London: Chatto & Windus, 1905), 46.

330 **"You never saw"**: RLS to Edward Burlingame, mid-April 1890, *Letters*, 6: 387.

330 **"like a flying fish"**: RLS to Colvin, April 30, 1890, *Letters*, 6: 389.

330 **"on the damp"**: Fanny Van de Grift Stevenson, *The Cruise of the "Janet Nichol" Among the South Sea Islands*, ed. Roslyn Jolly (Sydney: University of New South Wales Press, 2004), 50.

330 **"The first experience"**: Robert Louis Stevenson, *In the South Seas* (London: Penguin Books, 1998), 6.

331 **"in every stage of undress"**: Margaret Isabella Balfour Stevenson, *From Saranac to the Marquesas and Beyond*, ed. Marie Clothilde Balfour (New York: Charles Scribner's Sons, 1903), 76. (ULAN Press facsimile, 2023.)

331 **"beyond the reach"**: Stevenson, *In the South Seas*, 9.

332 **"It is wonderful"**: FVS to Sidney Colvin, December 4, 1888, Beinecke Collection.

333 **"quite *une femme*"**: Margaret Stevenson, *From Saranac to the Marquesas*, 203.

333 **"When I desired"**: Stevenson, *In the South Seas*, 12–13.

333 **"freak of fashion"**: FVS to Sidney Colvin, August 18, 1888, in E. V. Lucas, *The Colvins and Their Friends* (New York: Charles Scribner's Sons, 1928), 211.

334 **"the carcases of creatures"**: Stevenson, *In the South Seas*, 68 and 70.

334 "magnificent figure": FVS to Dora Williams, November 1888, Beinecke Collection.

334 "when you know": FVS to Colvin, December 4, 1888, *Letters*, 6: 234.

334 "The barbarous substance": Stevenson, *In the South Seas*, 72.

335 "civilization" and "savagery": In *Robert Louis Stevenson, Science, and the Fin de Siècle*, Julia Reid proposes that Stevenson's writing was a challenge to the contemporary scientific theory that European races were more advanced than primitive societies on the evolutionary scale.

335 "a sort of halfway house": Margaret Stevenson, *From Saranac to the Marquesas*, 170.

335 "What is a *haole*?" RLS to Charles Baxter, May 9, 1889, *Letters*, 6: 295.

336 "I cannot bear colonial people": FVS to Dora Williams, November 1888, Beinecke Collection.

336 "orgies": Field, *This Life I've Loved*, 161.

336 "make a little money": *Letters*, 6: 243.

337 "this was always": Field, *This Life I've Loved*, 214.

337 "mutual glee": RLS to Charles Baxter, February 18, 1889, *Letters*, 6: 249.

338 "And if you could": FVS to Sidney Colvin and Frances Sitwell, June 18, 1889, *Letters*, 6: 322.

338 "Words cannot depict": RLS to Alice Taylor, June 19, 1889, *Letters*, 6: 322.

338 "I have seen sights": RLS to Sidney Colvin, early June 1889, *Letters*, 6: 311.

338 "lovable fellow": RLS to Charles Baxter, April 12, 1889, *Letters*, 6: 286.

338 "you always love, worse luck": FVS to Colvin and Sitwell, June 18, 1889, *Letters*, 6: 320.

340 "O, Charles! what a crop": RLS to Charles Baxter, February 8, 1889, *Letters*, 6: 248.

340 "the last erect visage": Stevenson, *In the South Seas*, 209.

340 "plenty": Stevenson, *In the South Seas*, 214.

341 "becomes him admirably": Stevenson, *In the South Seas*, 212.

341 "an insight that became" : Fanny Van de Grift Stevenson, *The Cruise of the "Janet Nichol" Among the South Sea Islands*, ed. Roslyn Jolly (Sydney: University of New South Wales Press, 2004), Jolly, Introduction, 29.

342 "as odd-looking": Field, *This Life I've Loved*, 247.

343 "rolled like a mummy": Field, *This Life I've Loved*, 254.

343 "dropping off": Van de Grift Stevenson, *Cruise of the "Janet Nichol,"* 125.

344 "each producing a spark": Van de Grift Stevenson, *Cruise of the "Janet Nichol,"* 194.

344 "the loveliest rat": Van de Grift Stevenson, *Cruise of the "Janet Nichol,"* 68.

344 "It is needless": Van de Grift Stevenson, *Cruise of the "Janet Nichol,"* 121.

344 "I could feel her heart": Van de Grift Stevenson, *Cruise of the "Janet Nichol,"* 125–26.

345 "that I might take": Van de Grift Stevenson, *Cruise of the "Janet Nichol,"* 114.

345 "took possession": Van de Grift Stevenson, *Cruise of the "Janet Nichol,"* 133–34.

345 "half-breed Mexican": Ernest Samuels, *Henry Adams: The Major Phase* (Cambridge, MA: Harvard University Press, 1964), 29; Worthington Chauncery Ford, ed., *Letters of Henry Adams 1858–1891* (Boston and New York: Houghton Mifflin, 1930), 446.

347 "a supposed fiery gleam": Van de Grift Stevenson, *Cruise of the "Janet Nichol,"* 59.

347 "sombre fire": Stevenson, *In the South Seas*, 203.

348 "*the* big book": RLS to Marcel Schwob, August 19, 1890, *Letters*, 6: 401.

348 "He has taken into his Scotch": FVS to Sidney Colvin, May 21, 1889, *Letters*, 6: 303–4.

349 "Contrary to our expectation": S. S. McClure, *My Autobiography* (New York: Frederick A. Stokes, 1914), 192. (Forgotten Books facsimile.)

349 "the *visible* in them": Janet Adam Smith, ed., *Henry James and Robert Louis Stevenson* (Westport, CT: Hyperion Press, 1948), 198.

349 "peace of mind": RLS to Sidney Colvin, April 18, 1891, *Letters*, 7: 102.

350 "enabled him to distinguish": Roslyn Jolly, *Robert Louis Stevenson in the Pacific* (Farnham, England: Ashgate Publishing, 2009), 64.

350 "However dull it": Van de Grift Stevenson, *Cruise of the "Janet Nichol,"* 50.

350 "[Fanny] certainly takes": Heather Waldroup, "Picturing Pleasure: Fanny Stevenson and Beatrice Grimshaw in the Pacific Islands," *Women's History Review* 18 (2009): 1. Accessed at Taylor & Francis Online: tandfonline.com/doi/abs/10.1080/09612020802608074.

350 "word for word": Audrey Murfin, *Robert Louis Stevenson and the Art of Collaboration* (Edinburgh: Edinburgh University Press, 2019), 94. In comparing handwritten, transcribed, and published versions of Fanny's diary, Murfin writes that Fanny credited Louis for two long passages in her published diary, but she also included smaller ones verbatim or lightly edited that she did not specifically attribute to him.

350 "family venture": Murfin, *Robert Louis Stevenson and the Art of Collaboration*, 23.

351 "Breaths of the land breeze": Van de Grift Stevenson, *Cruise of the "Janet Nichol,"* 75.

SIXTEEN

353 "more human": Worthington Chauncery Ford, ed., *Letters of Henry Adams 1858–1891* (Boston and New York: Houghton Mifflin, 1930), 452 and 456.

355 "We have salad": RLS to Sidney Colvin, August 23, 1893, *Letters*, 8: 159.

355 "omelette of our hopes": RLS to Sidney Colvin, December 22, 1890, *Letters*, 7: 58.

356 "bright eyes": Carla Manfredi, *Robert Louis Stevenson's Pacific Impressions* (Cham, Switzerland: Macmillan, 2018), 209.

356 "like a grating": RLS to Colvin, December 22, 1890, *Letters*, 7: 56.

356 "no Samoan devil": Fanny and Robert Louis Stevenson, *Our Samoan Adventure*, ed. Charles Neider (New York: Harper & Brothers, 1955), 97.

356 "The life of the plants": RLS to Sidney Colvin, March 20, 1891, *Letters*, 7: 93.

357 "*Nothing* is so interesting": RLS to Sidney Colvin, November 2, 1890, *Letters*, 7: 20.

357 "Louis says that I have": Stevensons, *Our Samoan Adventure*, 31.

357 "My vanity, like": Stevensons, *Our Samoan Adventure*, 38.

357 "I plunged into": FVS to Sidney Colvin, January 1891, *Letters*, 7: 80.

358 "fish, human and beast": Stevensons, *Our Samoan Adventure*, 73–74.

358 "idealistic flexibility": Manfredi, *Robert Louis Stevenson's Pacific Impressions*, 214. Manfredi's discussion of the place of aitu in Samoan culture and analysis of the Stevensons' participation in colonial exploitation are especially enlightening.

358 "driving and callous overseer": Doug Munro and Stewart Firth, "Samoan Plantations: The Gilbertese Laborers' Experience 1867–1896," in Brij V. Lal, Doug

Munro, and Edward D. Beecher, eds., *Plantation Workers: Resistance and Accommodation* (Honolulu: University of Hawaii Press, 1993), 111.

359 "any exclusiveness becomes": RLS to Charles Baxter, March 20, 1890, *Letters*, 6: 381.

359 "chief and father": RLS to George Meredith, September 5, 1893, *Letters*, 8: 163.

359 "The inside of Java's knees": RLS to Sidney Colvin, June 24 or 25, 1891, *Letters*, 7: 140, and November 25, 1891, *Letters*, 7: 202.

360 "elderly and sick": RLS to Colvin, June 24 or 25, 1891, *Letters*, 7: 141.

360 "Dark as a wayside gypsy": Stevenson, "Dark Women," in Roger C. Lewis, ed., *The Collected Poems of Robert Louis Stevenson* (Edinburgh: Edinburgh University Press, 2003), 175.

361 "beyond dreams": RLS to Edmund Gosse, April 1891, *Letters*, 7: 106

361 "Everybody felt thoroughly": H. J. Moors, *With Stevenson in Samoa* (Boston: Small, Maynard & Company, 1910), 56. (Primary Source Edition.)

362 "A writer who amounts": Lloyd Osbourne, *An Intimate Portrait of R. L. S.* (New York: Charles Scribner's Sons, 1924), 132.

362 "You are the man": Robert Louis Stevenson, "The Enchantress," *Georgia Review*, Fall 1989, 559. The manuscript, originally entitled "A Singular Marriage," was thought lost for decades until English literature scholars David Mann and Susan Garland Mann rediscovered it at the Beinecke Library and published it for the first time in the University of Georgia journal.

362 "the lengths to which": Lena Wånggren, "Robert Louis Stevenson and the Marriage Debate: 'The Enchantress' in Context," *Scottish Literary Review* 12, no. 1 (Spring/Summer 2020). Accessed online: muse.jhu.edu/article/757386.

362 "He does me fathoms": Robert Louis Stevenson, "The Persons of the Tale," *Fables* (New York: Charles Scribner's Sons, 1910), 5.

363 "promoted apes": Robert Louis Stevenson, "The Scientific Ape," *English Literature in Transition, 1880–1920* 48, no. 4 (2005): 401 and 403.

363 "like a bone": Robert Louis Stevenson, *A Footnote to History: Eight Years of Trouble in Samoa* (New York: Charles Scribner's Sons, 1901), 25. (Leopold Classic Library, 2024.)

364 "the handful of whites": Stevenson, *A Footnote to History*, 24.

364 "It is impossible": RLS to Bob Stevenson, June 17, 1894, *Letters*, 8: 305.

364 "When his novels are forgotten": Roslyn Jolly, *Robert Louis Stevenson in the Pacific* (Farnham, England: Ashgate Publishing, 2009), 102, fn 60.

365 "very fury": RLS to the editor of *The Times*, July 19, 1892, *Letters*, 7: 338, fn 1.

365 "the extraordinary condition": Editorial, *Times* (UK), January 17, 1893, quoted in Jolly, *Robert Louis Stevenson in the Pacific*, 151.

365 "I see that romantic": Merlin Holland and Rupert Hart-Davis, eds., *The Complete Letters of Oscar Wilde* (New York: Henry Holt and Company, 2000), 789.

365 "the main currents": Sidney Colvin to RLS, March 21, 1894, *Letters*, 8: 279 fn.

365 "Please remember that": RLS to Sidney Colvin, April 24 or 25, 1894, *Letters*, 8: 281–82.

366 "Our friends at home": FVS to Edmund Gosse, May 1894, Beinecke Collection.

366 "Since Byron was": Evan Charteris, ed., *The Life and Letters of Sir Edmund Gosse* (New York: Harper & Brothers, 1932), 249.

367 "for all the pleasure": Arthur Conan Doyle to RLS, May 30, 1893, excerpt, *Letters*, 8: 50, fn 1.

367 "The fact seems": Edmund Gosse to George Armour, January 31, 1891, excerpt, *Letters*, 7: 106–7, fn 6.

367 "You don't know what news": RLS to Henry James, December 5, 1891, *Letters*, 7: 449.

367 "Throughout the island world": Robert Louis Stevenson and Lloyd Osbourne, *The Ebb-Tide: A Trio and Quartet*, in Robert Louis Stevenson, *Treasure Island and The Ebb-Tide* (London: Penguin Group, 2012), 225.

368 "troop of swine": RLS to Henry James, June 17, 1893, *Letters*, 8: 107.

368 "This is not the Stevenson": Unsigned review, *Speaker*, September 1894, in Paul Maixner, ed., *Robert Louis Stevenson: The Critical Heritage* (London: Routledge & Kegan Paul, 1981), 459.

369 "like a bullet": RLS to Sidney Colvin, November 3, 1890, *Letters*, 7: 27.

369 "is illegally married": Robert Louis Stevenson, *The Beach of Falesá*, in Barry Menikoff, ed., *Robert Louis Stevenson and "The Beach of Falesá": A Study in Victorian Publishing*, Original Text (Stanford: Stanford University Press, 1984), 124.

369 "I'm a white man": Stevenson, *The Beach of Falesá*, 137.

370 "deal fairly with": Stevenson, *The Beach of Falesá*, 186.

370 "Nobody thinks less": Stevenson, *The Beach of Falesá*, 186.

371 "most mutilated": Menikoff, *Robert Louis Stevenson and "The Beach of Falesá,"* Introduction, 5.

371 "that night": RLS to Sidney Colvin, January 31, 1892, *Letters*, 7: 231.

371 "No editor who knows": Menikoff, *Robert Louis Stevenson and "The Beach of Falesá,"* 87.

371 "bearded gentlemen": Roger Swearingen, *The Prose Writings of Robert Louis Stevenson* (London: Macmillan, 1980), 155–56.

371 "send his wife to hell": Menikoff, *Robert Louis Stevenson and "The Beach of Falesá,"* 87–88.

372 "clean out of the atmosphere": A. B. Walkley, "Review," *Black and White*, May 13, 1893, in Maixner, *Critical Heritage*, 415.

372 "Where or how": *New York Times*, April 9, 1893, quoted in Menikoff, *Robert Louis Stevenson and "The Beach of Falesá,"* 58.

372 "almost as good": George Lyman Kittredge, *Nation*, January 9, 1896, quoted in Menikoff, *Robert Louis Stevenson and "The Beach of Falesá,"* 98.

372 "You will know": RLS to Sidney Colvin, September 28, 1891, *Letters*, 7: 161.

373 "wordy, politic intrigue": A. T. Quiller-Couch, "From First Thoughts on 'Catriona,'" *Speaker*, September 9, 1893, in Maixner, *Critical Heritage*, 427.

373 "drawn a good petticoat": Andrew Lang, *Longman's Magazine*, November 1893, in Tom Hubbard, ed., *The Selected Writings of Andrew Lang* (Abingdon-on-Thames: Routledge Press, 2017), vol. 1.

SEVENTEEN

374 "deathly": Fanny and Robert Louis Stevenson, *Our Samoan Adventure*, ed. Charles Neider (New York: Harper & Brothers, 1955), 72.

374 **"going wrong in"**: FVS to Frances Sitwell, January 1890, Beinecke Collection.

374 **"The remedy is as bad"**: FVS to Frances Sitwell, September 1892, Beinecke Collection.

375 **"like a demented beast"**: Robert Louis Stevenson, "About my fields, in the broad sun," reprinted in Roger C. Lewis, ed., *The Collected Poems of Robert Louis Stevenson* (Edinburgh: Edinburgh University Press, 2003), 284–85.

375 **"anxious shrillness about nothing"**: RLS to Sidney Colvin, April 1, 1893, *Letters*, 8: 40.

376 **"the greatest whoremaster"**: RLS to Margaret Stevenson, May 21, 1893, *Letters*, 8: 81.

376 **"Well, there's no disguise"**: RLS to Colvin, April 1, 1893, *Letters*, 8: 39.

376 **"month's lark"**: RLS to Sidney Colvin, February 19, 1893, *Letters*, 8: 30.

377 **"ghostly track"**: Jane Bonnyman, *An Ember from the Fire: Poems on the Life of Fanny Van de Grift Stevenson* (Salzburg: Poetry Salzburg at the University of Salzburg, 2016), 23. Bonnyman drew attention to the footprint on the ceiling of Fanny's bedroom.

377 **"tired as a man could"**: RLS to Colvin, April 1, 1893, *Letters*, 8: 40–41.

377 **"extraordinary recuperative power"**: RLS to Colvin, April 1, 1893, *Letters*, 8: 41.

377 **"only with some old illusions"**: RLS to Margaret Stevenson, May 21, 1893, *Letters*, 8: 80.

378 **"As I look back"**: RLS to Anne Jenkin, December 5, 1892, *Letters*, 7: 452.

378 **"stormy petrel"**: Robert Louis Stevenson, "To the Stormy Petrel," in Lewis, *Collected Poems*, 300.

379 **"I wish I were able"**: Stevensons, *Our Samoan Adventure*, 221.

379 **"not often on his nose"**: Mrs. Robert Louis Stevenson, "Under Sentence of the Law: The Story of a Dog," *McClure's Magazine*, June 1893, 34.

379 **"I wonder what"**: Stevensons, *Our Samoan Adventure*, 221.

379 **"'Easily earn much more'"**: Frank McLynn, *Robert Louis Stevenson* (New York: Random House, 1993), 460.

380 **"Treat the savory bulb"**: Fanny Van de Grift Stevenson, "Housewife's Ramblings: I. Champagne Defli," *Philadelphia Inquirer*, October 1, 1893, 21. Fanny's recipe books are at the Beinecke Library and the Robert Louis Stevenson Museum in St. Helena.

381 **"sordid"**: Mrs. Robert Louis Stevenson, "A Backwoods Childhood," *The Woman at Home*, vol. 1, 1894. The essay also appeared with the same byline in the *Scranton Republican*, August 26, 1893.

381 **"Mrs. W"**: Fanny Van de Grift Stevenson, "At the Undertaker's: Early Recollections of a Noted Woman," *Philadelphia Inquirer*, September 3, 1893, 23.

382 **"was not only a writer"**: Margaret Mackay, *The Violent Friend* (London: J. M. Dent & Sons, 1968), 262.

382 **"After all there are only"**: RLS to Sidney Colvin, June 24, 1893, *Letters*, 8: 121.

382 **"quite wild with excitement"**: Stevensons, *Our Samoan Adventure*, 191–92.

382 **"I suppose if our house"**: Stevensons, *Our Samoan Adventure*, 197.

383 **"lawless, savage people"**: Roslyn Jolly, *Robert Louis Stevenson in the Pacific* (Farnham, England: Ashgate Publishing, 2009), 136.

383 **"called the Samoans"**: Stevensons, *Our Samoan Adventure*, 198 and 210.

383 **"idiotic Enthusiast"**: Stevensons, *Our Samoan Adventure*, 226.

383 "only friend": RLS to Sidney Colvin, December 28, 1893, *Letters*, 8: 214–15.

384 "There is only one way": Robert Louis Stevenson, "Address to the Samoan Chiefs, Vailima," in Robert Hoskins, ed., *Sophia Scarlet and Other Pacific Writings* (Auckland, New Zealand: AUT Media, 2008), 122.

384 "to follow the demand": Arthur Johnstone, *Recollections of Robert Louis Stevenson in the Pacific* (London: Chatto & Windus, 1905), 92.

385 "most pressing": RLS to Charles Baxter, October 14, 1890, *Letters*, 7: 16.

385 "For 14 years": RLS to George Meredith, September 5, 1893, *Letters*, 8: 163–64.

385 "I break down": RLS to Sidney Colvin, April 25, 1893, *Letters*, 8: 68.

385 "so much so that I have": RLS to Bob Stevenson, June 17, 1894, *Letters*, 8: 304.

385 "impotent and forgotten": RLS to H. B. Baildon, January 30, 1894, *Letters*, 8: 243.

386 "big presence and his welcome": RLS to Charles Baxter, late February 1891, *Letters*, 7: 88.

386 "cigarettes without intermission": RLS to J. M. Barrie, April 2 or 3, 1893, *Letters*, 8: 44.

386 "gratifying relapse": RLS to Lillie Hitchcock Coit, January 15, 1894, *Letters*, 8: 233.

387 "identities of sensation": RLS to Sidney Colvin, May 27, 1893, *Letters*, 8: 91.

388 "Hang a thief": Jennifer Speake, *Oxford Dictionary of Proverbs* (Oxford: Oxford University Press, 2015), 144.

388 "much more in harmony": Rosaline Masson, ed., *I Can Remember Robert Louis Stevenson* (Edinburgh: W. & R. Chambers, 1922), 263. Roger Swearingen drew attention to Lysaght's account in his discussion of the composition of *Weir of Hermiston* in *The Prose Writings of Robert Louis Stevenson* (London: Macmillan, 1980).

389 "He had hardly more": Isobel Strong and Lloyd Osbourne, *Memories of Vailima* (New York: Charles Scribner's Sons, 1902), 97.

389 "I see it unfold": Isobel Field, *This Life I've Loved* (Lafayette, CA: Great West Books, 2005), 284.

389 "like a bed of tiger lilies": Robert Louis Stevenson, *Weir of Hermiston*, Gillian Hughes, ed., *The Works of Robert Louis Stevenson*, New Edinburgh Edition (Edinburgh: Edinburgh University Press, 2017), xxviii.

390 "He felt her whole body": Stevenson, *Weir of Hermiston*, 99.

390 "attack of blood": RLS to Charles Baxter, May 9, 1889, *Letters*, 6: 294.

390 "I have in fact lost": RLS to Edmund Gosse, December 1, 1894, *Letters*, 8: 399.

390 "blank is a silly ass": RLS to Adelaide and Annie Ide, December 27, 1893, *Letters*, 8: 210, fn 1.

391 "What's that?": Belle Strong's Journal, December 4 or 5, 1894, in *Letters*, 8: 402. I have chosen to use Belle's recollections; other accounts of Louis's last words are similar.

391 "so that no foreign hand": Excerpt in "Dryburgh Abbey, Sir Walter Scott's Final Resting Place," Scotiana, scotiana.com/dryburgh-abbey-sir-walter-scott%E2%80%99s-final-resting-place.

392 "Tofa Tusitala": Belle Strong's Journal, December 4 or 5, 1894, *Letters*, 8: 403.

392 "Under the wide": Robert Louis Stevenson, "Requiem," in Lewis, *Collected Poems*, 88.

393 "You are nearest": Henry James to FVS, December 1894, Beinecke Collection.

394 "divined with genius": "Stevenson's Posthumous Masterpiece," *New York Times*, June 28, 1896, and "Stevenson's Last," *Literary World*, June 1896; both quoted in Stevenson, *Weir of Hermiston*, xlii.

394 "fine dandified talent": Graham Greene, "From Feathers to Iron," *Collected Essays* (New York: Viking Press, 1968), 79.

394 "He was very near": Mackay, *Violent Friend*, 311.

394 "My life, young man": Alexandra Lapierre, *Fanny Stevenson: Muse, Adventuress and Romantic Enigma*, trans. Carol Cosman (London: Fourth Estate, 1995), 17.

395 "wouldn't let Louis publish": FVG to Margaret Stevenson, November 1895, Beinecke Collection.

395 "inflict pain upon a snail": Codicil to the will of Robert Louis Stevenson, October 10, 1885, Beinecke Collection.

396 "this Seraph in Chocolate": W. E. Henley, "R.L.S.," *Pall Mall Magazine*, December 1901, xxv, in Paul Maixner, ed., *Robert Louis Stevenson: The Critical Heritage* (London: Routledge & Kegan Paul, 1981), 497.

396 "gentleness and kindness": Henry James to Sidney Colvin, September 28, 1899, Beinecke Collection.

396 "old grizzled lioness": Mackay, *Violent Friend*, 324.

396 "the only woman": Lapierre, *Fanny Stevenson*, 4.

397 "poor barbarous and merely instinctive": *Letters*, 1: 67.

398 "[I] would rather go": Nellie Van de Grift Sanchez, *The Life of Mrs. Robert Louis Stevenson* (Fairfield, CA: James Stevenson, 2001), 302.

398 "We are one": Fanny V. de G. Stevenson, "Anne," *Scribner's Magazine*, July 1899, 120.

399 "Teacher, tender, comrade, wife": Robert Louis Stevenson, "My Wife," in Lewis, *Collected Poems*, 184–85.

399 "never to have let": *Letters*, 1: 72.

400 "airy R L Stevenson": Linda Dryden, Stephen Arata, and Eric Massie, eds., *Robert Louis Stevenson and Joseph Conrad* (Lubbock: Texas Tech University Press, 209), 4.

400 "pitiful instance of the way": Linda Dryden, "How Robert Louis Stevenson's Reputation Was Shipwrecked by His Inner Circle," The Conversation, theconversation.com/how-robert-louis-stevensons-reputation-was-shipwrecked-by-his-inner-circle-55666.

400 "non-controversial writer of children's fiction": Dryden, "How Robert Louis Stevenson's Reputation Was Shipwrecked by His Inner Circle."

401 "a violent friend": RLS to Barrie, April 2 or 3, 1894, *Letters*, 8: 45.

401 "selective sympathy . . . whereby": Joseph Farrell, *Robert Louis Stevenson in Samoa* (London: MacLehose Press, 2019), 50.

402 "an inseparable sharer": Graham Balfour, *The Life of Robert Louis Stevenson* (London: Methuen and Co., 1906), 175. (Kessinger Rare Reprints.)

402 "Take thou the writing": Stevenson, *Weir of Hermiston*, 4.

SELECTED BIBLIOGRAPHY

There have been 130 years of extensive Stevenson scholarship. This bibliography is not an exhaustive list of the many biographies of Robert Louis Stevenson or those of Fanny Van de Grift Stevenson, or of their work, which can easily be found online. Instead, for the most part, it includes the relatively more recent books and essays that I found most interesting and informative.

BOOKS

Ambrosini, Richard, and Richard Dury, eds. *Robert Louis Stevenson: Writer of Boundaries*. Madison: University of Wisconsin Press, 2006.

Arata, Stephen, Richard Dury, Penny Fielding, and Anthony Mandal, eds., *New Edinburgh Edition of the Works of Robert Louis Stevenson*. Edinburgh: Edinburgh University Press, 2014–. Four volumes of this thirty-nine-volume definitive modern edition of RLS's work have been published to date. Each volume includes discussion of topics relevant to the work, such as composition, suppression, publication, reception, and influence.

Bathurst, Bella. *The Lighthouse Stevensons*. New York: Perennial, 2000.

Bell, Ian. *Dreams of Exile: Robert Louis Stevenson, a Biography*. New York: Henry Holt and Company, 1992.

Bonnyman, Jane. *An Ember from the Fire: Poems on the Life of Fanny Van de Grift Stevenson*. Salzburg: University of Salzburg, 2016.

Booth, Bradford A., and Ernest Mehew, eds. *The Letters of Robert Louis Stevenson*. 8 volumes. New Haven and London: Yale University Press, 1994–95.

Dryden, Linda, and Stephen Arata and Eric Massie, eds. *Robert Louis Stevenson and Joseph Conrad*. Lubbock: Texas Tech University Press, 2009.

Dury, Richard, ed. *Strange Case of Dr Jekyll and Mr Hyde, The Collected Works of Robert Louis Stevenson*, Centenary Edition. Edinburgh: Edinburgh University Press, 2004.

Farrell, Joseph. *Robert Louis Stevenson in the Pacific*. London: Maclehose Press, 2017.

Fielding, Penny, ed. *The Edinburgh Companion to Robert Louis Stevenson*. Edinburgh: Edinburgh University Press, 2010.

Harman, Claire. *Myself and the Other Fellow: A Life of Robert Louis Stevenson*. New York: HarperCollins, 2005.

Holmes, Richard. *Footsteps: Adventures of a Romantic Biographer*. New York: Vintage, 1985.

Jolly, Roslyn, ed. *The Cruise of the Janet Nichol Among the South Sea Islands: A Diary by Mrs. Robert Louis Stevenson*. Seattle: University of Washington Press, 2004.

Jolly, Roslyn. *Robert Louis Stevenson in the Pacific: Travel, Empire, and the Author's Profession*. Surrey and Burlington: Ashgate Publishing Limited, 2009.

Lapierre, Alexandra. *Fanny Stevenson: Muse, Adventuress and Romantic Enigma*. Translated by Carol Cosman. London: Fourth Estate, 1995.

Manfreddi, Carla. *Robert Louis Stevenson's Pacific Impressions: Photography and Travel Writing, 1888–1894*. London: Palgrave Macmillan, 2018.

Menikoff, Barry, ed. *Kidnapped, or the Lad with the Silver Button: The Original Text*. San Marino: Huntington Library, 1999.

Menikoff, Barry. *Robert Louis Stevenson and 'The Beach of Falesá': A Study in Victorian Publishing with the Original Text*. Stanford: Stanford University Press, 1984.

Miller, Elizabeth Carolyn. *Framed: The New Woman Criminal in British Culture at the Fin de Siècle*. Ann Arbor: University of Michigan, 2008.

Murfin, Audrey. *Robert Louis Stevenson and the Art of Collaboration*. Edinburgh: Edinburgh University Press, 2019.

Neider, Charles, ed. *Our Samoan Adventure,* by Fanny and Robert Louis Stevenson. New York: Harper & Brothers Publishers, 1955.

Reid, Julia. *Robert Louis Stevenson, Science, and the Fin de Siècle*. London: Palgrave Macmillan, 2009.

Sandison, Alan. *Robert Louis Stevenson and the Appearance of Modernism*. New York: St. Martin's Press, 1996.

Swearingen, Roger G. *The Prose Writings of Robert Louis Stevenson: A Guide.* London and Basingstroke: Macmillan, 1980.

Veeder, William, and Gordon Hirsch, eds. *Dr Jekyll and Mr Hyde after One Hundred Years.* Chicago and London: University of Chicago, 1988.

Walkowitz, Judith R. *City of Dreadful Delight: Narratives of Sexual Danger in Late-Victorian London.* Chicago: University of Chicago, 1992.

ARTICLES AND ESSAYS

Ames, Sarah. "'The Suicide Club': Afterlives." *Journal of Stevenson Studies* 8 (2011): 143–65.

Beattie, Hillary J. "Fanny Osbourne Stevenson's Fiction: 'The Nixie' in Context." *Journal of Stevenson Studies* 11 (2014): 127–50.

Colley, Ann C. "Robert Louis Stevenson's South Seas Crossings." *SEL Studies in English Literature, 1500–1900* 48, no. 4 (Autumn 2008): 871–84. https://doi.org/10.1353/sel.0.0034.

Davidson, Emma-Lee. "'The Game Is Up': The Evolution of *Treasure Island* as Imperial Critique." *Journal of Stevenson Studies* 13 (2016): 125–47.

Deciphering The Dynamiter: A Study in Authorship Attribution. "Who Wrote The Dynamiter?" 2023. http://thedynamiter.llc.ed.ac.uk/?page_id=223.

Doane, Janice, and Devon Hodges. "Demonic Disturbances of Sexual Identity: The Strange Case of Dr. Jekyll and Mr/s Hyde." *NOVEL: A Forum on Fiction* 23, no. 1 (Autumn 1989): 63–74. https://doi.org/10.2307/1345579.

Dryden, Linda. "How Robert Louis Stevenson's Reputation Was Shipwrecked by His Inner Circle." The Conversation, March 4, 2016. theconversation.com/how-robert-louis-stevensons-reputation-was-shipwrecked-by-his-inner-circle-55666.

Everett, Nancy. "Dora Norton Williams: A New England Yankee in San Francisco Bohemia." *Argonaut* 21, no. 1 (Spring 2010): 72–91.

Fielding, Penny. "A Dangerous Collaboration: Fanny Van de Grift Stevenson and Robert Louis Stevenson." *Dangerous Women Project*, January 6, 2017. https://dangerouswomenproject.org/2017/01/06/a-dangerous-collaboration.

Greene, Graham. "From Feathers to Iron." In *Collected Essays*, 79–82. New York: Viking, 1968.

Honaker, Lisa. "The Revisionary Role of Gender in R. L. Stevenson's *New Arabian Nights* and *Prince Otto*: Revolution in a 'Poison Bad World.'" *English Literature in Transition 1880–1920* 44, no. 3 (2001): 297–319. muse.jhu.edu/article/366571.

Katz, Wendy R. "Stevenson's Silverado Squatters: The Figure of 'the Jew' and the Rhetoric of Race." *Journal of Stevenson Studies* 4 (2007): 73–90.

Linehan, Katherine. "Revaluing Women and Marriage in Robert Louis Stevenson's Short Fiction." *English Literature in Transition, 1880–1920* 40, no. 1 (1997): 34–59. muse.jhu.edu/article/367111.

Manfredi, Carla. "Island Encounters in Focus: Photography and the R. L. Stevenson Family." *Victorian Review* 43, no. 1 (2017): 67–86. https://doi.org/10.1353/vcr.2017.0011.

Nabokov, Vladimir. "The Strange Case of Dr Jekyll and Mr Hyde." In *Lectures on Literature*, edited by Freedson Bowers, 179–206. London: Mariner Books, 2002.

Parfect, Ralph. "Robert Louis Stevenson's 'The Clockmaker' and 'The Scientific Ape': Two Unpublished Fables." *English Literature in Transition, 1880–1920* 48, no. 4 (2005): 387–400. https://doi.org/10.2487/Y008-J320-0428-0742.

Pritzker, Robyn. "Something Wicked Westward Goes: Fanny Van de Grift Stevenson's Californian Uncanny." *Humanities* 9, no. 2 (June 2020): 47. https://doi.org/10.3390/h9020047.

Sun-Joo Lee, Julia. "The Plot Against England: The Dynamiter." In *The American Slave Narrative and the Victorian Novel*, 131–43. Oxford: Oxford University Press, 2010.

Waldroup, Heather. "Picturing Pleasure: Fanny Stevenson and Beatrice Grimshaw in the Pacific Islands." *Women's History Review* 18, no. 1 (2009): 1–22. https://doi.org/10.1080/09612020802608074.

Wånggren, Lena. "Gender and Genre in Fanny Van de Grift's Periodical Writing." *The Review of English Studies (RES)* 72, no. 305 (June 2021): 520–39. https://doi.org/10.1093/res/hgaa104.

Wånggren, Lena. "Robert Louis Stevenson and the Marriage Debate: 'The Enchantress' in Context." *Scottish Literary Review* 12, no. 1 (Spring/Summer 2020): 123–42. muse.jhu.edu/article/757386.

DISSERTATIONS

Pritzker, Robyn Joanne. "Fanny Van de Grift Stevenson's Short Fiction: Gender and Genre in the Late Nineteenth Century Literary Imagination." PhD diss., University of Edinburgh, 2019. https://era.ed.ac.uk/handle/1842/36537.

Riggs, Roy Albert. "The Vogue of Robert Louis Stevenson in America, 1880–1900." PhD diss., Ohio State University, 1953.

IMAGE CREDITS

page 11 (*top*): Lloyd Osbourne, *Spearing Fish on Bow-sprit*, 1889, The City of Edinburgh Council Museums and Galleries, capitalcollections.org.uk; (*bottom*): Thomson Murray MacCallum, *Adrift in the South Seas* (Los Angeles, Wetzel Publishing Company, Inc., 1934)

page 12 (*top*): Wikimedia Commons; (*bottom*): Robert Louis Stevenson Museum, St. Helena, California

page 13 (*top*): Wikimedia Commons; (*bottom*): Unknown, *Stevensons in Company with Nantoki and Natakauti, Butar*, 1889, The City of Edinburgh Council Museums and Galleries, capitalcollections.org.uk

page 14 (*top*): Wikimedia Commons; (*bottom*): Michael Coghlan, *The Samoan Home of Robert Louis Stevenson*, photo taken September 26, 2016, uploaded to Wikimedia Commons on May 13, 2017. Via CC BY-SA 2.0.

page 15: Wikimedia Commons

page 16 (*top*): CBW / Alamy Stock Photo

INDEX